APPLYING ECONOMIC PRINCIPLES

Sanford D. Gordon

Alan D. Stafford

GLENCOE
Macmillan/McGraw–Hill

New York, New York   Columbus, Ohio   Mission Hills, California   Peoria, Illinois

Authors

Alan Stafford earned a Bachelor of Science degree in economics from the honors program at Western Michigan State University and Master's degrees in social studies education and business administration from the State University of New York. He served as a Peace Corps volunteer in Micronesia, taught in an urban high school for 12 years, and currently is an associate professor of economics at Niagara County Community College. He has taught courses sponsored by the New York State Department of Education and the New York Developmental Economics Education Program (DEEP). A recipient of 2 first place teaching awards from the New York State Council on Economic Education, he is coauthor of several economics texts.

Sanford D. Gordon earned a Ph.D. in economics from New York University. Active in the economic education movement since 1960, he served as the Executive Director of the New York State Council on Economic Education from 1979 to 1989. He is a recipient of the Calvin Kazanjian Foundation award for innovation in teaching economics and the first winner of the Bessie B. Moore Award for outstanding service and dedication to excellence and innovations in economic education. Dr. Gordon has authored many books on economics and economic education and has been adviser to numerous school districts, the New York State Education Department, banks, and local governments.

Reviewers and Consultants

Christine A. Blumberg
Social Studies Teacher
Burnt Hills—Ballston Lake
Senior High School
Burnt Hills, New York

Randolph J. Pachuta
Curriculum Specialist—
Social Studies
The School Board of Broward
County
Lauderdale Lakes, Florida

Peter Pitard
Department Chairperson,
Learning Handicapped
Grossmont High School
La Mesa, California

Harvey L. Prokop
Program Manager, Social
Studies
Educational Services Division,
*   San Diego City Schools*
San Diego, California

Delores Marie Robinson
Curriculum Specialist, Mentor
Teacher
Roosevelt High School
Fresno, California

Joseph Weintraub
Regional Administrator, New
*   York City Developmental*
Education Program
Adjunct Professor of
*   Economics*
Nassau Community College
Garden City, New York

James H. Wimberly
Social Studies Curriculum
Director/Secondary
Bibb County Board of
*   Education*
Macon, Georgia

Send all inquiries to:
GLENCOE DIVISION
Macmillan/McGraw-Hill
936 Eastwind Drive
Westerville, Ohio 43081

ISBN 0-02-822711-5 (Student Text)
ISBN 0-02-822712-3 (Teacher's Annotated Edition)

1 2 3 4 5 6 7 8 9
RRDC 99 98 97 96 95 94 93

CONTENTS

CONTENTS

CONTENTS

CONTENTS

PART 3 Understanding the Economy as a Whole   213

CONTENTS

CONTENTS

PART 4 Understanding International Economics 365

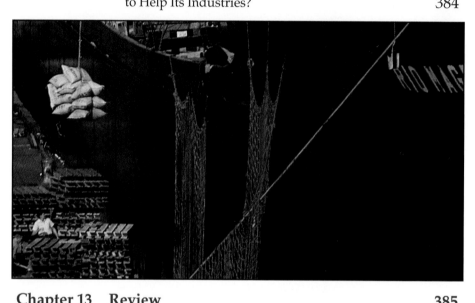

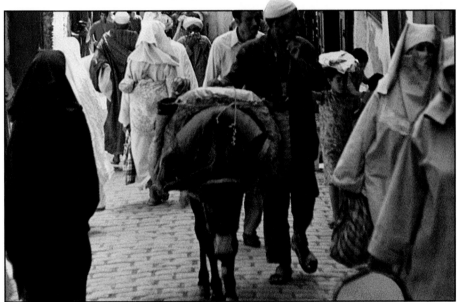

Chapter 15   *Alternative Economic Systems*   415

CONTENTS

FEATURES

FIGURES AND TABLES

FIGURES

FIGURES AND TABLES

Why Study Economics?

Economics has become an increasingly important high school course in recent years. This is partly because many people believe America as a nation will be better off if we all understand how our economy works. Another reason is this: If you understand how the economy works, you personally will be better off too.

All of us live in the economy, and we all must make economic choices. You will soon discover that you have been making economic choices all your life—even when you haven't thought of them as such. As you study economics, you will learn to make these decisions using logic and common sense. This does not have to be difficult, and it can be very interesting. It can also be profitable. The more you know about economics, the better equipped you will be to make choices that bring you the most satisfaction for your time and money.

How to Use This Book

This book will help you understand how economics and your life fit together. It is designed to do this in a way you will find easy to understand. The following features are especially important in using this book.

The Personal Narrative

Each chapter is divided into sections that begin with a Personal Narrative. The Personal Narratives are made-up stories that describe people who are roughly your age. The people in these stories experience problems that could be real. As you read the Personal Narratives, you will discover that principles of economics are at work in important events in the lives of these people. The same principles of economics also affect important events in your life.

Following each Personal Narrative is a section of test that explains the concepts that were demonstrated in the Personal Narrative. Together, the text and the Personal Narratives show how economics is a part of your everyday life. You'll find that the study of economics will help you understand what is happening in the world around you and will assist you in making better decisions.

Section-by Section Organization

This textbook is organized in sections, to enable you to concentrate on important individual principles. The list of Objectives at the beginning of each chapter shows the main principles to look for in each section. At the end of each section, the Self-Check questions help you briefly review what you have learned. The Applying What You Have Learned questions give you an opportunity to reexamine the Personal Narrative and other real-world situations.

Current Economic and Consumer Issues

Near the end of each chapter, you will find either a Current Economic Issue or a Current Consumer Issue. Current Economic Issues deal with economic questions that face the nation. As elected officials address each issue, their decisions will affect every American. Current Consumer Issues will likely affect you directly as you participate in making consumer choices. As you study such issues, you will discover that many problems of economics involve social and political values. That is one reason why people often disagree over what should be done to solve economic problems.

Developing Your Economic Skills

At the very end of each chapter, you will find a Developing Your Economic Skills feature. Each of these features gives step-by-step instructions on how to use a particular kind of skill that is important in economics. For example, one skills feature will show you how to read a table; another will show you how to interpret a bar graph. Each feature has a Skill explanation, an Application, and a Practice to give you hands-on experience in using the skill. Your teacher may ask you to study a particular skills feature when you first read the chapter or as a reference to review that particular skill.

Photographs and Figures

There are many photographs, tables, and graphs in this book. Each was included to illustrate one or more economic concepts. You have heard the saying, "one picture is worth a thousand words." The same is true of these figures. They provide information that would often take many written pages to communicate.

Each photograph is accompanied by a caption that explains a concept of economics. Each figure is explained in nearby text. Take the time to read these captions and explanations. They will make your work much easier in this course and in many other situations in the future.

TO THE STUDENT

Highlighted Vocabulary Terms

At the beginning of each section is a short statement of important terms and concepts that you will find in the section. Within the section itself, you will see that some terms are set in a heavy, dark type—these are the most important vocabulary terms. These terms are defined in the Glossary at the end of the book and are reviewed in each Chapter Review. As you read the text, if you forget exactly what a particular economic term means, look it up in the Glossary. The Glossary will define the term, and give you a page number where you can read more about it in the text.

Review Activities

Each chapter and part of the text is followed by a series of activities. All of these Activities will help you check your understanding of economic concepts. Many provide you with additional information. Some give you a chance to apply what you have learned about economics to new situations. Your teacher will probably assign some of these activities as classwork or homework. Don't be surprised if sometimes different students are assigned different activities. There is a wide selection of things to do, and your teacher has been trained to decide which are best for each student.

You may know little about economics right now. If you make a reasonable effort, that statement will not be true in a few months. You will discover that there is a logic about economics that tells you much about the way people behave and about the way things happen in the world. In learning those things, you will learn much that is valuable to you in your everyday life.

APPLYING
ECONOMIC
PRINCIPLES

1

Understanding the Fundamentals of Economics

Part 1 lays the foundation for your understanding of economics. It provides you with the meanings of many essential economic terms and concepts. You will learn what the basic economic questions are and how these questions are answered in different economic systems. You will examine the process through which resources are combined to create production and how products are distributed. And perhaps most importantly, you will learn how economists solve problems.

Life Is Economics

Objectives

In the sections of this chapter, you will learn:

A

why *scarcity* is the central economic problem;

B

how the choices we make cause us to pay *opportunity costs*;

C

how the *factors of production* combine to produce goods and services;

D

how economists use *models* to evaluate economic conditions and make predictions;

E

why people do not always agree in selecting the *rational choice*; and

F

how to interpret a graph that shows a *production possibilities frontier*.

Introduction

All your life, you will be dealing with economics. You have no choice: being born, living, and dying all involve economics. One way to define **economics** is to say that it is *the study of the decisions involved in producing, distributing, and consuming goods and services.*

In this chapter you will begin your study of economics by understanding the term *scarcity*. You will learn why we must make economic decisions and how each choice involves a trade-off of alternatives. And you will study the four factors necessary to produce goods and services.

Everyone in the United States consumes goods and services. Goods and services are things that satisfy human wants and needs. **Goods** are *tangible*—meaning that they are physical, touchable objects. **Services** are *intangible*—they are things that people do, not objects that can be touched.

Study the photograph on page 6. How many different goods and services can you identify in the photograph? Many of the people shown are working to produce products or to provide services that other people are buying. How many occupations can you identify? The people who are working are not only producing things for other people to buy, they are also earning money so they can buy products too.

The people in this street scene are producing goods and providing services—and also are buying the goods and services produced by other people.

You have studied a photograph of many people. Now look at the person in the top photograph on page 7. What sort of goods and services would this person want the most? What responsibilities does society have toward him? Do we owe him a basic income if he can't take care of himself?

Now look at the second photograph. What goods and services do children require? What is society's responsibility in providing for them? Do children deserve better treatment than adults? Should society treat a family that lives in poverty differently than the man in the preceding picture? How would you explain your feelings about this to someone else?

The third photograph shows individuals who are employed to make a product. What sort of help should be provided to them if they become unemployed? Do you believe that the unemployed should be treated differently from people who have never worked?

The final photograph is of a person who appears to be wealthy. Why do some people have many more things than others? Would you like to live like the man in this picture? What sort of choices might you have to make to be like him?

You have been asked many questions and given few answers in this introduction. There is an important reason for this: many economic issues concern *value judgments*. People often disagree over what is the "best" answer to an economic question. You

Economic decisions affect people who are living in many different kinds of circumstances. This is one reason why economic choices for a society may sometimes be difficult to make.

may feel one way about an issue while other people hold different points of view. This does not prove that you are right while others are wrong. It shows that there are different and conflicting ideas concerning economics. Still, decisions have to be made. It is important that we consider everyone's point of view when we decide what to do.

The best economic decisions are those that do the most good at the least cost. One reason for you to study economics is that by learning more you will have a better chance of making good decisions.

Section A Unlimited Wants and Limited Resources

This section introduces the concept of *scarcity* and explains why consumers, businesses, and governments must all make choices.

Personal Narrative

I Don't Have Enough

There's a hole in my right shoe. It's not a big hole, but it lets water in when it rains. Then I walk down the hall at school going "squish, squash." Everyone laughs as I go by. I really need a new pair of shoes.

I've only got $20 now. That's not enough. On Saturday I'll get paid $30 when I clean out Joe Rizzo's garage. Then I'll be able to afford a decent pair of shoes.

Joe Rizzo runs a garage where he fixes dents and paints cars. He works hard, but he doesn't do a very good job. He says he would do better work if he could afford new tools. Joe dreams a lot and buys lottery tickets. Joe's okay, but I don't want to end up like him.

I know what I want. I want to be able to just walk into a store and buy what I like. I'm tired of having to ask my mom for money that I know she really needs herself. Dad loads trucks for a living. The pay isn't very good, but it's all he can find. There never seems to be enough money by the end of the week.

Next year I'm going to graduate from high school. I hope I can find a good job, but I'm not sure that I will. My older brother graduated two years ago. He joined the Army because he couldn't find a decent job around here.

Sometimes I walk downtown just to look in the stores. I see people buying expensive things. Last week I watched a man buy a suit that cost $350. It doesn't bother me that he spent so much money; I would just like to be able to do it too.

Something happened to the man with the expensive suit that was kind of funny. It was raining when he left the store. A bus hit a pothole just when he got to the curb. It splashed him with muddy water. He may have had an expensive suit, but he was just as wet as I was.

There's a big park with a zoo downtown. On nice days I go in and watch the animals. I feel sorry for them because their cages are so small. On the other hand, they get fed every day. If they could choose, I wonder if they would take freedom or regular meals. There used to be lions in the zoo, but they were sold. It cost too much to feed them. Even the city can't afford to pay for everything.

Yesterday our landlord said that he is raising our rent by $30 next month. "Property tax went up," he said. Maybe it did, but I don't see them fixing the potholes, and the lions aren't back in the zoo.

It's almost three o'clock, time to go home. I still have a hole in my shoe and it looks like rain.

Unlimited Wants and Limited Resources

Scarcity is the economic term that describes a situation where there are not enough products available to satisfy people's needs or wants. Scarcity is based on two ideas. First, there is no limit to what we want. Second, there is a limit to our ability to produce goods and services that will satisfy our wants. This means that scarcity *always* exists. No matter how much we make, someone will always want more.

Consumers Must Choose

If we can't have everything we want, then we have to choose what we want the most. We usually make these choices when we decide how to spend our money. If you spend your money on a pair of shoes, that must be what you want most. Anything you pay for is scarce because you are giving up something of value to get it.

Businesses Must Choose

Businesses face the problem of scarcity too. If Joe Rizzo bought fewer lottery tickets he might be able to afford more tools. He can't pay for both.

The Government Must Choose

The government also is confronted with scarcity, and must make choices. Even if taxes go up, the government still has to decide what needs to be done. If resources are used to fix the roads, there may not be money left to hire as many teachers.

One example of government choice was the strategic defense initiative (SDI) or "star wars" program. In March 1983, Ronald Reagan announced a plan to develop weapons that would destroy attacking missiles before they could reach American cities or military installations. Spending continued on this program even after the breakup of the Soviet Union in the early 1990s. Today people disagree over whether SDI was a wise use for the nation's resources. It resulted in the development of the Patriot missile that helped protect American soldiers in the 1991 Persian Gulf War. Some people, however, believe the money could have been used in other ways that would have benefited more people.

Because resources are scarce, we must all make choices on how to use what we have. The SDI program was an economic choice on the government level, at a cost of many billions of dollars.

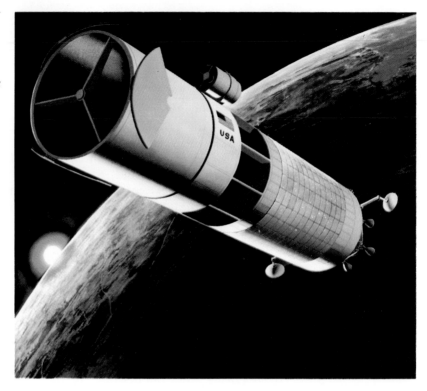

People, businesses, and the government are forced to choose. Part of this book will be devoted to showing you how these choices are made, and to helping you make good choices in your own life.

■ Self-Check

1. Why must we all make economic choices?
2. Why does scarcity always exist?

■ Applying What You Have Learned

Below you will find a list of people or organizations that were mentioned in the Personal Narrative. There was at least one thing that each didn't have enough of. Identify what each found to be scarce.

a. the person telling the story   d. the man with the suit

b. Joe Rizzo   e. the city

c. the brother   f. the animals in the zoo

Section B Everyone Pays Opportunity Costs

This section will explain how every choice involves *trade-offs* and *opportunity costs.*

Personal Narrative

If I Buy You a Pizza, I Can't Put Gas in My Car

Ted used to be my boyfriend. If I told you what I think of him now, they wouldn't print it. Last Friday Ted took me to a movie about some war hero. I didn't want to go, but he was all excited about it. I went with him to make him happy. I don't remember much about the movie. There were lots of guns and explosions. It was boring!

I was really starved when we got out of the theater around nine o'clock. Ted said, "Let's go to your place and see what your mom's got in the refrigerator." Understand, at home there would be nothing to do but watch television. That's boring! My two little brothers would have been screaming at each other and my mother would have been on the phone in the kitchen. Home was the last place on earth I wanted to be.

I told Ted I wanted to go to Eddy's Pizza to sit and talk. He said, "I've only got 15 dollars to last me until next payday. If I buy you a pizza I can't put gas in my car." Well, I was really mad. I told him that I only sat through his stupid movie because I was looking forward to going out for a pizza afterwards. He said I was selfish. I said he was cheap. Ted got me home in time to see the news. No one even noticed when I came in. I wonder what I'll do next Friday night.

Opportunity Costs

In the story above, Ted and his girlfriend both made choices. Economists call these kinds of choices **trade-offs,** meaning that you choose to give up one thing so that you can have something else instead. In making these choices, Ted and his girlfriend both paid what economists would call **opportunity cost.** Opportunity cost is a term used to describe the value of a second choice that you give up when you take your first choice. Ted refused to buy his girlfriend a pizza. She decided to tell him off. He took her home early. In each case the person got one thing but gave up something else in exchange. Ted, for example, will be able to drive to school next week, but when he gets there his girlfriend probably won't speak to him. Ted must have wanted the gas for his car most. He gave up his girlfriend's company. Ted's opportunity cost was the value he placed on his girlfriend's company.

Everyone pays opportunity costs. Each time you spend money you make a choice. You buy what you want most. When you do this, you give up the chance to buy something else instead.

Opportunity cost can also be paid in terms of time. If you take a job after school, you may have to give up the chance to join the basketball team.

Businesses Pay Opportunity Costs

Businesses must pay opportunity costs too. Many firms have invested in factories in Mexico. Money that has been spent there

The nation pays opportunity costs when it makes choices. The money spent on defense cannot at the same time be spent on health services, money spent on health services cannot at the same time be spent on education, and so on. When we pay the opportunity cost that goes with any choice, it means that we give up the value of the thing not chosen.

is money that won't be spent in the United States. Machines sent to Mexico are machines that can't be used here. Jobs for Mexican workers are jobs that American workers won't have. Businesses will receive earnings from their investments in Mexico, but they will give up the earnings they could have made from investments in the United States.

Governments Pay Opportunity Costs

Opportunity cost is also paid by the government. If the President asks for $30 billion for additional defense spending and Congress agrees, that $30 billion worth of resources will be unavailable for education or other purposes. At the same time, the money spent for education will be unavailable for the nation's defense, new housing, or health services. There is no way to be sure which type of government spending has the most value for the most people. Still, the choices must be made. And every time the government spends money an opportunity cost is paid, because the value of something else the government could have done is given up.

Everyone Makes Trade-Offs

Life is made up of a series of trade-offs in which we give up one thing in order to gain something else that we feel has greater value. We must make choices all of the time. So do businesses and governments. We all try to make decisions that give us the most value. Sometimes we succeed, sometimes we don't, but we have to go right on making choices and paying our opportunity costs.

■ *Self-Check*

1. What is a trade-off?
2. Why does every choice involve an opportunity cost?

■ *Applying What You Have Learned*

In the Personal Narrative, the people made many choices. You will find some of these choices listed below. Explain why you think each choice was made. Describe the opportunity cost that was paid for each choice.

a. The girl's choice to go to a movie she didn't really want to see
b. Ted's choice to go to a movie when he was short on money
c. Ted's choice to take his girlfriend home early

Section C   From Resources to Products

This section will explain how four factors—*natural resources, labor, capital,* and *entrepreneurship*—make production possible.

Personal Narrative

I Built a Dog House

I wish you could see my dog Washington: He's a pure-bred Afghan. My uncle gave him to me when he was just a puppy. I named him Washington because when I comb his hair he looks just like the picture on a one-dollar bill.

Washington and I had a problem. My mother said he was a "one-dog disaster area." He tracked dirt all over the house and his hair was on all of the furniture. My mom was mad when I first got the dog. She finally said I had to keep him outside or get rid of him. It doesn't get cold here, but it rains a lot. I decided that the only thing to do was to build Washington a dog house.

I went to the library and found a book that told me what I needed and how to do it. I borrowed $75 from my father. We went to the lumber yard to buy plywood, some two-by-fours, nails, shingles and paint. My father brought my supplies home in his truck.

A real problem was that I don't know how to use tools very well. The last time I had picked up a saw I ended up in the emergency room at the hospital. I made a deal with my neighbor Ed. In exchange for cutting his lawn for free, he said he'd help me build my dog house.

We worked on the job all last weekend. Sunday night I painted Washington's house. I don't think he likes it very much. He sits on the porch and whines, but Mom says he'll get used to it. Maybe he will, but I'm not sure.

From Resources to Products

In the story above, Washington's owner decided to build a dog house. Building the dog house is one example of **production,** which is the creation of any kind of good or service. To build the dog house, Washington's owner needed certain resources. **Resources** are all the things that are necessary for production. Washington's owner needed lumber, nails, shingles, and paint. He had to get help from someone who knew how to use tools. He got plans from the library and borrowed money to pay for his supplies. Finally he had to decide where to put the dog house when it was finished. All of these resources would then be called

factors of production by an economist. They are all necessary to produce goods and services.

The Four Factors of Production

Economists classify factors of production in four types (as shown in Figure 1–1). They are:

1. **Natural Resources**—things that are in their natural state and have not been changed by people. Examples would be crude oil in the ground, or trees before they are cut down to make lumber.
2. **Labor**—human effort that is applied to natural resources in producing goods and services.
3. **Capital**—the tools that are used by labor in making products. Capital can also be raw materials after they have been processed into various other forms. Money itself is not capital, but it can be considered capital when it is used to buy factories, machines, or anything else in the production process.
4. **Entrepreneurship**—the organization that is necessary to bring production about. This includes the owner or manager of a

Figure 1–1 *The Four Factors of Production*

The construction of the Atlantis *space shuttle required the use of the four factors of production: natural resources, labor, capital, and entrepreneurship.*

firm who organizes the other factors of production and takes the risks associated with running a business.

All four of these factors are necessary to achieve production.

■ *Self-Check*

1. Are all resources considered *natural* resources? Explain.
2. What are the four factors of production?

■ *Applying What You Have Learned*

The Personal Narrative contains examples of all four factors of production. From the story, make four lists:

a. examples of natural resources

b. examples of labor

c. examples of capital

d. examples of entrepreneurship

Section D How Economists Use Models

This section explains how people and economists all use *models* to understand how things work.

Personal Narrative

How Do You Talk to Someone You Don't Know?

Last summer we bought a house in the suburbs. Before we'd always rented, but Mom and Dad figured it was a good time to buy.

Before we moved in, my dad and I did a lot of work around the house. We ended up with a giant mound of trash. We set it all out just as the garbage truck arrived. It was such a hot day that we asked the two sanitation workers if they wanted a glass of some lemonade we had brought with us.

They accepted, so I poured them each a glass. But I couldn't think of anything to say. I always worry when I first meet someone new. I don't know what they're like. I'm afraid I'll say something foolish. My mom tells me to just look at them and talk about something I think they would be interested in. That's easy for her to say, but not for me to do.

As it turned out, it didn't matter, because they couldn't take time to stay and talk. They just drank the lemonade in two quick gulps and hurried on to finish their work.

I wonder what we would have talked about if they had been able to stay longer.

Using Models

What do you think of the situation described above? When you first meet someone, do you always know what to say? Do you know what things the person might be interested in and like to talk about? You might know what someone does for a living, but is there any way to guess other things about the person?

Although you could guess, there is no way for you to actually know what he is like without more information. Still, we all make judgments about other people without knowing very much about them. We often judge people based on our first impressions. If we later find that our first impressions were wrong, we just change our minds. It's not hard, people do it all the time.

Why do we try to guess what people are like when we don't know much about them? We do it because we want to know how to act. We feel safer if we know what to expect. An economist might say that when we do this we are making a **model**.

Like economists, weather forecasters use models to help predict some of the things that might happen in the future.

A model is a theory or an idea of what something is like or how something works. Models are made from incomplete information. We make models about people. Economists make models about how the economy works.

Models Are Based on Assumptions

If you want to predict what will happen to the price of gasoline, you study the factors that you think are the most important.

A list of all the things that might cause the price of gasoline to go up would be very long. No one could think of all the possible reasons at one time.

You would use a model because you know you will not have complete information when you make your prediction.

When we make models we often make assumptions. Assumptions are things that we take for granted as true. We use them as facts even though we can't be sure that they are. For example, I might assume that fancy restaurants are expensive. I might not even try a restaurant if I don't have much money. I would assume that I can't afford it. But I might be wrong. The prices at the restaurant might be quite reasonable. The quality of a model is no better than the assumptions that it is based on.

Models Can Be Revised

Economists use models to better understand the past or present and to predict the future. If an economic model results in a prediction that turns out to be right, the model can be used again. If the prediction is wrong, the model might be changed to make better predictions the next time.

Economists predict how much prices will change. They predict employment, or the number of cars that will be sold next year. They could make predictions about the effects of a tax cut. Sometimes economists' predictions turn out to be wrong, but they keep trying. We study these predictions because they help us make decisions about our own future.

Economic Predictions Affect Us All

Economists' predictions are more important than our own in at least one big way. Their predictions are used by the government and businesses when decisions are made that affect us all. Economic models and predictions are important to everyone. Many of the things you will study in this book concern economic models and how predictions are made.

■ *Self-Check*

1. Why do economists use models?
2. Do models always produce accurate predictions? Why not?

■ *Applying What You Have Learned*

In this section you have read about how economists and people in general try to make predictions so that they will know what to do in the future. Make some predictions of your own about the future of things you are familiar with. Below is a list of topics. Try to guess what will happen to each of them by the end of this semester. Put your name on your predictions. Seal them in an envelope and give the envelope to your teacher. Your class can open all the envelopes at the end of this semester and see how close you were. Think about things you could do to improve your chances of being right. Your teacher may want you to add other predictions to the list.

a. How much will a gallon of gasoline cost?
b. Who will have the #1 record on the top ten?
c. How many students will earn a *B* or better in this class?
d. How many students will have a job?

Section E   Making Rational Choices

This section discusses how people try to make *rational choices* using *positive* and *normative statements*.

Personal Narrative

My Mother Wants Me to be a Doctor

When my mother was a little girl, she had a dream about growing up to be a doctor. What she really did was get married at 17 and have five children in eight years. She never even finished high school. Twenty years later she still has her dream. She knows it won't ever come true for her, so now she wants it for me. The problem is I don't want to be a doctor.

What I like to do is write stories. That's what I'm good at. I get *A's* in English all the time. My math grades are bad and my science grades are worse. I was lucky to pass General Science last year. I tell my mom that it doesn't make any sense for someone who is lousy at math and science to try to be a doctor. She doesn't listen to me at all. She says, "Things are different today. Now a woman can be anything she wants to be. When I was a girl, everyone just expected women to be housewives. Think how much a doctor can earn. You could do something really important. You could save lives and be famous." When I tell her no one gets into medical school unless they have *A's* in science and math, she ignores me. She doesn't want to hear.

I have a lot of thinking to do about my career plans. I know that I can write well. I could go to college to learn how to be a reporter for a newspaper. I think there are lots of jobs in journalism. I'm sure that I would be happy writing for a living. The right choice for me is to study journalism and to forget about being a doctor.

Making Rational Choices

Like the young woman in the story, economists must often decide what is the right or *rational* choice. You have already learned in this chapter that economists study how decisions are made. Every time a choice is made something is given up. The woman in the story recognizes that she must choose between alternatives for her career. **Rational choice** is taking the things with greater value and giving up those with lesser values. That's the rational thing to do.

But which things have greater value? If everyone felt the same about what they did and did not want, it would be easy to decide how to use our resources. The problem is that we don't

Decisions about career goals are some of the more important rational choices that people must make. Like many other choices, they can involve both positive statements (which are based on fact and can be proven) and normative statements (which reflect personal values and will vary from one person to another).

all agree on what is best. When you make a decision just for yourself, it doesn't make much difference how others feel. But many of your decisions will affect other people who may not share your ideas. Making the best choices for groups of people is hard to do.

Positive Statements

Some things are facts. Last year's rate of inflation can be measured. We can count how many people were employed over the past year, or past five, or past ten years. And we know it is very likely that if nothing else changes, higher prices will cause lower sales. Economists call these things **positive statements** because they can be proven.

Normative Statements

There are other things that can be just as important as facts. These include things that cannot be proven and over which we may disagree. You might believe you deserve an *A* on your English report when your teacher only gave you a *C* −. The person who owns the hardware store might think that property taxes are already too high when the city council wants to increase them. The President might argue for less money for housing development and more for transportation, while Congress might see it entirely differently. These are areas where there is no "right" answer. What each person believes should be done depends on his or her individual values. Economists call these **normative statements.** Many of the things we will study in this book will be normative, and so will have no single answer upon which everyone can agree.

Social Values and Choices

Economic systems exist within social systems that are made up of traditions and values. Social values—such as equality, justice, and freedom—help determine the goals we set for our businesses. Differences of opinion concerning these "socio-economic" goals often result in conflicting normative statements.

Making rational choices about normative statements is a very difficult job. No matter what you do, some people will end up being better off while others will feel that they are worse off. What we try to do is make decisions that help more people than they harm. When you consider the fact that most people don't agree on what is best, you can see why this is hard to do.

Putting Rational Choices to a Test

Most governments have the right of eminent domain. This means that they may force people to sell private property for public use. In many cities, entire neighborhoods have been torn

In the process of redevelopment, many cities face choices between low-cost housing and new office buildings for businesses. These choices involve trade-offs. The costs and benefits of such choices are not always borne by all people equally.

down and replaced with new buildings. Sometimes people are forced to sell their homes so businesses can move into urban areas. Is this a rational choice for society? What is the role of value judgments in such a decision?

☐ *Self-Check*

1. How are positive statements different from normative statements?
2. Why is it easier to make a rational choice just for yourself than to make one that affects many people?

☐ *Applying What You Have Learned*

In the Personal Narrative, the young woman deals with both positive and normative statements in choosing a career path. Look back at the story and find

a. one positive and one normative statement made by the mother, and
b. one positive and one normative statement made by the young woman.

Section F Using the Production Possibilities Frontier

This section introduces the idea of a *production possibilities frontier*.

Personal Narrative

Should I Grow More Cucumbers or More Tomatoes?

My name is Ruth. My husband Dave and I own two acres of land just outside of town. Dave doesn't have much free time because he works in a local factory and studies economics in night school. I do most of the housework and take care of our two children. We are often short on money, so I raise vegetables and sell them at a roadside stand. Over the years I have found that tomatoes and cucumbers grow and sell well. Last year I decided growing anything else is too much work. My problem was to decide how much of each crop I should grow.

I kept track of what I grew last year and decided we own enough land to grow either 400 tomato or 200 cucumber plants. I could also grow some of each. An extra cucumber plant means two fewer tomato plants. In August I expect to harvest an average of ten tomatoes or five cucumbers per plant. Therefore, if I grew only tomatoes, I could harvest 4,000 a day in August.

$$400 \text{ plants x } 10 \text{ each } = 4,000 \text{ a day}$$

If I grew only cucumbers I could harvest 1,000 a day.

$$200 \text{ plants x } 5 \text{ each } = 1,000 \text{ a day}$$

I have drawn the graph below to help me decide what to do.

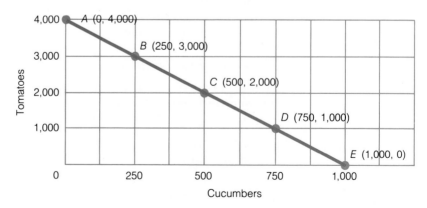

All graphs have two axes, a *y* or vertical axis, and an *x* or horizontal axis. In this case the *y* axis represents tomatoes I could grow while the *x* axis represents cucumbers. Each of the lettered points on the graph stands for a combination of the two crops I could produce. The amounts are shown in parentheses next to the lettered points. The first amount in parentheses is always the *x* axis (cucumbers) and the second amount is always the *y* axis (tomatoes).

If I could sell tomatoes for a higher price than cucumbers, I might choose to grow 4,000 tomatoes and no cucumbers (represented by point *A* on the graph). But I have found that I can't sell more than 2,000 tomatoes a day, so I have chosen to produce 2,000 tomatoes and 500 cucumbers (represented by point *C* on the graph). I have traded the production of 2,000 tomatoes for 500 cucumbers. This trade can be seen as movement from point *A* (0, 4,000) to point *C* (500, 2,000) on the graph.

I have drawn a line connecting points *A* through *E* on the graph. This line represents the different combinations of the two crops I could grow. I understand that economists would call this line a production possibilities frontier.

The Production Possibilities Frontier

A **production possibilities frontier** is a graph that shows the different combinations of two products that can be produced from a given quantity of the four factors of production. Each product is represented by an axis. Amounts of the products that could be produced are plotted along these axes. Suppose that a factory could produce either radios or TV sets. The table below could

The owners of this stand must decide how much of which products to grow and sell. A production possibilities frontier can be used in making such a decision.

represent the combinations of these two products that could be produced from the firm's resources *if* the firm is using its resources most efficiently.

Production Combinations

Combination	Radios	TV Sets
A	600	0
B	400	50
C	200	100
D	0	150

Each combination can be represented by a point on a graph:

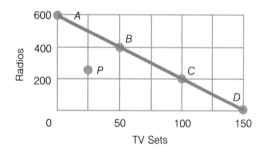

If a firm's actual amount of production appears *inside* the production possibilities frontier (see point *P*), the firm either is not using all its factors of production or else is using them inefficiently.

■ Self-Check

1. What does a production possibilities frontier mean?
2. How does a production possibilities frontier show trade-offs?

■ Applying What You Have Learned

Production possibility frontiers are economic models. They represent reality. They are not reality itself. Which of the following would be true regarding production possibility frontiers?

a. They don't tell you the price of the products.
b. They can only be used for two products at a time.
c. They don't provide any useful information.
d. They don't tell you how much of one product would have to be given up to get an additional unit of the other product.
e. They assume that there is no problem shifting production from one product to another.

CURRENT CONSUMER ISSUES

Should High School Graduates Come With a Guarantee?

Many Americans believe our high schools are graduating young people who have limited academic ability and few skills. Employers complain that they must often train new employees to read, write, and do simple math. The Los Angeles Unified School District in California has announced steps to try to reduce this problem.

Starting in 1994, graduates of Los Angeles high schools will receive a diploma and a written warranty. The warranty guarantees future employers that graduates have basic skills in reading, mathematics, and effective communications. It also guarantees that students have acquired thinking skills, such as problem solving and reasoning, as well as personal qualities, like self-management and responsibility.

Any employer who finds a 1994 (or later) graduate lacking in any of these areas may request remedial classes for the employee from the school district at no cost. The firm must continue to employ the worker to obtain this help.

Many community leaders and teachers doubt that the program will work. They suggest that if the schools provided an adequate education in the first place, a guarantee would not be necessary. Leaders of the teachers' union called it "smoke and mirrors" to take public attention away from other problems facing the schools. They pointed out that the board of education asked teachers to take a 3 percent pay cut to help reduce the district's budget problems two days after the warranty program was announced.

Do you believe warranties for graduates is a good idea?

Arguments in Favor of the Plan
1. It might make some students and teachers work harder.
2. It would assure employers that new employees would be able to complete certain tasks or they would receive free training.
3. It could make it easier for new graduates to find jobs.

Arguments Against the Plan
1. It would cost a great deal of money to carry out properly.
2. It requires even greater spending for future remedial programs.
3. It takes attention away from the real problems faced by schools.

What Do You Think?
If you were a taxpayer in Los Angeles, would you support this program? If you were a student? An employer? How does this situation relate to scarcity and opportunity costs?

Chapter 1 Review

What Have You Learned?

In this chapter you have learned the following important principles of economics:

- The central problem in economics is *scarcity*—the inability to produce enough goods and services to satisfy all of our wants.
- Scarcity exists because people will always want more than they can have.
- Because of scarcity, people, businesses, and the government must all make *trade-offs* in choosing the products they want the most.
- When a choice is made, an *opportunity cost* is paid. Opportunity cost is the value of the choice given up when the first choice is taken.
- Production—the creation of goods and services—requires four factors. The *four factors of production* are *natural resources, labor, capital,* and *entrepreneurship.* These factors exist in limited quantities, and therefore it is impossible for us to produce all the products we would like to have.

- To understand how the factors of production operate in the economy, we sometimes use *models.* Models are representations of reality, not the reality itself, and although they are not perfect, they do help us try to understand what will happen next in the economy.
- In making economic decisions we try to make the *rational choice.* This means that we try to make the choice that has the greatest amount of benefits compared to costs.
- Decisions may involve both *positive* and *normative* statements. Positive statements are statements of fact; normative statements are statements that express our values.
- Economic choices can often be illustrated with tables or graphs. One such graph—the *production possibilities frontier*—shows the different combinations of two products that can be produced from a fixed quantity of the four factors of production. It also shows what a firm (or nation) is capable of producing if it is using all of its resources efficiently.

Words and Terms

economics (p. 5)
goods (p. 5)
services (p. 5)
scarcity (p. 9)
trade-offs (p. 11)
opportunity cost (p. 11)
production (p. 14)
resources (p. 14)
factors of production (p. 15)

natural resources (p. 15)
labor (p. 15)
capital (p. 15)
entrepreneurship (p. 15)
model (p. 17)
rational choice (p. 20)
positive statements (p. 21)
normative statements (p. 22)
production possibilities frontier (p. 25)

Building Your Vocabulary

On a separate piece of paper, write the vocabulary word or term that best completes each of the following statements.

1. The value of your second choice that you give up when you take your first choice is _____.
2. The central problem in economics is _____.
3. _____ is the study of the production, distribution and consumption of goods and services.
4. An expression of fact is called a _____.
5. Raw materials that have not been processed are _____.
6. The creation of goods and services is called _____.
7. The resources necessary for production are classified as the four _____.
8. A graph showing the combinations of two products that could be made from a fixed set of resources is called a _____.
9. _____ is human effort that is applied to natural resources to produce goods and services.
10. An expression of a value judgment can be called a _____.
11. A factor that initiates and supervises production is called _____.
12. _____ _____ means making decisions such that the benefits to society are greater than the costs.
13. The tools that are used by labor in making products are _____.
14. A theory of reality used to make predictions is called a _____.
15. When you give up one thing for another, you are making a _____.
16. Tangible things that satisfy human wants and needs are _____.
17. Intangible things that satisfy human wants and needs are _____.
18. _____ are all the things necessary to produce goods and services.

Understanding Economics

Answer each of the following on a separate piece of paper.

1. What are the two ideas upon which *scarcity* is based?
2. Identify the *opportunity cost* John paid when he spent his $20 on a new pair of gloves instead of a new shirt.
3. Explain what people try to achieve when they make decisions or *trade-offs*.
4. Suppose a Native American chief told his people to cut down a tree with axes to make a canoe. Each of the *four factors of production* (natural resources, labor, capital, and entrepreneurship) would be used in making the boat. Identify the specific example of each from this situation.
5. Describe what models are and how they are used by economists.
6. Explain why the predictions made by economists can be more important than predictions we might make as private individuals.
7. According to the *production possibilities frontier* below, how many chairs would the firm have to give up to produce ten more tables?

Production Possibilities Frontier, Al's Furniture

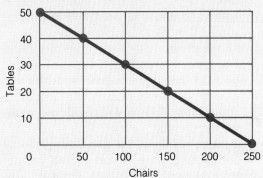

Chapter 1 Review

8. Describe the purpose of making a *rational choice*.
9. Explain the difference between *normative* and *positive statements*.

Thinking Critically About Economics

1. Suppose you won a contest and your prize was a free shopping spree at your local discount store. You could keep anything you carried out in three minutes. Make a list of at least five different products you would take. Explain why you would take each product.
2. Choose a product that you use frequently. Identify each of the four factors of production that were used to make it.
   a. What natural resources were used?
   b. What type of skills did the workers need?
   c. What type of tools were used?
   d. Describe the firm that made the product. Is it large? What else does it make?
3. Describe an important decision that you have made. Explain the opportunity cost you paid when you made this decision.
4. There are many types of models other than economic models. Two are weather maps and house plans. Describe at least three other types of models that you know about.
5. Read an editorial from your local newspaper. Copy three positive statements from the editorial and three normative statements. Be sure to identify which is which.
6. Find an article in a national magazine concerning an important decision made recently by the federal government. Answer each of the following:

   a. Describe the decision that was made.
   b. Identify a particular person or group of people who will be better off because of this decision. In what way will they benefit?
   c. Identify a particular person or group of people who will be worse off because of this decision. In what way will they be hurt?
7. You have four hours to clean your room and/or study for a math test. Draw a production possibility frontier showing the different ways you could use your time.

Consumer Skills Projects

1. Take a survey of students in your class, asking what they would do if they won $50 in a contest. Ask several adults the same question. Describe differences between the kinds of consumer choices these people would make. Suggest reasons why different people make different trade-offs when they make consumer decisions. Why can different decisions be examples of rational choices for different people?
2. Make a bulletin board for your classroom showing the factors of production that are combined into different consumer products you or other members of your family buy. The figure on page 15 in the text may give you some ideas of how to do this.
3. Make one collage of statements cut from newspaper advertisements that are normative and another of statements that are positive. Explain which statements would be most useful in helping people make rational consumer decisions.

Developing Your Economic Skills

Constructing a Line Graph

Skill: In this lesson you'll review how to read and construct a line graph (you already encountered line graphs on pages 24–26). A line graph is used to show the relationship between two sets of information. One set of information is represented by values on the horizontal or *x* axis. The other is represented by values on the vertical or *y* axis. To complete a line graph, you'll follow these three steps:

1. Assemble both sets of information in a table.
2. Plot the information as points on the graph and connect the points.
3. Interpret the graph.

Application: Suppose there is a $40 tax on property for each $1,000 of assessed value in your school district. To construct a graph of the relationship between property values and the amount of tax paid, you would first organize information in a table similar to the one below. This table has two columns. The left column is for assessed property values and the right is for the amount of tax.

Assessed Property Value	Amount of Tax
$20,000	$ 800
$40,000	$1,600
$60,000	$2,400
$80,000	$3,200

The information on the table can now be used to construct a graph. Let the vertical axis represent the assessed property value. The values on the vertical axis must go up from zero to the maximum assessed property value of $80,000. The axis is divided into equal units, each representing an additional $10,000.

Let the horizontal axis represent property taxes. The values on this axis must reach the maximum tax of $3,200. This axis is divided into equal units of $400 each.

Points are then plotted to represent combinations of values on the table. For example, point *A* represents a tax of $800 on property with an assessed value of $20,000. Point *B* represents a tax of $1,600 on property with an assessed value of $40,000. The rest of the points represent other combinations of taxes and assessed values from the table. A graph may be drawn by connecting the points that have been plotted.

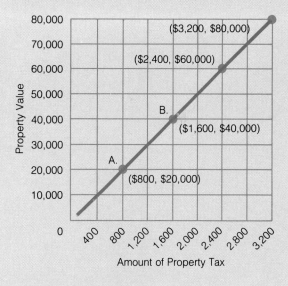

This graph shows there is a *positive* relationship (meaning that as one goes up, so does the other) between property values and the amount of tax owners must pay.

Practice: Graph the relationship between property values and the amount of tax paid in your community.

Economic Systems: Who Made the Rules?

Objectives

In the sections of this chapter, you will learn:

A

why economic systems developed and how the *division of labor* made *specialization*, and *wealth*, possible;

B

how *capitalism* deals with the economic questions *what, how,* and *for whom;*

C

how *profits* affect *allocation of resources* in capitalism; and

D

how a *command economy* functions.

Introduction

Who organized the first economic system? Did a cave man walk out of the jungle one day and say, "I think I'll open a taco stand"? The answer to the question is, "Of course not!" Still, someone did start the first economic system.

An **economic system** is a set of rules that governs what goods and services to produce, how to produce them, and for whom they are produced. People organize production in such a system to be more efficient in their use of resources. Improved productivity allows them to have more things and to live better lives. Before there were economic systems, individuals worked just for themselves or for their own families. No one became very skilled at anything because everyone had to do so many different jobs.

Economic systems allow specialization. People can do the things they are best at and trade for goods or services that others provide. When people specialize in the things they do well, total production is greater and people end up being better off.

In this chapter you will learn about different types of economic systems that exist or have existed in the world. You will find that each system has advantages and disadvantages. The system that is best for a country depends on the values and beliefs of the people it serves. People are not all the same. Because people are not all the same, there is no one economic system that is best for all countries.

Most of this chapter will be devoted to the American economic system, which is called **capitalism.** Capitalism is an economic system in which the means of production are owned and controlled by private individuals or groups. Governments play a limited role in capitalism. Most economic decisions are made in **markets** that exist when individuals buy and sell goods and services. This is why capitalism is sometimes called a *market* economy.

In the United States, economic decisions begin with consumers. This is not the case in many other countries. Some countries have **traditional** economic systems, in which economic decisions are based mostly on customs. You will learn more about traditional economies in Chapter 14.

At one time there were many countries that had **command** economies. Today there are few. In these countries most economic decisions are made by government authorities. Individuals have little choice in how these economic systems run. (You will learn more about command economies in Chapter 15.)

Although we refer to some economies as command economies and to others as capitalism, no economy is purely one kind or the other. All are *mixed*—meaning that even the most capitalistic economy will incorporate some aspects of a command economy, and even the most extreme command economy will incorporate some aspects of capitalism.

The American economy has matured and grown over the past two hundred years. The goods and services we produce and consume have changed. Some of our values are different from what they used to be. Most Americans feel a sense of responsibility for each other. We recognize the rights of individuals, but we also see a need to aid those who are unable to care for themselves. We are willing to give up some of our freedom and property for the good of the community.

As you read this chapter, you will realize that we do not have pure capitalism in the United States. You will learn how economic decisions are usually made in this country. Sometimes you will know of cases where our system does not work the way it is described in the text. Don't let this confuse you. Remember, we are studying how most of the American economy works most of the time. This chapter will teach you the basic ideas of capitalism. Later in the book you will learn why there are exceptions to the rules.

Section A How Economic Systems Developed

This section introduces the ideas of *specialization*, the *division of labor*, and *wealth*.

Personal Narrative

From Yesterday to Tomorrow

Thousands of years ago, on the banks of a small river, Grug (a cave dweller) lived with his relatives. Grug's family and other families grouped together as a unit, but each family took care of itself. Each family fished, hunted, gathered grain, made bread, and performed all of the other jobs necessary to their way of life. Although the family groups met socially at dances, they never traded the things that they made.

Poor Grug! He was most unhappy. You see, Grug was the best hunter that had ever been. He could sling stones two hundred paces and never miss his target. In an hour he could kill all the meat his family needed for a week. Grug loved to hunt.

The problem was that he was expected to do all the other "manly tasks" too. When he went fishing, he usually slipped and fell in the river. When he gathered grain, he got bored. If he tried to bake bread, he burnt his fingers. The only job he liked was hunting.

One day Grug decided to do nothing but hunt. From dawn to dusk he spent all his time hunting. He killed more animals than he could use, so he just left them lying around. Before long the village began to smell. People got angry with Grug. His wife scolded him for never fishing or gathering grain. The chief threatened to throw him into the river if he did not stop. Grug was in despair.

Then Grug had a wonderful idea. He remembered that his cousin Thump was a good fisher, his sister-in-law Buff made the best bread in the village, and his nephew Gerg could gather more grain than anyone else. When he thought about it, Grug realized that each person in the village was best at one particular job.

Grug asked the chief to call a meeting of the villagers. He promised to solve all of their problems. The chief agreed, but said if he didn't like what he heard, Grug would be useful as lion bait. At the meeting, Grug suggested that all the people do only the jobs they were good at and trade for the other things they needed. The villagers immediately saw the wisdom of his idea. They could each spend their time doing the things they liked to do best. Grug was saved from being lion bait.

As Grug's idea was put into practice, people found that they were better off than they had ever been before. Not only were people doing the jobs they liked best, but they were getting better at their jobs because they had more practice. They found that they could produce as many things as they needed in half the time. They had time left to sit in the sun and talk.

Some of this talk was about ways to improve production. The villagers built a dam to store water for the dry season, they discovered how to make bows and arrows, and they even discussed the possibility of traveling to the next village up the river to trade their furs for clay pots that were made there.

When the old chief died, Grug became the new leader. He lived a long and prosperous life in peace and happiness.

The Division of Labor

Of course the story of Grug never happened, but the economic concepts in the story are important and real. Grug lived in a traditional economy. What people did, and how they produced goods and services, was largely determined by customs. When Grug introduced new ways of doing things, he replaced old traditions with new ideas. Economists call his idea the **division of labor.** This means dividing the process of production into specific tasks. Each task is completed by the person who is best suited to that job. Workers become more efficient because each has a chance to practice his or her task.

Specialization Increases Productivity

The division of labor allows *specialization* of labor. **Specialization** occurs when individual workers concentrate their labor on single tasks, enabling each worker to become more efficient and productive. In Grug's village each person specialized in the task he or she liked best, and their productivity increased.

The division of labor also allows the development of **specialized capital.** In the first chapter of this text you learned that capital is one of the four factors of production. One example of capital is tools that are designed to increase the efficiency of a particular task in production. The dam and the bows and arrows that Grug's villagers made are examples of specialized capital. When everyone worked only for their own family, no one had the time to make these tools. The division of labor gave the villagers the time to invest in tools that increased their productivity and standard of living. They also had the time to consider trading with other villages, which could improve their lives by taking advantage of the skills of other people in other places.

Wealth Permits Investment

The tools and products that are accumulated in an economic system are called **wealth** by economists. For an economic system to grow, it must produce enough goods and services so that some people do not need to be involved in production for current consumption. They can build factories or machines that will make it easier to produce more goods and services. In Grug's village the division of labor gave the people enough time to build specialized tools that became the basis for increased production and wealth in the future.

Over time Grug's village could have grown into a city and then a nation. What started out as a traditional agricultural economy could have become a market or command economy. At some time the traditional values and customs might have been changed into a set of rules. A government would have developed that could formalize methods for changing these rules. The rules might have been written down as laws. Grug's ideas would then have become the basis of the nation's economic system.

In different parts of the world other people could have had other leaders and other ideas. They could have developed different economic systems to suit their own needs and beliefs. Still, all economic systems have some factors in common. They all concern the division of labor, specialization, and the accumulation of wealth. In the following sections you will learn about other things that economic systems have in common.

Examples of Increased Productivity

One of the best examples of the advantages offered by the division of labor and specialization is the introduction of the assembly line into automobile manufacturing by Henry Ford. This process cut the time necessary to assemble a car from a day and a half to 93 minutes. It also cut the price of a new car by over 50 percent. The assembly line itself is an example of specialized capital made possible through the accumulation of wealth. Its result was a major improvement in productivity.

Another example of the changes that can result from specialized tools can be seen in American agriculture. In 1910 it took over 13 million farmers to feed the United States population of just over 90 million people. Today fewer than 2.8 million farmers

Henry Ford's assembly line introduced division of labor and specialization—assigning a single task to each worker—into automobile production. The process greatly increased production and cut the price of new cars.

can feed a population that is more than two and a half times as large as it was in 1910. Table 2–1 shows how this change has taken place since 1910. This increased production is possible because of the improved tools farmers use today.

Table 2–1
Farm Employment and Production, 1910 through 1990
(values times 1,000)

Year	Acres Farmed	Farmers (full- and part-time)	Production Index (1977 = 100)	Total U.S. Population
1910	879,000	13,555	29	92,400
1930	987,000	12,497	34	123,200
1950	1,202,000	9,926	48	151,700
1970	1,102,000	4,523	66	205,100
1990	988,000	2,772	160	249,600

Source: *Statistical Abstract of the United States*, 1991; *Historical Abstract of the United States*, 1959.

The transition from the horse-drawn plow has been possible because the division of labor gives people the time necessary to create more efficient tools.

■ Self-Check

1. What is an economic system?
2. How does the division of labor improve productivity?
3. What must an economic system provide in order to grow?

■ Applying What You Have Learned

Look back at the story about Grug and find at least three examples of the division of labor. Name at least two benefits that come about from the division of labor.

Section B   The Basic Questions: *What, How,* and *For Whom?*

This section will introduce the basic economic questions of *what, how,* and *for whom.*

Personal Narrative   *Should We Sell Yogurt in the School Store?*

The school bookstore is in danger of going broke. Lina, the student manager, has called a staff meeting to discuss the problem. She is huddled with the student clerks and their advisor, Mr. Berkley, trying to think of a solution. The conversation begins:

Mike: So what's the problem, Lina? Haven't we sold enough pencils?

Lina: Oh be quiet! The problem is we've been paying clerks $4.50 an hour and we haven't earned enough money to cover their wages.

Mark: Why not just increase our prices? We could charge 25 cents for pencils and a dollar for pens.

Sharon: Yeah, and no one would buy anything at all. They would just do without or buy it at the discount store after school.

Ralph: We should sell candy bars and potato chips. We'd make a fortune!

Mr. B: We can't sell junk food, Ralph. The principal would close us down. She'll only allow us to sell school supplies and what she calls "nourishing snacks."

Sharon: So what's a nourishing snack? Tofu?

Mark: Don't be stupid! She means things like raisins, sunflower seeds and trail mix.

Ralph: No one's gonna buy that stuff. We may as well forget food. It's too bad; we could make a lot of money from candy.

Lina: Well, how about yogurt? The teachers would buy that.

Mark: How can we sell yogurt? We don't have a refrigerator to store it in.

Mr. B: There's an old one in my basement you could use. I think it still works.

Sharon: How about granola bars? They're healthy. You can get them with chocolate chips, honey and everything!

Ralph: Great idea! And we could sell popcorn. That's healthy too.

Mr. B: Slow down. The granola bars and yogurt may be okay, but there's no chance for popcorn. You know, there is another alternative.

Mark: What?

Mr. B: You could take a cut in pay to, say, $3.50 an hour, or you could have fewer clerks. Most of you just stand around as it is. You're not using your resources wisely.

Ralph: Oh, come on, Mr. B. We need the pay. For most of us it's the only spending money we get.

Mr. B: You may think you need the money, but you aren't earning it. Unless you can cut your costs or increase your income, the store will be closed, and then you will earn nothing. The decision is yours to make.

Answering the Basic Economic Questions

These students may not realize it, but their problems are the same ones all economic systems face. They are trying to decide *what* to sell, *how* to sell it and *who* should receive the benefits from what is sold. All economic systems must solve similar problems:

1. **What** goods and services should be produced?
2. **How** should these goods and services be produced?
3. **For whom** is the benefit of these goods and services being produced?

In capitalistic economic systems these decisions are made by people or by groups of people.

What?

The question *what* is answered every time people buy goods or services. When sales are made, stores usually order additional products to replace those that were sold. Manufacturers receive these orders and set their production schedules. They allocate resources to products that sell. Products that do not sell are not ordered and are not produced. In a market economy consumers determine what products will be made when they buy things.

How?

The question *how* is answered by producers according to what will yield the greatest profits. Capitalistic firms are in business to make money. One way to improve profits is to find the least expensive means of production. The least expensive way is also the most efficient way. Customers determine what will be made in capitalism, but entrepreneurs decide how to make it.

For Whom?

The question *for whom* refers to who will receive the benefits produced by the economic system. The question is answered ac-

Every economic system must answer three questions: what will be produced, how will it be produced, and who will receive the benefits of the production. When you buy something in capitalism, you are helping determine what will be produced. When you receive a paycheck, you are receiving some of the benefits of production.

cording to the value of a person's contribution to production. People work and earn money. The amount they earn usually depends on the value of their labor. A research chemist might earn $50,000 a year, while a janitor could earn only $14,000. Economists would explain much of the difference in their pay by pointing out the difference in the value of what they do. The chemist's labor contributes more to the final value of the product than that of the janitor. In capitalism, income usually determines how much people can buy. People who make more valuable contributions to production are paid better and usually receive more of what is produced.

Everyone knows about a person who has "made it." In capitalism, people who do well usually are those who are best able to answer the questions *what* and *how.* If you can do this, the *for whom* often turns out to be good for you.

For example, the "hula hoop" craze swept the nation in 1958. Suddenly it seemed that everyone was trying to spin a piece of colored plastic around his or her body without letting it fall to the ground. Doctors said it was bad for the back. Some people said it was a waste of time and money. But for the Wham-O company the product was a gold mine. This firm offered a product people wanted at a price they were willing to pay. They sold millions in only a few months. Eventually people got bored with the "hula hoop" and stopped buying it, but for a time Wham-O did very well.

The table below shows that some occupations command higher wages than others. Think about why this is the case. What does this have to do with the workers' contributions to production?

Table 2–2
Average Hourly Wages by Industry, 1991

Industry	Average Hourly Wage
Manufacturing	$11.22
Mining	$14.31
Construction	$14.01
Transportation/Utilities	$13.26
Wholesale Trade	$11.14
Retail Trade	$ 7.03
Finance, Insurance & Real Estate	$10.40
Services	$10.25

Source: *Employment and Earnings*, U.S. Department of Labor, Oct. 1991 (July data).

■ *Self-Check*

1. What do the questions *what* and *how* mean to economists?
2. How does a market (or capitalistic) economy decide who will receive the benefits from what is produced and sold?

■ *Applying What You Have Learned*

Look back to the story of Lina and her co-workers in the school store. They were trying to answer the questions of *what* and *how* so that the *for whom* could be for them. Study the conversation and find two statements that deal with *what,* two with *how,* and two with *for whom.*

Section C The Role of Profits in the Economy

This section will explain the relationship between *profits* and the *allocation of resources*.

Personal Narrative

If I Make It Big, I Can Retire When I'm 30

My name's Regina. I'm going to try running my own business. When I was about three my mother took me to see the boats at the dock one hot summer evening. She had promised to buy me a hot dog but the stand had gone out of business. I can still see all those people staring at me while I screamed because she couldn't buy what I wanted. I remember their faces a lot better than I remember the boats. Ever since that day I've had the idea that I could open up that hot dog stand and get rich. I saved my money and rented the stand. Next week I'm going to try.

I've worked for over a month cleaning and painting. It's been 20 years since the stand was used. I bought a new grill and a freezer. I had new wiring and plumbing put in. I ordered hot dogs, buns, ice cream bars and all the other things I need. The health department has been here to inspect my store. I even bought an insurance policy. I've spent over $10,000, and I haven't sold anything yet, but I'm not worried.

Every evening retired people come here from the village to fish and watch the sun go down. There are hundreds of them. There isn't a restaurant or fast-food store within a mile. Many of them bring sacks of food and sit on the dock to eat. They must be uncomfortable. I've bought 8 aluminum tables and 32 chairs. I'm sure those people will buy my food and sit at my tables. After I get this store going I can take my profits and start other stands on other docks all up and down the coast. I could retire when I'm 30!

Profits Allocate Resources

The young woman in the story above is going into business in a capitalistic economic system. Her purpose is to make a profit.

Profits Are an Incentive

Profit is the incentive (reason) for starting a business in capitalism. Any firm that makes a profit must be selling products customers want at prices they are willing to pay. The firm's cost of production must also be less than its selling price. Regina

Like Regina, the owner of this food stand is in business to make a profit.

thinks she knows what the people in her community want, but is she right?

Let's assume that Regina's stand is successful, and she makes a large profit. What would she do with it? She has stated that her plan is to expand her business. She would use her profits to buy more resources and start new hot dog stands. Her profits would enable her to allocate more resources to her business.

Profits Allocate Resources

The **allocation of resources** is a problem that must be solved in all economic systems. In capitalism, profitable firms are better able to afford scarce resources. Firms that are not profitable rarely have the money to buy scarce resources. Successful firms are profitable because they make products people want and sell them for prices people are willing to pay. These are the firms we would like to see grow, and in capitalism they do. The allocation of resources in capitalism is efficient because resources tend to be attracted to the most profitable firms.

The vast expansion of McDonald's would not have been possible if its early hamburger stands had not been profitable.

Profit is the basic incentive in capitalism, and it is also the basic method of allocation.

One example of a firm that was able to grow as a result of its profitability is the McDonald's Corporation. When the first McDonald's hamburger stand was opened in the 1950s, the price of a bag of french fries was 12 cents, hamburgers were 15 cents, and soft drinks cost 10 cents. Even in the 1950s these were low prices. People bought McDonald's products and the firm was a great success. Today there are McDonalds stores in every state and in many foreign nations. What did profits and the allocation of resources have to do with the success of this business?

■ Self-Check

1. What must a firm do to earn a profit in capitalism?
2. What do profits have to do with the allocation of resources in capitalism?

■ Applying What You Have Learned

In starting her business Regina plans to use various factors of production. Identify specific examples of each of the following:

a. Natural Resources
b. Labor
c. Capital
d. Entrepreneurship

Section D Economic Decisions in Other Systems

This section discusses how the basic economic decisions are made in *command economies*.

A Visit Home

My name is Mayling Wang. My great-grandfather came to the United States to build railroads in California in 1880. Although he had expected to return to China, he never went home. He later bought land here and grew vegetables that he sold to earn his living. Eventually he opened a store and became quite wealthy. Grampa Wang died before I was born, but a picture of him and his vegetable store hangs on the wall of our living room. When I was growing up I felt that in some way he was watching over me. I have always wanted to go to China to see the area where our family came from. A few years ago I took the trip back to China that my great-grandfather was never able to make.

I booked my trip through an American travel agency. However, when I reached China my travels were controlled by representatives of a Chinese government tourist organization. The hotels I stayed in were run by the government. The railroads I traveled on were owned and operated by the government. Even the tour guides who went with me were employed by the government. As I traveled I saw steel mills, clothing factories, and coal mines that were government owned and operated. One guide told me that Chinese doctors work for the government and that the hospitals are free because they are paid for by the government. I could tell that the guide was very proud of her country and its accomplishments.

Before going to China I read about the Chinese people's desire for less government control over their lives. On my visit I learned that during the 1980s people in China had been given some economic freedom. Many farms and small businesses were allowed to operate under private ownership. While this freedom increased the economic choices ordinary people could make, it did not change the basic character of the Chinese economy. Most businesses and resources remained in the hands of the government.

I visited my ancestors' hometown while I was in China. It is located along the banks of the Lijang River near Guilin. The countryside was very beautiful and the farmers seemed happy and successful. Many of them worked their own farms and decided what to grow for themselves. I have come to the conclusion that the people of China have more economic freedom than they had ten years earlier, but that their lives are very different from ours in the United States. I enjoyed my visit, but I don't think that I could adjust to a country where the people have so few freedoms and such limited opportunities.

Other Ways to Decide *What, How,* and *For Whom*

Mayling visited a country that doesn't have a capitalistic economic system. In 1992 in the People's Republic of China and a few other countries, the economic questions *what, how,* and *for whom* were mainly answered by the government.

Capitalism Compared to Command Economies

In capitalism people have the right to start businesses on their own. They decide what products to make according to what they expect to sell. They produce goods and services in the way they believe will earn the most profit. People receive income depending on the value of their contribution to production. Their income determines what they are able to buy. This is not how the economic system in China worked in 1992.

People in China live in a command economy. Such an economy attempts to make trade-offs between economic security and personal freedom.

Decisions in a Command Economy

In 1992 in the Chinese economy ordinary citizens did not help make most of the basic economic decisions. Instead, an agency of the government or a central planning authority made these decisions.

The people who set up this economic system believed that government officials would be better able to decide "what" products should be made. They argued that businesses in capitalism would make products for the rich and ignore the poor. They felt that their government would know what products were really needed.

They also believed that their government would be best able to decide how to make products. In deciding "how" to make goods and services they would consider what sort and number of jobs people needed. They would not allow unemployment because they would not be concerned about making a profit.

Finally, they felt their government would do a better job of deciding "for whom" products should be made. From their point of view, capitalism would cause some people to be very rich while others would be very poor. They were in favor of distributing products according to need.

It may be easier for you to understand how command economies work by considering the chart in Figure 2-1. The chart shows how goods and services and the factors of production move within a command economy. (A chart that portrays the

Figure 2-1 *Flowchart for a Command Economy*

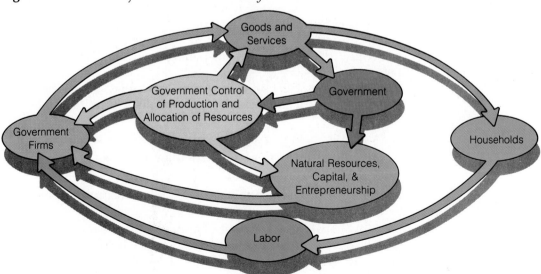

capitalistic economic system will be presented in Chapter 3.) You will notice that most of the factors of production on this chart are controlled by the government.

On the lower half of the chart, resources flow to the firms to be used for the production of goods and services. Only labor comes from households. Natural resources, capital, and entrepreneurship are supplied by the government. These factors are not bought and sold as they would be in the United States. They are allocated by the government, which also owns them.

On the top half of the chart, goods and services flow to the people and the government. The type and number of products that are produced are controlled by the government. The only choice people really have is whether or not to buy the products.

In Chapter 15 you will learn more about alternative economic systems that have government ownership and control over the means of production.

▪ *Self-Check*

1. How are the decisions of *what, how,* and *for whom* made in a command economy?
2. Why do people who believe in command economies think running businesses to earn a profit is a bad thing for most people?

▪ *Applying What You Have Learned*

In capitalism it is easy to tell how efficient competitive firms are by finding out how much profit they make. Profitable businesses are efficient businesses. When firms are owned by the government, as explained above, it is much harder to tell whether a firm is efficient or not. They are not in business to make a profit. If a firm only follows government plans, how can you know if it is being efficient?

Below you will find a list of mistakes that a business could make. Describe a likely result for a capitalistic firm if it made each mistake.

a. A firm is making a style of shirt that no one wants.
b. A firm has hired more workers than it needs.
c. A firm is making poor quality products.
d. A firm has trouble finding good workers because it pays too little.

Now consider what would happen if these same things happened to a firm that was owned and told what to do by its government. Why would it be difficult to tell whether such a firm is producing efficiently or not?

CURRENT ECONOMIC ISSUES

Achieving the American Dream

In recent years many Americans have not been able to achieve their dream of owning a home. High prices, low wages, difficulty in obtaining a loan, and other factors have kept young people, single parents, and some members of social and ethnic minorities from achieving home ownership.

In the early 1990s, Secretary of Housing and Urban Development (HUD) Jack Kemp proposed a program that allowed people living in public housing to buy homes from the federal government at low cost. In 1992 President Bush suggested that people be allowed to subtract up to $5,000 from their federal income tax when they buy their first home. In addition, most states offer low-interest rate loans that help people with limited incomes buy homes.

Although many people support programs that help others become home owners, some argue that these programs cost the government too much money. Others argue that the programs are not fair to middle-income people who do not receive such aid. Government aid to home buyers can cause other projects to lose money. It could also cause taxes to increase. For example, the money spent on Secretary Kemp's program could not be spent for other projects that might have benefited more people. Some people who qualified for this help felt angry because there were not enough homes or low-interest rate loans for everyone who wanted them.

Would you support these programs to help people buy homes? What is good and bad about this idea? Consider the following arguments:

Arguments in Favor of These Plans
1. They allow many low-income or disadvantaged people to own a home.
2. They help improve living conditions in many neighborhoods.
3. They help many people develop a sense of self-respect.

Arguments Against These Plans
1. They cost the government billions of dollars.
2. The government cannot provide such help to every qualified person.
3. They do not help many middle-income people own a home.

What Do You Think?
What do you think about the arguments above? Are there other factors that need to be considered? Try thinking about the issue as a problem in deciding the *for whom* question in an economic system. How do these plans answer this question in a different way from the way it would be answered in a pure market economy? Can you think of a better way to help more Americans become home owners?

Chapter 2 Review

What Have You Learned?

In this chapter you've learned the following important principles of economics:

- *Economic systems* organize production by establishing and enforcing rules.
- Economic systems increase the efficiency of production by creating a *division of labor*, which allows *specialization* of labor and capital. This also provides a method of accumulating *wealth*.
- Although there are many different types of economic systems, they all must answer the three basic economic questions, *what*, *how*, and *for whom*.
- *Capitalism* is an economic system in which the means of production are owned by individual people (not by the government) and the basic economic questions are answered through individual decisions.

- In capitalism, the question *what* is answered by the choices of consumers, *how* is answered according to the lowest cost of production, and the answer to *for whom* depends on the value of a person's contribution to production.
- The basic reason to run a business in capitalism is the desire to make a *profit*.
- Resources in a capitalistic economic system are *allocated* to the firms that make the most profit.
- In *command economies*, the means of production are owned by the government which also makes the basic economic decisions.
- All economic systems in the world today are *mixed*. They are mixtures of both capitalism and command economies.

Words and Terms

economic system (p. 33)
capitalism (p. 34)
market (p. 34)
traditional economy (p. 34)
command economy (p. 34)
specialization (p. 36)
specialized capital (p. 36)

division of labor (p. 36)
wealth (p. 37)
what? (p. 41)
how? (p. 41)
for whom? (p. 41)
profits (p. 44)
allocation of resources (p. 45)

Building Your Vocabulary

On a separate piece of paper, write the vocabulary word or term that best completes each of the following statements.

1. Splitting up the process of production into specific tasks is called the _____.
2. An _____ is a set of rules through which production is organized.
3. In capitalism, the question _____ is decided according to the value of a person's contribution to production.
4. Greater efficiency in production allows some people to produce _____ instead of making goods for current consumption.
5. In a _____ the three basic economic questions are answered by the government.
6. In a _____ economy, the question *what* is decided according to what is purchased.
7. _____ is an accumulation of products that have been produced.
8. In capitalism, the question _____ is decided according to the firm's costs of production and profits.
9. _____ is an economic system in which the basic economic questions are answered by individuals and not the government.
10. When people do one particular task and buy other things they need, there is _____.
11. In capitalism the _____ is decided according to the profits firms can make.
12. The desire to earn a _____ is the reason for starting a business in capitalism.
13. In a _____ the basic economic decisions are made according to traditions.

Understanding Economics

1. Explain what an economic system is.
2. Define the meaning of the division of labor and explain how it improves the efficiency of production.
3. Explain how specialized tools contribute to the creation of wealth.
4. Describe examples that show the way in which the three basic economic questions, *what, how,* and *for whom,* are answered in a capitalistic economic system. Be sure to provide a different example for each question.
5. Cite two things a firm must do in capitalism to be profitable.
6. Describe the relationship between profits and the allocation of resources in a capitalistic economic system.
7. Describe three differences between a command economy and capitalism.

Thinking Critically About Economics

1. Many communities used to have one-room schools where the teacher taught every subject to each grade level. Almost all of these schools have been replaced with large schools that employ many teachers who often teach several different classes in the same subject. Make a list of at least five different things that can be done better or more efficiently in larger schools than in the old one-room schools.
2. Choose a small independent local grocery store. Which of the following items does it sell? Explain why the store does or does not stock each of these items.

Chapter 2 Review

a. Chinese noodles
b. frozen TV dinners
c. goldfish food
d. fresh pineapples
e. fresh spinach
f. Russian caviar

3. Look up and make a list of salaries that are being offered for at least five different jobs being advertised in a "help wanted" section of your local newspaper. Explain why each of these jobs commands a different salary.

4. Choose a local business that has closed down recently. Answer the following questions concerning this firm.
   a. What products did the firm sell?
   b. Why did the firm close?
   c. What do you believe the owners could have done to save their business?

5. Choose a local business that is successful. Answer the following questions concerning this firm.
   a. What products does the firm sell?
   b. What factors have made the firm successful?
   c. What do you feel are the most important differences between this success-

ful firm and the one you described in question 4?

6. List at least six different things that can be done by the owner of a capitalistic firm in the United States that could not be done by the director of a firm in a command economy.

Consumer Skills Projects

1. Write a story or draw a picture that demonstrates differences in how computers (a specialized tool) have changed the way we make consumer choices in the past 50 years.

2. Draw a map of your neighborhood including the stores where you shop. Explain what the location of these stores has to do with your choice to buy goods or services from them. How much more could these stores charge before you would shop somewhere else?

3. Interview an elderly person about changes in government regulations of consumer products that have taken place in his or her lifetime. Does this person believe these changes have been helpful or harmful for most people?

Developing Your Economic Skills

Interpreting a Table

Skill: This lesson shows you how to read a table to find data and answer questions about numeric relationships (*numeric* means *dealing with numbers*). To interpret the table, follow these steps:

1. Read the table title to identify the subject matter of the table.
2. Examine the categories in the table to determine the types of information the table provides.
3. Examine the data of the table to interpret any relationships between the categories.

Application: How valuable is an education? In capitalism, greater education should cause the value of a person's contribution to production to increase—and the person's income should increase accordingly. Study the table below, which provides information that relates educational achievement with earnings for two different groups.

Earnings by Education Level and Sex, 1988
(average for adults 25 and older)

Years of School Completed	Sex	
	Men	Women
8 years or less	$18,903	$11,710
1 to 3 years of high school	$22,430	$13,834
4 years of high school	$27,139	$17,336
1 to 3 years of college	$31,543	$21,310
4 or more years of college	$40,415	$25,674

Source: *Statistical Abstract of the United States, 1991.*

The title of this table tells you that its topic is *earnings*, and that the table's data will be arranged according to *educational level* and *sex*. The title also tells you that the information was valid for the year 1988, and

that the earnings shown are the averages for adults 25 and older.

Now look at the categories of the table. At the far left is the list of vertical (up and down) categories, under the heading "Years of School Completed." At the top of the table is the list of horizontal (across) categories, under the heading "Sex."

To use the table, you will pick a specific vertical category and a specific horizontal category, and find the amount of earnings that corresponds to *both* categories. It's even easier than it sounds. Try these questions:

1. How much more did the average man with four or more years of college earn than the average man with four years of high school? (To answer this question, find the appropriate levels of education on the vertical axis. Read across to find the average earnings for men at those levels. Calculate the difference between the two levels.)
2. How much more did the average man with 1 to 3 years of college earn than the average woman with the same level of education? (To answer this question, find 1 to 3 years of college on the vertical axis. Read across to find the average earnings for men and for women. Calculate the difference between the two levels of earnings.)

This table allows you to answer questions about differences in income that are related to education and sex. It does not explain *why* there are differences. Tables can provide information, show relationships, and suggest areas for additional study.

Practice: Write a paragraph that examines and interprets information on a table found in your local newspaper.

Part 1 Review

Summary of Major Economic Concepts

In Part 1 you have learned the following basic economic principles, which will become the foundation for your learning in the next three parts of this book:

- The central problem for all economic systems is *scarcity*, which forces people, businesses and governments to make choices in which *opportunity costs* are paid.
- The *production* of goods and services requires each of the scarce *factors of production: natural resources, labor, capital*, and *entrepreneurship*.
- *Models* are used to help us understand economic relationships and predict the future.
- Economists try to make *rational choices* in which the benefits of a decision are greater than its costs. Rational choices are more difficult to make when they involve *normative* statements (values) rather than *positive* statements (facts).
- Economic relationships are often demonstrated through the use of tables and graphs.
- *Economic systems* organize production by establishing rules that result in greater efficiency through *specialization* and a *division of labor*.
- Although there are many economic systems, they all answer the basic economic questions of *what, how,* and *for whom*.
- *Capitalism* is an economic system in which the means of production are owned by people and the basic economic questions are answered through individual decisions.

- In capitalism, businesses are run to make a *profit*, which allows firms to have more resources allocated to them.
- In *command economies* the means of production are owned by the government, which also makes the basic economic decisions.
- All economic systems in the world today are *mixed*.

Understanding Economic Concepts

Each of the following questions emphasizes one or more of the important economic concepts you have learned in Part 1. An important concept is listed in parentheses after each question. Answer each question in complete sentences that *show you understand the meaning* of the concept. The first question has been answered for you as an example.

1. Why can't we all have everything that we want? (discuss *scarcity*)
   (*Answer:* We can't all have everything we want because we do not have enough resources to produce all the goods and services we would like.)
2. When we choose to buy the product we want the most, what are we giving up? (discuss *opportunity cost*)
3. What types of resources are necessary to create goods and services? (discuss the *four factors of production*)
4. What tools do economists use to help them predict the future? (discuss *economic models*)
5. How do economists try to make decisions? (discuss *rational choice*)
6. How do economic systems increase the efficiency of production? (discuss *specialization* and the *division of labor*)

7. What basic questions must all economic systems answer? (discuss *what, how,* and *for whom*)
8. In general, what type of economic system does the United States have? (discuss *capitalism*)
9. In capitalism, how do we decide which firms will receive more resources? (discuss *profit* and *allocation*)
10. In general, what type of economic system does China have? (discuss *command economy*)

Writing About Economics

Each of the questions below requires you to write a brief essay. Be sure to include each of the following in your answer:

■ Demonstrate your understanding of the identified economic concept(s) in your essay.
■ Explain how the economic concept(s) is involved in the situation.
■ Describe how you would resolve the situation and on what basis you would make your decision.

1. Your mother gave you $5 to buy school supplies you need for your math class. As you are walking to the store you pass a movie theater that is showing a new horror show you really want to see. Tickets to the movie cost $5. You have no other money to spend. Do you buy the math supplies or go to the movie? (discuss *opportunity cost*)
2. You can't find a summer job, so you are considering going into business for yourself. You received an *A* on a wooden letterbox you made in your shop class. You think you could sell them door-to-door for about $5 each. You are going to make a list of the things you need before you actually decide whether to try making

and selling the boxes. Do you think you would go into the letterbox business? (discuss *natural resources, labor, capital,* and *entrepreneurship*)
3. You have started a business with three of your friends, cutting grass and doing gardening in your neighborhood. You have so many customers that you are having trouble getting all the work done. At the present, each of you goes to a different house and does all the work. One of your friends has suggested that all of you go to the same house at the same time to get the work done in a hurry. Another wants to buy some electric hedge trimmers and a weedcutter. Do you believe these are good ideas? (discuss *specialization* and the *division of labor*)
4. You own an appliance store. Your business has not been doing well lately. Although sales of radios and TV's have been good, you have sold few washing machines and refrigerators. It has taken too long to have appliances fixed by sending them back to the factory. You are thinking of hiring someone to fix them in your store. Finally, your four employees have demanded an increase in their salary, which you really can't afford. What would you do about each of these problems? (discuss the basic economic questions, *what, how,* and *for whom*)

Discussing Economics

The following paragraphs describe economic proposals that have been the topic of recent public debate. For each, decide whether you support or do not support the proposal, and think about how you would present your opinion to the rest of the class. When you present your opinion to the class, follow these steps:

Part 1 Review

■ Identify and describe the controversial issues of the proposal.
■ Clearly state the decision you have reached.
■ Explain why you think your choice is the best one.

1. It has been suggested that rationing should be used if there is ever another gasoline shortage such as the one that occurred in 1973. One plan would give coupons to licensed drivers that would allow each driver to buy ten gallons of gasoline each week. Drivers not using their coupons would be allowed to sell them to other people for whatever price they could get.

   What would be the costs and benefits of such a plan? Who would be affected? Would you support the plan?
2. Many towns pass zoning laws that limit the use of land within their communities. Some types of zoning laws limit the height of new construction. Others deal with commercial vs. residential use, and others may deal with maintaining public access to coastlines and beaches.

   In one type of zoning law, new residents must have at least an acre of land to build on, and new multiple-unit construction (such as apartment buildings) is not allowed. What purposes do you think such a restriction might have? What are the costs and benefits, and who is affected by the rule? Would you support this zoning law?

Problem-Solving in Economics

Chapter 1

1. Look at a recent copy of a local newspaper. Find examples of choices that were made by a person, by a business, and by the government. For each:
   a. Describe the choice that was made.
   b. Identify what scarce resources were used.
   c. Describe an alternative choice that could have been made.
2. Make a list of four different decisions you have recently made. Explain why you made each decision and what opportunity cost(s) you paid for each.
3. Choose a product that you use every day. Identify as many factors as you can that were used in making the product. Classify each factor as a natural resource, labor, capital or entrepreneurship.
4. Below you will find a list of six statements. Explain why each one is a positive or a normative statement.
   a. There were about 250,000,000 people living in the United States in 1990.
   b. The unemployment rate in the state of West Virginia declined from 1985 to 1989.
   c. The President of the United States is the most important man in the world.
   d. Watching television is a waste of time.
   e. Most prices went up in 1992.
   f. It is wrong for Americans to buy Japanese cars.

Fatal Traffic Accidents Involving Alcohol

Ages		16–17	18–21	22–24	25–34	35–44	45–54	55–65	65+
Accidents per	(1983)	19.45	31.50	26.40	18.16	7.82	7.59	4.26	2.67
100,000 drivers	(1989)	13.70	26.21	23.64	15.58	9.26	6.42	4.03	2.60

5. In 1985 the federal government threatened to reduce highway aid to any state that did not increase its legal drinking age to 21. This policy was based on many assumptions concerning automobile accidents and the ability of young adults to use alcoholic beverages responsibly. Make a list of the assumptions you believe this rule was based on. Do you believe that these assumptions were a reliable way to predict the future? Explain why you do or do not believe 21 to be a reasonable legal drinking age. The table above should help you.

6. As you near graduation from high school, you need to think about what you will do next. You might try to find a job. You could go on to college or to a vocational school. Think of at least two alternatives for what you would like to do after high school. Make a list of reasons for and against each alternative, and decide which of the alternatives represents the most rational choice. Explain why you prefer that alternative.

Chapter 2

1. Jerry is doing very poorly. Jerry used to sell many orders of hamburgers and fries in his little restaurant. Last year a fast-food chain opened a store down the street. They sell their hamburgers and fries for less than Jerry can possibly charge, and they have orders ready in seconds while Jerry only cooks to order. Explain what Jerry's problems have to do with (1) the division of labor, (2) specialization, (3) specialized tools and (4) the accumulation of wealth. What would Jerry probably have to say about his new competition? What would Jerry's customers say? If you were Jerry, what would you do?

2. Think of a product that was used five to ten years ago that people don't want any more. What might have happened to the firm that made this product? On a separate sheet of paper, write the name of the product. Then describe what may have happened to the producer. Be sure to explain how the questions *what*, *how* and *for whom* are related to your description.

2

Understanding How Individuals and Businesses Make Economic Decisions

Part 2 shows how the decisions of individual consumers and businesses affect a capitalistic economy. Economists call this the study of *microeconomics*, meaning that it focuses on specific elements within the economy.

In this part you will learn how spending and production decisions by consumers and businesses relate to the laws of demand and supply. You will explore the effects of competition in the economy. And you will look at the roles of workers and labor organizations in a market economy.

Demand and Supply

Objectives

This chapter discusses how demand and supply function in a market economy. In the sections of this chapter, you will learn:

A

how the movement of elements in the economy can be demonstrated using a *circular flow model;*

B

why people buy more or less of a product (the *determinants of demand*) and what the *law of demand* means to a market economy;

C

how the principle of *diminishing returns* and the *law of supply* affect the economy;

D

how the market adjusts to *surpluses* and *shortages* and tends to move toward a *point of equilibrium;*

E

how *elasticity* of demand affects prices.

Introduction

It's Monday morning, your third week in Economics. Your teacher calls on you and asks, "How much is a granola bar worth? Would you pay a dollar for one?"

Your answer, "It depends."

"It depends on what?"

"Well . . . it depends on how big it is."

"What else?"

"It depends on how hungry I am, or how much money I've got, or whether it's a type that I like."

"Anything else?"

"It depends on whether or not you'll call on someone else if I buy your granola bar!"

In this chapter you will learn how we decide what things are worth. In some ways it is a very easy problem. A product is worth as much as someone is willing to pay for it. But that answer is really too easy. There are many different factors that affect how much customers are willing to pay.

Economists have organized these factors into what they call the theories of demand and supply. When these two theories are studied together, they explain the way prices are set and how firms decide which goods and services to produce.

Section A The Elements of an Economic System

This section introduces the *circular flow model,* the *factor market,* and the *product market.*

Personal Narrative

My Father Was a Farmer

My name is Brad. For as long as I can remember, my family lived on a farm in Iowa. My great-great-grandfather settled here in the 1870s. With every generation we bought more land and grew more food. I thought we had the best possible life. We lived and worked together and in most years we were pretty well off.

By 1980 we owned nearly a thousand acres and rented about five hundred more from our neighbor, Mr. Sims. He had retired from full-time farming. Sometimes we hired him when things got busy in the spring or fall.

We grew corn on most of our land. We also raised hogs and kept a vegetable garden to supply us with produce for a roadside stand. Our corn was sold through the local co-op to a firm in Davenport. Some of it was shipped down the Mississippi River and sent to other countries. We also bought our seed and fertilizer through the co-op.

Our busiest time each year was during the harvest season. There was no way that our family members alone could handle everything that had to be done. So each September we would hire workers to help just during the harvest.

We did most of our shopping in Cedar Rapids, which was about twenty miles south of our farm. I liked going to the city because there was always something to see or do. You might not believe 110,000 people is much of a city, but if you almost never saw more than a hundred people at a time you would think otherwise. My father would drop my brother and me at a mall and give us $25 to spend. At the time we thought it was great. We would buy a shirt or a pair of jeans and go to a movie.

Life on the farm was not easy. It seemed like there was always too much to do and not enough time to do it. But we lost the farm in 1985, and now when I look back, those seem like the best times of my life.

The Circular Flow Model

In the story at the left, Brad described his life on a farm, and he explained part of the role farms play in the American economy. Following this section, you'll look at the economics of Brad's farm using what economists call the **circular flow model.**

The circular flow model is a chart that economists use to show how economic systems work and how firms and people fit into these systems. Figure 3–1 shows one of these charts.[1]

The circular flow model is made up of four boxes, which are connected in a circle by two sets of arrows that point in opposite directions. The box on the left side represents all businesses. The box on the right side represents all households. The top box is for the **product market,** where all sales of consumer products take place. The bottom box is for the **factor market,** where all sales of the factors of production (natural resources, labor, capital, and entrepreneurship) take place.

The arrows of the inside circle are labeled with dollar signs ($). They represent the flow of money through the economy. The arrows of the outside circle represent the flow of goods and services and the flow of factors of production.

Figure 3–1 *Simplified Circular Flow Model*

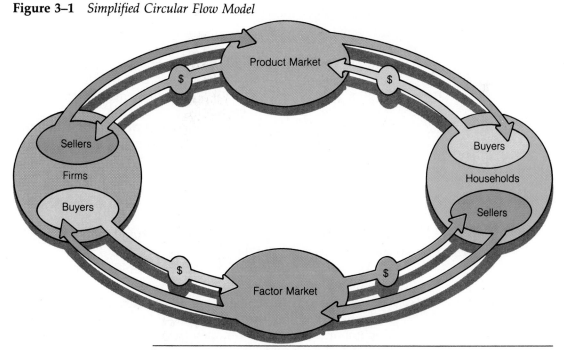

The top part of the model shows what happens when a household consumer buys a product. Suppose that you (like Brad in the story) buy a new pair of jeans. Money would flow from you (the buyer on the right-hand side of the model) through the product market (at the top of the model) to the firm that made the jeans (the seller on the left-hand side of the model). This is across the top part of the model from right to left. In return, a pair of jeans flows across the top of the model from left to right. The jeans go from the firm through the product market to you (a household buyer).

Households provide factors of production to firms in the form of labor they sell, natural resources they own, or in savings they invest. For these factors they are paid wages, rent, and interest.

The bottom part of the model shows what happens when a firm buys any of the factors of production. Suppose that you take a job in a clothing store. You are "selling" your labor to the store. Labor moves from you (the seller on the right-hand side of the model) to the firm. In return, you receive wages from the firm (the buyer on the left-hand side of the model). Money (in the form of wages) flows from left to right through the factor market. Labor and other factors of production flow from right to left through the factor market.

The value of money flowing through the model in a counter-clockwise direction is exactly equal to the value of goods and services and factors of production that flow in a clockwise direction.

All transactions can be placed in a circular flow model. This shows that they are all related to each other, just as all parts of the economy are related to each other.

This is a *simplified* circular flow model. It does not include the government or the banking system. It does give us a foundation to build on. We will refer back to this model in the chapters that follow.

■ *Self-Check*

1. In what part of the circular flow model would the sale of crude oil to a refinery take place?
2. In what part of the circular flow model would the sale of a color television set take place?
3. What can be said about the value of products and factors of production that flow through the model in a clockwise direction and the value of money that flows in a counterclockwise direction?

■ *Applying What You Have Learned*

In the Personal Narrative, Brad described events that included the following transactions. Show where each fits in the circular flow model by placing its letter in the correct location on the circular flow model you have been given by your teacher. (You may be asked to sketch one yourself.)

a. selling vegetables at a roadside stand

b. renting land from Mr. Sims

c. hiring extra workers during harvest

d. going to a movie

e. selling corn to a co-op

f. buying seed

g. buying gas to drive to Cedar Rapids

h. hiring Mr. Sims

i. buying a pair of jeans

Like Brad living on the farm, most of us fit into the circular flow model in many ways.

PROFILE

Adam Smith
(1723–1790)

To many economists, Adam Smith was the most important contributor to the development of the theory of capitalism. He is remembered for his famous book, *The Wealth of Nations*, which was published in 1776, the year of the American Declaration of Independence. In this book, he asked and explained how capitalism answered the basic questions of *what, how* and *for whom*.

Smith believed that consumers were the starting point of production. They made their wishes known in the market place through what they bought. Businesses profited if they supplied what consumers demanded. If the government allowed the forces of demand and supply to operate without interfering, consumers would find the best goods at the lowest prices. Businesses, following their own self-interest, would try to produce the best goods at

the lowest prices so that they could make the most profits. As if guided by an "invisible hand," consumers, producers, and the factors of production would be brought together, helping them all get the largest part possible of what they wanted.

Smith said that the economy would function best if government would practice *laissez faire*, or a hands-off policy toward the market. He believed competition in free markets—the laws of supply and demand—would ensure good quality products at fair prices.

Smith also believed in the division of labor. He encouraged everyone to specialize in what they produced best and to exchange their products for what others produced. If this was done, he said, everyone would have more goods and services.

Born in Scotland, Smith became a professor of moral philosophy at Glasgow College. A brilliant lecturer, he was also absentminded, timid, and never married. When he became older, he was given the highly paid position of customs collector. Smith's theory of capitalism greatly influenced the development of the American economic system.

Section B The Law of Demand

This section will introduce *demand*, the *law of demand*, the *demand schedule*, the *demand curve*, and the *determinants of demand*. The section will also introduce the terms *substitute goods* and *complementary goods*.

Personal Narrative

He Used to Say, "Everyone's Got to Eat"

I think I was about four years old when I realized that our farm was a business and not just the place we lived. I remember my father talking about the weather and the corn wilting in our fields. It was 1972 and there was a drought in Iowa. Our corn production was down by about ten percent. In the whole country it was only down about one percent, but that didn't do us any good. We thought things looked really bad. But life never works out the way you expect. 1972 turned out to be one of our best years.

That was the year of the Russian grain deal. President Nixon agreed to sell millions of bushels of grain to the Soviet Union. Our crop may have been smaller, but the price we got for our corn went up. We got $1.08 per bushel in 1971. In 1972 the price reached $1.57. We earned almost a third more from our crops that year. The price we were paid for our hogs went up about 15 percent too.

1973 was even a better year. By then the export of U.S. grain to Russia was in full swing. They had a bad harvest. Our crops weren't all that great either, but the price of corn reached $2.37 per bushel. That was more than twice what we got two years before. Our costs had stayed almost the same. We earned more money than we had ever made before.

I was just five years old in 1973, so I didn't really understand, but I do remember my father saying, "Everyone's got to eat, and I don't care if they're a Russian or an American."

Demand

Economists would say that Brad's family's farm did well in 1972 and 1973 because of a growth in demand. **Demand** is a willingness to buy a product at a particular price. Demand occurs when a product is actually sold. Just wanting or needing something is not demand unless you buy the product too. There is a **law of demand,** which states that people will buy more of a product at a lower price than they will buy at a higher price, if nothing else changes.

Demand Schedule

It is possible to make a table that shows how many products could be sold at different prices. Economists call these tables **demand schedules.** An example of a demand schedule is shown in Figure 3–2. The schedule shows how many of "Joe's Picnic Tables" can be sold at various prices. Joe can sell more tables at a low price than he can at a high price. This demonstrates the law of demand.

Demand Curve

To the right of the table is a graph that shows a **demand curve.** It is drawn from the information shown on the table. A demand curve shows what quantities will be in demand at various prices. Its vertical (up and down) axis represents price. Its horizontal (across) axis is for the quantity demanded. All normal demand curves slope from the upper left-hand corner of the graph to the lower right-hand corner. This is a _negative slope._ A negative slope shows that if one of the values goes up, the other will go down. (The demand curves used as examples in this chapter are straight lines because this makes them easier to read and understand. Real demand curves usually bend toward the corner of the graph. In Section A of Chapter 4 you will study a demand curve that does bend.)

Figure 3–2

Demand Schedule for Joe's Picnic Tables

Price	Number of Tables Sold
$70	10
$60	20
$50	30
$40	40
$30	50

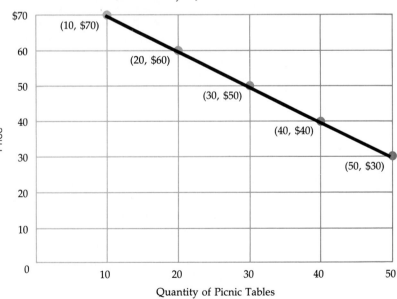

Demand Curve for Joe's Picnic Tables

Changes in Demand

Demand does not always stay the same. There are a number of factors that will cause demand to either increase or decrease. Economists call these the **determinants of demand**. This name sounds much harder than the idea is. The determinants of demand are listed below.

1. *Tastes:* Consumers don't always want the same things. Items that are popular now may not sell in the future. Thirty years ago many students carried slide rules to school. Now they use pocket calculators instead of slide rules. The demand for calculators has increased. The demand for slide rules has decreased.

2. *Income:* If income increases, people can afford to buy more products. As a result, demand will grow. On the other hand, if income goes down, demand will decrease. There is a direct relationship between income and demand.

3. *The price of related products:* Many products can be substituted for each other. If the price of butter went up, more people would buy margarine instead. The demand for margarine would increase. If the price of hot dogs at the ballpark went down while the price of hamburgers stayed the same, many fans would buy hot dogs instead of hamburgers. The demand for hamburgers would decrease. Economists call these products **substitute goods** because they can be used *in place of each other*.

Demand for American corn has been increasing due to an increase in the number of potential customers (one of the determinants of demand).

Other products are **complementary goods.** These products are used *with each other*. Gasoline and automobiles are an example. If the price of gasoline went up to five dollars a gallon, fewer people would drive cars. The demand for cars would decrease because of the increase in the price of a complementary good, gasoline.

4. *Number of potential customers:* If the number of people either increases or decreases in an area, it will change demand in that area. In the 1980s houses in California were in great demand because so many people moved there. At the same time demand for houses in parts of the Northeast fell as people moved to other parts of the country.

If demand for a product increases, its demand curve will move to the right on the graph. If demand for a product decreases, its demand curve will move to the left.

In 1972 and 1973, demand for American corn increased. The biggest reason was our large exports to other parts of the world, particularly to the Soviet Union. The number of our customers and size of their orders increased and so did the demand. Table 3–1 shows our corn exports for 1971–73.

Table 3–1
Exports of U.S. Corn, 1971–1973
(in millions of bushels)

Year	Amount Exported	Total Production
1971	796	5,641
1972	1,258	5,573
1973	1,200	5,643

Source: *Statistical Abstract of the United States, 1975.*

■ *Self-Check*

1. When does wanting a new coat become demand?
2. If the price of a product increases, what should happen to the number sold?
3. Factors such as tastes, income, the price of related products, and the number of customers can all change demand. What is the name economists have given these things?

■ *Applying What You Have Learned*

In this section you've learned about four determinants of demand. What event can you find in the Personal Narrative that caused a change in one of the determinants? Which determinant changed, and what was the effect on demand?

Section C The Law of Supply

This section will introduce the ideas of *supply, law of supply,* a *supply schedule,* a *supply curve,* and *diminishing returns.*

Personal Narrative *Many Other People Thought the Same*

The 1970s were the "golden years" for our farm. We grew more and more corn and the price kept going up. By 1979 we were getting $2.52 per bushel and our production was up 40 percent from 1973. When the price hit $3.10 a bushel in 1980, we began to think we were going to be like the Rockefellers. The same was true of many other farmers in the country.

Of course it cost us money to increase our production. We bought 200 more acres of land and started renting from Mr. Sims. We bought new tractors and lots of other equipment. The price of fertilizer went up too. In 1980 we had to pay almost three times as much as we did in 1973, because of the increase in the price of oil.

We borrowed most of the money we needed to expand our production. In 1973 our farm was almost free and clear. By 1980 our debt was over $900,000. We had to pay 12 percent interest on the loan, but our income was up. We thought we had nothing to worry about. We didn't really understand what was happening to farming all over the world.

After 1980 our problems never seemed to end. In 1981 U.S. exports to other countries began to fall. Scientists invented "miracle seeds" that started the "Green Revolution." Countries that had been our customers grew all the food they needed for themselves. Some of them even started to export grain to compete with us. Not only was our production up, but the production of all U.S. farms had increased by about 40 percent. There was more food available than there were people who could afford to buy it. Supplies had been greatly increased while demand had stayed almost the same.

Supply

Economists would say that Brad's family was in the business of *supplying* food. **Supply** is the term given to the quantity of products that a firm is willing to sell at a particular price.

When firms first start production, they find the cost per unit goes down as they make more products. However, after they reach a certain level of production, the cost of producing additional items increases. This can be the result of paying overtime, of hiring less skilled workers, or simply the result of overcrowding. Economists call this **diminishing returns.**

*The law of supply states
that at higher prices,
producers will offer more
products for sale. When
the price of corn went
up, American farmers
made the investments
necessary to increase production. But at the same
time, food production
was also increasing in
some of the nations that
had been customers for
U.S. grain.*

When costs of production grow, firms require higher prices to produce more products. Higher prices make up for their higher costs. Therefore, at higher prices producers offer more products for sale than they would be willing to offer at lower prices. This is called the **law of supply.**

Supply Schedule

It is possible to make a table that shows how many products would be supplied at different prices. Economists call these tables **supply schedules.** You can see a supply schedule for Joe's picnic tables in Figure 3–3. Joe will be willing to sell more tables if he is able to charge higher prices.

Joe builds picnic tables on his weekends. If he builds more tables, he has to give up more of his free time. He is willing to give up more of his free time if he can sell the tables at higher prices. The price of tables determines how many Joe will make. This demonstrates the law of supply.

Supply Curve

To the right of the table is a graph that is called a **supply curve.** It is drawn from the values on the table. Its vertical (up and down) axis represents price. Its horizontal (across) axis is for the quantity supplied. These are the same values that appeared on the graph in the preceding section on demand.

Figure 3–3

Supply Schedule for Joe's Picnic Tables

Price	Number of Tables Supplied
$70	50
$60	40
$50	30
$40	20
$30	10

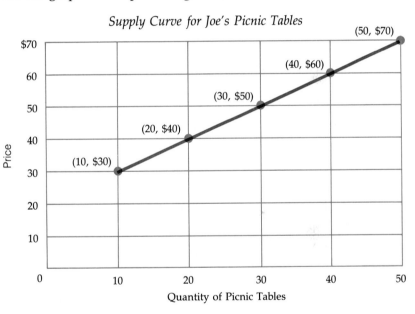

Supply Curve for Joe's Picnic Tables

All normal supply curves slope from the lower left-hand corner of the graph to the upper right-hand corner. This is a positive slope. A positive slope shows that if one of the values goes up, the other will go up too.

Changes in Supply

The number of items a firm is willing to supply does not always stay the same. Suppose that the price a firm is able to charge does not change when its cost of production goes up. This increase in cost would cause the firm to offer fewer products for sale at the current price. The firm's supply curve would move to the left on the graph.

On the other hand, if the firm's cost of production fell, it would be willing to offer more products for sale at the current price. In this case the firm's supply curve would move to the right on the graph.

The prices firms are able to charge for their products are often set by powers that are beyond their control. This is usually the case with farmers. There are so many farmers that none of them has the power to set the price alone. The number of products that farmers produce depends on their cost of production and the price they expect to receive when they harvest and sell their crops.

In the late 1970s and early 1980s, higher prices caused farmers to produce more corn. Table 3–2 shows this growth. (1980 was an exception because of a drought.)

Table 3–2
U.S. Corn Production,
1977–1982
(in millions of bushels)

Year	Total Production
1977	6,505
1978	7,268
1979	7,928
1980	6,639
1981	8,119
1982	8,235

Source: *Statistical Abstract of the United States, 1979–1987.*

▪ Self-Check

1. According to the law of supply, what will happen to the number of products a firm offers for sale when prices go down?
2. What will happen to the cost of additional units of production when a firm starts having diminishing returns?
3. What will happen to the number of products a firm will offer for sale if its cost of production increases while prices remain the same?

▪ Applying What You Have Learned

In the Personal Narrative at the beginning of this section, why did the farmers decide to make the investments necessary to increase production?

Section D Surpluses, Shortages, and Equilibrium

This section will introduce the ideas of *equilibrium, surpluses,* and *shortages.*

Personal Narrative

Some Years Were Good, and Some Years Were Bad

When we planted our crops in the spring, we never knew what we would be paid when we harvested them in the fall. Prices were high for a while and then they were low. I didn't know why. My father told me it had something to do with how much grain the United States sold to other countries and how big the harvest was, but at the time I didn't understand.

I did know that our business worked in a strange way. Some years we had very poor crops. There was too much rain, or too little rain, or winter would set in too early. My mother would get all worried. Many of those years turned out to be good, because the price for the corn we did harvest was high.

In other years the crop was wonderful. We could produce as much as 115 bushels per acre. But in many of those years the prices were low and we actually ended up losing money. Every time I thought I understood, something new would happen to make me confused. In the end I decided to let my father worry about it.

In the 1970s and early 1980s farm prices went up almost every year. In 1984 they turned around and started going down. In 1985 the price fell to $2.54 a bushel. You might think that was a pretty good price. After all, in 1973 we had been excited about $2.37 a bushel. What you need to remember is inflation. Between 1973 and 1985 the prices of things we had to buy to run our farm more than doubled. What was even worse was the interest on our debt. When we borrowed money in the 1970s, the interest rate was only about 10 percent. By 1983 we had to pay 20 percent or more on some of our loans. Do you know how much 20 percent is when you're in debt almost a million dollars? It works out to be close to $200,000 a year. There was no way we could pay our bills. In 1985 the bank took our farm and sold it for a song. We got almost nothing at the auction because many other farmers were in the same situation. More farms were being sold than there were people to buy them.

The price for corn changed from year to year because of changes in its demand and supply. In the 1970s and early 1980s the demand for corn grew more rapidly than its supply. The result was higher prices. After 1983 the supply of corn exceeded its demand and prices fell. No individual farmer could do anything about it.

Determining Equilibrium

Economists demonstrate what happened to Brad's family through the use of a combined demand and supply schedule, and by drawing demand and supply curves on the same graph. You can see a graph and a demand and supply schedule for picnic tables in Figure 3–4.

These are the same demand and supply schedules and curves that you studied in Sections B and C of this chapter. On the graph, you can see that the demand and supply curves intersect at a point that has been labeled *E*. Economists call this the **point of equilibrium.**

Figure 3–4

Demand and Supply Schedule for Joe's Picnic Tables

Price	Number of Tables Demanded	Number of Tables Supplied	Surplus or Shortage
$70	10	50	+40
$60	20	40	+20
$50	30	30	0
$40	40	20	−20
$30	50	10	−40

Demand and Supply Curves for Joe's Picnic Tables

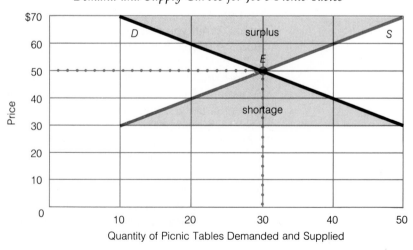

Quantity of Picnic Tables Demanded and Supplied

On this graph, the point corresponds to a price of $50 and a quantity of 30. (The colored dots show you how to find these numbers. Read straight across to find the number on one axis and straight down to find the number on the other axis.) This means that at a price of $50, consumers are willing to buy 30 picnic tables *and* Joe is willing to supply 30 tables. The demand and supply schedule shows the same information for the row corresponding to $50. At this price, the quantity demanded is equal to the quantity supplied. When demand and supply are the same, the economic system is said to be at equilibrium.

In economic theory, the point of equilibrium indicates the price and quantity at which a product will be sold in a competitive market economy.

Suppose Joe thinks he can sell all of his picnic tables at a price of $70 each. This makes it worth his while to produce 50 tables. But the demand curve shows that he would only sell 10 tables at that price. There would be a **surplus** of 40 tables. A surplus is the amount of a product that a firm offers for sale in excess of the quantity customers are willing to buy. The surplus is shown as the upper shaded portion on the graph. Joe would be forced to lower his price to eliminate his surplus. The market price would fall to the equilibrium price.

If Joe thought the equilibrium price was $30, he would only make 10 tables, but he would find he had 50 customers who wanted to buy them. There would be a **shortage** of tables. A shortage is the amount of a product customers want to buy in excess of the quantity a firm offers for sale. This shortage is shown as the lower shaded portion on the graph. Joe would be encouraged to raise his price and produce more tables until the number of tables he was willing to supply was equal to the number his customers wanted to buy. The market price would increase to the equilibrium price.

You can see that market prices tend to move *toward* the equilibrium point. When surpluses exist, prices fall. When shortages exist, prices rise. Given a reasonable amount of time, the market price should become the same as the equilibrium price.

In Brad's story you saw how these forces work. The price of corn in any year is the result of the interaction of demand and supply. Figure 3–5 shows a graph and a table of corn prices for the years 1972–1982. If there is a large increase in demand, the result will be a shortage and an increase in price. If there is a large increase in supply, there will be a surplus and a decrease in price. No single farmer is big enough to have any power over price. All farmers are forced to accept the price the market gives them.

Figure 3–5
Price of Corn per Bushel, 1972–1982

Year	Price per Bushel
1972	$1.57
1973	$2.37
1974	$3.03
1975	$2.54
1976	$2.15
1977	$2.02
1978	$2.25
1979	$2.52
1980	$3.10
1981	$2.50
1982	$2.68

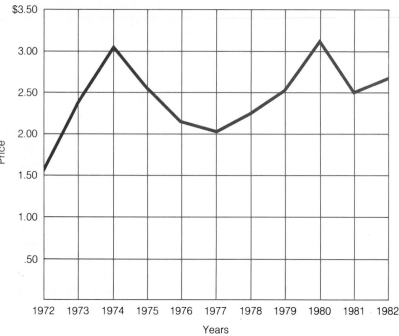

Line Graph of Price of Corn per Bushel, 1972–1982

Source: *Statistical Abstract of the United States, 1975–1987.*

■ *Self-Check*

1. Where would you find the point of equilibrium on a graph of a product's demand and supply?
2. If a firm charges a price above the equilibrium price, why will it eventually be forced to lower its price?
3. If a firm charges a price below the equilibrium price, why will it probably increase its price?

■ *Applying What You Have Learned*

In the Personal Narrative for this section, Brad described how in some years the farm made good profits even though crops were poor, and in some years the farm made no profit even though crops were good. Explain how this could have been so, based on what you have learned about shortages and surpluses. Suppose that in a particular year Brad's family's farm produced a poor crop (say, because of a single batch of bad seed), but all the other farmers had good crops. Would this affect the farm's profits in the same way as a shortage due to all the farmers having poor crops?

Section E Elasticity

This section will introduce the concepts of *elasticity, price elastic demand,* and *price inelastic demand.*

Personal Narrative

Every Time We Grew More Food, the Price Went Down

A few years ago I finally understood why we had so much trouble on our farm. One of my teachers explained it to me. The problem was that people all over the world need to eat about the same amount of food every year. The price doesn't make much difference; if people can afford to buy food, they will eat.

When there is a bad year for crops, prices go up because people are trying to buy the same amount of food even though there is a shortage. If there is a good harvest, the opposite happens. There is a surplus, and prices fall.

In the 1970s crops were bad in many other countries, particularly in the Soviet Union and Africa. Demand for American food grew throughout the world. Food prices went up rapidly. This encouraged farmers to plant and harvest more crops everywhere.

It takes farmers a long time to adjust their production. If prices are high in September, you can't just go out and grow more corn. It takes years to clear new land and buy new machinery. With prices high, production gradually kept growing until there was more food than people wanted to buy. There was a surplus and prices fell.

A problem farmers faced was that food prices were almost the only prices that fell. The things farmers had to buy kept getting more expensive. The biggest problem for many American farmers was that they had gone so far into debt. They still had their payments to make when their income went down. Many of them simply could not pay their bills, so they lost their farms.

You might say that we were good farmers but poor business-people. My father thought that the government should have helped us out. I'm not really sure what should have been done, but I know we paid a price.

Elasticity of Demand

The problem Brad described is called **elasticity** by economists. It refers to the effect that a change in price has on demand. If people want about the same amount of a product no matter what its price, economists say the demand for the product is **price inelastic.**

The demand for some foods is inelastic. For example, the price of salt has little effect on the amount consumers will buy. There are two major reasons why the quantity of salt demanded does not change very much when its price changes. First, even if the price of salt tripled, it still would cost the average family less than a few pennies a day to satisfy their total demand. Second, there is no good substitute for salt. For these reasons, the demand for salt is very inelastic. Basic staples (products that consumers cannot do without) such as bread and milk have inelastic demands. They are viewed as necessities. However, steak, expensive chocolates, and artichokes are luxuries, high-priced and easily substituted. They have **price elastic** demands. When their prices go up, sales fall rapidly.

We can study what happens to staple food prices through the use of a series of graphs.

1. Figure 3–6 shows the world demand (the D curve) and supply (the S curve) for food in 1971, before the price of food went up. Notice that the demand curve is steeply sloped. This shows that people want about the same amount regardless of price. (On the graph, P and Q represent the equilibrium price and the amount of sales.)

Figure 3–6

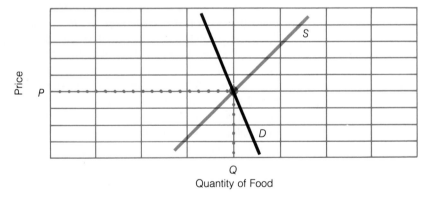

2. Figure 3–7 shows the supply curve moving to the left when many countries had poor crops in 1972 and thereafter. On the graph, P^1 and Q^1 represent the equilibrium price and sales for 1971; P^2 and Q^2 represent the same factors for 1972. There is a significantly higher equilibrium price in 1972 (from P^1 to P^2) but the amount of food sold is down only a little (from Q^1 to Q^2).

Figure 3–7

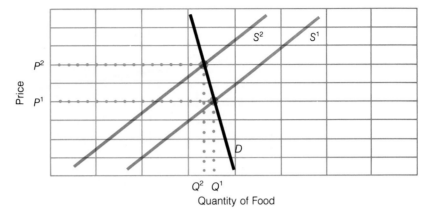

Quantity of Food

3. Figure 3–8 shows the supply curve shifting out to the right (from S^2 to S^3). This is the growth in world food production that had occurred by the mid-1980s. There is a lower equilibrium price. Notice that the amount of food sold has stayed almost the same in all of these graphs.

Figure 3–8

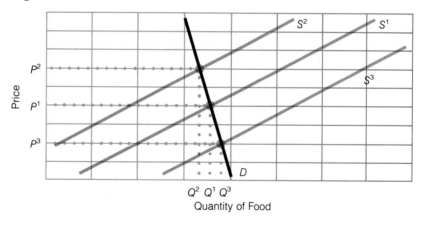

Quantity of Food

Although the demand for most foods is inelastic, there are many products whose demand is price elastic. For these products a small change in price brings about a larger relative change in the amount of the product that is bought. Elastic demand curves tend to be more horizontal than inelastic demand curves. Study the graphs for a type of granola bar in Figures 3–9, 10, and 11.

Figure 3–9

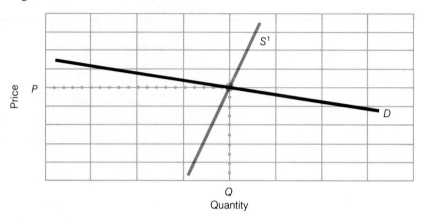

Figure 3–10

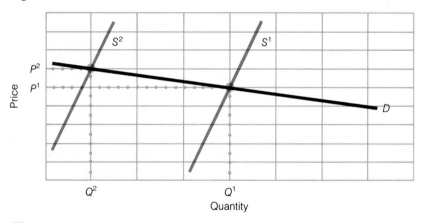

Figure 3–11

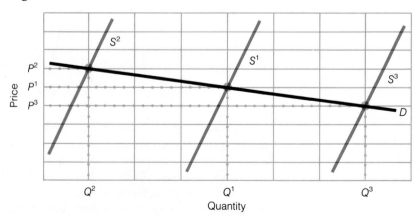

1. The demand curve for "Nutty" granola bars is quite elastic. Figure 3–9 shows its demand and supply, and the current equilibrium price *(P)* and sales *(Q)*.

2. If the firm's workers got a wage increase, the supply curve would shift to the left (Figure 3–10) because the cost of production would rise. There would be a higher equilibrium price. The number of granola bars sold would fall rapidly because people would substitute some other type of snack.

3. If the firm bought new machines to replace its workers, it could shift its supply curve to the right (Figure 3–11). There would be a lower equilibrium price and the number of granola bars sold would increase rapidly.

The effect of elasticity can be seen in the Arab–Israeli war of 1973. This war led to an increase in the price of crude oil from about $2.60 to $11.00 for every 40-gallon barrel. That price was more than four times greater than it had been. Even with this large increase in price, the importation of oil into the United States fell by less than one tenth. However, the high price did encourage exploration for more oil in other parts of the world. It also encouraged conservation in all countries. By the mid-1980s there was a surplus of oil and its price fell to as low as $7.00 a barrel.

Medicines are price inelastic. Because they are necessary and are used only to meet specific needs, consumers will want about the same amount of medicines, regardless of the price.

Cosmetics are generally price elastic. Because consumers can do without them if necessary, sales of cosmetics are likely to fall if their prices go up.

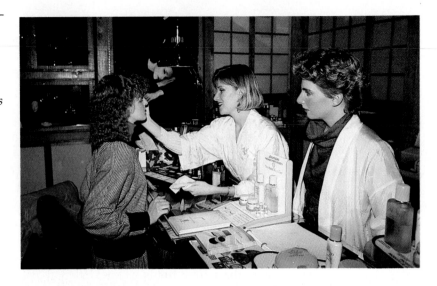

■ Self-Check

1. What is the term that describes the relationship between a change in price and the resulting change in the number sold?
2. When a small change in price results in a relatively larger change in the number demanded, is the demand considered price elastic or price inelastic?
3. Will products that are very important to us and that have no close substitutes have demand that is price elastic or price inelastic?

■ Applying What You Have Learned

In the Personal Narrative that begins this section, you read about a product—corn—for which demand is price inelastic. Below you will find a list of products. Using the criteria you've learned in this section, decide for each whether the demand is likely to be price elastic or price inelastic.

a. the demand for one brand of toothpaste
b. the demand for trips to Florida in July
c. the demand for a heart disease medicine
d. student demand for tickets to a reading of early English poetry by your teacher
e. the demand for tickets to a concert put on by the most popular rock group in the country
f. the demand for water by people lost in a desert

CURRENT CONSUMER ISSUES

What Value Is There In Designer Clothing?

How much would you be willing to pay for clothes that have been designed by a famous person? Every year American consumers spend billions of dollars for designer fashions that can cost twice as much as similar (but less well-known) garments.

Consumers give different reasons why they choose to buy designer clothes. One common reason is that a famous designer would have his or her name placed only on a quality product. However, this may not be the case. Although a famous person designs these clothes, some garments may be poorly constructed or made from inferior materials.

Other consumers may pay for designer clothing because they like the way these garments look on models in advertisements. They seem to believe that they will also look like the models, or be more popular if they wear these clothes. A problem is that professional models work constantly to keep their weight and appearance at an acceptable level to get assignments. Their income depends on maintaining a professional model's appearance. They also have the advantage of make-up artists and current photographic technology.

One thing consumers can be sure of is that they will pay more for designer clothing than other garments. When famous people design clothing they receive royalties (a percent of sales) for the right to use their names. This forces the businesses to charge higher prices to pay for their higher production costs.

Is buying designer clothes a wise choice for most consumers?

Arguments in Favor of Buying Designer

1. They may have better quality than other garments.
2. They may help people appear to be more attractive.
3. They may help people to be more popular.

Arguments Against Buying Designer

1. They may not have superior quality.
2. They are not likely to make people appear more attractive or make them more popular than they already are.
3. They will cost more than other similar garments.

What Do You Think?

Think about the clothing you own. How much of it is made up of designer clothing? Do you believe the money spent to buy such garments represents a rational choice for most consumers? How do firms that offer designer fashions try to influence the determinant of demand: *tastes?* Would you choose to buy designer clothing if you could afford to?

Chapter 3 Review

What Have You Learned?

In this chapter you've learned the following important principles of economics:

- Money, goods and services, and factors of production flow through the economy. Economists use a chart called the *circular flow model* to demonstrate this flow.
- *Demand* refers to the amount of a product that is sold at a particular price. The *law of demand* states that if nothing else changes, more products will be sold at lower prices than at higher prices. This relationship can be shown on a *demand schedule* or on a graph called a *demand curve*.
- Factors called the *determinants of demand* can change demand. They include tastes, consumer income, the price of related goods, and the number of customers.
- *Supply* is the number of products a firm is willing to sell at a particular price. The number of goods and services a firm is willing to supply in capitalism depends on the price its managers believe they will be able to charge and their expectations of earning a profit.
- As a firm increases its production, it experiences *diminishing returns*. This term describes situations where the cost of production per item increases as the number of products manufactured goes up. Due to diminishing returns, after a certain level of production businesses require higher prices to produce greater quantities of a product.
- The *law of supply* states that if nothing else changes, more products will be supplied at higher prices than at lower prices. This relationship can be shown on a *supply schedule* or on a *supply curve*.
- Changes in the costs of production will change the number of items a firm is willing to supply at a particular price.
- A product's demand and supply curves intersect at a point that is called the *point of equilibrium*. This point indicates the product's market price and the quantity that will be sold. Any price above this price would result in a *surplus* that would force the price down. Any price below this price would result in a *shortage* that would force the price up.
- The sensitivity of the quantity demanded to a change in price is called *elasticity*. When a change in price causes a greater percentage change in the quantity sold, the demand is *price elastic*. If a change in price causes a smaller percentage change in the quantity sold, the demand is *price inelastic*.
- Products with price elastic demand tend to be those that are less important to the consumer and easily substituted. Items with price inelastic demand are often those that are important and difficult to replace or do without.

Words and Terms

circular flow model (p. 65)
product market (p. 65)
factor market (p. 65)
demand (p. 69)
law of demand (p. 69)
demand schedule (p. 70)
demand curve (p. 70)
determinants of demand
  (p. 71)

substitute goods (p. 71)
complementary goods
  (p. 72)
supply (p. 73)
diminishing returns (p. 73)
law of supply (p. 74)
supply schedule (p. 74)
supply curve (p. 75)

point of equilibrium (p. 78)
surplus (p. 79)
shortage (p. 79)
elasticity (p. 81)
price inelastic demand
  (p. 81)
price elastic demand (p. 82)

Building Your Vocabulary

On a separate piece of paper, write the vocabulary word or term that best completes each of the following statements.

1. The number of products that a firm is willing to sell is also known as the number it is willing to _____.
2. _____ is when a good or service is actually sold.
3. Consumer goods and services are sold in the _____.
4. The four factors of production are sold in the _____.
5. If a change in price results in a smaller relative change in the quantity sold, the product involved probably has _____.
6. If a change in price results in a larger relative change in the quantity sold, the product involved probably has _____.
7. A table that shows the number of items that could be sold at various prices is called a _____.
8. A graph that shows the number of items a firm would be willing to sell at various prices is called a _____.
9. The fact that after a point the costs of production per item increase as the number produced grows shows _____.
10. A chart that shows the flow of money, goods and services, and the four factors of production is called a _____.
11. A table that shows the number of items a firm would be willing to sell at various prices is called a _____.
12. A graph that shows the number of items that would be sold at various prices is called a _____.
13. Two goods that are used together are called _____.
14. Two goods that can be used in place of each other are _____.
15. A market price above the equilibrium price will result in a _____ of the product.
16. The principle that says people will buy more of a product at a lower price than they will at a higher price (if nothing else changes) is the _____.
17. A market price below the equilibrium price will result in a _____ of the product.
18. The relationship between a change in price and a change in the quantity sold is called _____.
19. A product's supply and demand curves will intersect at a _____.
20. Factors that can cause a demand curve to move to the left or right are called _____.
21. The principle of economics that states that at higher prices producers will be willing to offer more products for sale than at lower prices is called the _____.

Chapter 3 Review

Understanding Economics

1. Describe three different transactions that would take place in the product market.
2. Describe three different transactions that would take place in the factor market.
3. Explain why just wanting or needing a good or service is not the same as the demand for the product.
4. In each case below, identify the specific determinant of demand that is causing demand to change.
   a. The demand for snow tires in Chicago increases when a weather forecast predicts a blizzard.
   b. The demand for tea decreases when the price of coffee falls.
   c. The demand for specialty foods decreases in a recession.
   d. The demand for housing increases in the suburbs of a city that is having a crime wave.
5. Explain two reasons for the principle of diminishing returns.
6. Indicate whether supply would increase or decrease in each of the following situations.
   a. The cost of a product's basic raw material goes down.
   b. The workers who produce a product receive a 10 percent wage increase.
   c. A new machine is purchased that cuts raw material waste in half.
   d. The firm converts its electric furnace to natural gas.
7. Answer each of the following questions in relation to elasticity.
   a. If the demand for a product is price elastic, will a change in price cause a larger or smaller relative change in

the number sold?
   b. Would you expect the demand for medicine to be price elastic or price inelastic? Explain.
   c. If a firm raised the price of its brand of dish soap, would you expect the relative change in the quantity sold to be greater or smaller?

Thinking Critically About Economics

1. Describe how either you or a relative of yours who has a job fits into the circular flow model. Be sure to discuss both the factor and product markets.
2. Suppose that you own a store that sells women's shoes. Describe three different things you could do to try to increase the demand for your product (hint—cutting price is not one).
3. List three items you buy that are important to you. For each, explain why your demand for the product is either price elastic or price inelastic.

Consumer Skills Projects

1. Make a poster with examples of how changes in each determinant of demand could change a consumer's decision to buy a new car.
2. Take a poll of the number of television sets students have. Suggest possible reasons why different families have made different decisions concerning the number of sets to own. What other consumer decisions do people often make when they own television sets?

Developing Your Economic Skills

Using a Demand and Supply Graph

Skill: This lesson will show you how to use a graph of demand and supply that shows a change in market conditions from one year to the next. You will follow these steps:

1. Locate the equilibrium points for both years on the graph.
2. See how price and number of units sold changed from one year to the next.

Application: Imagine that a major American car manufacturer experienced a surplus, and took actions to correct the problem. A graph of demand and supply can be used to show what happened.

   In the first year the equilibrium price for the firm's cars was $14,200, and at that price 1,120,000 cars were sold. Because of a recession in the following year, demand fell. However, the firm continued to produce at the same rate, resulting in surplus product. These events are shown on the graph.

   The first year's demand has been plotted on the graph. It intersects with the firm's

supply curve at the equilibrium price of $14,200 (labeled *E 1st year* on the graph). At this price, the firm sold all 1,120,000 units of its production. In the following year, a recession caused demand to shift to the left (this shift appears as movement from *D 1st year* to *D 2nd year* on the graph). The firm was not aware of this change, and its costs of production were still the same as in the first year. The firm produced another 1,120,000 units of its product and tried to sell them for the same price of $14,200.

   The firm discovered it could only sell 1,040,000 units of its product at the old price. It had a surplus of 80,000 units. This surplus is labeled on the graph, and it is the difference between 1,120,000 (the quantity sold in the first year) and 1,040,000 (the quantity sold in the second year). To eliminate the surplus, the firm offered lower prices and reduced its level of production. Eventually the firm found that at an equilibrium price of $13,800 it could sell all of the 1,080,000 products it could supply.

Practice: Write a paragraph that summarizes how to use a graph of demand and supply.

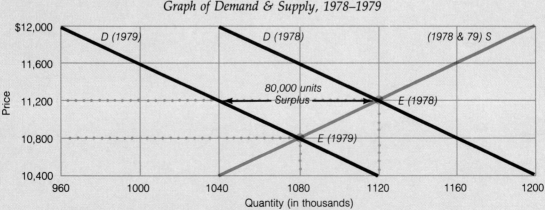

Graph of Demand & Supply, 1978–1979

Source: *Facts on File*, 1979.

The Consumer and the Economy: Getting What You Pay For

Objectives

In the sections of this chapter, you will learn:

A

how the principle of *diminishing marginal utility* causes people to buy many different products rather than only a few;

B

how *consumer sovereignty* and the *"invisible hand"* influence producers' decisions on what to make and sell;

C

the need for *consumer protection* and the trade-offs involved;

D

how businesses attempt to influence consumer demand through marketing.

Introduction

You have been told that we have a free market economy. But is it really true? Do Americans have the power to make the decisions of *what, how,* and *for whom?*

We all know that sometimes there is a difference between what is supposed to happen and what does happen. In this chapter you will learn about economic decisions people make and about limitations on their rights to make these decisions.

In our mixed capitalistic system, the government has a responsibility to protect consumers from unfair business practices and from inferior or dangerous products. To do this, the government limits or influences the decisions consumers make.

In the United States, businesses try to influence consumer decisions. Economists may say that consumers control the economy, but businesses try to affect what their customers do. Business policies that influence both the government and people limit consumer freedom.

American consumers do have a strong voice in controlling our economic system, but they don't have total control. Both the government and businesses limit their economic freedom. In many cases this is to the consumer's advantage. In some cases it may not be. Often there is a trade-off between freedom of choice and consumer protection.

Section A How We Make Spending Decisions

This section introduces the principle of *diminishing marginal utility.*

What Should I Do With My Pay?

Harry's whole life is his restored classic sports car. He polishes it and waxes it and cleans it and tunes its engine. About the only time he doesn't spend with his car is when he is at work or asleep.

It took Harry almost five years to save enough money to buy his car. He started when he was only 14 by delivering papers. When he reached 16 he got a job cleaning cars for a used car dealer. At 18 he started selling the used cars. Harry never earned much money, but he saved every penny he could.

Harry doesn't have much of a social life. He almost never dates because it costs too much money. Most of his clothing comes from secondhand stores. Last week he invited a girl out, but when she found that he only wanted her to help him wash his car, she went home.

Harry is 19 years old now. Last week his younger brother asked him what he does with the money he earns. Harry said, "I'm saving for another car!"

Diminishing Marginal Utility

Most people wouldn't want to live like Harry. We all try to get the greatest possible enjoyment from our lives. This usually means that we do many different things with our time and buy many different products with our money. Harry is different from most people. He is only interested in one thing, his car.

If you really like something, why don't you spend all of your money buying just that product? Economists call the reason **diminishing marginal utility.** Diminishing marginal utility means that each additional unit of a product is less useful to you than the one that came before it.

If you had no shoes, your first pair would be worth a lot to you. The second pair you buy might also be important, but it would not be as desirable as the first. Each additional pair of shoes would have less value to you.

Harry spent all his savings to buy one thing—a classic car. Will he spend all his future savings to buy a second car, and then a third? The principle of diminishing marginal utility says no. When you already have one car (or any other product), each additional unit is less valuable than the one that came before it.

Diminishing marginal utility is why an individual's demand curve for products slopes down from the upper left-hand corner of a graph to the lower right-hand corner. Suppose the demand schedule and curve in Figure 4–1 belong to you.

Figure 4–1

Demand Schedule

Price of Shoes	Number You Would Buy
$70	1
$65	1
$60	2
$55	3
$50	4
$45	5
$40	6
$35	8

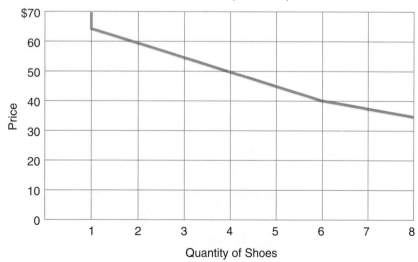

Your Demand Curve *for Pairs of Shoes*

One of the best measures of a product's value is the amount people are willing to pay for it. In the demand schedule in Figure 4–1, notice that you are willing to pay $70 for the first pair of shoes. You are not willing to buy a second pair until the price falls to $60. The second pair is not worth as much to you as the first. When the price reaches $55, you are willing to buy a third pair, which is worth even less to you.

The graph of your demand curve shows the same principle. As the price goes down, you will be willing to buy more pairs of shoes. This is why the graph slopes down from left to right. The graph and demand schedule demonstrate the principle of diminishing marginal utility.

The end of World War II reduced our demand for certain types of weapons. Although the military continued to use some of these weapons, many that had been built for the war were sold for scrap. They no longer provided enough utility to justify the cost of keeping them in service.

Think back to the question, "If you really like something, why don't you spend all your money buying just that product?" The answer is that after you have a few of them, they aren't so important to you any more. You will spend your remaining money on other products that have greater value to you now.

Even Harry may get tired of classic sports cars after he has two or three. He might become interested in other products then.

Businesses and governments also are subject to diminishing marginal utility. For example, the defense budget for the United States totaled $290.2 billion in 1988. That amount was broken down into the specific types of spending listed in Table 4–1. Why does the Defense Department distribute its spending in so many different programs? If a weapon is successful, why doesn't the government buy great numbers of just that one weapon? What does this have to do with diminishing marginal utility?

Table 4–1
Defense Spending, 1988
(billions of dollars)

Purpose	Amount	Purpose	Amount
General Purpose (largely pay)	$114.9	Training, medical	$37.3
Strategic Forces	$ 19.8	Supply & Maintenance	$24.9
Research & Development	$ 28.4	Intelligence & Communication	$28.3
Guard and Reserve	$ 16.9	Air & Sealift	$ 4.4
Administration	$ 6.7	Support to other nations	$ .8

Source: *Statistical Abstract of the United States*, 1991.

■ Self-Check

1. According to the principle of diminishing marginal utility, why would customers be willing to pay more for their first television set than they would pay for a second television?
2. If you really like a product, why don't you spend all of your money buying just that product?

■ Applying What You Have Learned

Make a list of five different items that you actually spend money on. Rank them according to their importance to you, most important first and so on. Estimate the number of each item you buy in a year. Does the importance of the items and the number you buy match up? Why or why not? What does this tell you about diminishing marginal utility and the price you are willing to pay for a product?

Section B Consumer Sovereignty

This section introduces the ideas of *consumer sovereignty* and the *invisible hand*.

Personal Narrative

Baggy Pants Are Out This Year

"The trick to making money in the fashion industry is knowing what people want to buy before they do." That's a quote from one of my college instructors. Although I didn't say it first, I believe in it completely.

I graduated ten years ago with a degree in merchandising. After working in different women's clothing stores for several years, I opened "JoAnn's Cheap Boutique." I sell the latest fashions at a discount price. Most of my customers are young working women who want to look up-to-date but can't afford to spend much money. Every year I go to shows in New York to see what the expensive stores will be selling. Then I take a trip to the West Coast and buy imitations of the same styles—made in Hong Kong, Singapore, Taiwan or someplace else in East Asia. I can sell clothing for about half the name-brand price.

There are some dangers in this business. Quality can be a problem. Sometimes the garments just fall apart, but that doesn't happen very often.

A real danger is buying products that no one wants. It happens from time to time. There's just no way to avoid it. Last year I ordered a dozen cocktail dresses of blue silk with big pink polka dots. I thought they were striking. My customers didn't agree. I almost had to give them away. I sold one to someone who wanted to wear it to a costume party.

Most of the time I guess right about what will sell. I have a friend who owns a store on the other side of town. She ordered hundreds of pairs of baggy pants. I told her they would be out of style this year but she didn't believe me. I was right. Now she has to figure out some way to unload them.

This is a high-risk business, but the profits are good when you guess right.

Consumer Sovereignty

Firms that are profitable sell products people want at a price they are willing to pay. At least most of the time, customers are in control of what is made in a competitive economic system. They also have a strong impact on both quality and market price. Economists call this idea **consumer sovereignty.**

The principle of consumer sovereignty says that in a competitive economy, customers determine what is made by choosing what they will buy. To stay in business, a clothing manufacturer must make the goods people want and must sell them at competitive prices.

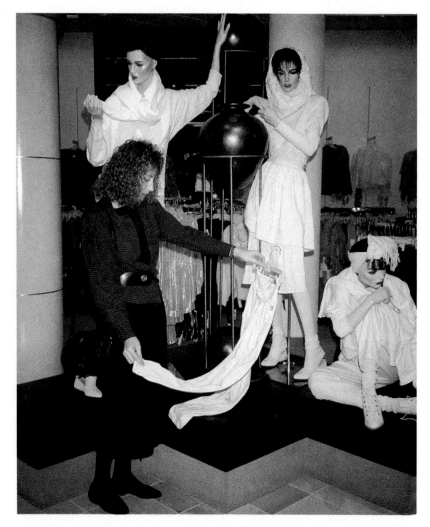

The word *sovereign* means "ruler" or "one who is in charge." Consumer sovereignty means that the consumer is in charge of the economy. Manufacturers must make what customers want to buy if they expect to remain in business.

However, it is not enough to produce goods and services people want. The quality of the products must also be satisfactory. Inferior quality will lead customers to return merchandise and eventually to stop patronizing a business entirely.

Businesses must charge competitive prices even if they are selling quality products people want. When "a better mouse trap" is made, the world will not beat a path to the inventor's door if the price is one hundred dollars per trap.

According to the principle of the "invisible hand," businesses in a market economy must offer products consumers want, and at the lowest possible prices. In this sense, business owners must serve the interests of society if they are to serve their own interests.

The Invisible Hand

Adam Smith (see the Profile in Chapter 3) wrote about the "invisible hand" and what it had to do with competition. In a market economy, owners run businesses to make a profit. To earn profits firms must provide products people want at competitive prices. This serves the interests of society. Therefore, by attempting to serve their own self-interest (to earn a profit) business owners supply products customers want at the lowest possible prices. To Smith, the **"invisible hand"** was the self-regulating market that controlled profit, products, and prices. Consumer choices ruled the market.

In the story at the beginning of this section, JoAnn is able to make a good profit because she sells products her customers want at a price that is lower than her competition. When she makes a mistake and buys low quality garments or products that don't sell, she pays for her mistake through reduced profits. If she made too many mistakes, she would lose her business. Firms can only make a limited number of errors before they fail.

Every year both large and small businesses get into financial trouble. One example involved a large steel firm. On July 17, 1986, the second largest steel producer in the United States, the LTV Corporation, filed for bankruptcy. Its last profitable year had been 1981. The firm estimated that it had lost roughly one billion dollars in the preceding two years. Its failure was the result of reduced demand and lower prices for its primary product, steel. An attempt to move into oil production in the 1970s had contributed to the firm's problems by increasing debt and reducing its cash reserves.

Table 4–2 shows that at least part of LTV's problems may have been the result of both a smaller total market and more foreign competition.

Table 4–2
U.S. Steel Production & Imports (in millions of tons)
and
Imports as a Percentage of U.S. Production, 1979–1985

Year	U.S. Production	Imports	Imports as a Percentage of Total U.S. Production
1979	136.3	17.5	12.8%
1980	111.8	15.5	13.9%
1981	120.8	19.9	16.5%
1982	74.6	16.7	22.4%
1983	84.6	17.1	20.2%
1984	92.5	17.2	18.6%
1985	88.3	24.3	27.5%

Source: *Statistical Abstract of the United States, 1987, 1991.*

■ Self-Check

1. Why do firms have to sell products customers want in order to earn a profit?
2. What is the relationship between the "invisible hand" and the intention of business owners to earn a profit?

■ Applying What You Have Learned

In the Personal Narrative for this section are two examples of fashion products that consumers didn't want. Explain how the principle of consumer sovereignty will affect how many pink polka dot dresses and baggy pants will be manufactured in the next year.

Section C Individual Freedom and Consumer Protection

This section introduces issues related to *consumer protection*.

Personal Narrative

My Uncle Smokes a Pack a Day

My uncle calls himself an "individualist." He can't stand having other people tell him what to do. He seems to feel that rules were made for him to break. Most of the things he gets upset about are silly and not very important. He does things like walking in the "out" door at the supermarket. Somehow it makes him feel important or independent or something. I never could understand what he thinks he's proving.

Some of the things he does are dangerous and not very smart. He refuses to wear a seat belt. It's not because he doesn't think they make driving safer, it's because the law says he is supposed to wear one. He wore them occasionally before the law was passed. Now he won't put them on "out of principle."

I think the thing that bothers him most is the Surgeon General's cancer warning on cigarette packs. He must have told me a thousand times that this rule is an "infringement on his personal freedom to choose how to lead his life." He thinks the decision to not allow tobacco advertising on TV is "unAmerican." He smokes a pack a day. I sometimes wonder if he will die in an auto accident or of cancer.

Last year my uncle bought a used car. It was a 1989 model and he thought he got a really good deal. His exact words were, "Man, did I take him for a ride!" After about a week, things started to go wrong with the car. The radio stopped working and the brakes started to pull to the left. Worst of all, the transmission began to smoke. It cost him over $1,800 to get everything fixed.

He tried to get the dealership to pay for the work, but they refused. It was something about the "as is" clause on the bill of sale. My uncle called the state Attorney General's office to complain. They said there was nothing they could do. It was a legal contract and my uncle had signed it. Although it's been over a year since this happened, I can still count on him to gripe about the "useless government" at least once a day. I guess my uncle is an "individualist" until it concerns his wallet.

Consumer protection takes many forms. Since 1964, the U.S. government has required that cigarette manufacturers put health warnings on their products.

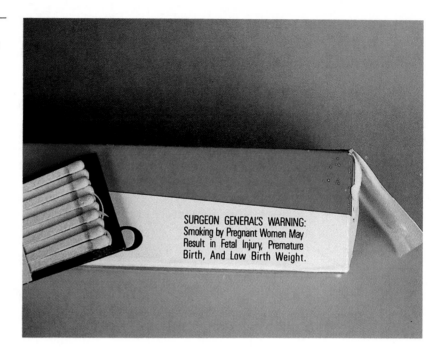

SURGEON GENERAL'S WARNING: Smoking by Pregnant Women May Result in Fetal Injury, Premature Birth, And Low Birth Weight.

Why Consumer Protection?

For a competitive market economy to work efficiently, both buyers and sellers must understand the product that is being sold and the conditions under which the exchange takes place. Two hundred years ago most products were fairly easy to understand. When Joe sold Fred a wagon in 1790, they probably both knew what was being exchanged.

Now products are much more complicated. The average consumer does not know how a TV set really works, or understand microchips, or realize the possible side-effects of various medications. Few people can read legal contracts and know exactly what they mean. If this is the case, does the government have a responsibility to protect us from unscrupulous producers and potentially harmful products? Most people would say the answer to this question is "Yes." The real problem is to decide how much protection is enough.

The U.S. government has a long history of **consumer protection**. In 1964, cigarette manufacturers were forced to put a health warning on their products. The "Truth-in-Lending Act" of 1968 requires businesses to tell customers the actual interest rate they will be paying on installment purchases. The Food and Drug Administration assures extensive testing before new medications can be prescribed in this country. Automobile manufacturers have been required to meet federally mandated pollution, safety, and fuel efficiency standards.

What Are The Trade-Offs?

Consumer protection is a very complicated issue. Although consumers benefit from these rules, they also pay a cost. In meeting federal regulations, businesses are forced to spend additional money. This added cost is passed on to customers in the form of higher prices. It has been estimated that the safety and pollution control equipment on the average 1990 automobile added about $1200 to its price.

Government regulations may reduce competition. Government rules are often very expensive to follow. This makes it harder for new firms to get started, or for small firms to stay in business. If only large firms can afford to meet government regulations, the result could be fewer firms in each industry, resulting in less competition and higher prices.

Government regulations can slow down the acceptance of new ideas and reduce this nation's ability to compete in the world market. Extensive testing of new products not only costs money, but also takes time. People who could benefit from new medicines or products are forced to do without while they are being approved. This process can go on for years. Some other countries have few requirements. Their firms can provide new products much more quickly. This gives them an advantage in establishing control over new markets throughout the world.

Consumer protection is a trade-off. There is no one right answer to the question, "How much protection is enough protection?" There are value judgments for answers.

A case where government protection was necessary occurred in the late 1950s when thalidomide, a drug that was intended to help people sleep, was marketed. It was first used in West Germany and eventually in the United States. After several years of use, it was found to cause deformities in children whose mothers had used the drug in their first three months of pregnancy. Before the drug was recalled in 1961, it was estimated to have caused the malformation of about 8,000 children throughout the world. The drug had been approved by various government agencies in different countries. Who should be responsible for the costs of caring for the people who were harmed by thalidomide?

■ *Self-Check*

1. Why is consumer protection more necessary today than it was two hundred years ago?
2. Why can increased consumer protection cause higher prices?
3. What is one trade-off made for greater consumer protection that *does not directly involve prices or money?*

■ *Applying What You Have Learned*

1. At the beginning of this section you read about the reaction of the narrator's uncle to the federal government's health warning on cigarette packages. What do you think of the following federal regulations? Explain why you think each is either justified or unjustified.
   a. The health warning on cigarettes
   b. The list of ingredients on breakfast cereal
   c. The pollution control equipment on cars
   d. The truth-in-lending rules for credit purchases

2. Below you will find a picture of a street in some major city. There are several different products or activities in the picture that are regulated by the government. Identify as many of them as you can, and describe why you think the regulation is or is not necessary.

How many regulated products and activities can you find in this scene?

Section D Advertising and Consumer Demand

This section will introduce issues related to *advertising*.

Personal Narrative

The Man on TV Said I Should Buy It

Sherry is home alone, watching TV. Outside, the wind screams around the house while rain beats against her window. Lightning strikes nearby, there's a crash of thunder and the lights flicker. On the screen, a form gradually appears in a brown uniform and starts to sing, "Aren't you hungry? . . ." It's just another ad. Sherry tries to ignore it. Soon they'll have the "Late Night Fright Show" back on and she can see the rest of "The Fungus That Ate Chicago."

Sherry thinks, "There seems to be advertising everywhere you go. Get on a bus, you see advertising. Take a ride in the country, you see advertising. Go to the movies, you see advertising. What's the point? No one pays any attention to it. Advertising is just a waste of money."

The next morning, Sherry takes the morning paper as she leaves for work. She notices that her favorite store has shoes on sale for half price and makes a mental note to stop to buy a pair on her lunch hour.

Sitting on the bus, she glances through the help-wanted section. Sherry's sick of her job but she can't afford to quit before she finds something better. There's nothing new today so she turns to the theater section. A new play has just opened. There is an ad in the newspaper, with quotations from different reviewers. She decides to get her boyfriend Ken to take her to it.

Riding along with nothing particular on her mind, Sherry passes a florist's shop that has a big sign in the window, "Don't Forget Mother's Day." She thinks, "Oh good grief! I've got to send Mom some flowers or she won't forgive me for a year."

She overhears two women talking behind her, ". . . and then I asked her how she got so thin? and she said 'Well, I saw this ad on TV for the *Stay Thin Fat Reduction Plan* and they had memberships for half price all this month, so I just went down and joined and they worked it all off me before I really knew what happened. It really was so easy. Why, I'm down to just 180 now, and I'll bet I can fit into a size 16 before long.' "

Finally Sherry reaches her desk. Her secretary knocks on the door and hands her a letter. She thanks him and opens it quickly. It's from her boss, John Fuller Grey III. He is offering her the job of assistant to the vice president of advertising if she wants it.

Increasing Demand

Advertising is very much a part of the American economy. In 1991 over 120 billion dollars were spent nationwide on different types of advertising. That was over 2 percent of all spending in the country that year. You could also think of it as about $480 for every man, woman, and child in the United States.

Firms advertise because they want to increase the demand for their products. They hope this will increase their sales and profitability. There are essentially two types of advertising. They are:

The two major types of advertising are informative advertising and persuasive advertising.

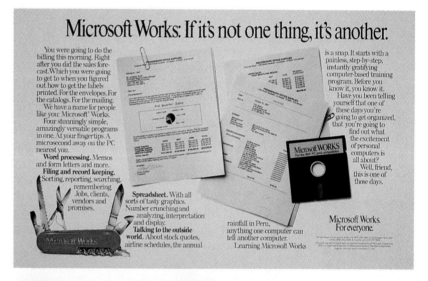

■ **advertising that is intended to inform**
Such advertising tells customers of price or quality differences. This improves their knowledge and should increase their demand for the products that have a price or quality advantage.

■ **advertising that is intended to influence or persuade**
Such advertising attempts to change the customer's tastes or preference for the product being promoted.

Clearly, advertising that is intended to inform is beneficial to the customer in particular and the economy in general. It assists consumers in getting better prices for quality products. It also helps efficient firms earn a profit.

A problem is the possibility that some advertising is either false or misleading. With this possibility in mind, the Federal Trade Commission was given the responsibility of preventing "false and deceptive advertising of goods, drugs, curative devices, and cosmetics." It is against the law to knowingly make false claims about a product.

Another debated issue is the value of advertising that is intended to influence or persuade. For example, it has been suggested that advertising on Saturday morning cartoon shows has convinced America's children to demand breakfast cereals that have too much sugar and too little nutritive value. Some countries have made it against the law to use children in any advertising or to direct advertising to an audience made up largely of children.

■ *Self-Check*

1. Why do firms advertise their products?
2. What is the difference between advertising that is intended to inform, and advertising that is intended to persuade?
3. Why do some people feel advertising that is intended to persuade can hurt consumers?

■ *Applying What You Have Learned*

Although Sherry did not think much of advertising, she used and benefited from it in many ways. Give five specific examples of advertising from the story and identify each example as an attempt to inform or to persuade.

CURRENT CONSUMER ISSUES

How Should We Regulate Cigarette Advertising?

After the government outlawed cigarette advertising on television and radio in the 1970s, tobacco companies concentrated their advertising in the print media and on billboards. RJR Nabisco created one of the most successful advertising campaigns for Camel cigarettes in 1989 based on "Old Joe," a cartoon camel. Many people believe RJR Nabisco's ads persuaded the nation's youth to ignore health warnings and take up smoking.

In 1992 Dr. Joseph R. DiFranza stated he hoped that information he had helped gather would lead to a complete ban on cigarette advertising. Dr. DiFranza had helped carry out one of three studies completed in 1991 by the American Medical Association that found the Camel ads were very successful in reaching children. One study found that a group of six-year-olds were almost as likely to recognize "Old Joe" as they were Mickey Mouse.

The Surgeon General of the United States, Antonia Novello, called on magazines and retailers to voluntarily refuse to accept advertising or to sell products with the likeness of "Old Joe." She called such advertising "deplorable" and declared, "It's time that we invite 'Old Joe' Camel himself to take a hike."

RJR Nabisco claimed that its ads were directed to fun-loving and sophisticated adults. However, its estimated share of the under-18 market increased from less than 1 percent in 1989 to 33 percent in 1992. RJR Nabisco argued that to force it to eliminate the ads would deprive the firm of its constitutional right of free speech.

Do you think RJR Nabisco should have been forced to stop using "Old Joe" advertisements to protect young people?

Arguments in Favor of Banning the Ads

1. It could have reduced the number of young people who smoke.
2. It could have reduced the costs of medical care for people who became ill from smoking.
3. It could have caused other tobacco firms to direct less advertising to young people.

Arguments Against Banning the Ads

1. It would limit the right of RJR Nabisco to free speech and to earn a profit.
2. There is no absolute proof that "Old Joe" ads did cause more young people to smoke.
3. It would have limited the rights of consumer choice.

What Do You Think?

Consider the arguments for and against banning the "Old Joe" advertisements. Could a friendly-faced cartoon camel influence your decision to smoke or not? Do you support the original ban on television and radio advertising of tobacco products?

Chapter 4 Review

What Have You Learned?

In this chapter you've learned the following important principles of economics:

- Consumers distribute their spending between many different products because of the principle of *diminishing marginal utility*. This principle tells us that as consumers buy more units of a particular product, each additional unit is less valuable to them. Therefore, consumers receive more value when they purchase many different goods and services.

- In capitalism, firms must sell products people want to buy at prices they are willing to pay. Consumers control the goods and services that are produced through what they purchase. This idea is called *consumer sovereignty*.

- In capitalism, firms are in business to make a profit. To do this they must offer products consumers want at competitive prices. By working to protect their own interests, firms serve the interests of the consumer. This idea is called the *invisible hand*.

- As the American economy has become more complex over the past two hundred years, our need for government involvement and *consumer protection* has grown. Although consumers benefit from government protection, they also pay for additional costs that result from government regulation and reduced competition.

- We can often see competition between businesses in advertising. Advertising can be divided into two general classifications. *Informative advertising* provides consumers with additional information to help them make rational choices in how they spend their money. *Persuasive advertising* attempts to convince consumers that they need a particular product.

Words and Terms

diminishing marginal utility (p. 94)
consumer sovereignty (p. 98)
invisible hand (p. 100)

consumer protection (p. 103)
informative advertising (p. 108)
persuasive advertising (p. 108)

Building Your Vocabulary

On a separate piece of paper, write the vocabulary word or term that best completes each of the following statements.

1. When a firm pays a famous person to promote its product, it is using _____.
2. When the government regulates the type and quality of products that can be advertised and sold, it is involved in _____.
3. The idea that firms must produce the products that sell is called _____.
4. When a firm prints the contents of its product on posters in large red letters, it is using _____.
5. An example of the _____ happens when a business owner's self-interest causes the firm to offer products for sale that are similar in price and quality to those of competitors.
6. I don't care about my third hamburger as much as I did my first because of _____.

Understanding Economics

1. Explain why a firm that sold wooden wagon wheels would have difficulty staying in business.
2. Joe wants to earn a profit in his tire business. There are many other tire stores in town. Explain what the "invisible hand" will force him to do.
3. Explain why most people believe the government should regulate the kind of chemicals that can be sprayed on plants that will be used for food.
4. Describe the trade-off that is made when the government tells farmers not to use a chemical that would kill insects that eat their crops.
5. Describe two different advertisements that you believe are helpful to consumers. Include an explanation of how you think they benefit the consumers.
6. Describe two different advertisements that you believe could be harmful to consumers. Include an explanation of how you think they hurt the consumers.

Thinking Critically About Economics

1. John just bought a new jacket for $60. Although he likes his new jacket, he would not be willing to pay more than $30 for a second one. Explain how this situation demonstrates diminishing marginal utility.
2. In the mid-1960s a popular style of dress was called the "sack." This garment looked very much like a potato sack. It was difficult to tell what someone who wore one looked like. Describe what you feel the result would be if a store tried to sell "sack" dresses now. Explain what this has to do with consumer sovereignty.
3. Imagine a store that tried to sell new au-

tomobile tires for five hundred dollars each. Also assume that many of these tires failed after several thousand miles of use. Clearly such a firm could not stay in business for very long. Explain what this has to do with the invisible hand.
4. If the government passed a law that required all restaurants to have the nutritive value of the food they served analyzed and printed, it might help consumers follow their diets or to eat more nourishing food. However, consumers would also pay a cost for this form of protection. Describe three specific costs that would have to be paid.
5. Write an advertisement that informs the consumer about a specific product. Write a second advertisement for the same product that is intended to persuade.

Consumer Skills Projects

1. Most states have laws that limit smoking in all public places. Take a survey of the students in your class concerning such laws. Do they feel that these laws are justified or not? Ask them to complete the same survey among their parents or other adult relatives. Do adult opinions differ from those of your fellow students? You could ask them to identify the adults interviewed as smokers or nonsmokers to see how their answers varied.
2. Choose five products that are sold in many stores in your area. Survey the price charged for the exact same products in as many stores as possible. Are the prices more or less the same? Are there any other factors that affect the quality of the product? Describe how your results relate to the idea of a competitive market.

Developing Your Economic Skills

Using Line Graphs to Compare Data

Skill: In this lesson you will learn how two different sets of data can be compared on the same line graph. To complete this lesson, you will follow these steps:

1. Study the data in the table to determine the type of information it provides.
2. Examine the line graph to see the relationship between two sets of data.
3. Consider the possible causes of the relationship between the two sets of data.

Application: Is there a direct relationship between the money automobile producers spend on advertising and the number of cars they are able to sell?

When automobile manufacturers suffer from low car sales there are a number of ways they may react. They could reduce their costs by cutting advertising budgets. This policy, however, might result in even fewer sales and greater losses. Another alternative would be to keep their advertising budgets unchanged and hope that their sales would soon pick up. The third alternative would be to increase their advertising spending to try to encourage more sales.

The data in the table below and on the following graph will show you which of these three strategies was taken by automobile manufacturers during the 1980s and the degree to which their policy succeeded. The table below shows us the advertising budget for print media (magazines and newspapers) of American automobile manufacturers from 1984 through 1989. It also indicates sales of American cars in these years. By examining the table you will see that spending for advertising grew in each year during this period of time (at an average rate of 11.2 percent per year). Car sales, however, showed little relationship to the amount of advertising spending. In some years sales fell even though advertising grew.

The data in the table has been used to create the graph that follows. Study the graph. The horizontal axis indicates the years from 1984 through 1989. Because the amount of money spent and the number of cars sold cannot both be shown on the same axis, two vertical axes are used. The left-hand axis shows spending for advertising in millions of dollars. The right-hand axis shows the number of cars sold in thousands. The two lines on the graph demonstrate that there appears to be little relationship between advertising spending and car sales. There may, however, be other factors such as broadcast advertising or foreign automaker advertising that affect car sales. What other explanations could be offered for declining sales? What other types of data could be investigated in order to provide a clearer picture of the relationship between advertising and sales?

Spending for Print Media Advertising by U.S. Automobile Producers, 1984–1989

Year	1984	1985	1986	1987	1988	1989
Advertising Spending (in $ millions, adjusted for inflation)	$473	$525	$550	$612	$694	$734
Sales of U.S.-Made Cars (in thousands)	7,621	8,002	7,516	7,085	7,105	6,807

Advertising and Sales of U.S. Cars, 1984–1989

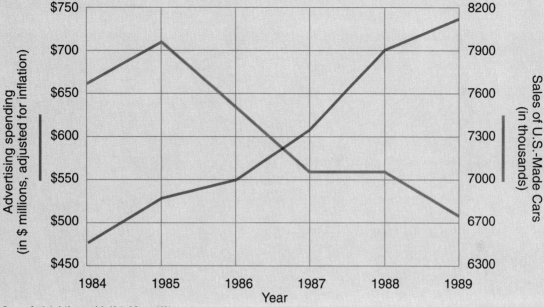

Source: *Statistical Abstract of the United States*, 1991.

Practice: Graphs can be used to show relationships between many kinds of data. Think of events and situations that may have cause/effect relationships that change over a period of time, collect the data, and build a graph similar to the graph above. Time units along the bottom of the graph may be in hours, days, months, etc. For example, is there a relationship between the number of minutes or hours you study for tests and your test scores over a period of weeks? Is there a relationship between the number of students in your economics class who bought lunch in the school cafeteria each day of the week and the number of students in the class who ate breakfast each day?

Business and the Economy

Objectives

In the sections of this chapter, you will learn:

A

how businesses can be organized as *sole proprietorships*, *partnerships*, or *corporations*;

B

how *fixed* and *variable costs* are involved in the operation of a business;

C

how *average fixed costs* affect profits; and

D

how businesses obtain and pay for the resources they need.

Introduction

It is one thing to dream about running your own business but it is something quite different to actually do it. Many people think of business ownership in terms of independence, freedom and profits. They tend to overlook competition, responsibility, and the possibility of failure.

In this chapter you will study the different types of business organizations that are common in the American economy. You will discover that each type of business organization has advantages and disadvantages in different situations.

In the second and third sections of the chapter you will investigate how businesses make decisions. The costs of production are particularly important to the profitability of businesses. By controlling these costs firms are able to improve their return. All business decisions are related to the costs of production.

Most businesses require an outside source of money to operate. In many cases this source may be found in the banking community. Corporations, however, are able to raise money through the sale of stocks and bonds. These and other sources of money will be presented in the last section of this chapter.

Section A Forms of Business Organization

This section introduces the basic forms of business organization in the United States: the *single proprietorship,* the *partnership,* and the *corporation.* It introduces the terms *limited* and *unlimited liability* and *limited life,* and explains the function of *stocks* and *corporate bonds.*

Personal Narrative

I Want to Be the Boss: How Should I Begin?

Rita and Joshua worked together at Sal's Diner for almost five years before they got married. He cooked and she waited on tables. They had talked about going on a honeymoon to Hawaii, but they used the money to open their own restaurant instead.

The place wasn't much of a restaurant at the start. Actually it was an old bookstore, 15 feet wide and 40 feet deep. After they put in a small kitchen, there was room for only six tables and a few chairs at the counter. They chose the location because it was cheap and it was right in front of a bus stop. Every morning and evening hundreds of people would wait outside their door for the bus. They thought some of those people would come inside and buy food.

Rita and Joshua were both right and wrong about their location. Many people did wait for a bus in front of their business, but few came in. One day Rita talked with some of the waiting people. She asked them if they had ever thought of going in to eat. She found that many wanted to buy food but were afraid of missing their bus if they went inside.

Rita thought she had an idea to solve the problem. She told Joshua that they needed to move the kitchen to the front of the store, put in a window, and sell hot dogs and hamburgers like a fast-food restaurant. Joshua said, "Great, so where do we get the money to do it with? Did you win the lottery or something?"

There was a real problem: Rita and Joshua didn't have any money left. Finally Rita's father, Paul, helped them out. He was retired and had saved for his old age. Rita convinced him to become a partner in the business. They gave him a one-third interest in exchange for $20,000. He didn't have to work; he just had to put in his money. Paul's lawyer drew up the necessary papers and they all signed them.

With a quick-service window in the front of the store, business grew rapidly. Soon they took out the tables and counter so they could expand their kitchen. They sold complete take-home meals.

They specialized in Mexican and American food. In the morning they sold coffee, rolls, and breakfasts-to-go. At the end of their second year they had paid off all of their debts and even had a few thousand dollars put away in a bank.

Rita and Joshua decided it was time to expand. If they could make a good profit in front of their bus stop, why not in front of other bus stops too? Joshua found three other locations that looked promising. Rita, Joshua, and Paul estimated that they needed at least $130,000 to set up the other locations and another $20,000 for inventory. Paul's lawyer suggested they form a corporation. He said that he knew of a number of people who would want to invest in such a successful business. Rita, Joshua, and Paul received 10,000 shares valued at $10 each for their existing business. The lawyer and his friends bought 15,000 shares for $150,000 providing the money necessary for expansion.

Eventually professional managers were hired to run the other stores. The chain became very successful. Rita and Joshua work at their original store, but they also receive dividends from the income made at the other locations. They no longer control the business, but they are content to collect their share of the profit. Next year they are going to take a fifth anniversary trip to Hawaii.

Forms of Business Organization

The three basic forms of business organization in the United States are the **single proprietorship,** the **partnership,** and the **corporation.** Each form has both advantages and disadvantages.

Single Proprietorship

The single proprietorship is the easiest type of business to organize. This partially explains why it is the most common form of business organization. Proprietorships place full responsibility on the single owner. This gives individual owners the power to make decisions, but it also prevents them from sharing their responsibilities with others. Proprietors are personally accountable for all financial obligations of their firm. Their personal property can be taken by the courts to satisfy claims on the firm. This is called **unlimited liability.** In addition, proprietorships can have difficulty raising funds because they are limited to the financial resources of the individual owner. Finally, proprietorships have **limited life**—when the owner dies, the business must be reorganized. Completing this process can take a long time and can hurt the firm's competitive position in its market.

The single proprietorship is the most common form of business organization. A partnership—a legal joining of two or more individuals—is the least common form. Corporations are a less common form of organization than single proprietorships, but they generate by far the larger amount of receipts.

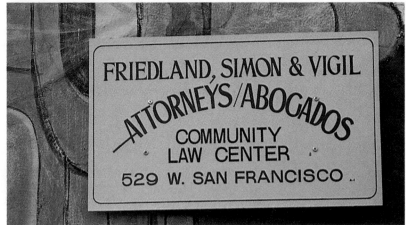

Partnership

Partnerships are a legal joining of two or more individuals in a business. This is the least common form of business organization. There are two important advantages of partnerships over proprietorships. First, partnerships can raise more money because they have the financial resources of more than one person to call on. Second, they allow individuals to share expensive capital or services necessary to particular types of business. For example, doctors often become partners so that they can share the costs of a nurse or a lab.

Individuals who join as partners must be very careful because they are financially responsible for personal as well as business debts of their partners (except for those debts specifically exempted in the contract under which their partnership was formed). Like proprietorships, partnerships have unlimited liability and limited life. If one partner leaves, other partners are required to pay his or her debts. The courts can take a partner's personal property to satisfy debts of other partners. If a partner dies the firm must be reorganized.

Corporation

The corporation is the most difficult form of business organization to establish. However, it offers a number of important advantages over other forms of business organization. Corporations are able to raise money through the sale of either *stock* or *corporate bonds*. Corporate *stock* is a unit of ownership in the firm. It entitles the owner to share in the profits the firm makes. A *corporate bond* is a loan to the firm. Interest must be paid on the loan for some specified time, after which the loan must be repaid.

A corporation is recognized as a legal person before the law. This means that if a corporation is sued or fails, individual owners cannot lose more than they have invested in the firm. This is called **limited liability.**

Legal control of a corporation is determined through a majority of the *voted* stock. If an owner dies or fails to vote his or her stock, the firm will continue to operate. This gives the corporation the advantage of **unlimited life.**

Table 5–1 organizes the characteristics of the three forms of business in a format that will help you remember them. Table 5–2 compares the three forms in terms of how many businesses of each kind exist and the amount of receipts each kind generates. Notice that although sole proprietorships are the most numerous form of business organization, corporations generate by far the greater receipts.

Table 5–1
Characteristics of Business Organizations, Compared

	Single Proprietorship	Partnership	Corporation
Ease of organization	Easiest	Moderately difficult	Most difficult
Capital generally available for operation	Least	Intermediate	Most (best able to raise capital)
Responsibility	Centered in one person	Spread among partners	Policy set by directors; president supervises day-to-day operation
Incentive to succeed	Centered in one person	Spread among partners	Spread among many people
Flexibility	Greatest	Intermediate	Least
Ability to perform varied functions (production or purchasing, accounting, selling, etc.)	Dependent on one individual's versatility	Dependent on capabilities of two or more individuals	Best able to employ individuals with different capabilities
Possibility of conflict among those in control	None	Most prone to conflict, especially if partners have equal interest in business	Chain of command reduces internal conflict; wide ownership minimizes disagreement
Taxation	No corporate income tax	No corporate income tax	Corporate income tax
Distribution of profits or losses	All to proprietor	Distributed to partners in accordance with terms of partnership agreement	Profits retained or to stockholders as dividends; losses reduce price of stock
Liability for debts in event of failure	Unlimited	Unlimited, but spread among partners	Limited to each stockholder's investment
Length of life	Limited by one individual's life span (or until he goes out of business)	Limited (partnership is reorganized upon death or withdrawal of any partner)	Unlimited (with ownership of shares readily transferable)

Source: Adapted, with permission, from Conover, Berlye, and Gordon, *Business Dynamics* (Mission Hills: Glencoe Publishing, 1989), p. 479.

▰ *Self-Check*

1. What is the difference between the unlimited liability of proprietorships and partnerships, and the limited liability of corporations?
2. Why do doctors or lawyers often become partners?
3. Name at least two advantages of corporations.

Table 5–2
Forms of Business Organization by Number, Receipts,
and Percentage of Total,
1960–1987
(number in thousands)
(receipts in billions of $)

	1960	1970	1980	1987
Proprietorship				
number	9,090	9,400	12,702	13,091
% of total	81%	78%	76%	71%
receipts	171	238	506	611
% of total	16%	11%	7%	6%
Partnership				
number	941	936	1,380	1,648
% of total	8%	8%	8%	9%
receipts	74	93	292	411
% of total	7%	5%	4%	4%
Corporation				
number	1,141	1,665	2,711	3,612
% of total	11%	14%	16%	20%
receipts	849	1,751	6,361	9,186
% of total	77%	84%	89%	90%

(The figures for receipts include the value of
mergers and other assets that are sold from one
firm to another. This explains why receipts are so
large. Nevertheless, it is an indication of business activity.)

Source: *Statistical Abstract of the United States,* 1991.

◼ *Applying What You Have Learned*

Rita and Joshua chose to allow their firm to become a corporation. Although they kept partial ownership, they lost control of the firm because they did not hold more than 50 percent of the stock. Write a new end to the story, starting when Joshua began to look for other locations. What might happen if other shareholders disagree with him? How might Rita and Joshua keep control of the firm themselves? Could they accomplish their expansion and keep control? What danger might there be in this course of action? Include the answers to these questions in your ending.

Section B The Costs of Production

This section will introduce the ideas of *fixed* and *variable costs*.

Personal Narrative

How Much Does It Cost To Run a Business?

When Rita and Joshua went into business, they had no idea how much it was going to cost. They knew about the equipment and supplies they had to buy, but the costs of a license from the city to run a restaurant and many other expenses were a surprise. It seemed that there was a new surprise that cost them money every time they turned around. Their biggest unexpected cost was for an insurance policy. They paid $583 a month for liability protection. Their agent said it was because people had gone "sue crazy." The reason did not make them feel any better about spending more money.

Rita and Joshua started with $35,000. Before they opened their door they had spent almost all of it. Joshua made the following list of costs to help keep track of where the money went.

Kitchen equipment	$4,542	Furniture	$2,232
Dishes & utensils	$2,627	Wiring & plumbing	$2,769
Rent for six months	$3,920	License & fees	$ 520
Insurance, 1/2 year	$3,500	Food inventory	$3,434
Paper products	$1,356	Cash register	$ 862
Utilities	$ 792	Advertising	$ 550
		Total	$27,104

These were only expenses that were related to their business. There were also personal costs they had to pay. When they left Sal's Diner they lost their medical insurance, retirement plan, and paid vacation. They had to take care of their living expenses while they got the restaurant ready to go. All of these things either had to be paid for or done without. Medical insurance alone cost them $387 a month.

The day they sold their first fried egg they were down to less than $500. It is not surprising that Joshua didn't see how they could move the kitchen to the front of the store and start selling fast food. Without additional funds they couldn't afford it.

Costs

Economists have divided the costs of production into two groups, *fixed costs* and *variable costs*.

Mortgage payments on a building are an example of fixed costs. Such costs are paid regardless of how many (or how few) products are made. The raw goods delivered by the truck are variable costs. Such costs vary according to how many products the company decides to make.

Fixed Costs

Fixed costs are expenses that must be paid no matter how many products the firm manufactures. Mortgage payments and property taxes are two examples of fixed costs. Banks and the city government don't care how many products a firm makes or sells. If a firm owes them money they expect to be paid.

Variable Costs

Variable costs are expenses that change with the number of products produced. Wages and raw materials, such as eggs, are examples of variable costs. These expenses will increase as production grows.

Controlling Costs

Many people who are first starting businesses underestimate their fixed costs. This frequently causes them to charge too little for their product and to overestimate their ability to make profits. They think, "The meat in a hamburger costs twenty cents. The bun and condiments add another six cents. I can sell it for fifty cents and make almost a quarter profit." Reasoning like this ignores the cost of insurance, rent and other fixed costs. It probably costs more than fifty cents to make a hamburger.

One way to reduce the importance of fixed costs is to increase the number of products you sell. For example, if your store has fixed costs of $100 and you sell 100 items, there is one dollar of fixed cost per item. However, if you can increase your sales to 1,000 items, the fixed cost per item will go down to just ten cents. The more items sold, the lower the fixed cost per item. This is one reason that high volume stores like McDonald's Restaurants can afford to have lower prices than low volume stores. You could say that Rita and Joshua's restaurant became a high volume store when they put in their quick-service window.

According to tax returns filed with the Internal Revenue Service, the debt of all corporations in the United States grew from $2,034 billion in 1980 to $4,286 billion in 1987. This was an increase of over 110 percent in seven years. During the same period of time, the interest paid by these corporations grew from $345 billion to $500 billion, for an increase of only 71 percent. The increase in interest paid was smaller because interest rates fell during these years. Consider what these lower interest rates did to the firms' cost of borrowing. Can they be sure these rates will remain low in the future?

Study Table 5–3. What happened to profit as a percentage of sales between 1979 and 1989? Why might this have happened?

Table 5–3
Sales and Profits of Manufacturing Corporations, 1979–1989
(in billions of dollars)

	1979	1981	1983	1985	1987	1989
Sales	$1,742	$2,145	$2,114	$2,331	$2,378	$2,745
Profits before taxes	$154	$159	$133	$137	$159	$182
Profits as a percentage of sales	8.8%	7.4%	6.3%	5.9%	6.9%	6.6%

■ *Self-Check*

1. What is the difference between fixed and variable costs?
2. Do people who are first starting businesses more frequently underestimate fixed or variable costs?
3. What is one way to reduce fixed costs per item?

■ *Applying What You Have Learned*

Joshua listed various costs that he and Rita paid in the story above. On a separate piece of paper, list the 12 expenses and identify each as a fixed or variable cost.

Section C Reducing Average Fixed Costs

This section will discuss the idea of *average fixed costs*.

Personal Narrative

I Could Earn a Bigger Profit if I Sold Popcorn Too

When Rita and Joshua first opened their restaurant, they had a very limited menu. They sold hot dogs, hamburgers, french fries, soft drinks, coffee, and very little else. Their store was so small that they couldn't sell many things. They studied the people who waited for the bus in front of their store. Most of them were lower middle income workers. Rita and Joshua sold food that they considered "safe," instead of more varied and interesting items.

After they changed to quick service and take-out food, they had space for a bigger kitchen. Rita wanted to cook Mexican food. Joshua thought they would do better by opening early to sell breakfasts and by stocking snack food. He wanted to sell popcorn. There was a park across the street where children and old men fed pigeons. He said they would buy lots of popcorn. Rita and Joshua compromised. They did both.

Actually, Paul convinced them that expanding their menu was a good idea. He pointed out that a large part of their expenses were fixed costs. They had to pay rent, insurance, license fees and heat whether the store was open one or twenty hours a day. "How much more would it cost to come in early and cook breakfasts?" he asked. "Would it be expensive to stock candy bars, ice cream and other snack food for children on their way home from school?" Paul said they should try to keep their store busy all of the time.

It turned out that they sold much more Mexican and snack food than anything else. Rita was a good cook. Her tortillas sold as quickly as she made them. A local newspaper did a story about their business. After that they had more customers than they could handle. It was about this time that Joshua began thinking of expansion.

Reducing Average Fixed Costs

Businesses often find that they can make a larger profit when they stay open for longer hours or sell more things. This can be the result of reducing *average fixed costs*. Fixed costs—such as rent, property tax, and fire insurance—must be paid no matter how many products are made or sold. The **average fixed cost** is the total of the fixed costs of operating the business, divided by the number of units produced or sold.

This restaurant can reduce its average fixed costs by staying open for longer hours and adding items to the menu. The fixed costs do not change, but the number of products sold should go up.

Suppose a store sells shirts for $30 each and has fixed costs of $100 a day. If it sells 10 shirts a day, it would have an average fixed cost of $10 per shirt.

$100 in fixed costs ÷ 10 shirts = $10 per shirt

If the store could increase its sales to 20 shirts a day by lowering its price to $28 each, it could reduce its average fixed costs per shirt to $5.

$100 in fixed costs ÷ 20 shirts = $5 per shirt

The store owners would discover that by lowering their price they could both reduce their average fixed cost per item and increase their profits. Here's how it would work:

Suppose the store had a variable cost of $12 for every shirt it sold. When it sold 10 shirts, it would have made $8 profit per shirt.

price	$30
variable cost	− 12
average fixed cost	− 10
profit per item	$ 8

The store would have made a total profit of $80 a day.

shirts sold	10
times profit per shirt	× $8
total profit	$80

If the store could sell 20 shirts a day by lowering its price to $28 it would increase its profit.

price	$28
variable cost	− 12
average fixed cost	− 5
profit per item	$11

The store would make a total profit of $220 a day.

shirts sold	20
times profit per shirt	× $11
total profit	$220

The store could accomplish the same result by selling other products. If it sold ties and gloves, it could reduce the average fixed cost per item. This explains, at least in part, why stores often choose to sell many different types of merchandise.

Large businesses are often better able than smaller firms to reduce their average fixed costs through volume selling. This is one reason that large discount stores can afford to have lower prices than small neighborhood stores.

It is possible for firms to become too large to operate efficiently. However, in most cases large firms are more efficient than small ones. You will learn about the advantages and disadvantages of large firms in Chapter 6.

◼ *Self-Check*

1. Why do firms often try to reduce their average fixed costs?
2. If a firm has an average fixed cost per item of $8 when it sells 200 items a day, what would its average fixed cost per item be if it sold 800 items a day?
3. What reason, mentioned in this section, do firms have for selling many different types of merchandise?

◼ *Applying What You Have Learned*

In the story at the beginning of this section, find two things that Rita and Joshua did to reduce their average fixed costs. What effect, if any, did these actions have on the *fixed* costs? What effect did they have on the amount of products sold?

Section D Rent, Interest and How Businesses Obtain Money

This section explains how businesses obtain money to pay for the factors of production. New terms include *rent, interest, profit, prime rate, bond, stock, dividend, capital gain,* and *shareholder.*

Personal Narrative

If I Borrow $50,000 I Can Open Up Another Store

After their first location became a success, Joshua wanted to open up new stores as rapidly as possible. He was afraid other people would imitate their idea after the newspaper article was published. Joshua found three locations that looked promising. They were all at bus stops and near office buildings. After careful study, Rita and Joshua decided that they needed at least $50,000 for each new store. The problem was where to get the money.

They had almost all of their own money tied up in the first store. Paul was unwilling to "put all his eggs in one basket" by giving them the rest of his retirement savings. Besides, it would not have been enough. They discovered that they would have to find an outside source for the needed funds.

The banks were their first stop, but they had little luck. The loan officers all said about the same thing. They were very happy that Rita and Joshua were successful, but they still didn't think they were a good risk. They had only been in business a year and a half. Restaurants are more likely to fail than most other types of business. There was little market for their used restaurant equipment. Rita and Joshua had nothing else to pledge for collateral. The most they could borrow from a bank would be about $30,000 and they would have to pay 14 percent interest. This just wasn't good enough.

When Rita and Joshua told Paul about their problem, he suggested they see his lawyer. They made an appointment and described the situation to the attorney. He was very interested and helpful. He told them about the possibility of forming a corporation. He liked their business and said he would be willing to invest $10,000 in it himself. He said he could also find other investors.

Rita asked how much of the stock Paul and they would receive. The lawyer suggested 40 percent. He agreed that 40 percent was not a controlling interest, but he pointed out the fact that their total investment so far was less than $50,000. He also reminded them that they lacked managerial training and the legal knowledge to run all four stores at once. Eventually they agreed. The lawyer drew up the necessary papers. Six months later they had four locations open.

Obtaining Resources

To run a business it is often necessary to use resources that belong to other people. Rita and Joshua didn't own any buildings. They had a lease to *rent* from someone else. One definition for **rent** is payment for the use of a resource that belongs to someone else. Rent may be paid on natural resources (such as land) or on capital (such as a building, or a truck, or money). One way of renting capital is to borrow money.

Loans

Borrowed money is really a borrowed claim on resources. Rita and Joshua wanted to borrow $150,000 to open three new stores. They would have used someone else's money to buy the resources they needed. To use someone else's money they would have had to pay *interest*. **Interest** is payment for the current use of someone else's money.

The amount of interest that must be paid depends on several factors: the risk for repayment of the loan, the demand and supply for loanable funds, the length of time for repayment, the cost of administering the loan, and the competition in the market.

In this presentation we will concentrate on the market—that is, the demand and supply of money. It is possible to draw a demand and supply graph for loanable funds, like the one in Figure 5–1, which shows the interest rate that banks charge to large corporations that have low risk. The price of money (interest rate) is on the vertical axis. The amount or quantity of money that is loaned out is on the horizontal axis.

Figure 5–1 *Demand and Supply for Loanable Funds*

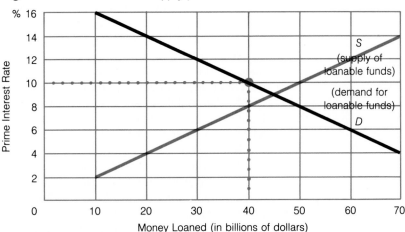

One way to obtain the use of resources is to borrow money from a bank. When you do this, you pay interest. The interest rate that banks charge their best customers is called the prime rate.

In this case the equilibrium interest rate would be 10 percent and 40 billion dollars would be loaned at that rate. But if the loans involved greater risk, the lenders would require higher interest rates, and so the equilibrium interest rate would be higher. Rita and Joshua's loan would have been a high-risk loan, which explains why the bank wanted 12 percent interest to lend them money. If a large, low-risk company such as General Electric wants to borrow money, it would pay the **prime rate.** This is the lowest rate banks charge to their best customers (the 8 percent equilibrium rate in this case). Look at Table 5–4, below, and con-

Table 5–4
Average Prime Interest Rate,
1981–1990

Year	Prime
1981	18.87%
1982	14.86%
1983	10.79%
1984	11.51%
1985	9.93%
1986	8.33%
1987	8.21%
1988	9.32%
1989	10.87%
1990	10.01%

sider what must have happened to the demand and supply of loanable money between 1981 and 1990.

Bonds

Corporations can also raise money by selling bonds. A **bond** is an I.O.U. that a firm sells. The purchaser of a bond is in effect making a loan to the corporation. A bond requires the firm to make interest payments over a specific period of time to the owner of the bond, and to repay the original amount of the loan, or principle, on a specific date in the future. Bonds usually have longer terms, which means they do not have to be repaid as quickly as loans from banks. Although the firm that issues a bond will not cash it in until the date that it is due, bonds can be sold to other people. If bonds could not be sold, few people would buy them in the first place. Few people would be willing to give up access to their money for such long periods of time.

Large corporations often borrow money by selling bonds. Small firms can't do this as easily because they are not as well known or widely trusted. Purchasers of the bonds could find it difficult to sell their bonds to someone else. Therefore, they would be unlikely to buy the bonds in the first place.

Stock

Rita and Joshua finally got the money they needed by forming a corporation and selling stock. A share of **stock** is a unit of ownership in the corporation. People who invest in stock give up the use of their money in exchange for a share of ownership in the firm and a portion of future earnings the corporation might make.

Any investment in a corporation involves some risk. The firm could fail, causing the stock owners to lose their investments. To take such a risk, stock owners must expect to earn more from their stock than they could from a bank, where there is little or no risk.

It is possible to earn a profit from stock in two ways—from *dividends* or from a *capital gain*. **Dividends** are a share of the corporation's profit. They must be approved by a vote of the stockholders. A **capital gain** occurs when stock can be sold for more than it originally cost to buy. The value of stock will go up if the firm does well or if investors believe that it will do well in the future. This will cause more people to want the stock and fewer people to sell it. The value of stock is determined by demand and supply. The following example shows how demand and supply affected the value of stock in Archer Communications, Inc., an electronics company.

In 1988 stock in Archer Communications, Inc., sold for 50 cents a share. By 1990, it had climbed to $20 a share. However, Archer Communications' sales were only $2 million in 1989, and the firm had lost $17.5 million since it was organized. Some may ask why anyone would pay $20 a share for a firm that was losing money. The answer is that many people thought Archer Communications was going to make large profits in the future.

Managers of Archer Communications said the firm had a new type of sound system (called Qsound) that was superior to any other method of reproducing sound. Coca-Cola and the Nintendo Company were interested in using Qsound in advertisements and video games. Recording companies announced their interest. Many people tried to buy Archer stock, but those who owned the firm's stock did not want to sell. The value of the stock rose rapidly.

In 1990 disaster struck. The sound system was not successful when used in advertisements. Potential customers began to back out of agreements, stating that they would reconsider buying the product after its quality had been tested. By then, most of Archer's stock owners wanted to sell, but no one wanted to buy. The total value of all of the firm's stock fell to $75,000 or less than half a cent per share.

Changes in sales or profits, rumors of a possible take-over, news of a technological breakthrough, or changes in dividends, all can change the demand and supply for a firm's stock and therefore its price. Even the best market analysts have difficulty explaining changes in stock prices on all occasions.

■ *Self-Check*

1. What is one way in which rent and interest payments are similar to each other?
2. Why are large, established businesses often able to borrow money at lower interest rates than small, new businesses?
3. If the price of a type of stock goes up, what does this suggest about the quantity of that stock being demanded and the quantity being supplied?

■ *Applying What You Have Learned*

To expand their business, what two methods of raising money did Rita and Joshua consider? In so doing, which of the four factors of production were they attempting to obtain?

CURRENT ECONOMIC ISSUES

The Fixed Cost of Medical Equipment

During the 1980s and early 1990s the cost of medical care in the United States increased at about twice the rate of other prices. One of the biggest causes for this rapid price increase was the cost of new types of medical devices. Magnetic resonance imaging machines (MRIs), for example, were purchased by many hospitals and private clinics in the 1980s at a cost of roughly $3 million each. MRIs allow doctors to take a series of pictures of the insides of patients to see what is happening to their bodies. This procedure is particularly valuable for people who suffer from various forms of cancer or who have had strokes.

The typical fee for one series of MRI pictures is between $800 and $1,200. Some patients have had a series completed every few weeks over many months. It has been suggested that some MRI sessions have not been necessary but were completed to help pay for the cost of the MRI machines. When a hospital buys one of these machines it has a very large fixed cost it must pay. The actual cost of using the machine is about $200 for each session. The rest of the fee can be used to pay off the cost of the machine. Hospitals can pay for their machines more rapidly by serving many patients.

One possible solution to this problem would be to allow fewer hospitals to purchase expensive medical devices. Many doctors argue that their patients would either have to be moved from one hospital to another for different treatments they need, or do without them. They believe the extra quality care is worth the cost.

Would you support a plan that limits hospital spending on expensive equipment?

Arguments in Favor of the Plan
1. It would probably reduce the cost of medical care.
2. Hospitals and doctors would have less reason to prescribe unnecessary treatments.
3. Patients might have more money left over for other purposes.

Arguments Against the Plan
1. Many patients might not receive the best treatment possible.
2. Patients might have to be moved to another hospital risking their health and causing discomfort.
3. Medical devices would be even more expensive to buy if fewer of them were produced and sold.

What Do You Think?
Should the government regulate the number of expensive medical devices that could be purchased in any area of the country? What would happen to the fixed cost of buying and using these machines if such a plan was started?

Chapter 5 Review

What Have You Learned?

In this chapter you've learned the following important principles of economics:

- There are three principle forms of business organization in the United States: the *single proprietorship, partnership,* and *corporation.* Each form has advantages and disadvantages. Of the three, there are more single proprietorships in this country, but the corporation dominates production.

- All firms must consider both *fixed* and *variable* costs of production. Fixed costs remain the same regardless of the level of production, while variable costs increase with the level of production.

- Firms may try to control the effect of fixed costs by increasing their level of production. This will spread out their fixed costs among more products and reduce the *average fixed cost* per item.

- Most businesses need to use other people's capital from time to time. They may pay other people *rent* to use their buildings, machines, or money.

- Many businesses borrow money to buy the resources they need. When they do, they pay *interest* for the use of someone else's money. The amount of interest that must be paid depends on the risk associated with the loan, the length of time over which the loan must be repaid, and the demand and supply of loanable funds.

- Corporations may raise money by selling *stock.* A share of stock is a unit of ownership in a corporation. It entitles the owner to share in the corporation's earnings. Corporate profits paid to stockholders are called *dividends.* Stockholders may also benefit from a *capital gain,* which occurs when they sell their stock for more than the original purchase price.

- Corporations often raise money by selling *bonds.* A bond is a form of loan through which the firm is required to pay interest to the owner of the bond and to repay the bond on some specific future date. The owner of a corporate bond does not own part of the corporation.

- Firms that are profitable are best able to raise additional money. These firms are able to buy more resources, grow, and become more important to our economic system.

Words and Terms

single proprietorship (p. 117)
partnership (p. 117)
corporation (p. 117)
unlimited liability (p. 117)
limited life (p. 117)
limited liability (p. 119)
unlimited life (p. 119)
fixed costs (p. 123)
variable costs (p. 123)

average fixed cost (p. 125)
rent (p. 130)
interest (p. 130)
prime rate (p. 131)
bond (p. 132)
stock (p. 132)
dividend (p. 132)
capital gain (p. 132)

Chapter 5 Review

Building Your Vocabulary

On a separate piece of paper, write the vocabulary word or term that best completes each of the following statements.

1. Payments for labor, natural resources, and capital are usually examples of _____ of production.
2. _____ is a unit of ownership in a corporation.
3. _____ means that when one of the owners dies, the firm must be reorganized.
4. The most common form of business organization in the United States is the _____.
5. The form of business organization that has the greatest total sales in the United States is the _____.
6. The least common form of business organization in the United States is the _____.
7. A share of the profit paid by a corporation to its shareholders is a _____.
8. People who own stock in a corporation enjoy _____ because they can't lose more than the value of their investment.
9. If the owner of stock dies, the corporation will continue to function because it has _____.
10. Property taxes, rent and insurance are examples of _____ of production.
11. Payment for the use of someone else's resources can be called _____.
12. One way to earn a profit from owning stock is to sell it for more than it cost. This is called a _____.
13. The fixed cost per unit of production is called the _____.
14. Payment for borrowed money is called _____.
15. An obligation to pay interest over a period of time and to repay a loan, sold by corporations is called a _____.
16. The interest charged to a bank's best customers is the _____.
17. _____ means that the owners are personally liable for the debts of the firm.

Understanding Economics

1. Describe three different advantages that the corporate form of business organization has over either a single proprietorship or a partnership.
2. Identify a local business. Make a list of fixed costs this business would have to pay. Make a second list of its variable costs.
3. Explain why it might be less expensive *on an average* to raise a child in a large family instead of as an *only child.*
4. If you had $2,000 and wanted to make a safe investment in a firm, explain why you might choose to buy a corporate bond instead of buying the firm's stock.
5. Suppose someone else was quite wealthy. Explain why that person might be interested in buying stock in the firm instead of a bond.
6. Explain why the most profitable firms are the ones that will also probably pay the lowest interest rates and tend to grow more than less profitable firms.

Thinking Critically About Economics

1. Three different firms are being organized. Below you will find basic informa-

tion about each. Choose the form of business organization that would be best for each firm. Explain your answers.

Firm A is being formed by a group of lawyers. They need to rent a large office, buy a law library that will cost thousands of dollars, hire secretaries and assistants, and rent an expensive computer.

Firm B is being formed to manufacture home appliances. This firm will require a large factory and many expensive machines. It will be in competition with many other firms and will need to spend large amounts of money on advertising and distribution to break into its target market.

Firm C will sell snack food near a local park. The store will not be large but it will be open long hours. The person who runs the store will be responsible for both preparing the food and keeping financial records.

2. John rents a large store where he sells sporting goods. His rent is $1,000 a month. Although business has been good, John has found that he really has more space than he needs. On the other hand, he does not want to move because of his excellent location. John has considered selling camping equipment in his store too. Explain how this could help his business by *lowering average fixed costs per item sold*.

3. I sell bicycles in my store for $110 each. My fixed costs are $50 a day. It costs me $80 to buy and put together a bicycle. I sell an average of 10 bicycles a day. What is my total profit each day now? Should I lower my price to $100 if I could then sell 20 bicycles a day?

4. Sharon owns a proprietorship that makes straw hats. She employs five workers and has sales of about $180,000 a year. She recently received an order from a mail-order firm for $500,000 worth of hats. Sharon must expand her business and she will have to use someone else's money to do it. Describe three different ways she might raise the money she needs.

5. Mark bought stock in a corporation that has a history of paying large dividends. Barbara bought stock in a different firm that makes good profits but pays almost no dividends. This firm invests its profits back in its business. As a result, it has grown very rapidly. Explain how Barbara could make as much money from her stock as Mark does from his.

Consumer Skills Projects

1. Make a chart that includes possible advantages and disadvantages for consumers who seek medical services from a doctor who is: A. a single proprietor; B. a partner; C. an employee of a corporation.

2. Identify a business from which you often purchase goods or services. Make a list of steps the owners of this firm could take to reduce their costs and allow them to lower the price they charge consumers. Would all of these steps be good for consumers?

3. Identify a major corporation that produces products you often buy. Graph the value of this firm's stock over several months. Write an essay that describes how changes in the value of this firm's stock may have been influenced by how well it serves its customers.

Developing Your Economic Skills

Using Tables to Help Make Decisions

Skill: In this lesson you'll learn how data can be analyzed through the use of tables to help make economic decisions. To complete this lesson you'll follow these steps:

1. Study the firm's costs of production and sales as they currently exist.
2. Study the projection of the costs of production and sales as they would be after an expansion.
3. Compare the data from the two tables to determine whether the firm should expand.

Application: Based on your analysis, should your business grow?

Suppose you owned a florist shop. Your business has done well. Sales totaled $280,000 last year. You have wondered if you should open another store on the other side of town. To make your decision you need to compare your costs and earnings as they are now with what you believe they would be with a new store. The first table will help you by providing a list of your current costs. The total cost is listed at the bottom of the table along with the firm's sales. The firm's profit can be found by subtracting the cost of production from its sales.

You did not pay yourself a salary but you keep the profit.

If you open the new store, you expect that its sales would be about $252,000. You expect that 10 percent of your current customers would buy from the new store because they live closer to its location; as a re-

Current Costs of Production and Sales

Rent	$ 9,600
Labor (3 workers @ $15,000 each including all fringe benefits)	$ 45,000
Utilities (electricity, heat, water)	$ 6,200
Insurance	$ 1,800
Payment on bank loan for store equipment	$ 5,300
Inventory for sale (flowers, pots, etc.)	$130,000
Advertising	$ 15,000
Delivery trucks	$ 20,000
All other costs	$ 3,100
total cost now	$236,000
total sales now	$280,000
current profit	$ 44,000

sult, sales at the old store would fall slightly, and would also be about $252,000.

You believe most of the costs would double if you open a new store but you know that some would not. For example, advertising would cost you no more because you could advertise for both stores at the same time. The cost of inventory for each store would fall by 10 percent to $117,000. You believe that you could use the same delivery trucks for both stores, but the total cost would increase to $30,000 because of extra driving. You would require four workers at the new store because you could not work at both locations yourself. All other costs would be the same at the new store as they are at the old.

Projected Costs and Sales for Both Stores

	Old Store Before Expansion	Both Stores After Expansion	
		Old Store	New Store
Rent	$ 9,600	$ 9,600	$ 9,600
Labor (3 + 4 workers at $15,000 each)	$ 45,000	$ 45,000	$ 60,000
Utilities (electricity, heat, water)	$ 6,200	$ 6,200	$ 6,200
Insurance	$ 1,800	$ 1,800	$ 1,800
Payment on bank loan for store equipment	$ 5,300	$ 5,300	$ 5,300
Inventory for sale (flowers, pots, etc.)	$130,000	$117,000	$117,000
Advertising	$ 15,000	$ 7,500	$ 7,500
Delivery truck	$ 20,000	$ 15,000	$ 15,000
All other costs	$ 3,100	$ 3,100	$ 3,100
cost		$210,500	$225,500
total cost	$236,000		$436,000
sales		$252,000	$252,000
total sales	$280,000		$504,000
total profit	$ 44,000		$ 68,000

How can you consider all of these ideas at once to make the right decision? One answer is to compare all these amounts on the same table.

The left column will list the same costs of production as those in the first table. The two columns to the right list the projected costs of the old and new stores. By adding the totals for the two right-hand columns together, you can find the total cost of both stores after an expansion. You have esti-mated that each store will have sales of $252,000 for a total sales of $504,000. The table tells you your total cost will be $436,000. Therefore, you project your profit to be $68,000 if you open the new store. $68,000 is better than $44,000 so you decide to open the new store. The tables have helped you organize data to make a decision.

Practice: Determine what effect opening a third florist store would have on profits.

Perfect and Imperfect Competition

Objectives

In the sections of this chapter, you will learn:

A

how businesses operate in *perfect* and in *imperfect competition;*

B

how various kinds of *monopolies* can exist;

C

how *horizontal* and *vertical combinations* are formed;

D

how there are *economies* and *diseconomies of scale* in having a large business;

E

how the government tries to maintain *workable competition.*

Introduction

There is a popular belief that big businesses usually make big profits. This is often not the case. Remember that profit needs to be looked at in terms of what was done to earn it. If I invest $10,000 and earn $2,000 a year in profit, I am doing very well. The $2,000 is 20 percent of my investment. However, if I invest $100,000 and earn the same $2,000 in profit, I am only earning 2 percent on my investment. I would not be very happy. I could have done better by putting my money in a bank.

A firm's profitability often depends more on the type of market it sells in than on its size. Firms that provide products consumers want with little competition are more likely to make profits than firms in highly competitive markets.

In this chapter you will learn about the differences between firms that operate under perfect competition and those that do business in imperfect markets. The costs and benefits of each type of market to the economic system will be explained. If there were no advantages to monopolistic firms, there would be less of a problem in getting rid of them. The fact is, like so many economic problems, large firms that operate in imperfect markets have both a good side and a bad side.

Some businesses, like these stands in a farmer's market, are engaged in near perfect competition. Other businesses, such as electric utility companies, operate in conditions of imperfect competition. Perfect and imperfect competition both have advantages and disadvantages for the economic system as a whole.

The government of the United States tries to prevent firms from getting so large and powerful that they can take advantage of the consumer. You will learn about government antitrust policy in this chapter. You will find that there is widespread disagreement over what role the government should play in maintaining competition.

Section A Perfect Competition

This section will introduce the ideas of *perfect competition, diversification,* and *the market as a regulator of the economy.*

One in a Million

My name is Ron. I run a filling station and convenience food store. My business is located on a major highway that leads into a big city. There are discount stores, fast-food restaurants, and other filling stations all around my store. Once last year I tried to count all the filling stations within a mile of my location. I stopped after I got to thirty. As you might guess, my business is very competitive.

My customers care about one thing, the price I charge. I don't service cars. I have nothing to offer but a low price. At least once a day I drive around my neighborhood to be sure that no one is charging less than I am. I want my customers to know that they will always get the lowest price from me.

In recent months my profit margin has been getting smaller. With the fall in the price of crude oil and gasoline in early 1986, competition between filling stations became fierce. It seemed that prices went down every day. My customers were thrilled, but I was not so happy.

I have already tried to cut costs by installing self-service pumps. I have diversified into selling soft drinks and groceries. On a hot day I actually earn more from selling ice than from gasoline. I'm not getting rich, but I am getting by. I feel that if I can hang on, other firms will eventually go under and I will be able to charge a higher price. I have great hopes for the future.

Perfect Competition

Ron runs his business in a market that is close to **perfect competition.** In perfect competition (as in Ron's business) customers don't care very much whose product they buy. They look for the lowest price. Ron is forced to sell his product at the same or a lower price than his competition. If he tries to charge more than his competition his customers will buy from someone else. Firms in perfect competition are called "price takers" because they have no control over the price they can charge.

A firm in perfect competition can increase its profit only by cutting its costs of production or by increasing its sales. That is probably why Ron installed self-service pumps. The new pumps cut his labor cost and increased the number of customers he could serve.

A firm in perfect competition will lose customers if it raises its prices above those of the competition. Therefore, firms in perfect competition can increase profits only by cutting costs of production or by increasing sales. Diversification—such as selling both gasoline and groceries—is a common way of increasing sales in competitive markets. It also reduces the average fixed cost per item sold.

Diversification

A common step taken by competitive firms is to sell additional types of products. Economists call this **diversification.** There are at least two advantages to this action. First, the additional types of products might encounter less competition, and so could earn a larger profit. Second, diversification should reduce the average fixed cost per item sold. For example, if you have to be in your store to collect money for gas, you might as well collect for dairy foods, groceries, and magazines, too. It wouldn't cost much more to stock these items and they could add to profitability. This is why many self-service gas stations are also convenience food stores.

The Market as a Regulator

If there are too many firms in a competitive market, profits will be low. This should cause some of the less efficient firms to close. This would reduce the supply of the product and increase its price. Ron hopes this will happen. If other filling stations close, he may be able to charge more for his product.

If there are only a few firms in a competitive market, profits are more likely to be high. This encourages additional firms to enter the market. The additional firms increase the supply of the product and reduce its price. Through demand and supply the market helps to regulate the number of firms serving the consumer.

Customers in a perfect competitive market should benefit from low prices. One possible danger is that in attempting to reduce costs competitive firms may cut services or reduce quality. Many filling stations no longer service cars. They believe that the cost of providing service is greater than the return they could earn.

Figure 6–1 shows a graph concerning some industries that are quite competitive. The graph shows the numbers of these firms that existed in 1972 and 1988. Why do you suppose some grew in number while others fell?

It has been suggested that there can be too much competition. If there are many competitive firms in an industry, it is unlikely that any will be able to make a large profit or accumulate

Figure 6–1   *Retail Stores in 1972 and 1988*

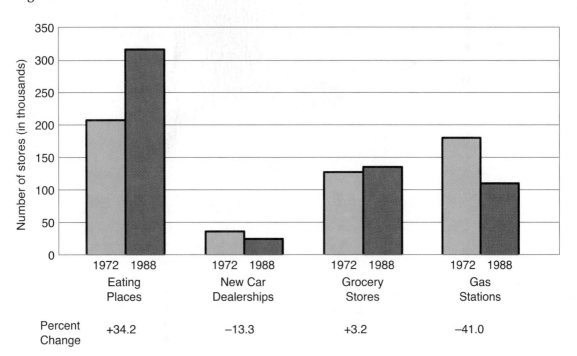

Source: *Statistical Abstract of the United States,* 1981, 1987, 1991.

When the market is competitive, customers should benefit from lower prices. But there can also be drawbacks to such competition, which could include lower quality products or services.

large amounts of wealth. This could reduce their ability to invest in research and new technology that would lower production costs or improve quality. It might also reduce their ability to ride out a downturn in the economy. The problems experienced on many farms in the early 1990s are an example of this.

■ _Self-Check_

1. How do customers of competitive firms decide where to make their purchases?
2. Why have many firms in competitive markets chosen to diversify?
3. Why do some people believe that there can be too much competition?

■ _Applying What You Have Learned_

The types of businesses people can start for themselves are almost always very competitive. There are many reasons for this fact. Below you will find a list of characteristics. Explain why each is common among competitive firms.

a. low initial investment

b. limited skill and training necessary

c. not many employees

d. easy to buy necessary resources

Section B Monopolies

This section will discuss aspects of *imperfect competition*, including *perfect monopoly*, *monopolistic competition*, *oligopoly*, and *natural monopoly*.

Personal Narrative

One of a Kind

My name is Gary. I own a filling station and garage in a small town in Nebraska. There isn't another filling station within 20 miles of my business. Most of my customers are local people and farmers. Now and then I get a tourist who is lost. I have no competition worth considering.

I charge about ten cents more per gallon for gasoline than stations in the big city. My customers have no real choice. They would use more time and gas driving to another filling station than they could possibly save. Sometimes people complain, but I always point out that I wash their windows and check their oil for free.

Another difference between my business and big city filling stations is the fact that I don't have as many customers. If I am going to make as much profit, I have to make more from each one.

Actually, I am very careful to treat my regular customers well. I often go out to farms to work on tractors and farm equipment. I only charge $25 an hour for my work, although I know many big city garages charge $40 or more. If any of my repairs aren't done right, I fix them for free. I try to buy up-to-date equipment for my shop. Without a good profit, the quality of my service would be lower.

Once I got really worried. The state considered putting a major highway through this town. If that had happened, new filling stations would have been opened and I would have had competition. The highway was finally built 20 miles to the north, but I learned a lesson. I decided to do whatever I could to prevent competition. For example, I keep my prices reasonable. I am afraid high prices might encourage someone else to go into competition with me.

Imperfect Competition

Gary's business is almost a perfect monopoly. A **perfect monopoly** is a firm that is the only supplier of a product that has no close substitutes. Consumers either have to buy the product from the monopoly or do without. Monopoly power has been called the power to set prices. Monopolists can charge high prices without worrying about the competition. This fact tends to increase the profitability of monopolistic firms.

Monopolistic competi-
tion *means that there are
many firms producing
products that are almost
the same. Such firms rely
heavily on advertising to
convince customers that
there is a difference and
that their products are
better. If successful, they
are able to charge a
higher price and make
more profit.*

There are several factors, however, that limit how high a wise monopolist would raise his or her price. One problem is that high prices will reduce the number of people who are able to afford the product. High prices and low sales cause the fixed cost per item to be large. A monopolist might choose to have lower prices and greater volume to reduce fixed cost per item.

A second danger is that high prices will encourage competition or the substitution of other products by the consumer. For example, it has been suggested that some of the aluminum industry's problems today are the result of their high prices in the past. High aluminum prices encouraged other firms to enter the market and consumers found ways to use substitutes, such as plastic, instead.

There are very few perfect monopolies, but there are many industries that have some of the characteristics of monopolies. Businesses in these industries operate in **imperfect competition.** Imperfect competition exists when businesses are large enough to have some, but not complete, control over the prices they can charge their customers. Industries that sell in such imperfect markets can be divided into three groups—*monopolistic competition, oligopoly,* and *natural monopoly.*

Oligopoly *refers to a sit-uation where there are only a* few *producers of products that are similar, with a high degree of inter-dependence between them. American automo-bile manufacturers have been oligopolies, but in recent years foreign com-petition has reduced their market power.*

Monopolistic competition occurs when there are many producers of products that are almost the same. Firms in such a market try to make customers believe that the similar products are actually different. Each producer uses advertising to convince the customer that his brand is superior. Firms that are successful have a monopoly on their name and reputation more than on their product. Customers are willing to pay more for the product because they associate its name with quality or value. Many beauty products, soaps, household cleaners, and over-the-counter medicines fall into this group.

Oligopoly occurs when there are a few suppliers of the same product in the market. Because there are so few, the acts of any supplier may affect prices, production, or sales in the industry as a whole. Generally oligopolists avoid price competition, focusing instead on the differences of their products and advertising brand names. If a few large firms attempt to set prices or to divide up the market among themselves, the law may impose heavy fines or even prison sentences.

Look at Table 6–1. It shows the percentage of total U.S. production supplied by the four largest firms in different industries. This value is given a special name: *The Four-Firm Concentration Ratio*. What conclusions can you draw from this information concerning which types of businesses were monopolistic?

Table 6–1
Four-Firm Concentration Ratios

Industry	Percentage of U. S. Production Supplied by Four Largest Firms
1. Motor Vehicles	94%
2. Chewing Gum	93%
3. Window Glass	89%
4. Sewing Machines	31%
5. Household Detergent	80%
6. Tires	71%
7. Canned Beer	66%

Source: Department of Commerce, *Annual Report.*

In today's world economy, the concentration ratios above are not the threat to the consumer they used to be. For example, in 1990 imported cars accounted for over 25 percent of all auto sales in our country. Competition has helped protect the consumer.

Natural monopoly occurs when a product or service requires such large capital investments (fixed costs) that it would be inefficient to have more than one firm in the area. Utilities such as natural gas and electricity suppliers are good examples of such firms. The cost of producing and delivering electricity or natural gas is so high that it would be terribly wasteful to have more than one firm supply these products in any location. These firms have to be monopolies.

The local, state, or federal government has power to grant a permit, certificate, or franchise to a public utility. Most public utilities in the United States are privately owned. Local governments do own and operate airports, transit systems, sewage disposal systems, and water systems. Public utilities are a major factor in the United States economy. Altogether as natural monopolies they rank second between financial institutions and manufacturers in total assets.

The government in each state has established **regulatory agencies** to set rates that natural monopolies can charge. These agencies are boards appointed by the executives of the states. They are responsible for protecting the public from the abuse of market power by natural monopolies.

Natural gas producers tend to be natural monopolies. The fixed costs of such firms are so great that it would be inefficient to have more than one in an area. Natural monopolies are allowed to operate only under licensing and regulation by the government.

■ Self-Check

1. What are two factors mentioned in this section that limit how high monopolists will raise their prices?
2. What characteristic tells you that a market has imperfect competition?
3. What three types of imperfect markets were mentioned in this section?

■ Applying What You Have Learned

In the story on page 147, Gary has a number of advantages over similar firms in a city. Most of these advantages concern lower costs. Explain why Gary would have to pay less for each of the following.

a. property tax
b. insurance
c. hired help
d. cost of original building

PROFILE

Joan Robinson
(1903–1983)

Joan Robinson was one of the most important economists of the 20th century. She is best known for her work on monopolistic competition. Her work, and that of John Maynard Keynes (see Chapter 12), was influenced by Alfred Marshall at Cambridge University in England. During the forty years that she taught at Cambridge, Robinson came to different conclusions concerning competition than Marshall. She explained these ideas in her book, *The Economics of Imperfect Competition*.

Alfred Marshall had believed that the natural condition of markets was competition. He felt competition would keep prices close to business costs, and profits would be held to a reasonable level. He said firms would easily enter or leave markets as demand changed. However, Robinson asked, "Is that the way the world is? No!" It is more likely, she said, to have monopoly-like conditions. Frequently a few large firms, oligopolies, dominate the market. They usually control enough sales to be able to affect prices. This allows these firms to make large profits. With this money they can try to control larger parts of the market and have even more influence over prices.

These ideas led Robinson to the possibility of monopolistic competition. She reasoned that even in cases when many firms were selling in a market, each one would try to gain some control over price. If firms could make their product appear to be different and more desirable than that of their competition, they would be able to charge a higher price to earn a greater profit.

In later years, Robinson became a critic of capitalism and of the economics profession. She believed important problems, such as the way in which wages are set outside of the market, and the impact of world trade on competition, were being ignored. Some might call Joan Robinson the conscience of the economics profession.

Section C Combinations and Big Business

This section discusses how large businesses have developed, and introduces the ideas of *horizontal* and *vertical combinations*.

Personal Narrative

A Discount Store Opened Up In Town and I May Lose My Business

I've run a hardware store in a small town for over 20 years. Most of my customers rely on me for minor repairs and personal service. I fix screens and broken windows. When a lock is broken, I replace it. I never charge a high price for my services. A lot of people in this area are retired and can't afford to pay too much. I have been able to make a decent profit by selling lawn mowers, tools and other items at about a 50 percent mark-up. I have found that as a result of stocking many replacement parts, the turnover of my inventory is very slow. That means I have a lot of money tied up in merchandise that takes a long time to turn into cash. I know my prices are a little higher than some of the big stores. On the other hand, I make up for higher prices with quality service.

Until recently I had no effective competition. Customers had to drive eight miles to get to another hardware store. But last year a big discount store opened up in town. They sell lawn mowers that were made in Hong Kong, for almost one hundred dollars less than my price. Their tools are less expensive than mine, but many of them are low quality. In general they don't service any of the products they sell.

Most of their employees are kids just out of school. The store pays minimum wage. This saves them money, but their clerks don't know anything about the products they sell. If a customer asks a question, no one can answer it. They won't fix screens or broken windows. When something they sold breaks, it gets sent back to the factory. The customer won't see it for weeks.

People keep bringing me things from the discount store to fix. I don't stock parts for the brands they sell. I often can't repair them at all. If I can, I have to send for parts, which takes time. I charge extra for my trouble. Some of my customers are angry with me because they think I charge too much.

My biggest problem is that people just keep buying things at the discount store. I charge $89.99 for a ceiling fan that works and which I could fix if necessary. They charge $49.99 for one that looks about the same. All the customers see is the price. They think they can save $40, so they buy the cheaper product. It often breaks after a month or two. This doesn't change the fact that my sales are down at least 40 percent from last year.

I'm afraid that I won't be able to make ends meet if things don't get better. I still have to pay the rent. If my store does close, many of my customers will lose too. Next time they need a window fixed, there won't be anyone to call.

Small Business—Big Business

When one type of business grows, there is a good chance that some other type of business will shrink or fail. Change involves a trade-off between what was and what will be. It is important to remember that a firm is not just a business. A firm is a source of income for both its owners and its employees. Businesses provide services to customers. Even when a business fails, there were probably some customers who would have wanted to continue buying that firm's products. Businesses pay taxes. When businesses in an area close, it is more difficult to provide government services there.

There are advantages and disadvantages to the economy from both small and large businesses.

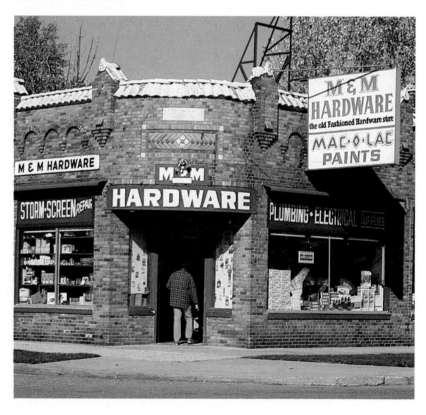

Large businesses may be able to offer lower prices and a wider selection than smaller businesses. Smaller businesses, on the other hand, may be able to develop closer relationships with the consumer—and may provide better service.

The growth of big business in the United States led to either the failure or takeover of many small firms. Smaller businesses often could not match the price of larger firms with more capital. Customers often gained in terms of price, but may have lost in other important ways.

Large firms have been accused of being cold and impersonal. It is more difficult to develop a close relationship with customers when a firm has thousands of them to serve. Many people believe that small firms provide better service than large businesses.

The possibility of monopolization is also a danger. If large firms eliminate small firms, they may eventually gain monopoly power and raise prices. Monopolies probably have less reason to provide quality service than competitive firms.

The Emergence of a Monopoly

Two ways in which firms sometimes join together are *horizontal* and *vertical combinations* (Figure 6–2). The growth of Standard Oil in the late 1800s provides an example of both.

Figure 6–2   *Horizontal and Vertical Combinations*

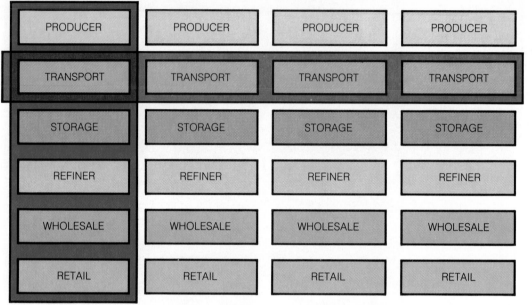

Vertical Combination

The bar that runs from left to right shows a horizontal combination—*in which firms that do the same thing (in this case transport) join together. The bar that runs up and down shows a* vertical combination—*in which firms that perform different steps in producing a product join together.*

A Horizontal Combination

In 1865 the firm of Rockefeller and Andrews (eventually to become Standard Oil) was only one of many oil producers in this country. In the late 1860s and early 1870s, this firm bought out and merged with many other firms that took oil from the ground. In doing so, Standard Oil became a **horizontal combination.** Horizontal combinations are formed when firms that do the same thing join together. The combination's greater capital then allows it to become more efficient and sell its products for a lower price than its competition.

A Vertical Combination

In the late 1870s, Standard Oil joined with firms that performed different steps in the process of converting crude oil into finished products. Standard Oil became a **vertical combination.** A vertical combination is formed when firms that perform differ-

Standard Oil began as an oil producer, taking oil from the ground. It bought out firms that did the same thing (forming a horizontal combination), and later merged with firms that performed other steps in the process (forming a vertical combination).

ent steps in producing a product join together. By 1880, Standard Oil was able to take oil from the ground and process it to sell to the final customer without the need of any other firm. It controlled most of its costs of production. Standard Oil was able to sell its final product for less than its competition. Soon it had little competition. By 1880 it provided over 90 percent of the oil products sold in this country.

What do you think would be the costs and benefits of such a monopolistic firm to the economy as a whole?

■ *Self-Check*

1. When one type of business grows, what is likely to happen to some other type of business?
2. How is a horizontal combination formed?
3. Why were vertical combinations often able to sell their products for less than their competition?

■ *Applying What You Have Learned*

1. Make a list of five specific problems that could develop for customers or the community if the hardware store in the story above went out of business. Identify who would pay the cost.
2. Write an advertisement that the owner of the hardware store could have printed in a local newspaper, designed to convince customers to buy at his store instead of at the discount store. Include at least four specific reasons.

Section D Advantages and Disadvantages of Big Business

This section introduces the ideas of *economies* and *diseconomies of scale*.

Personal Narrative

A Discount Store Opened Up In Town and I Can Buy For Less

I've lived in the same small town for 20 years. I used to deliver milk for a living, but I'm retired now. I live off a small pension and Social Security. I do okay, but I have to be careful how I spend my money.

For years I've had to shop at the local hardware store whenever I needed some nails or a hammer. I always felt I was paying too much, but I had no alternative. Last year a discount store opened up in town. They sell their products for at least 20 percent less than the hardware store. I think it's great!

The best example I can think of is my new lawn mower. I checked the price at the hardware store just to be sure. He wanted $219 for his. The discount store sold me one for just $139. So far I haven't had any trouble with it, and I've had it almost a year.

I wasn't so lucky with the ceiling fan I bought. I got a good price. It was only $49.99, but it broke after I had it for just three months. They boxed it up and sent it back to the factory. I was supposed to get it back in four weeks. That was two months ago and I still haven't seen my fan. The other problem is I had to put it up, take it down, and eventually I will have to put it up again. I don't like working on a stepladder very much, but I don't have any choice. I can't afford to have anyone else do it.

Last week my dog Muffy tried to chase a cat by running through a screen door that was locked. He chased the cat, but the screen got a dog-size hole in it. I took it to the hardware store to get it fixed. He charged me twenty dollars. While he was taking my money he complained about how much the discount store had cut into his business. He said they only stocked commonly purchased items and did not service what they sold. He suggested that he might have to do the same to stay in business. He might be right, but I don't feel too sorry for him.

Economies and Diseconomies of Scale

As businesses grow larger they often have advantages over small businesses. Economists call things that make a large firm more efficient than a small firm **economies of scale.** Some examples of economies of scale are:

- the ability to buy resources or products in quantity at lower cost
- the ability to afford more efficient tools and have workers specialize so they can be more efficient
- the ability to distribute fixed costs among more products*
- the ability to afford more research and development

The importance of economies of scale is demonstrated by the fact that so many firms have grown larger. Firms are in business to make a profit. If they could not be more efficient and make larger profits by growing, they would stay small.

It is possible for firms to become too large. A firm that has grown too large or too quickly suffers from **diseconomies of scale.** A diseconomy of scale is anything that causes an increase in the costs of production per unit made when a firm grows. Some examples of diseconomies of scale are:

- inability to coordinate large scale production
- less personal service for the customer
- less personal commitment to the firm by employees
- greater difficulty in meeting the specialized needs of different customers

*You learned about this problem in Section C of Chapter 5.

This large automobile firm has several important advantages over smaller firms. The things that tend to make a larger firm more efficient than a smaller one are called economies of scale.

Although there are diseconomies of scale, they are often not as important as economies of scale. If this were not true, most firms would not want to grow.

Costs and Benefits from a Monopoly

In the late 1800s, Standard Oil and other monopolistic firms were accused of taking advantage of consumers to make unreasonably large profits. John D. Rockefeller denied these claims and stated that consumers had benefited from Standard Oil's market power.

Rockefeller agreed that Standard Oil was able to make significant profits. However, he suggested that these profits were the result of efficiency and not monopoly power. According to him,

It's possible for an increase in size to have disadvantages for a firm. For example, if this small, specialized automobile firm were to expand too rapidly, it might run into difficulty in coordinating large scale production. This would be a diseconomy of scale.

profits earned were largely used to invest in more efficient production, more careful control of quality, and in research and development. Rockefeller argued that as a result of Standard Oil's market power, prices were lower than before the company had come to dominate the oil industry. He believed that he was not exploiting customers but helping them.

Rockefeller's arguments were not accepted by the courts. Standard Oil was forced to break up into several smaller companies in 1914. What is clear is that because of Standard Oil's growth, many small firms were eliminated, and in the process many individuals had been hurt. Whether this was good or bad for the country as a whole was a matter of one's point of view. As usual there was a trade-off between costs and benefits.

Table 6–2 provides the price of oil in this country between 1870 and 1920. It also contains information about prices in general. What other information would help you decide whether or not Rockefeller's point of view was correct?

Table 6–2
Oil Prices, 1870-1920

Year	Price of Oil per Barrel	Percent Change From 1870	Inflation for All Products from 1870
1870	$3.86	—	—
1880	$ .94	−76%	−12%
1890	$ .77	−80%	−14%
1900	$1.19	−69%	−12%
1910	$ .61	−86%	+ 6%
1920	$3.07	−20%	+120%

Source: *Historical Abstract of the United States, 1957.*

■ *Self-Check*

1. How has the importance of economies of scale been demonstrated?
2. What reasons did John D. Rockefeller give for Standard Oil's ability to earn large profits?
3. What did the courts do to Standard Oil in 1914?

■ *Applying What You Have Learned*

Make a list of four different problems that might occur for a customer who bought from a large discount store instead of a local hardware store.

Section E The Government's Role in Competition

This section will discuss the role government plays in maintaining competition in our economic system and the ideas of *workable competition* and *antitrust policy*.

Personal Narrative

I Can't Understand My Phone Bill

I got my phone bill yesterday. It was seven pages long. There was a page for the total bill, and one each for long-distance out-of-state, long-distance within-the-state, long-distance itemization, local billing, local itemization, and a final page to explain what the rest of it said. I'd need a college degree to understand it. I just pay it and don't ask questions.

A few years ago I could understand my bill. It was only two pages long. There was one page for long-distance and another for everything else. Not only was it easy to understand, it also cost much less.

Phone bills are the best example of things I don't understand, but not the only one. I work for an airline. I take luggage on and off airplanes. The airline I work for went bankrupt in 1985. They closed down for a while. Later they started flying again. I got called back to work and was happy to go, but my pay was about 20 percent less than it had been before. The courts had said the airline could cut wages while they were trying to reorganize.

I've been trying to look at this the way an economist would, and it seems to me that the distribution of certain costs and benefits in the economy has changed. People who make many long-distance calls are paying less. People who only make local calls pay more. Many airline workers have taken wage cuts, while passengers pay less to fly. Someone told me that these changes are partly the result of government attempts to maintain fair competition in these industries. I can see that trade-offs are being made. I feel bad because I believe I have paid more of the costs. Other people probably feel happy because they have received more of the benefits. I'm not really sure what's fair.

I read a few years ago that General Electric has purchased the RCA corporation. RCA owns the NBC Television Network. The article said that General Electric is now the second biggest supplier to the military. The article said the firm was becoming a conglomerate by merging with other businesses. A conglomerate is a firm that is powerful in many different markets. The article went on to say that ownership of a television network could give General Electric power to influence public opinion on its work as a military contractor. I don't understand what it was all about, but the newspaper sure didn't think it was right.

There are so many things that go on that I don't understand. Sometimes I wonder if it makes much difference to me. Then I get my phone bill and I realize that these things do affect me whether I understand them or not.

Workable Competition and Antitrust Policy

The government of the United States has the responsibility to maintain a competitive market economy. It is impossible to have perfect competition, but we can have **workable competition.** Workable competition means that there is a reasonable balance between the benefits provided by large monopolistic firms and

The break-up of AT&T was an example of government antitrust policy. The break-up had mixed results. What was once one phone company for the entire nation was broken into seven independent firms, each responsible for local service in its own area.

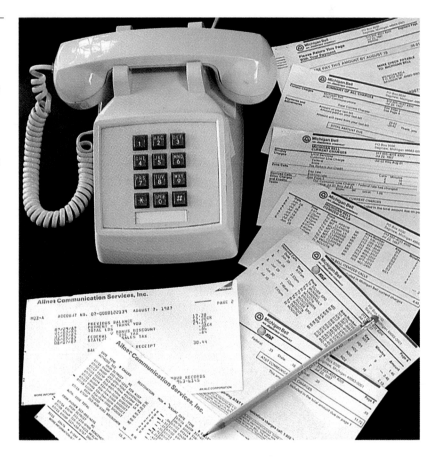

those provided by competition. The government tries to prevent firms from getting so large that they can abuse the public's interests. In cases where monopolies are necessary, the government regulates what the firms can charge.

Government efforts to maintain workable competition is called **antitrust policy.** Antitrust policy is the result of a number of laws. The most important antitrust law is the *Sherman Antitrust Act* of 1890. This law said that plans to restrain trade or attempts to monopolize production were against the law. Although this law has been amended over the years, it is still the basic rule in controlling the growth of monopolies in this country. A firm that is found guilty of violating antitrust laws can be fined or even broken up into smaller businesses.

In the early 1900s the government successfully took a number of large monopolistic firms, including Standard Oil, to court and forced them to be broken up into smaller businesses. The goal of this policy was to create more competition. Many economists doubt that these prosecutions accomplished very much for the average consumer.

In the past 20 years the government has often negotiated settlements with large, possibly monopolistic firms. The case of AT&T (the phone company) is a good example. In 1974 the Justice Department took AT&T to court, accusing the firm of monopolizing telephone service. The court case dragged on for years and cost billions of dollars. In August of 1981 the government asked that charges be dropped against AT&T. Federal Judge Harold H. Green refused to drop the charges and required AT&T to submit a plan for breaking up the phone system. A plan was eventually approved on August 5, 1983.

This plan called for AT&T to "spin off" its local phone companies into seven new, independent firms. In exchange, AT&T (now 80 percent smaller) could move into the computer industry where it might compete with another monopoly, IBM. IBM was also being tried under antitrust laws at that time, but this case was eventually dropped by the government. AT&T also received the right to continue in long-distance communications. This agreement went into effect on January 1, 1984.

Each part of the country now has its own phone company, separate from AT&T. A survey reported that in the first two years of operation local phone companies averaged a 35 percent increase in their rates. This was at a time when inflation in general was about 4 percent a year. In these same years long-distance rates have declined. There is some question about whether or not local customers benefited from this agreement.

Government deregulation of the airlines greatly increased competition in that industry. More airlines, with more flights, entered the market place, and prices fell. There may have been trade-offs, however, in quality of service and in safety.

Another example of the effect of government regulation can be seen in the airline industry. Before 1978 the Civil Aeronautics Board regulated the number of airlines and flights that could serve any location in the United States. The Airline Deregulation Act of 1978 gradually reduced and eliminated most barriers to new airlines. Table 6–3 shows the growth in the number of U.S. airlines after deregulation.

Following deregulation, airline prices generally declined. In some cases they fell by more than 50 percent. The mid-1980s witnessed a number of airline mergers and a slight increase in prices. The market was doing its work, first correcting for regu-

Table 6–3
Number of Certified Air Route Carriers, 1975–1989
(passengers and revenues in millions)

Year	Number of Carriers	Number of Passengers	Revenues	Industry Profit or (Loss)
1975	35	205	$14,974	$ 134
1978	35	275	22,275	1,319
1980	72	297	32,947	(228)
1985	86	382	45,931	1,337
1988	66	455	63,589	3,446
1989	62	453	69,147	1,868

Source: *Statistical Abstract of the United States,* 1987, 1991.

lated prices that protected inefficient carriers. Later, it eliminated the inefficient firms and adjusted firm size to conform to economies of scale.

Where is Antitrust Policy Today?

For many years our country's antitrust policy reflected a suspicion that too much economic power can interfere with the democratic process by giving owners of large businesses political power. However, as competition from other countries has become stronger, our antitrust policy has shifted. This change has led to deregulation of some industries to allow more competition, and to ignoring size when it could result in improved efficiency. The major emphasis in antitrust policy today is to prevent price-fixing agreements.

■ *Self-Check*

1. What do economists call a reasonable balance between the benefits provided by large monopolistic firms and those provided by competition?
2. What can happen to a firm that is found guilty of violating antitrust laws?
3. Why was AT&T required to "spin off" its local phone companies before it could expand into the telecommunications and computer industries?

■ *Applying What You Have Learned*

In the Personal Narrative, a number of trade-offs were made. Describe three of these trade-offs. Then identify groups that benefited and those that paid a cost.

CURRENT CONSUMER ISSUES

Should Newspapers Be Allowed to Merge?

The table below demonstrates that the number of daily newspapers has been falling in recent years.

Year	1975	1980	1985	1989
Number of Daily Newspapers	1,819	1,744	1,701	1,626

You might think that the loss of 193 newspapers in 14 years is no problem. However, most of the decline happened in major cities. Most small town papers have stayed in business.

Many large cities now have only one newspaper. These newspapers have a form of monopoly-like power. They control much of the printed news and advertising consumers in their communities see. Newspapers that have no competition might choose not to cover controversial topics to avoid offending certain readers.

Some people have suggested that to guarantee consumer access to more than one paper city newspapers should not be allowed to merge. In 1989 a court decision allowed the *Detroit Free Press* and the *Detroit News* to join their production and distribution operations. Both papers had been losing money. Both papers are now published under a degree of shared management, and they are smaller than they once were.

Although the merger probably saved several hundred jobs, some Detroit residents are upset. They believe they have less choice in what they read. The cost of newspaper advertising has increased, which may have caused businesses to increase consumer prices. Some people have suggested that Detroit's consumers have less access to advertisements that could help them make better consumer choices.

Do you believe this merger is a good idea? How would it affect you or your friends if you lived in Detroit?

Arguments in Favor of the Plan
1. It prevented the failure of a newspaper and saved jobs.
2. It allowed the owners to make a profit.
3. It assured consumers that they would have two papers.

Arguments Against the Plan
1. It created some monopoly-like power for the newspapers.
2. It resulted in higher advertising costs that may have been passed on to consumers in higher prices.
3. It reduced the advertising that Detroit's consumers see.

What Do You Think?
Consider the arguments for and against the merger. How would you protect the rights of consumers, advertisers, newspaper owners, and their employees?

Chapter 6 Review

What Have You Learned?

In this chapter you have learned the following important principles of economics.

- There are many different types of markets, ranging from *perfect competition* to *perfect monopoly*. The way in which these markets function determines their impact on the economic system.
- Firms in perfect competition have no control over market price because there are many businesses that supply the same product. Firms in perfect competition often try to improve their profitability by *diversifying* into other types of production. This may allow them to reduce their average fixed costs and enter into less competitive, and more profitable markets.
- Firms in perfect competition may earn profits that are relatively low. This may result in such firms being less able to invest in new and more efficient means of production. They may also be less able to withstand a downturn in the economy. For these reasons, some economists believe that it is possible to have too much competition.
- A firm that is a perfect monopoly is the only producer of a product that has no substitutes. Such a firm may set its prices at any level consumers are willing to pay. Perfect monopolies are likely to make a larger profit than more competitive firms.
- There are few or no perfect monopolies in the United States, but there are many firms that have some ability to set their own prices. Firms with some monopoly-like power have been classified into three groups. In *monopolistic competition* there are many producers of similar products that are differentiated through advertising. In *oligopoly* a few interdependent firms produce similar products. *Natural monopolies* are firms with such high fixed costs that it would be inefficient to have more than one in any area.
- Many large firms have been formed through combinations of smaller firms. *Horizontal combinations* are formed when firms that produce the same product join together. *Vertical combinations* are formed when firms that perform different steps in the process of producing a product join together. Many vertical combinations grew to have monopoly-like power because they were better able to control their costs of production.
- Large firms often have advantages over smaller firms in the same market. Such advantages are called *economies of scale*. In

Words and Terms

perfect competition (p. 143)
diversification (p. 144)
perfect monopoly (p. 147)
imperfect competition (p. 148)
monopolistic competition (p. 149)
oligopoly (p. 149)
natural monopoly (p. 150)

regulatory agency (p. 150)
horizontal combination (p. 156)
vertical combination (p. 156)
economies of scale (p. 159)
diseconomies of scale (p. 159)
workable competition (p. 163)
antitrust policy (p. 164)

some cases small firms have advantages over larger firms in the same market. These are called *diseconomies of scale.*

■ The government has taken an active role in controlling the growth of businesses with monopoly-like power. It has recognized that some large firms are necessary and tries to achieve *workable competition.* This is a trade-off between the advantages offered by competition and those offered by large size.

■ The basic law used in government *antitrust policy* has been the *Sherman Antitrust Act* of 1890. Under this law, various firms have been broken up into smaller firms. The intent of this policy has been to ensure a reasonable level of competition and to prevent unnecessary monopolization of markets.

■ In recent years the government's antitrust policy has allowed more U.S. firms to combine. One possible reason for this is the need for American firms to be large enough to compete successfully in international markets with large firms from other countries.

Building Your Vocabulary

On a separate piece of paper, write the vocabulary word or term that best completes each of the following statements.

1. A governmental organization that sets prices and quality standards for monopolistic firms is called a _____.
2. When firms that perform different steps in a process join together, it is called a _____.
3. Firms that have no control over the market price they can charge because many firms provide the same product are in _____.
4. An economic system that has a reasonable trade-off between the advantages of competition and large businesses is

said to have _____.
5. An _____ exists where there are a few suppliers of the same kinds of products in the market, who may affect prices, production, or sales.
6. Government laws and decisions that are intended to control the power of monopolistic firms are part of _____.
7. Conditions that give a large firm an advantage over a smaller firm in the same market are called _____.
8. _____ exists when there are many firms that make similar products and that rely on advertising to attempt to convince customers that they offer a better product.
9. Many firms have tried to improve their profitability through _____ into other types of production.
10. When firms that produce the same good or service join together a _____ is formed.
11. A firm that is the only producer of a product that has no substitutes is an example of a _____.
12. Conditions that result in a large firm having a disadvantage compared to a small firm in the same market are _____.
13. A _____ exists when firms have very high fixed costs making it inefficient to have more than one in any area.
14. _____ exists when businesses are big enough to have some, but not complete, control over prices they can charge.

Understanding Economics

1. Explain why small stores that sell groceries often make very small profits. What does this have to do with their competition?
2. Many small stores that used to only sell groceries now sell hardware, sand-

Chapter 6 Review

wiches, and clothing too. Explain why they have diversified into these other markets.

3. Suppose you opened up a stationery store in your neighborhood and made very high profits. Describe what would probably happen over time that would force you to lower your prices and reduce your profitability.

4. List three different types of products that are sold in monopolistic competition. Describe how specific brands attempt to convince their customers that the products they sell are better than other similar products.

5. Most utilities are natural monopolies. Explain why it would make no sense to have more than one utility serve an area.

6. Describe the different types of firms that would have to join together to make a hamburger chain a vertical combination.

7. In 1987 the General Motors Corporation produced almost 50 percent of the cars manufactured in the United States. American Motors, going out of business, barely made .7 percent of our cars. Describe three different economies of scale that GM probably enjoyed over AMC.

Thinking Critically About Economics

1. Suppose that you own a business in a large shopping mall that sells clothing designed to be worn by young people. There are at least ten other stores in the mall that sell similar clothes. As things stand now, your store sells in an almost perfectly competitive market. Describe three different things you could do to try to improve your profits.

2. Almost all of the commercial aircraft

used in the United States are manufactured by one of three firms: the Boeing Corporation, McDonnell Douglas, or the Lockheed Corporation. Explain why it is probable that this industry is an example of an oligopoly.

3. Suppose that the government decided that it would be good to have competition in the electric utility industry. With this in mind, all large electric companies would be broken up into smaller firms that often serve the same areas. Explain three different reasons why this would result in inefficient delivery of the product, electricity.

4. Many small farms have been bought out and joined into large farms in the last few years. This is an example of a horizontal combination. Describe three advantages that these larger farms could have over small farms that remain.

Consumer Skills Project

1. Visit various stores that would have sold only one type of product in the past. Examples would be grocery, dry goods, sporting goods, or stationery stores. Make a list of products the stores now sell that are not related to their original market. Explain how consumers may be better served because these stores have diversified.

2. Go to a library and look up advertisements for air fares from 10 years ago. Find out what the current air fares are to the same locations. Write an essay that explains the effect these price changes may have had on consumers. What might they have to do with the deregulation of the airline industry?

Developing Your Economic Skills

Using a Table to Compare Prices

Skill: In this lesson you will use a table to compare prices charged by firms in a competitive situation with prices charged by firms in a monopoly-like situation. To complete this lesson, you'll follow these steps:

1. Determine the prices of the same products at convenience stores and at stores in a competitive environment (a shopping mall).
2. Use two columns in a table to compare prices from the two types of stores.
3. Use a third column to compute the amount of savings to be had by shopping at the more competitive stores.

Application: How much can I save if I go to the mall?

Jerry lives in a subdivision about five miles from a major shopping mall. There is one convenience store close to his home. Jerry always felt its prices were high, but he never bothered to figure out how high they were. Last week his teacher gave him an assignment to find out how much more convenience stores charge on an average than stores at the mall.

Jerry went to the nearby convenience store and found the prices of six items he buys. He then did the same for one of several department stores at a large mall. The items are listed on the left side. The next two columns are for the convenience store price and the mall price. The final column lists the differences between the two.

To find how much greater the convenience store's average price was than the mall store's average price, divide the total mall store price of $16.16 into the total sav-

Items Jerry Buys	Convenience Store Price	Mall Price	Savings
Model airplane glue	$ 1.29	$ .99	$ .30
A new baseball	$ 4.39	$ 3.69	$ .70
A box of candy	$ 5.25	$ 4.73	$ .52
A package of socks	$ 4.79	$ 3.47	$1.32
Batteries for a radio	$ 2.59	$ 1.99	$ .60
A box of hamster food	$ 1.59	$ 1.29	$ .30
Totals	$19.90	$16.16	$3.74

ings of $3.74. The answer is .237, which is the same as 23.7 percent. On an average, the convenience store charged 23.7 percent, or almost one fourth, more than the mall store for the items Jerry buys.

Why was there so much difference in prices between these stores? One possible reason the stores at the mall charge lower prices is that they are more competitive. If one mall store charged more than another, Jerry would choose to shop at the store that charged less.

Owners of convenience stores have some monopoly-like power. Their customers do not have an easy alternative to buying their products, because there are usually no other stores nearby. These stores can charge higher prices but only up to a point. If they charge too much, most people will choose to go to the mall.

Practice: Choose six items that you could buy at a nearby convenience store and in a shopping mall. Visit the stores and prepare a chart similar to the one above.

Labor and the Economy: "I Built a Railroad, . . ."

Objectives

In the sections of this chapter, you will learn:

A

how labor fits into the *circular flow model*, how the principle of *diminishing marginal productivity* affects the demand for labor, and how the demand and supply of labor result in an *equilibrium wage rate;*

B

about the functions of *unions* in our economy and about laws intended to protect and to limit the rights of workers;

C

how the *collective bargaining* process works; and

D

why there is wide disagreement over *minimum wage laws.*

Introduction

Labor has a special place in a competitive market system. You learned in Chapter 1 that it is one of the four factors of production. However, labor has two roles in the economic system. It is part of the production process, but it is also the basic source of *demand.* Workers earn income. Income allows people to buy products. Every new job is a source of both production and demand. Lost jobs reduce production and workers' ability to consume.

Another important distinction is that labor is provided by the people that the economic system is intended to serve. Labor is not just a resource or the force that allows consumption. Serving people who provide labor is the central goal of the economy.

This chapter discusses how wages are determined. You will find that no firm willingly pays employees more than they are worth. Setting wage rates requires measurement of the value of labor. The value of labor is the price that the market sets. However, wages in the long run depend on businesses' ability to sell the products that are produced.

There is the possibility that workers could be paid less than they are worth. Many people believe that this has not only happened in the past but is also happening at the present. Labor unions were or-

Like workers of today, the workers on this railroad at the turn of the century were providing labor. By doing so they earned income, which allowed them to buy goods and services.

ganized in this country to protect workers and to improve their compensation. This chapter describes both union organizations and the relationship between unions and management.

The final section of the chapter deals with minimum wages. There is a difference of opinion between many economists, government officials, and labor leaders concerning the effects of minimum wages. Some people believe that these laws help the poor while others say they do more harm than good. You will study both sides of this debate.

There is a good chance that you will be personally involved with labor organizations in the future. The information in this chapter can help you understand what these organizations do and how they affect your life.

Section A How Wages Are Set

This section reviews the circular flow model as it relates to *derived demand* and supply for labor. It also presents the concepts of *diminishing returns* and the *equilibrium wage rate*.

Personal Narrative

Sure I'd Like a Job, But How Much Will It Pay?

I'm 23 years old and I need a job. I've been out of work for almost six months. Soon my unemployment benefits will be used up. If I can't find work soon, I may have to go on welfare so my kids can eat.

I used to work at a factory that manufactures electric mixers. I didn't have a very exciting job. I put screws into a motor on an assembly line. On the other hand, it was a union job and paid well. I got over $10 an hour and had good fringe benefits. For someone with only a high school education, I thought I was doing well.

It didn't work out that way. The company's sales were down. They closed one production line and laid off everyone that had less than seven years in. I had just been hired. I was one of the first to go.

The company sent me an "informational" letter. It explained that foreign competition had forced them to lower the price of their mixers. They said the firm was in danger of going bankrupt. However, it suggested the possibility of new investments and calling back workers if the union would reopen their contract and discuss wage reductions. That was almost three months ago and nothing has happened yet.

Whenever I apply for a job, they ask me what I can do. The fact is, I'm not trained to do much of anything. I can tighten screws or move boxes. I can't read a blueprint. I was never very good with numbers. I can drive a truck, but I've had a couple of accidents and speeding tickets. About the best thing I can say is that I get to work on time and I try hard. That doesn't seem to be enough to get a good job.

I can find lousy jobs. If I was willing to take a job that paid five or six dollars an hour, I could be working now. The problem is that five or six dollars an hour is ten to twelve thousand dollars a year. There is no way I could support my family on that. If we went on welfare we could get over $8,000 a year in benefits. I wouldn't have to work or pay taxes. If I can't earn a reasonable wage, it makes more sense to me to just stay home.

The Circular Flow Revisited

Study the circular flow model in Figure 7–1. It is the same one you saw in Chapter 3, except that demand and supply curves have been added in the factor and product markets. This shows that the forces of demand and supply control prices in both of these markets.

Labor is sold for wages in the factor market. Money to pay these wages is earned by businesses in the product market. The amount of money that any firm can pay for resources (including labor) is determined by what it earns in the product market. The demand for any factor of production is called **derived demand.** This means that in the long run a firm will only buy (demand) a factor of production if there is demand for the firm's final product. Demand for factors of production is a derived demand because it comes from the demand for the final product.

The amount a firm is willing to pay for labor or any other factor of production depends on the price it is able to charge for its final product. In the preceding story, the electric mixer company was forced to lower the price of its product because of foreign competition. As a result, it was unwilling or unable to pay

Figure 7–1   *The Circular Flow Model with Demand and Supply Curves*

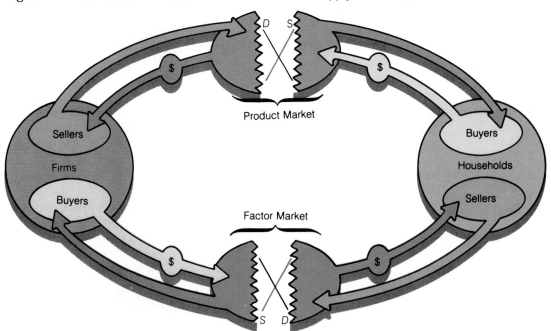

as many workers ten dollars per hour. No firm will pay a worker ten dollars an hour if the worker's labor is only worth five dollars an hour. If prices go up or down, the value of labor to the firm will also go up or down.

Diminishing Returns

Firms do not always have the time or ability to change their machines or the buildings in which they operate. Under these circumstances, they can only increase production by adding more workers and raw materials. When firms use this method, they find that the corresponding increase in production keeps getting smaller. The name for this is **diminishing returns.** It happens because there is a limit to how many workers can use a tool or a machine at a time. After some point, adding more workers or raw materials won't increase production because they will have no tools to use or space to work in.

Demand for Workers

As a firm hires its first workers, the amount of product they are able to produce increases, because some minimum number of workers are needed to run the firm's machinery. However, a point will be reached when each additional worker will add fewer additional products. This idea is called **diminishing marginal productivity** and it is a more specific example of diminishing returns. Studying Table 7–1 will help you understand diminishing marginal productivity.

Table 7–1

Number of Workers	Total Items Made	Additional Items Made (Marginal Physical Product)	Market Price	Value of Added Worker (Marginal Revenue Product P × MPP)
0	0	—	$50.00	—
1	5	5	$50.00	$250.00
2	11	6	$50.00	$300.00
3	16	5	$50.00	$250.00
4	20	4	$50.00	$200.00
5	23	3	$50.00	$150.00
6	25	2	$50.00	$100.00

With no workers, the firm was closed and nothing was sold. When the first worker was hired the firm was able to make five items a day. The addition of a second worker enabled the firm to use all of its machines and increased production by six items, which was more than the first worker. The number of additional units of product that are produced when another worker is hired is called the **marginal physical product,** or MPP. The MPP for the second worker was six items a day. As additional workers were hired, the MPP in column #3 on the table started to go down. This is an example of the principle of diminishing marginal productivity.

If the price of the product was $50 and labor was the only cost of production (this would be impossible, but it makes this example easier), the first worker would be worth $250 (in the table you will see that 5 items × $50 = $250). The second worker, who increased production by six items, was worth $300. The value of additional workers eventually went down because of diminishing marginal productivity.

Suppose you are worker number 6. What is your value to the business? Would the firm be willing to pay you $150? Workers will only be demanded by employers if they add more value to the firm's production than their cost. Since the value of the sixth worker shown on the table is only $100 the firm would not be willing to pay you $150.

The graph in Figure 7–2 has been drawn from Table 7–1. It shows the firm's demand curve for labor.

Figure 7–2 *Demand for Labor (value of added worker)*

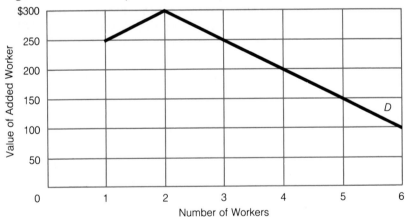

Supply of Workers

The number of people who are willing to work depends on the wage they can earn. The percentage of people 16 years of age or older who are either working or looking for work is called the

labor force participation rate. When wages are high, the number of people who look for work is greater than when wages are low. Suppose the table in Figure 7–3 shows the number of workers who would be willing to work for the firm above at different wage rates. The graph to the right is the firm's supply curve for labor.

Figure 7–3   *Supply of Workers*

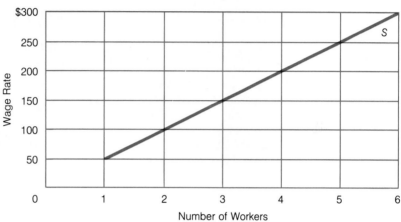

Wage Rate	Number of Workers
$300	60
$250	50
$200	40
$150	30
$100	20
$ 50	10

Equilibrium for Wages

It is possible to combine the two graphs from Figures 7–2 and 7–3 into one graph that shows the demand and supply for labor. This has been done in Figure 7–4. It results in an **equilibrium**

Figure 7–4   *Demand and Supply for Labor*

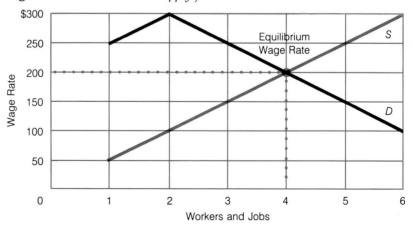

In the Great Depression, most businesses sold fewer products. As a result, the demand for labor fell, causing lower equilibrium wage rates. Many workers were unable to find a job at any wage rate. Businesses that could not sell products did not have sufficient reason or ability to hire workers.

wage rate, where the number of jobs and workers are exactly the same. In this example the equilibrium wage rate is $200 per week and the number of jobs is 4.

The Great Depression of the 1930s provided an example of changes in the equilibrium wage rate. Between 1929 and 1931 consumer prices fell by almost 27 percent. The value of retail sales fell by about half. One result of this was an increase in the unemployment rate from about 3 percent in 1929 to nearly 25 percent in 1933. Wage rates for industrial workers fell by about 22 percent between 1929 and 1933. Reduced prices and sales caused workers to be worth less to employers. Fewer workers could find jobs and those who did were paid less. However, because prices fell, each dollar a worker earned bought more products. Poverty in the Great Depression was more the result of not having a job than of receiving lower wage rates.

When comparing wage rates over long periods of time, bear in mind the difference between *money wages* and *real wages*. The term **money wages** refers to the number of dollars workers receive for their labor. The term **real wages** refers to how much the money wages will buy. Money wages were much higher in the early 1990s than they were in the late 1980s, but because of higher prices they bought less. This means that real wages had gone down.

■ *Self-Check*

1. What is the name of the market in which natural resources, labor, capital, and entrepreneurship are sold?
2. What is the meaning of the term *diminishing marginal productivity?*
3. If a firm is able to charge a higher price for its product, what will happen to the number of workers it is willing to employ at its current wage rate?
4. If wage rates increase, what should happen to the number of people who want to work?

■ *Applying What You Have Learned*

Answer the following questions from the graph below.

a. At a wage rate of $250, how many workers would want jobs?
b. At a wage rate of $250, how many jobs would be available?
c. At a wage rate of $250, would there be a surplus or shortage of workers?
d. At a wage rate of $250, how big would the surplus or shortage be?
e. What is the equilibrium wage rate in this example?

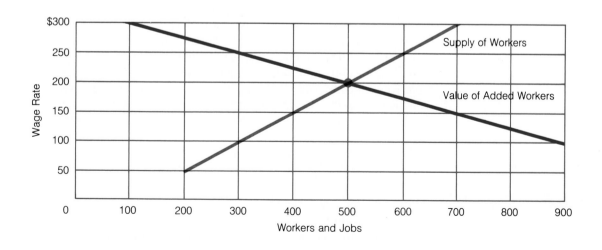

Section B Labor Unions in the Economy

This section will distinguish between *craft* and *industrial unions* and will introduce the terms *injunction, closed shop,* and *right-to-work law.*

Personal Narrative

I Want a Living Wage

No matter how many hours I put in at work, my paycheck isn't large enough for me to support my family. Even if I work fifteen hours of overtime I only earn $330 a week before taxes. Last year I earned just over $14,000 total.

My job is watching a machine stuff fruits or vegetables into cans at a local cannery. As long as the machine works, I have nothing to do. If it misses a can or jams, I have to shut the line down before it shoots food all over the place. The work is easy but boring. Did you ever watch peaches getting mushed into a can for eight or more hours a day? If you fall asleep you get fired. The foreman says he can get five people to replace any of us. He's probably right. I only get $5.27 an hour, but many people would be happy to get that.

The cannery isn't a very safe place to work. There are sharp pieces of metal all over the place and they cook the food with steam. If something goes wrong, people can get hurt. Last year a woman over in packing got her hand caught in a machine and lost three fingers. They gave her some sort of compensation, but not enough to live on. She can't get a different job because she can't use her hand. She supports her children through social security disability.

Another problem is the fact that they close down production at least four months every year when there is no fresh food to can. We can collect unemployment insurance while we are off work, but it just won't stretch far enough. That's why we all work extra hours when the factory is working. No one ever turns down overtime.

The company pays for medical insurance now, but ten years ago they didn't. A union tried to organize the workers. At about the same time we got a 5 percent raise and the medical insurance. They said there was no connection, but I think there was. The management didn't want a union. There were rumors all over the plant. One was that they would close down and move out of state if we voted for a union. When the vote came in, the union lost 87 to 52. I wonder if my life would be different today if we had joined that union.

What Are Labor Unions

Labor unions are organizations that attempt to improve the working conditions of their members through joint (collective) action. Through unions, workers are able to negotiate with management as a group instead of as individuals. The worker in the story above believed the possibility of a union being formed caused management to provide workers with medical insurance. Although she could be wrong, it is clear that unions have helped to improve working conditions, wages, and benefits for many Americans.

Types of Unions

Labor unions can be divided into two basic types: *craft unions* and *industrial unions*. A **craft union** is sometimes called a *horizontal* union because it is made up of workers who all have the same skill. An example of a craft union would be one made up entirely of electricians. The American Federation of Labor (AFL) united various craft unions into a national organization in 1886. Since the late 1800s, craft unions have been reasonably successful in improving the compensation and working conditions of their members. It is possible that management may have been willing to cooperate with them because such skilled workers would have been difficult to replace.

Industrial unions, which are sometimes called *vertical* unions, are formed by all the workers who are employed in a particular industry. The United Mine Workers was an early example of an industrial union. Industrial unions organize skilled, semi-skilled, and unskilled workers. In the late 1800s and early

On many occasions, workers have formed labor organizations and chosen to go on strike in an attempt to improve their pay or working conditions. You can trace the history of some of the more noteworthy strikes in the United States through this illustration and those on the following pages.

In the Pullman Strike of 1894, the United States army was called in to prevent violence.

In the steel strike of 1919, management eventually was able to force workers to return to work on management's terms, and, to a large extent, to destroy the union organization.

The sitdown strikes of the 1930s led to the recognition of the United Auto Workers as a bargaining agent for workers in the U.S. automobile industry.

After World War II, a series of strikes led to the passage of the Taft-Hartley Act of 1947, which limited union powers.

Professional football players struck and eventually returned to work on management terms in 1987.

1900s, industrial unions had little success in improving the compensation or working conditions of their members. This may have been because most of their members were unskilled and easy to replace. In 1935 the Congress of Industrial Organizations (CIO) was formed to unite various industrial unions into a national organization. For the next 20 years there was competition between the AFL and the CIO for membership. This finally led to the joining of the two organizations in 1955 into the AFL-CIO.

Labor Legislation

In the 1800s, state governments showed great hostility toward labor unions and took actions intended to limit the power of unions. The law that was used most effectively against union actions was the Sherman Antitrust Act. You will recall from Chapter 6 that this law said actions to restrain trade were illegal. Federal judges ruled that strikes were planned and intended to restrain trade. Strikes were therefore against the law. If a union went on strike, the management could use the Sherman Antitrust Act to request that a court issue an *injunction* against the strikers. An **injunction** is a court order to stop doing something. A person refusing to obey an injunction can be found in contempt of court and be fined, jailed or both.

The use of the Sherman Act against strikes was stopped after the passage of the **Clayton Act** in 1914. This law said that it was not the intent of Congress to have the Sherman Act used against labor or farm organizations.

The **National Labor Relations Act,** or **Wagner Act,** of 1935 was intended to guarantee the right of workers to organize in unions and bargain collectively. Among other things, the law said that employers could not discriminate against workers who tried to organize unions. It also required management to negotiate with any union that organized more than half of the firm's workers. The Wagner Act was upheld by the Supreme Court in 1937. A number of other laws that were also favorable to unions were passed under Franklin D. Roosevelt in the 1930s and in World War II. As a result, union membership grew rapidly.

Following World War II, the nation's economy was hurt by a series of crippling strikes. Public opinion turned against unions. Congress passed the **Taft-Hartley Act** over President Truman's veto. The purpose of this law was to limit the unions' ability to disrupt the economy. The law made it illegal for federal employees to strike. It outlawed *closed shops* for any firm that was involved in interstate commerce. A **closed shop** was one that required workers to join the union before they could be employed. States were allowed to pass **right-to-work laws,** which prevented workers from being forced to join or pay union dues. The most important part of the law was thought to be the power given to the President of the United States to seek court injunctions against strikes that harmed the national interest. This power has been used occasionally, with varying degrees of success.

Union Membership

After 1935, union membership grew in this country, both in total number of workers organized and as a percentage of all workers. This growth continued until 1960. Since then, union membership has fallen. Table 7–2 will help you see how union membership has changed over the years.

Table 7–2
Labor Force and Union Membership, 1900–1990
(in thousands of workers)

Year	Labor Force	Union Membership	Union Membership as a Percentage of Labor Force
1900	27,640	791	2.9%
1920	40,282	5,034	12.5%
1930	47,404	3,632	7.7%
1940	53,299	8,944	16.8%
1950	60,054	15,000	25.0%
1960	72,100	23,600	32.7%
1970	82,800	22,600	27.3%
1980	106,900	20,900	19.6%
1985	115,500	20,800	18.0%
1990	124,787	20,465	16.4%

Sources: *Historical Abstract of the United States*, 1957, and *Statistical Abstract of the United States*, 1991.

An example of the difficulty of enforcing the Taft-Hartley Act injunction occurred in 1978. In December of 1977, 160,000 coal miners had gone out on strike, seeking both higher wages and protection of benefits for retired miners. The strike dragged on for almost 3 months with no sign of a settlement. On March 6, representatives of President Carter went to the Federal District Court in Washington, D.C., and requested a court order be issued requiring the miners to return to work. A temporary order was issued, which was to be effective on March 9. This order was to be transmitted to 1,400 officials in the labor union by U.S. Marshals. But because incorrect legal papers were filed, these orders were never delivered.

Fewer than 100 of the 160,000 miners ultimately returned to work as a result of the order. The District judge refused to make the return to work order permanent, because the government had failed to provide evidence that the strike would cause irreparable harm to the national health and safety. Non-union workers at some mines had kept coal production at about 50 percent of its normal level, and most areas of the country were suffering no bad effects from the strike.

The mine owners and union eventually settled for a 39% increase in compensation over three years. They did this without direct intervention by the government. However, the threat of a government takeover of the mines or of an imposed settlement may have speeded the agreement.

■ Self-Check

1. What are the two basic types of labor unions?
2. According to the National Labor Relations Act, when is management required to negotiate with a union?
3. What has happened to union membership as a percentage of the labor force since 1960?

■ Applying What You Have Learned

1. Reread the Personal Narrative about the worker in a cannery. Describe at least five different problems the worker has that a union might be able to solve.
2. Now reconsider the problems mentioned above from the management's point of view. Describe what they would have to say about each problem.

Section C Labor-Management Relations

This section will introduce the process of *collective bargaining* and terms that are related to this process.

Personal Narrative

Daddy's out on Strike

My father is a member of the Oil, Chemical and Atomic Workers Union. When I was 8 years old, he had a job working for the BASF corporation in Geismar, Louisiana. We weren't getting rich, but he earned enough in his steady job that our family didn't have to worry about paying the bills. In 1984, when his union's old contract was almost over, the management locked the 1,200 union members out of the plant. The company managers ran the plant for a while and then hired new workers to replace the union members. Those were hard economic times and many people were willing to take these jobs even when it meant crossing union picket lines. BASF even said its old workers could come back to work if they would cross the picket lines. A few did, but most did not.

Talks were held between the business and the union, but they went nowhere for many years. I remember my father telling me the union wasn't "going to take being walked on anymore." He said that he was willing to "stand up for what's right" even if he lost everything he had. I know he thought he was right, but my mother was awfully worried about how they were going to be able to feed us. Eventually she took a job as a waitress in a local restaurant. She didn't earn much, but we managed.

When the union leaders realized that they weren't succeeding at the bargaining table, they took their case to the press. They planted pickets in the community to tell people what had happened to them. Their story made the national news and even some international newspapers.

Finally in September of 1989, BASF invited the union to start negotiations again. After being locked out of the Geismar plant for more than five years, the union finally signed an agreement with BASF management. This might sound like it was the end to my father's troubles, but it wasn't. Each month, 10 union members were offered their jobs back. It took over a year before my father was offered his job back. By then he had been out of work for 6½ years. I'm not sure he showed the management that the union wouldn't be walked on anymore.

In 1986 and 1987 workers at United States Steel (USX) went on strike for job security. The company had cut back jobs because it was losing business to foreign steel competitors. In 1986 USX closed its plants in a lockout. The strike failed to achieve many of the workers' objectives.

Resolving Conflict

Unions are formed when workers join together in an organization that is intended to negotiate labor contracts with management. Unions attempt to improve the working conditions and pay of their members by negotiating as a group instead of as individuals.

Over the years, unions have negotiated improvements in working conditions, benefits, and wages for their members. Although such improvements are good for workers, they cause increased costs for employers. Some people suggest that high labor costs have reduced the ability of American firms to invest in new equipment. If this is true, it would at least partially explain why some American firms have not invested as much in new capital as their foreign competition. It is possible that high wages for workers at BASF may have contributed to union members losing their jobs.

Unions are supported through the dues paid by their members. Unions often negotiate for **union shops.** When there is a union shop, workers are required to join the union within some specific period of time after they are hired. Unions may negotiate for an **agency shop** as an alternative to the union shop. When there is an agency shop, workers must either join the union or pay an "agency fee" to the union, which is usually equal to the union dues. This fee supports the services that the union must legally provide to all workers in a union-protected group.

The Taft-Hartley Act of 1947 allowed states to choose to pass right-to-work laws. In the mostly non-industrial states that have these laws, workers cannot be required to join a union or pay a fee to a union if they don't want to. It is more difficult for a union to organize and bargain successfully in such states.

Collective Bargaining

Unions and management negotiate contracts through a process that is known as **collective bargaining.** This means that the union's elected representatives bargain for all the workers as a group instead of each worker bargaining as an individual.

In the collective bargaining process, each side has "weapons" they can use to try to gain their objectives. These weapons include the following:

Union Weapons

a. *Slowdowns*—employees do less work.

b. *Boycotts*—unions encourage members and the public not to buy the firm's products. *Secondary boycotts,* where unions ask the public not to buy from a firm's suppliers, are illegal.

In the late 1970s, Chrysler Corporation and the United Auto Workers reached an agreement through the process of collective bargaining.

c. *Sit-down strikes*—union members occupy a plant to prevent other workers from taking their jobs.

d. *Strike*—workers withhold their labor from the firm. Strikes that are carried out without the approval of union leadership are called *wildcat strikes*.

e. *Picket lines*—union members march around plants to discourage other workers from entering to do the work.

f. *Union labels*—unions encourage the public to buy only products that were manufactured by union workers.

g. *Political action committees*—unions often form groups that are intended to put pressure on politicians to support union points of view in the government.

Management Weapons

a. *Injunctions*—the firm obtains a court order to stop striking or picketing.

b. *Lockouts*—the firm closes the plant to try to force the union to agree to its terms.

c. *Strikebreakers*—the firm hires other workers to take strikers' jobs.

d. *Relocation*—the firm moves the plant to another place where workers may agree to lower wages and benefits.

The objective of negotiations is a mutually acceptable agreement. No one "wins" when a dispute halts production.

Figure 7–5 shows the number of strikes involving 1,000 or more workers, and the number of work days lost in these strikes. Think how much these strikes cost the economy. In 1970 the average American worker earned about $30 a day. The 52.8 million lost days cost workers over one and one half billion dollars in lost wages. Owners lost profits, the government lost tax revenue, and all Americans lost the benefit they could have received from products that were not produced.

The Government's Role

The government can assist in the negotiation process in an attempt to prevent or shorten strikes. There are several steps that can be taken by the government to help solve a labor dispute:

Government Tools

a. *Mediation*—an unbiased person (one who doesn't favor either side over the other) listens to each side and suggests a solution.

Figure 7–5 *Strikes and Total Days Lost, 1950–1989 (strikes involving 1,000 workers or more)*

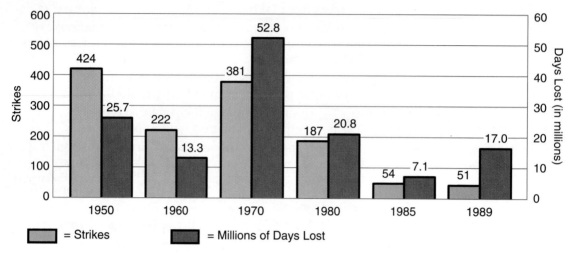

Source: *Statistical Abstract of the United States,* 1956-1991.

b. *Voluntary arbitration*—labor and management agree that an unbiased person should determine a solution.

c. *Compulsory arbitration*—the law *requires* that a solution be determined by an unbiased person. (This is done in several other countries and in some cases on a state level, but is not done on a national level in the United States.)

◼ *Self-Check*

1. What does a right-to-work law say?
2. What is the process through which unions and management negotiate contracts called?
3. When there is a strike, what would each of the following groups stand to lose?

   a. workers b. management c. government d. consumers

◼ *Applying What You Have Learned*

Many unions agreed to wage and benefit cuts in the early 1980s. In the mid-1980s they wanted to have these cuts restored. Many firms resisted this. Describe two arguments on this issue from the union's point of view and two from the management's point of view.

Section D Minimum Wages and Employment

This section will discuss the impact of the *minimum wage* on *marginal workers*.

Personal Narrative

I've Got Some Good News and Some Bad News

When I went back to work in 1992 I earned the minimum wage, $4.25 an hour. After one year I worked my way up to $4.75 an hour. Now there's talk of increasing the minimum to $4.75 or $5.00. If they do I doubt my boss would pay me any more than that. I would probably be back to earning the minimum wage again. I could look for a better job but I don't think I'd find one. I can only work a few hours in the middle of the day while my kids are in school.

I'm not sure what the minimum wage is intended to accomplish. There is no way a person could live on $4.25 an hour if they had no other source of income. Everyone who works here only plans to make a little extra money. Some of us are housewives, others are retired and on Social Security. Many of the workers are young and live at home with their parents. No one is the basic wage earner in their family.

Often I feel "used." I work just as hard as other employees. I'm smarter than most, yet I get paid a low wage. It doesn't seem fair. My neighbor is a baked goods clerk at the grocery store. They have a union. She earns $7.73 an hour and gets benefits. Her store put in new cash registers last year that read the item's product code. All she has to do is drag things across an electric eye while the machine does all the work. About the only thing she has to offer that I don't is that she can work nights. Her children are grown. I could go in nights too if my husband didn't work a swing-shift at his plant. We never know what his schedule is going to be.

If the government is going to increase the minimum wage, I wish they would make it high enough to do me some good. Why shouldn't it be $7.00 an hour? Then I would feel better about my job.

The Impact of Minimum Wages

The first federal **minimum wage** was established at 25 cents an hour in 1938 by the **Fair Labor Standards Act.** This rate was increased at various times over the years. It was raised to $4.25 an hour in 1991.

The woman in the story could not have supported herself on the minimum wage. Without her husband's income, she would have been forced to find a better paying job or to rely on government support. Some people believe the minimum wage provides little help for the working poor. Others argue that it prevents exploitation of those workers who often have no union to protect them.

Minimum wages were originally opposed by the AFL because there was a fear that the minimum wage might also become the "maximum wage." Union leadership assumed that this law would eliminate normal wage increases. Although this has not happened, there are many different points of view concerning the success and impact of minimum wage laws.

An increase in the minimum wage increases costs of production for firms that pay this wage. Firms that pay wages that are already higher than the minimum wage are not affected directly by such increases. Firms with minimum wage employees could react to their increased cost in a number of ways. They could:

a. accept a smaller profit;
b. increase prices to their customers;
c. pay no more than the minimum wage;

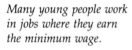

Many young people work in jobs where they earn the minimum wage.

d. lay off some workers;

e. purchase labor-saving machines;

f. replace low-skill workers with higher-skilled workers who are more productive;

g. move the firm or some production to a low wage country;

h. close down.

The deciding factor for these firms is whether a worker's value is more or less than what the worker must be paid. If an employee adds four dollars an hour to the value of production, it makes little sense to pay him five dollars an hour. An increase in the minimum wage will cause fewer jobs that pay the minimum wage.

Most people who earn the minimum wage are called **marginal workers** by economists. This means that their wage is not their only means of support. Young people, retired workers, homemakers, and the poor who receive government aid can be marginal workers. The fact that such individuals have other sources of income does not make their jobs any less important to them. People who are willing to work for $4.25 an hour often need the money.

Minimum wages are paid most frequently to the young and the elderly. Table 7–3 demonstrates this.

Workers who earn the minimum wage and have other means of support in addition to their wages are known as marginal workers. Young people, people of retirement age, and the poor who receive government aid are often in this category.

Table 7–3

Age group	Percent of Group Who Earned Minimum Wage, 1990
16–19	18.9%
20–24	6.5%
25–64	3.1%
65 and over	9.1%

Source: *Bureau of Labor Statistics*, 1990, 1991.

People who earn the minimum wage tend to have less education than other workers. Some people believe higher minimum wages cause many who earn the minimum wage to be laid off. Table 7–4 tends to support this idea. It shows that unemployment rates in 1982 were higher for people with less education. An increase in the minimum wage of 25 cents an hour in 1981 may have contributed to this higher rate of unemployment.

Table 7–4

Years of Education	1982 Unemployment Rate
less than 12 years	12.5%
12 years	8.5%
college graduate	3.0%

Source: *Statistical Abstract of the United States*, 1991.

It is possible that higher minimum wages could do more harm than good if they increase unemployment among people with low incomes. They could also prevent young people from getting their first jobs and a chance for work experience.

■ *Self-Check*

1. Why aren't all firms affected equally by increases in the minimum wage?
2. What are marginal workers?
3. Why do some people feel higher minimum wages help the poor while others believe they harm the poor?

■ *Applying What You Have Learned*

1. The woman in the Personal Narrative suggested that the minimum wage should be increased to $7.00 an hour. Describe four possible negative results for workers if such a change took place. Explain why each might happen.
2. In the preceding section is a list of reactions a firm could have to higher minimum wages. Choose the three that you feel are most likely and explain why you feel this way.

CURRENT CONSUMER ISSUES

What Should You Look For in a Job?

Statistics show that more than half the students in the United States will hold one or more jobs before they graduate from high school. Although some students need to work to help support their families, the majority choose to take jobs for other reasons. Some are looking for spending money. Others want to save for a future goal.

Imagine that you are looking for work. You plan to save most of your earnings to pay your tuition to a business school you hope to attend after high school. Your career goal is to become a human resource manager for a large business because you like working with people. You also have an interest in protecting the environment and enjoy being outside as much as possible.

After applying to many businesses and having a number of interviews, you are offered two jobs. A fertilizer plant offers a beginning wage of $11.50 an hour with good benefits and regular raises. The job is unloading toxic materials. You would be required to wear special protective clothing and to have regular medical check-ups. The work would be outside, but you would have little opportunity to talk to other people.

In the other job you would work in the complaint and return department of a large garden equipment store. Your wage would be $5 an hour, and you would spend most of your time trying to make dissatisfied customers happy.

Although you don't think you would like the work at the fertilizer plant very much, you are tempted by the higher wage. Would you consider taking this job under these circumstances?

Arguments in Favor of Working at the Fertilizer Plant
1. It would pay more than twice as much as the other job.
2. It would allow you to save enough money to pay your tuition to a business school.
3. You would not need to keep it forever. You could look for a better job later.
4. There are good benefits and potential raises.

Arguments Against Working at the Fertilizer Plant
1. It has nothing to do with your career goal.
2. It may be dangerous to your health.
3. Working with people at the store would be better career experience.
4. It could involve you in putting toxic materials into the environment.

What Do You Think?
Almost all decisions we make involve trade-offs between costs and benefits. What would you include on a list of the arguments for and against taking the job at the garden equipment store?

Chapter 7 Review

What Have You Learned?

In this chapter you have learned the following important principles of economics.

■ *Labor* is one of the factors of production, but it is different than the other factors. Labor not only helps to produce goods and services, it also provides the basis for consumption. Workers who earn wages buy products to provide a market for the goods and services they produce.

■ Wage levels depend on the value the market places on an individual's labor. In the long run, labor's value is determined by the price of the product that it is used to make.

■ As firms start making goods, additional workers result in increasing levels of production. But eventually a level of employment will be reached where additional workers create smaller amounts of additional goods. This idea is known as the principle of *diminishing marginal productivity*.

■ The American labor movement developed as a means of improving working conditions through collective action. Labor organizations that began in the 1800s can be divided into two groups: *craft unions* and *industrial unions*. Members of craft unions all shared the same skill. Members of industrial unions were all employed in the same industry. Generally, craft unions were more successful in improving the compensation of their members, possibly because skilled work-

ers were more difficult for employers to replace.

■ Many laws have been passed that have affected the ability of labor organizations to function in the U.S. economy. They include the *Sherman Antitrust Act of 1890*, the *Clayton Act of 1914*, the *National Labor Relations Act of 1935*, and the *Taft-Hartley Act of 1947*.

■ Labor organizations negotiate contracts with management through the *collective bargaining* process. In these negotiations, each side has "weapons" that they can use to attempt to achieve their objectives. Labor "weapons" have included slow-downs, use of union labels, boycotts, strikes, wildcat strikes, sit-down strikes, picket lines, and political action committees. Management "weapons" have included injunctions, lockouts, strikebreakers, and relocation.

■ The government has frequently participated in settling labor disputes through methods that include mediation, voluntary arbitration, and, in some cases, compulsory arbitration.

■ The first *minimum wage* was established under the *Fair Labor Standards Act of 1938*. There is a wide debate over the effect of minimum wages on this nation's poor. Some people feel higher minimum wages reduce the number of jobs poor people can find. Others believe that without minimum wages, poor people would be taken advantage of and be worse off than they are.

Words and Terms

Sections A and B
derived demand (p. 176)
diminishing returns (p. 177)
diminishing marginal productivity (p. 177)
marginal physical product (p. 178)
labor force participation rate (p. 179)
equilibrium wage rate (p. 179)
money wages (p. 180)
real wages (p. 181)
labor unions (p. 182)
craft union (p. 183)
industrial union (p. 183)
injunction (p. 185)
Clayton Act (p. 185)
National Labor Relations Act (p. 185)
Taft-Hartley Act (p. 186)
closed shop (p. 186)
right-to-work law (p. 186)

collective bargaining (p. 190)
slowdown (p. 190)
boycott (p. 190)
sit-down strike (p. 191)
strike (p. 191)
wildcat strike (p. 191)
picket line (p. 191)
union label (p. 191)
political action committee (p. 191)
lockout (p. 191)
strikebreaker (p. 191)
relocation (p. 191)
mediation (p. 191)
voluntary arbitration (p. 192)
compulsory arbitration (p. 192)
minimum wage (p. 193)
Fair Labor Standards Act (p. 193)
marginal workers (p. 195)

Sections C and D
union shop (p. 189)
agency shop (p. 189)

Building Your Vocabulary

Sections A and B

1. An _____ is a court order to stop an activity.
2. If additional workers result in smaller amounts of added production, there is _____.
3. When a contract required workers to join a union before they could be employed, there was a _____.
4. The _____ guarantees workers the right to organize a union.
5. A _____ is a labor organization made up of workers who all have the same skill.
6. An _____ is a labor organization made up of workers who all work in the same industry.
7. The wage rate that results in the number of individuals who are willing to work being just equal to the number of jobs offered by firms is called the _____.
8. The _____ said that the Sherman Act was not to be used against labor organizations.
9. A _____ prevents workers from being required to join a union.
10. The demand for labor is a _____ because it depends on the demand for labor's final product.
11. The _____ gave the President of the United States the power to request a court order to force striking workers to return to work.
12. The term for the additional products produced when another worker is hired is the _____.

Chapter 7 Review

13. The percentage of people 16 years of age or older who are either working or looking for work is called the _____.

14. The number of dollars a worker earns is called _____.

15. The quantity of products workers are able to buy with the dollars they earn is called _____.

16. _____ explains why adding more workers and raw materials won't always increase production.

17. _____ are organizations that attempt to improve working conditions of their members through collective bargaining.

Sections C and D

18. If a firm closes to try to force a union to agree to its terms, there is a _____.

19. A _____ is when a union decides to withhold labor from a firm in an attempt to achieve a labor objective.

20. When a law requires an unbiased person to determine a solution to a labor dispute, the law provides for _____.

21. The _____ provided for the first minimum wage.

22. If union members occupy a plant to prevent other workers from taking their jobs, there is a _____.

23. Moving a plant to another place where workers may agree to lower wages and benefits is called _____.

24. _____ is when an unbiased person listens to each side in a labor dispute and suggests an answer.

25. If labor and management agree to allow an unbiased person to settle a labor dispute, they have agreed to _____.

26. If workers are required to pay a fee to a union they don't join, there is an _____.

27. When a union forms a group that puts political pressure on government officials, it is called a _____.

28. People who earn the minimum wage are generally _____.

29. A _____ happens when union members go out on strike without the approval of their union leaders.

30. A _____ is when employees do less work in a period of time to put economic pressure on management.

31. If union members march around a plant to discourage other workers from entering, they are in a _____.

32. Labor organizations use a _____ to encourage the public to buy products made by union members.

33. A worker who is hired to take the job of a striking worker is called a _____.

34. The lowest wage rate a person can be paid under the law is the _____.

35. When workers are required to join a union within a specific period of time after they are hired, there is a _____.

36. The process through which unions and management negotiate labor agreements is called _____.

37. A _____ is when a union encourages people not to buy a firm's products in an attempt to put economic pressure on the firm.

Understanding Economics

1. Suppose a firm has a large saw that needs two people to operate it. The first worker hired can cut only ten logs an hour. The second worker increases production to thirty logs an hour. Explain why hiring a third worker might add only five more logs per hour. What does

this have to do with diminishing marginal productivity?

2. A firm has been selling table lamps for $40 each. For some reason these lamps suddenly become very popular and the firm finds it can sell many of them for $50 each. Describe the effect this event would have on the number of workers the firm would like to hire and the wage rate it would be willing to pay.

3. Explain why a union formed by aircraft engineers would often be more successful than one formed by the workers at a car wash.

4. Suppose that the nation's railroad workers had been on strike for the last two months. The economy was suffering. Many factories had been closed down and thousands of workers had been laid off. Describe what the President could do through the Taft-Hartley Act to try to resolve the situation.

5. Assume that you have been given the job of mediating a strike between the workers in a grocery store and its management. Make a list of at least five things you would want to know before you suggested a solution.

Thinking Critically About Economics

1. A local firm spent $50 million on new computer-controlled production equipment, which will assemble cameras automatically. Make a list of the types of workers who would be harmed by this investment. Make a second list of those who would be helped.

2. In the early 1980s, many large unions agreed to what were called "concessionary contracts," in which they actually accepted lower rates of pay and benefits. Describe three different reasons they may have had for doing this.

3. Describe several problems that a "right-to-work law" might cause for a union that was trying to organize a new plant.

4. In 1960, union membership was more than 30 percent of the total labor force. In 1990 about 16 percent of all workers belonged to unions. Describe three different reasons that you believe could have helped cause this change.

5. In recent years a number of firms have chosen to lock their workers out when an old contract expired, rather than let them continue to work under the old contract. Explain what a firm could accomplish by doing such a thing.

6. Write an argument in favor of a lower minimum wage for young workers between 16 and 19 years of age. Write a second argument against such a minimum wage law.

Consumer Skills Projects

1. Take a survey of ten adults of various ages and economic situations. Ask if they make buying decisions based on whether products are made by union members. Do they feel union-made products have superior quality? Do they see anything wrong with buying products that were not made by union labor? Discuss your findings with your class.

2. Interview a local union leader. Discuss the goals and purposes he or she sees for the local union organization. Ask this person to explain how consumers benefit from buying union-made products. Discuss your interview with your class.

3. Interview the owner of a local business. Ask this person to describe his or her feelings toward union organizations. In what ways does this person feel unions have helped or harmed consumers? Discuss your interview with your class.

Developing Your Economic Skills

Using Line Graphs to Compare Trends

Skill: In this lesson two line graphs will be drawn together to show changing trends. By studying the graphs you will be able to compare these trends. To complete this lesson, you'll follow these steps:

1. Identify the trends that are shown on the two graphs.
2. Study the graphs to see what has happened to each trend.
3. Compare the trends to each other.
4. Suggest possible reasons for changes in the trends.

Application: Has the minimum wage kept up with inflation?

Many young people earn the minimum wage when they take their first job. In 1992 the minimum wage was $4.25 an hour. Twenty-five years earlier the minimum wage was only $1.40 an hour. You might think the minimum wage was much smaller in 1967, but can you be sure? If you consider inflation, the 1992 minimum wage could have less purchasing power. The graph at right shows the long-term trend for changes in the minimum wage and prices.

On the graph, the percentage change in prices and the minimum wage between 1967 and 1992 is shown by a scale that appears on both vertical axes. The years are listed across the horizontal axis, from left to right. Growth in the minimum wage between 1967 and 1992 is shown with a black line, while the increase in prices is shown with a red line. (There are flat places on the graph of the minimum wage because there were many years in which it did not change. The

minimum wage changes only by direct government decision, but inflation changes automatically in response to economic conditions.)

The graphs show you what the percentage increase in each value was in comparison to its level in 1967. For example, locate the year 1978 on the horizontal axis, and read directly up to locate the corresponding points on the two line graphs. You'll see that in 1978 prices had increased by about 95 percent from 1967, while the minimum wage had increased by a little less than 90 percent over the same years.

The graph shows you that the growth in the minimum wage roughly kept up with the increase in prices until the late 1970s. After 1979 the trend for prices went up much more rapidly than growth in the minimum wage. Between 1981 and 1989 there was no increase at all in the minimum wage.

What reasons can you think of that could explain this situation? Why didn't the growth in the minimum wage keep up with inflation in recent years? Could it have anything to do with the recession of 1981–82? Do you believe it might have something to do with the political party that held power in Congress or the White House?

Practice: Copy advertised prices for similar food items, building supplies, and apartment rent from a current newspaper, a ten-year-old paper, and a five-year-old paper at your library. What is the percentage of increase for each? (To get percent divide the amount of increase by the original price.) Build a simple graph that shows different rates of price increase for three items.

Inflation and Changes in the Minimum Wage (as a percentage of 1967)

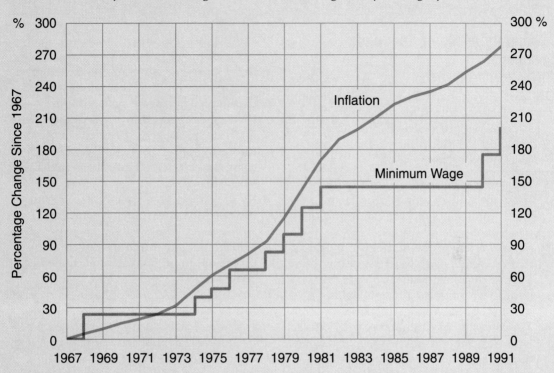

Part 2 Review

Summary of Major Economic Concepts

In Part 2 you have learned the following basic economic principles concerning the decision-making processes of businesses and individuals. These principles are part of what is called *microeconomics*.

- The *circular flow model* is used to demonstrate the flow of money, goods and services, and factors of production through the economy.
- *Demand* refers to the number of products that consumers will purchase throughout a range of prices, while *supply* is the number of products a firm is willing to sell throughout a range of prices.
- The forces of demand and supply interact with each other to reach a *point of equilibrium*, which indicates the market price and the quantity of a product that will be sold. In a competitive market, prices above equilibrium result in a *surplus*, which tends to force the price down. Prices below equilibrium cause a *shortage*, which tends to force the price up.
- The *elasticity* of demand is a measure of demand's responsiveness to a change in price. If the percentage change in the quantity of a product demanded is greater than the percentage change in price, the demand is *price elastic*. When the percentage change in quantity of a product demanded is smaller than the percentage change in price, the demand is *price inelastic*.
- As consumers buy more of a particular product, they experience *diminishing marginal utility*. This means that each additional unit of the product has less value to the consumer. Because of this, consumers distribute their purchases among many different goods and services.
- In *capitalism*, consumers control the products that are produced through what they buy. This idea is called *consumer sovereignty*. In their effort to serve their own interests, producers in capitalism are forced to supply products people want at competitive prices. This idea is called the *invisible hand*.
- As the American economy has grown, the need for government involvement and *consumer protection* has increased. Consumers pay a cost for government protection in higher prices and reduced competition.
- The three basic forms of business organization in the United States are the *single proprietorship*, *partnership*, and *corporation*. Each form has important advantages and disadvantages.
- All firms must take into consideration both *fixed* and *variable* costs of production. Businesses often increase production to reduce the *average fixed cost* per unit.
- Most businesses need to use capital that belongs to someone else. This leads firms to *rent* property or machines, and to borrow money from banks or through the sale of *bonds*. Corporations sell *stock*, or units of ownership, to raise money.
- There are many different types of markets, ranging from *perfect competition* to *perfect monopoly*. Firms in perfect competition have no control over the prices they can charge, while perfect monopolies set their own prices. Although there are few, if any, perfect monopolies in the United States, there are many firms that have some degree of monopoly-like power. These include firms engaged in *monopolis-*

tic competition, *oligopolies*, and *natural monopolies*.

■ Large firms often have advantages over their smaller competition; these advantages are called *economies of scale*. In some cases the small firms have advantages over larger competitors; these advantages are called *diseconomies of scale*.

■ Our government has used regulation and *antitrust policy* to try to achieve *workable competition*. This is a trade-off between the advantages offered by competition and those offered by large size.

■ *Labor* is different from other factors of production because it also provides the basis for consumption. Workers who earn wages buy products to provide a market for the goods and services they produce.

■ Wages depend on the value the market places on an individual's labor. As more workers are hired in a firm, a point will be reached where additional workers bring about smaller increases in production. This is called *diminishing marginal productivity*.

■ The labor movement attempts to improve working conditions and compensation through *collective bargaining*. Labor organizations can be divided into *craft* and *industrial* unions. Workers in craft unions have the same skills, while members of industrial unions are employed in the same industry.

■ Many laws have been passed that affect the labor movement. They include the *Sherman Antitrust Act of 1890*, the *Clayton Act of 1914*, the *National Labor Relations Act of 1935*, and the *Taft-Hartley Act of 1947*.

■ Labor organizations and management have many tools that they use in the collective bargaining process. Our government often participates in this process through *mediation, fact-finding,* and *volun-*tary and *compulsory arbitration*.

■ The first minimum wage was established under the *Fair Labor Standards Act of 1938*. There is a wide debate over the effect of minimum wages on this nation's poor.

Understanding Economic Concepts

Each of the following questions emphasizes one or more of the important economic concepts you have learned in Part 2. The important concept is listed in parentheses after each question. Answer each question in complete sentences that *show you understand the meaning* of the concept. The first question has been answered for you as an example.

1. What figure do economists use to show the relationship between different markets in our economic system? (Discuss the *circular flow model*.) (*Answer:* Economists use the circular flow model to show the flow of money, goods and services, and factors of production through the product and factor markets.)

2. What should happen to the number of products a firm sells if similar products become more expensive? (Discuss *determinants of demand* and *substitute goods*.)

3. If a firm's workers receive a wage increase, what will happen to the number of products it is willing to sell? (Discuss *supply* and *costs of production*.)

4. If a firm produces more products than it can sell at its current price, what will it be forced to do? (Discuss *surplus* and *equilibrium*.)

5. Why do consumers distribute their spending among many different types of products? (Discuss *diminishing marginal utility*.)

6. What products do firms produce in capitalism? (Discuss *consumer sovereignty*.)

Part 2 Review

7. What is one reason for the increased government involvement in our economic system? (Discuss *consumer protection*.)

8. Why are most large firms organized as corporations? (Discuss *stocks* and *bonds*.)

9. Why do many firms want to increase their level of production? (Discuss *average fixed costs*.)

10. What are two ways for a person to earn money from owning stock? (Discuss *dividends* and *capital gain*.)

11. How have many of the larger firms been formed from smaller ones? (Discuss *horizontal combinations* and *vertical combinations*.)

12. Why is it necessary that certain types of firms have monopoly-like power? (Discuss *natural monopolies*.)

13. What does our government try to achieve through its regulation and antitrust policy? (Discuss *workable competition*.)

14. Why can't all workers make the same contribution to production? (Discuss *diminishing marginal productivity*.)

15. How has the government frequently participated in the collective bargaining process? (Discuss *mediation*, and *voluntary* and *compulsory arbitration*.)

Writing About Economics

Each of the questions below requires you to write a brief essay. Be sure to include *each* of the following in your answer:

- Demonstrate your understanding of the identified economic concept(s) in your essay.

- Explain how the economic concept(s) is involved in the situation.
- Describe how you would resolve the situation and on what basis you would make your decision.

1. Your shoe store has not been doing well lately. Although you stock quality products and sell them at low prices, you believe many people don't know your store exists. You would also like to increase sales so it would be easier to pay your rent. What should you do? (Discuss the *determinants of demand, informative advertising*, and *average fixed costs*.)

2. After seeing an advertisement for the "Handy Dandy Garden Tool" on television, you ordered one for $29.95 plus $4.95 shipping. The advertisement showed a beautiful woman digging in her garden with no effort at all. When you got the tool, it turned out to be much like an ordinary hoe that you could buy for about $10.00 in any hardware store. You are angry and feel you have been cheated. Why do you think you decided to buy the product? What should you do? What will eventually happen to the firm that sells the product? (Discuss *persuasive advertising, consumer protection*, and the *invisible hand*.)

3. You manufacture house paint. You have recently merged with a firm that discovered a new chemical that makes paint stick to wood for at least ten years. It has been patented by the government so no one else can use it. Although your paint is good, you know many other brands of paint are good too. How do you convince customers to buy your paint? (Discuss *monopolistic competition*, and *informative advertising*.)

4. You work as a lawyer for the government. Your job is to help make sure firms don't have too much monopoly-like power. A large chemical firm has asked permission to buy another large chemical producer. Although the new firm would control about 35 percent of the chemical market, you also believe that it would be quite efficient. Should you recommend approval of the merger? (Discuss *horizontal combination, antitrust policy, economies of scale,* and *workable competition.*)

Discussing Economics

The following paragraphs describe economic issues that have been the topic of recent public debate. In each situation, there is no one answer or point of view that all Americans can agree to. For each issue, decide whether you support or do not support the proposal, and think about how you would present your opinion to the rest of the class. When you present your opinion, be sure to

■ identify and describe the issue
■ explain what you would do
■ explain why your choice is the best choice

1. In some states it is against the law to ride a motorcycle without a helmet. In others, wearing a helmet is a matter of personal choice. How can this be? Supporters of requiring helmets argue that accidents are more than a matter of individual choice. They point out that the government has been forced to pay for injuries resulting from motorcycle accidents. The government also has supported the families of accident victims. Taxpayers do pay a cost when people are injured in motorcycle accidents. If helmets reduce injuries, they would also re-duce the burden on the taxpayers. Finally, insurance premiums seem to be higher in states with no helmet laws.

People who feel helmets should be a matter of choice ask, "Where do you draw the line? There is some risk in everything we do. Should we pass a law that requires us all to walk because people are killed in automobile accidents? We can't eliminate risk, so why take away personal freedoms?"

Do you believe the government should require motorcycle helmets?

2. In a number of states, large nuclear power projects have been started and then abandoned or converted to other types of fuel. This has occurred in the states of Washington, Michigan, and Illinois. The electric companies that started these projects have lost billions of dollars. They would like to pass their loss on to their customers in the form of higher prices. In many cases, state regulatory agencies have prevented them from recovering all of their loss in this way. This forces the firms to pay their costs in some other way. They can cut dividends to stockholders. They can reduce wages and benefits for employees. They can reduce spending for service and maintaining their equipment. Electric utility companies argue that these alternatives are unfair and will hurt ordinary people who live in the area, as well as the utility companies themselves.

If you were in charge, would you allow electric utility firms to pass such costs on to their customers?

3. In some states it is against the law for public employees to go on strike. In other states such strikes are legal. Supporters of laws that outlaw public employee strikes believe that the services provided by public workers, such as po-

Part 2 Review

licemen, firemen, teachers and sanitation workers, are so important that they should not be allowed to strike. Others wonder why doctors, nurses, and telephone workers are allowed to strike in these states. They ask, "Are these workers any less important to the public? Do such laws result in unequal rights?"

If you were in charge, would you allow public workers to go on strike?

Problem-Solving with Economics

Chapter 3

1. Below you will find a list of events. For each event, state whether the result would be an increase or decrease in demand for the particular product.
   a. demand for all products when taxes go up 10 percent
   b. demand for diapers when there is a baby boom
   c. demand for snow shovels at the start of December
   d. demand for popcorn at the theater when the price of peanuts goes up
   e. demand for hospital beds as people live longer
   f. demand for all products when many people get better jobs
   g. demand for fish nets at the start of a salmon run
   h. demand for canvas shoes when leather becomes very expensive
2. Consider the following list of events that would change a firm's costs of production. For each, decide whether the event would increase or decrease the cost of production and whether this would cause the firm's supply curve to move to the left or to the right over a period of time.
   a. The firm's workers are paid 10 percent more.
   b. The firm has to pay more for heat.
   c. The firm buys more efficient trucks.
   d. The firm installs pollution controls.
   e. The firm buys a computer system.
   f. The firm spends money on training.
3. Answer the questions based on the supply curve below:
   a. At $5.00 how many toys would be offered for sale?
   b. What price would result in twenty toys being offered for sale?
   c. If the price went from $3.00 to $5.00, would the number of toys supplied increase or decrease?
   d. If the price went from $3.00 to $5.00 how many more or fewer toys would be supplied?
   e. At $2.00 how many toys would be supplied?

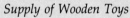

Supply of Wooden Toys

4. Below you will find a list of events. For each event state whether the result would increase or decrease the equilibrium price if nothing else changed.
   a. Consumer income goes up 10 percent.
   b. Labor costs increase by 10 percent.
   c. The cost of raw materials goes down by 10 percent.
   d. The product being sold becomes very popular.
   e. The government reports the product causes cancer.
   f. The product's raw materials become less expensive.
   g. The price of a product that could be used instead goes up.
   h. Other countries stop buying this product.

Chapter 4

1. Suppose you are going on a survival camping trip. The rules are that you can only take five items with you besides the clothes you wear. You may only take things you can carry ten miles into the forest *on your back*. (No cars, TV's, etc.) On a separate piece of paper, list the items you would take in order of their importance, most important first and so on. Briefly explain each choice.
2. The financial success of a professional sports team depends on its ability to please the fans. In many ways this concerns consumer sovereignty. List five different things management could do to encourage attendance at their games. You must be reasonable. They can't give away free tickets or beer or do anything else that would cost more than it could earn.
3. How could you explain the trends in advertising shown in the table below?

Advertising Expenditures for Newspapers and Television, 1950–89
(in millions of dollars)

	1950	1960	1970	1980	1989
Newspapers	2,076	3,703	5,745	14,794	32,368
% of total	36.3%	31.0%	29.3%	27.7%	26.1%
Television	171	1,590	3,596	11,366	26,891
% of total	3.0%	11.1%	18.3%	21.2%	21.7%

Chapter 5

1. Describe three different businesses. For each, identify the type of organization that would be best suited to the business and explain why. Provide one example each of a proprietorship, a partnership, and a corporation.
2. Assume that you are going to go into the bicycle manufacturing business. List five specific examples of fixed costs and five examples of variable costs you would need to pay.
3. It probably costs between $5,000 and $7,000 on an average to educate a student in your school district. In general it is less expensive to provide an education in large schools than in small ones. Explain what this has to do with average fixed costs.
4. In a number of foreign countries, workers are guaranteed a job and a wage by their employers no matter what. If these firms find that their products aren't selling, they may have to pay their workers for doing nothing. This means that labor can be a fixed cost to these firms. Explain why these firms could be willing to sell their products to the United States for less than it cost them to make them.
5. The following table shows the average interest rates paid by banks for large time deposits between 1980 and 1990.

Part 2 Review

Study the table and then answer the questions that follow.

Year	Interest
1980	13.07%
1981	15.91%
1982	12.27%
1983	9.07%
1984	10.11%
1985	8.73%
1986	8.06%
1987	7.86%
1988	8.39%
1989	7.86%
1990	7.52%

a. Why did corporations have to promise higher dividends to sell new stock in 1981 than they did in 1990?
b. How would these higher dividends affect the ability of firms to invest in new equipment?
c. If the economy is doing poorly and many businesses do not want to expand or produce more products, what would probably happen to the demand for resources? What would probably happen to the amount of rent paid to use resources that belong to someone else?

Chapter 6

1. Competitive firms are "price takers." They can only charge what their competition charges.
   a. Describe an industry that is made up of firms in perfect or near perfect competition. Explain why each firm must charge the same price.
   b. If all the firms in a competitive market try to make as many products as they can, total production will grow. What is this likely to do to the market price in the industry?
   c. Why have some economists suggested that competitive firms are their own worst enemies?
2. Americans buy products from monopolistic and competitive firms every day. List two specific examples each of products that consumers buy from (a) competitive firms; (b) firms in monopolistic competition; (c) oligopolies; (d) natural monopolies.
3. Think of a local example of a large business. Make two lists. On one, list four advantages the firm has because it is large. On the other, list four disadvantages it may have because it is large. Be specific.
4. Many other countries have decided that their governments should own large firms that tend to be monopolistic. In Great Britain, for example, airlines, railroads, steel mills and power companies either belong to or have belonged to the government. Explain why you do or do not believe this would be a good idea for the United States.
5. Assume that there was only one firm that produced all of the soft drinks in the country. Suppose the government forced this one large firm to be broken up into at least ten smaller firms. Explain what would probably happen to each of the following:
   a. the number of workers in the industry
   b. the total cost of distribution and advertising

c. the number of different soft drinks on the market
d. the market price of soft drinks
e. the quantity of soft drinks sold

Chapter 7

1. Each of the following events would tend to either increase or decrease wage rates. For each, tell which it would do and explain why.
   a. The entry of many new, young workers into the labor force would _____ wages because _____.
   b. An increase in the imports of inexpensive products from other countries would _____ wages because _____.
   c. Inflation would _____ wages because _____.
   d. An increase in government aid to the poor would _____ wages because _____.

2. Two arguments concerning unions are stated below. Evaluate each one. Explain why you feel the argument is right or wrong.
   a. Unions are bad for the economy. They cause higher wages, which lead to higher prices. Higher prices mean fewer people will be able to buy products, so there will be lower sales, fewer jobs, and less growth in the economy.
   b. Unions are necessary because they force wages up to a reasonable level. Reasonable wages mean workers can buy products. With no unions, businesses would pay low wages. Few people would have enough money to buy products. Sales would be low. Workers would be laid off and the economy would not grow.

3. Suppose that you represent a union involved in a contract dispute. Which labor "weapon" would you consider using first, and why? Suppose that you represent management involved in the same dispute, which management "weapon" would you consider using, and why? For both labor and management, what alternatives could you try before turning to any of the available "weapons"?

4. In 1983 President Reagan suggested that a lower minimum wage of $2.90 an hour be established for workers who are 16–19 years old. Give two arguments in favor of such a plan and two against it.

3

Understanding the Economy as a Whole

Part 3 will help you understand how the major parts of our economy fit together into a system. Economists call this *macroeconomics*, and it means you will be looking at the economy as a whole. In this part you will study several methods we use to measure the value of production. You will explore the role of the government in our economic system. You will grapple with the problems of inflation, unemployment, and poverty. You will learn about money, banking, and government regulation of the financial system. Finally, you will study government policies that are intended to help the economic system work and satisfy the needs of the people. Part 3 gives you an overall picture of the American economy.

Ethanol's Good for the Economy and Environmen

GIVE 'EM AN EARFUL

Measuring the Economy: Made in America

Objectives

In the sections of this chapter, you will learn:

A

how the value of the *Gross Domestic Product* is measured through the *expenditure* and *income* approaches, and why the *underground economy* makes it hard to measure GDP;

B

the difference between *nominal, real,* and *per person* GDP, and why changes in GDP do not always result in similar changes in our standard of living;

C

how the *four phases* of the *business cycle* affect the sales of *durable* and *nondurable* goods, and how economists use *leading indicators* to try to predict the phases of the cycle.

Introduction

"Have some wine," the March Hare said [to Alice] in an encouraging tone.

Alice looked all round the table, but there was nothing on it but tea. "I don't see any wine," she remarked.

"There isn't any," said the March Hare.

Lewis Carroll, *Alice in Wonderland*

In Wonderland, Alice discovered she couldn't have something that wasn't there. The same is true of the economic system. People can't have what isn't produced. Our material standard of living depends on our economy's productivity.

Economists, businesspeople, politicians, and many other people are concerned with what we are able to produce. In this chapter you will learn how we measure the value of our production and how productivity helps determine our standard of living. You will find that we use several different methods of measurement. There are problems with each method. The government must make an "educated guess" when it reports the value of production.

There are different opinions concerning how economic productivity relates to the quality of life. Remember, quantity and quality are not always the same thing. Having more goods and services will not do us much good if we are all sick from pollution.

Section A   What Is the Gross Domestic Product?

This section will introduce the *Gross Domestic Product* and explain its measurement through the *expenditure* and *income* approaches.

Personal Narrative

More Is Better, Isn't It?

A door slams, "SMASH," feet run across the floor, "THUD, THUD, THUD," there is panting in the next room, "WHEEZE, WHEEZE." Someone is trying to get herself under control. The door slowly opens and your daughter Alison steps gracefully into the room. "Daddy," (you know you're in trouble) "Can you be a dear and *please* lend me $20 until next week? I found the most wonderful little top at the mall and it's on sale for 30 percent off." You know the chance of her ever paying you back is about as good as that of snow in July. You try to ignore her, but she pokes you in the ribs.

"You think I'm made of money! Last week it was new shoes, and the week before you had to have a bathing suit. You always want something and your closet is stuffed with things you never wear. You need to learn a little self control. When I was your age I didn't have more than two pairs of jeans to my name!"

Alison starts to pout. "Those old things are out of style. I can't wear them. Do you want everyone to laugh at me? I don't care about your stupid jeans. Those were the old days anyhow. You don't care about me at all!" She makes a snuffling noise and looks a little like your neighbor's basset hound.

Now she's gone too far. You're angry because she's trying to use you. You bellow, "Alison, go to your room and stay there until I tell you to come out!"

Alison disappears up the stairs. "WaaaaaaaaH!"

The next morning she is all smiles in her new top.

How to Compute the Gross Domestic Product

Like Alison, we would all like to have more things. However, there is a limit to what we are able to buy. Our nation's income is determined by the amount we produce. In the early 1990s the most frequently used measure of the value of production became the **Gross Domestic Product.** The GDP is defined as the retail market value of everything produced in the country in a year, regardless of who owns the firm that made the products.

Before 1991 the standard measure of production had been the Gross National Product (GNP). Slightly different than the Gross Domestic Product, the GNP includes interest and the dividends or profits of foreign firms received by residents of this country. The GDP excludes these payments. This may sound complicated, but it isn't really. Imagine you owned 100 shares of stock in a French corporation that paid you $500 last year in dividends. The value of this income would be included in the GNP, but not in the GDP because it was not the result of production and earnings that took place in the United States. Most economists believe that GDP is a better measure of production than GNP.

The government spends millions of dollars every year measuring the Gross Domestic Product. There are two basic methods that are used to calculate GDP. They are the *expenditure* approach and the *income* approach.

The Expenditure Approach

It is possible to compute the value of GDP by adding together all the spending for new goods and services produced in a year. This is called the **expenditure** approach. It is based on the fact that someone must pay for all new production. Therefore, it is possible to measure production by measuring spending. When Alison bought her new top, her spending became part of the measurement of GDP through the expenditure approach.

In the expenditure approach, spending is organized into four categories: (1) consumer or consumption spending, (2) government spending, (3) business spending, and (4) net spending by foreign purchasers.[1] The spending in all four categories is totaled to obtain the GDP. Figure 8–1 shows how GDP was distributed in these four categories in 1990.

Figure 8–1   *Distribution of Spending as a Percentage of GDP in 1990*

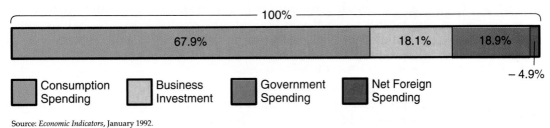

Source: *Economic Indicators,* January 1992.

---

[1]Net foreign spending is the difference between what foreigners buy from us and what we buy from them.

The 18.9 percent on this graph that shows government spending does not include all money the government controlled. Government transfer payments made to individuals for programs such as Social Security and welfare are included in "Consumption Spending."

The Income Approach

We can also calculate the GDP by counting all of the income earned in producing the GDP. As you might guess, this is called the **income** approach. The idea behind this method is that if income depends on the value of production, then it is possible to measure the value of production by measuring income. When Alison's father earned the money he gave her, this income became part of the measurement of GDP through the income approach.

The income approach is a relatively easy method of measuring GDP because most income is reported to the Internal Revenue Service. These values include wages, profits, rent, interest, some taxes, and the cost of wearing out capital (machinery). A problem with this method is the underground economy, which will be discussed later in this section.

Problems in Computing GDP

There are a number of problems that must be overcome to measure GDP. In several areas care must be taken to avoid including production that does not actually exist. **Double counting** is one danger. If a firm buys a wheel for $10, polishes it, and sells it for $12, it only added $2 worth of value. The government must be careful not to count the firm's contribution to GDP as $12. To do so would be double counting. Some other firm produced the wheel's first $10 of value. This value would already have been counted as part of GDP.

Spending for products produced in some other year is not part of GDP. If you bought a used car for $4,000, that spending would not be a part of GDP. The car was not part of this year's production. The same can be said for buying corporate stock that used to belong to someone else. One person's money is traded for the other person's stock. Although the value of the service provided by the broker is new production and part of GDP, the value of the stock itself is not.

Some areas of production are not included in the GDP. Only work that is paid is counted. When you paint your own house, no value is added to GDP. If you paint your neighbor's house for

$800 and report the payment to the government, it is counted as part of GDP. In both cases a house is painted, but the value of only one would be added to GDP. Homemakers create value every day, but it isn't figured into the GDP since they are not paid a wage.

The Underground Economy

One of the greatest problems in accurately measuring GDP is the **underground economy.** Many people work, produce value and are paid, but do not report their income to the government. This is often against the law, but it still happens. For example, if you pay your neighbor $100 to clean your garage but he does not report this income to the government, reported GDP will be less than real GDP. Underground production causes reported GDP to be smaller than actual production really is.

Some production goes unreported because it is against the law. Some people earn income from selling drugs or from gambling. Although our government attempts to prevent such transactions, there is clearly demand and supply for these goods and

The income of illegal aliens is not likely to be reported to the government, and so is not included in the GDP.

services. Such production is not included in the GDP, but it is part of our economic system.

Why Measure GDP?

Some people believe that economists are inclined to measure nearly everything measurable. Measuring GDP, however, has practical value to the United States and the American people. By measuring the changes in the growth of GDP annually, economists are able to track the health of the economy. When the GDP fails to grow significantly, it is a sign that there may be underlying problems in the nation's economy. Then government officials may offer suggestions and take steps to influence the direction of the economy. If the overall GDP grows substantially, it indicates that economic policies do not need fixing. However, the relationship between GDP and our quality of life is not always clear or something we all agree on. In the next section, you will learn about methods of evaluating the meaning of the GDP.

◼ *Self-Check*

1. What is the meaning of the term *Gross Domestic Product?*
2. What are the two methods used to measure the value of GDP?
3. How does the underground economy cause our measurements of GDP to be inaccurate?

◼ *Applying What You Have Learned*

1. Identify each of the following as something that would or would not be considered in measuring the GDP.

   a. The narrator of the story above collects his week's pay.
   b. Alison buys a new top at the mall.
   c. John buys Frank's used car.
   d. John has aluminum siding put on the house.
   e. Sara deposits $110 in her bank account.
   f. Roger cuts his grass.
   g. Your teacher gives you a test.
   h. Your mother pays you $3 to clean your room.

2. It has been said that the "American Dream" is to see your children have a better life than you have. The idea of a better life for most people means having more things. List four things you would like to have in your life that your parents didn't have. Explain why each is important to you.

Section B What GDP Really Means

This section will discuss the difference between *real* and *nominal* values and the relationship of GDP per person to the quality of life.

Personal Narrative

If We're So Rich, Why Aren't We Happy?

When my father got a job as a draftsman in 1978, he earned $12,800 a year. He tells me that he was really happy at the time. The pay was enough to buy a house and a new car the next year. He couldn't pay cash, but he was able to borrow the money he needed. He got a mortgage for only 8 percent. Now he's a project leader and earns $35,500. He complains that he's poor all of the time.

Of course my father's life has changed. He got married and had three children. The old house was too small, so we moved into a four bedroom split-level in 1988. The new mortgage was at 12 percent. My brothers eat as much as an army (according to my mother). We're still paying on our minivan, which is three years old. Next week my brother has to go to the orthodontist for braces.

My father's job has changed, too. There used to be nearly 30 people in his department. Now there are only twelve. The difference is that they have started to use computer-aided drafting. The computer does most of the work in less than half the time. They just don't need as many people. My father was smart. He went to school to learn how to use the new technology. That's why he's in charge of the department.

My parents are worried about how they're going to pay for my brothers' and my education. They can't save very much with all their payments. My mom says she'll try to find work in a year or two when my youngest brother is older. That isn't going to do me much good. In two years I'll already be in college.

For all of our problems, I know we are better off than many other people. We have a nice place to live, enough food, and my father's job is secure. Many of my friends at school are much worse off. Some of them have parents who have lost jobs. Others come from homes where there's only one parent to do everything. Some students wear nothing but hand-me-downs and secondhand clothes.

We know a lady named Mrs. Armstrong, who has a room above a fish store. She's a widow and has to live off her husband's Social Security. After she pays her rent and utilities, there's almost nothing left. When she was younger she used to do mending. That's how we got to know her. Now she doesn't see very well, so she has no extra income. Once a day a local church group brings her a warm meal. Her life must really be depressing.

On the other hand, my cousin Tara lives in a suburb about ten miles out of town. Her father is an "information systems director" for a local bank. He does something with computers that earns him a big salary. They just got back from Hawaii and are talking about an in-ground pool. They never worry about money.

Cutting GDP Down to Size

The American GDP in 1991 was more than twice as large as it was in 1975. For a number of reasons, this does not mean our standard of living was two times better. Like the family in the story, many Americans do not have as many things as they want, or even as many as they had in the past. Part of this may be the result of people wanting more goods and services than we can produce. It may also be the result of changes in who receives the products we produce. The distribution of income is related to this problem and will be discussed in Section C of Chapter 10.

Adjustments to the GDP

GDP is often reported in **nominal values.** This means it has not been adjusted for inflation. Between 1980 and 1991, consumer prices increased 50 percent. Therefore, a large part of the growth in GDP was the result of higher prices and not increased production.

The value of GDP can be adjusted for inflation. GDP increased 107 percent between 1980 and 1991. However, when inflation is taken into account, the **real value** growth in GDP was only about 50 percent.

This 50 percent can be adjusted again for population growth. Between 1980 and 1991, U.S. population increased by 12 percent. There may have been more production in 1991, but it had to be divided among more people. The real increase in GDP *per person* in these years was about 18 percent.

GDP and the Quality of Life

Even this figure does not tell you how people lived. We need to know what kind of products were manufactured and who got them. For example, unadjusted military spending increased by over 130 percent between 1980 and 1991. This exceeded the rate of inflation in those years. Therefore, part of any real increase in production between 1980 and 1991 went to military spending.

Another important measure of the economy is the average wage workers earn per hour, adjusted for inflation. This is the **real hourly wage rate.** Between 1980 and 1991, this rate declined about 2 percent. This means that on an average, people had to work more hours in 1991 to buy the same products they could buy in 1980.

There is also a question of the type of additional consumer goods that were produced. Production of housing totaled over 12 million units between 1980 and 1990, but government-supported low-income housing increased by only 127,000 units in the same

An apparent increase in the GDP can be caused by an increase in prices. To obtain the real value growth in the GDP, the figures must be adjusted for inflation.

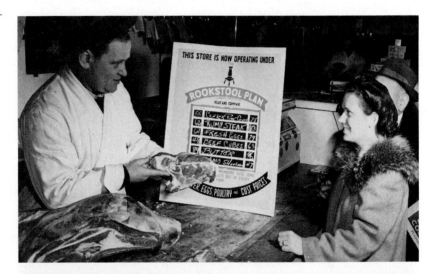

years. Most of the new housing units that were built were for the rich and middle class. It is possible that poor people were able to move into the units that were vacated by higher income people. However, few lower income people were able to move into new housing units.

Another example is that there were billions of dollars worth of video games produced in these years. Some people probably believe that these games added little to our quality of life.

Income is not evenly distributed. Additional production is concentrated in the type of products that are sold to people who have the greatest income. People do not share equally in the benefits of increased productivity. The issue of whether or not our distribution of income and GDP is fair is something we are not all likely to agree on. It is certain that as you grow older you will be asked to help make decisions concerning government programs that redistribute income.

■ Self-Check

1. What is the difference between nominal and real values?
2. Why is there a difference between the rate of growth in real GDP and the rate of growth in real GDP *per person?*
3. What is one reason why we can't be sure people live better when the real GDP per person goes up?

■ Applying What You Have Learned

1. When additional products are made, how much do they add to the quality of life? Not everyone agrees on the value of different types of products. Below you will find a list of percentage increases in production or shipments of specific items in the United States between 1985 and 1989. Explain how much each added to the quality of life *in your opinion.*

    a. Color television shipments grew from 16,894,000 to 20,955,000 sets.
    b. Car telephone production grew from less than 10,000 to more than 1,081,000.
    c. Personal computer shipments grew from 4,025,000 to 4,737,000.
    d. Air conditioner shipments grew from 2.9 million to 4.9 million.

2. Make a list of four things that add to your quality of life but which do not involve money or goods and services. Explain why each is important to you.

Section C Life Within the Business Cycle

This section will introduce the ideas of the *business cycle* and of *leading indicators,* and will introduce the terms *durable goods* and *nondurable goods.*

Personal Narrative

I've Got a Job!

As long as I can remember, my parents have worried about my father getting laid off. It seemed to happen about every three or four years. He's employed by a firm that makes parts for semi-trucks. Whenever trucks sold, he worked long hours and we lived well. When trucks didn't sell, he got laid off. Then we did without many things. I understood why my father's job depended on how well trucks sold. What I didn't understand was why they sold well some years and poorly at other times.

I learned some of the answers in school. Sometimes there are recessions in the economy. This is a period of time when sales are low, businesses make less profit, and there is unemployment. There are different theories about what causes recessions, but their result is clear. They make life much harder for many people.

When there is a recession, people and businesses are afraid to take risks. They would rather not buy things on credit. The possibility of not being able to make payments worries many people. Products that are expensive usually have to be bought on credit. As a result of this, fewer expensive items are sold in a recession. Inexpensive items are not affected as much because businesses and people do not have to borrow to buy them.

Semi-trucks are very expensive. When there is a recession, their sales go down and my father is laid off. I decided to get a job where this wouldn't happen. I figured that people would have to eat no matter what, so I decided to go into the food business. I went to school to learn retail management, and now I'm the assistant manager of a large grocery store. If there is a recession, I should still have my job.

Phases of the Business Cycle

Economists have studied changing trends in production for hundreds of years. They have identified a **business cycle** which they define as the repeated rise and fall of economic activity over time. The business cycle has been divided into four sections as shown in Figure 8–2: (1) *expansion,* (2) *peak,* (3) *contraction* and (4) *trough.* Recessions occur in the lower part of this cycle.

Not all sections of the economy are equally affected by the business cycle. Manufacturers of *durable goods* are hurt more by recessions than producers of consumer or *nondurable goods*. A **durable good** is a product that has an expected life span of several years and tends to be relatively expensive. When people or businesses are concerned about their economic future, they often put off the purchase of such items, in some cases by repairing old ones. Examples of durable goods include cars, refrigerators and furniture. The father in the story above helped to produce trucks, which are durable goods. When the economy went into a contraction, truck sales fell and he was laid off.

Figure 8–2   *Phases of the Business Cycle*

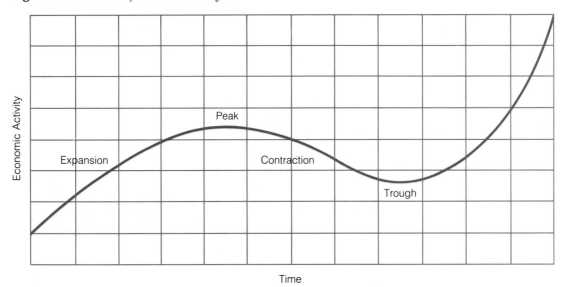

Nondurable goods—such as food or clothing—are intended for immediate use and are frequently less expensive. They are often purchased for cash instead of on credit. Sales of nondurable goods do not go down as much in a recession.

Forecasting

It is clear that businesses would benefit from knowing when a business cycle is going to come. This would help them plan their production and employment levels. The Department of Commerce reports what are called **leading indicators.** These are economic factors that usually change before the rest of the economy changes. These leading indicators include building permits, changes in inventories, and new orders for consumer goods. If inventories are falling, businesses will have to reorder new goods to replace those that have been sold. This would be a sign that the economy should improve. These and other indicators give us an idea of how the economy will be doing in the future.

There is no guarantee that leading indicators are always correct. They could not predict Iraq's invasion of Kuwait, which helped cause a recession in 1990. Still, they are more often right than wrong.

Businesses pay close attention to leading indicators. When they are down, businesses are less likely to invest or hire new workers. If they are up, businesses spend more. Later in this text you will see that government leaders also study the business cycle in their attempts to form good economic policies.

Figure 8–3 shows percentage changes in leading indicators and in the real GDP over ten years. By studying the indicators it is possible to estimate what will soon happen to production in the economy.

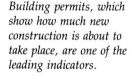

Building permits, which show how much new construction is about to take place, are one of the leading indicators.

Figure 8–3   *Changes in Leading Indicators and Real GDP, 1979-1989*

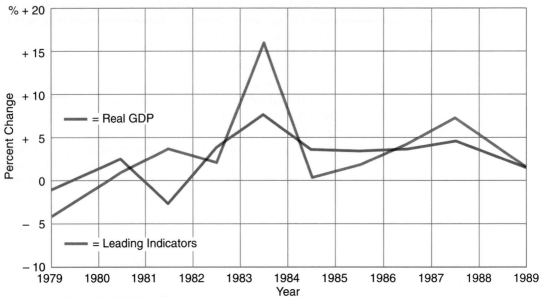

Source: *Statistical Abstract of the United States,* 1991.

■ *Self-Check*

1. What are the four phases of the business cycle?
2. What is the difference between durable and nondurable goods?
3. Why are businesses interested in leading indicators?

■ *Applying What You Have Learned*

In the Personal Narrative of this section, you read of the effects of a recession on a person employed in the manufacture of durable goods. Identify each of the following products as being a *durable* or *nondurable* good.

>   *Item*
> a. refrigerator
> b. shampoo
> c. gasoline
> d. shoes
> e. television set
> f. radio batteries

CURRENT ECONOMIC ISSUES

What Should Be Done About the Underground Economy?

The government loses billions of tax dollars each year from people who fail to report and pay taxes on all or part of their earnings. When some people cheat on their taxes, the rest of us pay more than our fair share.

What should be done about people who don't report their income? One suggestion has been to tax spending instead of earning. Then it would be harder to avoid taxes. Many European countries use *value-added* taxes to tax spending indirectly.

Value-added taxes require manufacturers to pay a tax on the products they produce. For example, if a firm made boats that sold for $1,000 from materials which cost $400, it would pay a tax on the $600 of value that it added.

Prices would be much higher if we had value-added taxes, because the tax would become part of the price of the products we buy. But with value-added taxes, people who do not report income would still pay taxes when they spend their earnings.

There could be some problems with a value-added tax. These taxes tend to be regressive because poor people have to spend a larger part of their income than rich people. Income that was saved or invested would not be taxed. Value-added taxes would be costly for firms due to extra bookkeeping expenses. Value-added taxes may discourage people from spending because of higher prices, reducing both sales and jobs.

How would a value-added tax affect you or your friends? What would be good or bad about the plan?

Arguments in Favor of the Plan
1. It would make it harder to avoid paying taxes.
2. It would reduce the tax burden on those of us who do not cheat.
3. It would encourage people to save and invest, which could cause growth in the economy.

Arguments Against the Plan
1. It could put more of a tax burden on the poor.
2. It would add to the cost of running a business.
3. It could discourage people from spending, which might reduce employment.

What Do You Think?
Consider the arguments for and against the plan. Do you believe the costs or benefits of the plan would be greater? What is the basis for your point of view? What other plans might discourage people from cheating on their taxes?

Chapter 8 Review

What Have You Learned?

In this chapter you've learned the following important principles of economics:

■ The government uses different ways to measure the value of *Gross Domestic Product*, which include the *expenditures approach* and the *income approach*.

■ The government's measurement of Gross Domestic Product is difficult because it must avoid *double counting* and take the *underground economy* into consideration.

■ There is no general agreement over the relationship between the size of our Gross Domestic Product and the quality of life in the United States. Inflation, population growth, the type of products being made, and their distribution all affect this relationship.

■ Our Gross Domestic Product is used as one measure of the *business cycle*. In the past, our economic system has experienced both *recessions* and periods of *expansion*. The business cycle does not affect all businesses equally. In general, businesses that produce *durable goods*, which are relatively expensive, will be affected more by a recession than businesses that produce less expensive *nondurable goods*.

■ The government helps us to predict future economic trends by preparing *leading indicators*. These are factors that tend to change before the rest of the economic system changes. Although it is impossible to be accurate all of the time, generally the leading indicators have provided us with a reasonable picture of what will happen to the economic system in the near future.

Words and Terms

Gross Domestic Product
  (p. 216)
expenditure approach
  (p. 217)
income approach (p. 218)
double counting (p. 218)
underground economy
  (p. 219)

nominal values (p. 222)
real values (p. 222)
real hourly wage (p. 223)
business cycle (p. 225)
durable goods (p. 226)
nondurable goods
  (p. 226)
leading indicators (p. 226)

Building Your Vocabulary

On a separate piece of paper, write the vocabulary word or term that best completes each of the following statements.

1. Economic activities that produce value that is not reported to the government are part of the _____.
2. Prices that are not adjusted for inflation are _____.
3. Prices that are adjusted for inflation are _____.
4. An economic factor that tends to change before the rest of the economic system changes could be used as a _____.
5. The method of measuring GDP that involves counting the value of all earnings is called the _____.
6. Fluctuations up and down in overall economic activity is called the _____.
7. The method of measuring GDP that involves counting the value of all expenditures is called the _____.
8. The retail market value of all goods and services produced in a year is called the _____.
9. Products that last for several years and tend to be expensive are called _____.
10. Products that are intended for immediate use and tend to be relatively inexpensive are called _____.
11. The average wage that workers earn per hour, adjusted for inflation is the _____.
12. If the full value of a tire is added to GDP by a firm that only markets the tire, they would have made the mistake of _____.

Understanding Economics

1. Explain why the purchase of a new machine for a factory would be included as a part of GDP while the purchase of a used car would not.
2. List and describe the four types of spending that make up the expenditure approach to measuring the value of GDP.
3. List and describe the types of earning mentioned in this chapter that make up the income approach to measuring the value of GDP.
4. Describe an example of how double counting might happen *other than the one which is described in this chapter.*
5. Explain why the underground economy represents a problem in measuring the GDP accurately.
6. Suppose you were told that you would earn $60,000 a year in 2008. Explain why this information would tell you little about the standard of living you might enjoy. What other information would you need to have before you could evaluate how well you could live in 2008?
7. Explain why we can't be sure that everyone will be better off if real GDP goes up 10 percent over the next five years.
8. Explain why durable goods industries are affected more by recessions than nondurable goods industries.
9. Explain why a firm might not choose to invest more money or hire more workers if the leading indicators were down for five months in a row.

Chapter 8 Review

Thinking Critically About Economics

1. Explain three different reasons why the GDP is not a perfect measure of the quality of life in the United States.
2. In 1991 the minimum wage was $4.25 an hour. In 1935 it was $0.25 per hour. Describe the information you would need to have before you could compare the minimum wages in these two years with accuracy.
3. Describe three different transactions that would be part of the underground economy.
4. In 1990 Congress approved legislation that provided $2.4 billion to fund an increased war on drugs in this country. Explain how such a use of GDP adds to the quality of our life.
5. In 1991–92 there was a recession in the United States. In this time the sales of new cars fell by 11.5 percent, while the sales of dairy products increased by 2.3 percent. Explain why this happened.
6. If business inventories are falling, the average hours worked per week is going up, and there is an increase in the number of new building permits, we would expect the economy to be in an expansion phase of the business cycle. Explain why each of these indicators would show that the economy would grow in the near future.

Consumer Skills Projects

1. Go to your library and ask the librarian to help you find a copy of a recent *Statistical Abstract of the United States* or a *World Almanac*. Look up the most recent GDP you can, and the GDP for ten years earlier (for example, 1992 and 1982). Draw one graph for each year that shows what part of the GDP went to these areas: (a) Personal Consumption Expenditures, (b) Gross Private Domestic Investment, (c) Net Export of Goods and Services, and (d) Government Purchase of Goods and Services. List any changes that have occurred in the distribution of GDP. Compare your results with the information in Figure 8–1.
2. Ask your parents or guardians how much they earned at their first jobs, what they did, when this was, and how old they were at the time. Many of you probably already have a job. Compare the wages paid for starting jobs now with the ones which your parents earned. Who was able to buy more with their income? Looking up the rate of inflation in a *Statistical Abstract of the United States* or *World Almanac* should help you complete this project.
3. You may remember the recession of 1991–92. If you do, you can answer these questions yourself. If you do not, ask your parents or other older relatives to answer them for you.
   a. Did anyone in your household lose or change their job in the recession?
   b. Was there anything that your family had to do without because of the recession? If so, what?
   c. Who did the members of your family feel was responsible for the recession? Why did they feel this way?
   d. When the recession was largely over, did your family live the same way they had before it began?
   When you have completed this, compare your answers with those of other students. What conclusions can your class draw from these results?

Developing Your Economic Skills

Using Dollar Values and Percentage Values in Graphs

Skill: This lesson will demonstrate that change measured in dollar amounts often does not provide the same meaning as change expressed as a percentage. To complete this lesson, follow these steps:

1. Study two graphs. One will show numeric change while the other will show percentage change.
2. Draw conclusions from each graph and compare these conclusions.
3. Consider how different conclusions can be reached from the same basic data.

Application: Do we save enough?

The part of Gross Domestic Product people have after they pay their taxes is called Disposable Personal Income (DPI). People may either spend or save this money. In recent years the part of DPI that people save has changed significantly. The bar graphs below demonstrate the change in savings.

The first graph shows how much Americans saved in each year. The amount of savings is listed on the vertical axis and the years appear on the horizontal axis. This graph shows you that Americans saved almost $80 billion more in 1990 than they did in 1970. You might conclude that we save more than we used to. In a way you would be right, because a larger number of dollars were saved. But did Americans save as large a part of their disposable income? The second graph answers this question.

The second graph lists the *percentage* of disposable income Americans saved in each year. Although both graphs are based on the same data, conclusions drawn from the second graph are likely to be quite different from those of the first. This graph shows we saved a smaller part of what we earned in 1990 than in 1970.

Which graph do you believe gives a more accurate picture of what has happened? Why is it easier to evaluate change that is expressed as a percentage?

Practice: Find five advertised items in a newspaper that give regular and sale prices for each. Prepare charts that compare percentages saved with dollars saved on each item.

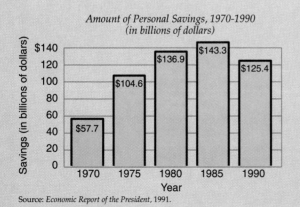

Amount of Personal Savings, 1970-1990
(in billions of dollars)

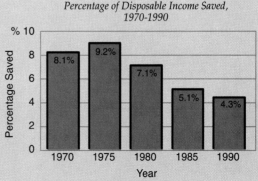

Percentage of Disposable Income Saved,
1970-1990

Source: *Economic Report of the President*, 1991.

Government's Role in the Economy

Objectives

In the sections of this chapter, you will learn:

A

why the government provides *public goods and services*, methods of correcting for *negative externalities*, and a mechanism for *redistribution of income;*

B

how taxes are selected according to basic *principles of taxation* and can be either *progressive, regressive,* or *proportional;*

C

how the government decides how to spend revenue; and

D

how government borrowing results in the *national debt*.

Introduction

If you don't own a car now, there is a good chance that you will in the next few years. Imagine what it would be like to own a car if there were no roads to drive on. You could not possibly afford to build your own roads. If the government did not build roads, your car would do you little good.

There are many goods and services people would not be able to afford if they were not provided by the government. These products are called *public goods*. Public goods and services include roads, schools, police and fire protection, and our national defense.

In this chapter you will learn about the differences between private goods and public goods. You will study the trade-offs that are made when we decide how much personal income to give up to support the production of public goods. You will discover that there is often disagreement over the kind and quantity of public goods that should be supplied by the government.

Public goods and services can only be provided if resources are allocated to them. This means there must be a way for the government to raise money to pay for these goods and services. In this chapter you will study how the government taxes and how it spends money.

Government spending has a major impact on our lives. About one out of every three dollars spent each year passes through the government. What the government does with money is very important to the rest of the economy.

The final section of this chapter deals with government borrowing. By 1992 the federal debt had grown to almost four trillion dollars. This was almost $16,000 for every man, woman, and child in the country. You will study the impact of this debt on our lives and evaluate its importance to your future.

There are many goods and services that people would not be able to afford if they were not furnished by the government. Goods and services that are provided to the people by government on an equal basis are called public goods and services.

Section A Public Goods and Services

This section will introduce the terms *public goods and services, private goods, principle of exclusion,* and *externality.* It will also describe our government's *redistribution of income.*

Personal Narrative

I Took a Bus to School This Morning

When I left for school this morning, my parents were arguing about taxes again. I could still hear my father when I got on the bus. It was a relief to be able to talk to my friends. The trip was slow and bumpy because the road was all torn up from construction. They are putting in sewers to the new waste treatment plant. At the corner of Main and Third the light was out, so a policeman directed traffic while some other men fixed it. We got to school late, but I didn't care. We were going on a field trip to traffic court that morning anyhow.

Every year the government classes have to go and see people get fined for speeding and stuff. We only stayed an hour. It was kind of interesting to hear all those stories about why they shouldn't have to pay their fines. We got back to school in time for lunch.

I ate with my best friend Mark. He gets his lunch free because his father is disabled and can't work. We don't talk about it much. He was all excited because his hockey team is going to play in the new municipal arena this year.

In sixth period a fire engine went roaring past the school. We all raced to the window to look. Actually we didn't care about the fire, it was just an excuse to stop doing our English assignment. Miss Gregg shouted at us. She told us to get back to work, but we managed to kill five minutes.

Our assignment was to write an essay about what our parents do for a living. My father is a civilian employee at the Air Force base outside of town. He works on jet engines. He used to be in the service, but he retired after 20 years. Now he gets a pension and earns a salary too. I don't know why he worries about taxes so much. He has plenty of money. I think the real problem is that he wants to buy a big expensive fishing boat. Now he puts our canoe in at the state park. If he gets a big boat, he'll have to rent a slip at the lake.

I wonder if they'll start arguing about taxes again when my father gets home.

The Need For Public Goods and Services

Goods and services provided to the people by government on an equal basis are called **public goods and services.** Many of the events in the story above involved public goods and services.

When the American economy was starting to grow two hundred years ago, most people were farmers. They didn't need many things that they could not buy or make for themselves. However, as businesses grew, people often found they needed many things they could not afford. The need for inexpensive transportation is a good example of this. Farmers and businesses wanted canals and ports, but did not have the money to build them. The government recognized the need and provided these things as public goods.

In the early days of our nation's history, people could buy or make for themselves most of the things they needed. But as businesses and cities grew, many things were needed—for example, transportation systems—that could not be provided by individuals alone.

At one point early in our history, many families educated their own children. However, as specialization increased, so did the need for public schools, so that all children could get an education and contribute to society. Without public schools only the children of the rich could become educated. Such a situation would make it harder for many people to contribute as much as they could to production.

The need for public goods and services has grown in many areas. The invention of the automobile led to the construction of the interstate highway system. In the past hundred years, many state and national parks have been established. Modern medicine has become so expensive that many people could not afford medical care unless the government helped them pay for it.

As production in the United States has become more specialized, it has become difficult for individuals to do many things for themselves. As a result, it has become necessary for the government to supply more goods and services. It is likely that this trend will continue into the future.

Characteristics of Public and Private Goods

Citizens can use most public goods on an equal basis. Even our military protects us equally whether we are rich or poor. Up to some point most public goods can be used by more people without additional cost to the government. A park will cost no more to have 100 people enjoy it than it would cost for 50. Public goods may not be free, but they are not subject to the **principle of exclusion.** When goods are not subject to the principle of exclusion, it means that no one can say, "It's mine, you can't use it." **Private goods,** on the other hand, are owned by individuals and *are* subject to the principle of exclusion. Owners of private goods have the right to prevent other people from using them.

Correcting for Externalities

It is possible for resources to be allocated improperly in a competitive economic system. When this happens, the government can take action to correct the problem. For example, businesses that are run to earn a profit can harm the environment. A factory may find it less expensive to dump wastes in a river than to provide proper disposal. Such an action would hurt people who live downstream of the factory. It would be a wasteful use of some of our resources.

Improper disposal of hazardous wastes is an example of a negative externality—in which people who neither use nor produce the product are hurt in some way by it.

This kind of a situation is called a **negative externality** by economists. It happens when someone who was neither the producer nor the consumer of a product pays a cost associated with the product. The people who live downstream of a polluting factory pay a cost in sickness or lost property values, even if they have nothing to do with the product itself. In recent years the government has forced many firms to reduce or eliminate their pollution of the environment. In doing so, the government is correcting a weakness in the economic system.

An example of how government can take action to protect citizens and to correct negative externalities occurred in Missouri in 1983.

Times Beach, Missouri, used to be the home of about 2,400 people. In December of 1982, the Centers for Disease Control recommended the evacuation of Times Beach because tests showed the presence of the chemical dioxin in the soil. The levels of dioxin were from 100 to 300 times the amount the government had set as the maximum safe level.

Investigations found that oil containing dioxin had been sprayed on roads in Times Beach in the early 1970s to keep down dust. The oil was purchased from a firm that had made chemicals for the U.S. government. That firm had gone out of business.

In January of 1983 the town was declared a federal disaster area. All homes were bought by the government at a total cost of $33,500,000. Local residents were given aid in relocating to other communities. 800 truckloads of debris were moved from the town and buried in a landfill.

The town of Times Beach, Missouri, was said to be contaminated with dangerous chemicals. To correct this negative externality, the federal government bought the homes and evacuated the people.

Ten years after the evacuation scientists changed their minds. New research showed that levels of dioxin in Times Beach were not as dangerous as people had been told. The federal official who had ordered the evacuation said he should have told the Times Beach citizens, "we may be wrong."

The government decision to buy the homes in Times Beach corrected a negative externality regardless of whether anyone had been harmed. Residents had suffered at least a financial loss because the value of their homes had gone down. This loss was corrected by the government action.

Redistribution of Income

Most Americans share a set of values that are not part of the competitive market system. We agree that no one should be without basic food and shelter in this country. The government attempts to provide minimal support for Americans who are unable to support themselves. There is wide disagreement concerning how much help should be given, what form it should be in, and to which individuals it should go. However, there are few people who believe there should be no public support for the poor at all.

To meet basic needs the government provides welfare, unemployment compensation, and Social Security payments. These

Figure 9–1   *Federal Payments to Individuals, 1965–1990*

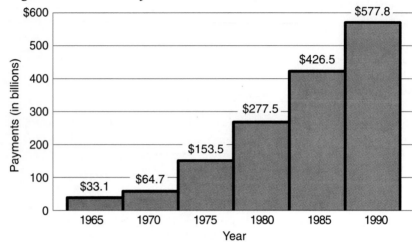

Source: *Statistical Abstract of the United States,* 1991.

are examples of the **redistribution of income** by the government. Income is taken from some people through taxes and given to others through **transfer payments** and **transfers in kind.** Transfer payments are payments in cash. Transfers in kind are nonmonetary payments. Transfers in kind include food stamps, free medical care, and low-cost housing.

Federal support for Social Security, welfare, and other similar programs is included in what is classified as Payments to Individuals in the federal budget. These payments grew more than 16 times between 1965 and 1990, as shown in Figure 9–1. This rate of growth was much larger than the increase in prices in those years. The federal government now spends the largest share of its budget on Payments to Individuals.

▉ *Self-Check*

1. How is it possible to tell whether something is a public or a private good?
2. Why has the need for public goods and services increased over the past 200 years?
3. What is a negative externality?

▉ *Applying What You Have Learned*

Make a list of at least six different public goods or public services that were referred to in the Personal Narrative for this section.

Section B Taxes and the Economy

This section discusses government taxes. It introduces the basic principles of taxation, and the concepts of *progressive, regressive,* and *proportional* taxes.

Personal Narrative

I Got My First Paycheck Today

Two weeks after I started work at my uncle's hamburger stand in 1992 I got my first paycheck. I had worked 28 hours at $4.25 per hour. I figured I'd get $119.00 or a few dollars less once they deducted taxes. Well, it was more than a few dollars. I had $9.10 taken out for Social Security, $5.56 for federal withholding, and another $2.94 for state income tax. That's $17.60 I didn't get. It may not seem like a lot of money, but to me it's important.

I borrowed my mother's car, took my $101.40 and went to buy a dress. I paid a 50 cent toll on the way to town. I parked in a municipal parking lot and put a quarter in the meter.

The dress I wanted was on sale, marked down from $100.00 to just $59.99, or at least that's what the tag said. I had to pay 8 percent sales tax, which brought the price to $64.79. Another $4.80 in tax down the drain.

When I got back to the car, the meter had expired and there was a $10.00 ticket on the windshield. It was not turning out to be my day. On the way home I put $5.00 worth of gas in the car to keep my mother happy. A sign on the pump said that federal and state taxes add 20 cents to the price of each gallon of gas.

At the end of the day there was just $25.11 left. I had my dress, but the government in one way or another had $33.90 of my pay. I got out my calculator and figured that this was about 28 percent of what I had earned. I know the government's important, but this just doesn't seem fair to me.

Principles of Taxation

The government needs money to carry out its responsibilities. Most of the money governments spend is gathered through taxes. It is important that taxes be fair, easy to understand, easy to collect, and not harmful to the efficient operation of the economy.

Economists have identified two basic principles of taxation. Under the **benefits received principle,** taxes are paid by those who benefit from the government service supported by the tax.

Gasoline taxes are an example of the benefits-received principle. Drivers are the people who benefit from roads, and so they pay the gasoline sales tax that helps maintain roads.

For example, gasoline taxes are used to maintain our roads. If you drive on the roads, you buy gas and pay the tax.

The **ability-to-pay principle** is based on the belief that those who have the greatest income should pay the highest tax rates. Most income taxes are based on this principle. Individuals with more taxable income pay a higher tax rate. They should be better able to afford the tax.

In addition to these basic principles of taxation, two other characteristics of taxes are often found in our tax system. Some taxes are intended to encourage greater production and efficiency. They follow what is called the **productivity principle.** For example, in 1981 the federal government allowed firms that purchased new equipment to deduct 10 percent of the cost from their federal income tax. The purpose of this law was to encourage business investment and to improve the efficiency of production.

Another characteristic of many taxes has been called the **least-likely-to-offend principle.** Tax laws are passed by politicians who usually want to be reelected. When tax increases are needed, politicians may try to find a way to do it that voters won't notice. This can result in taxes that are not fair or efficient. Taxes on liquor and cigarettes, sometimes called "sin" taxes, may be examples of this type of law.

The Burden of Taxation

All taxes can be classified as either *progressive, regressive,* or *proportional.* The terms refer to the *percentage of income* paid by people at different income levels. In **progressive taxation,** people with *higher* incomes pay a greater percentage of their income in tax than do people with lower incomes. In **regressive taxation,** people with *lower* incomes pay a greater percentage of their income in tax than do people with higher incomes. In **proportional taxation,** all people pay the same percentage of their income in tax.

Federal, State, and Local Taxes

Federal Taxes

The **personal income tax** is the federal government's most important source of revenue. This tax is progressive, but less so than before the tax law was changed in 1990. There are now three personal income tax brackets—15 percent, 28 percent, and 31 percent. All taxpayers pay one of these three ratios. The rate paid depends largely on the amount of the taxpayer's taxable income. Those with the larger incomes pay the higher tax rates.

Social insurance taxes are the second greatest source of income for the federal government. These taxes are proportional for wage earners up to a maximum taxable income. After reaching this level they become regressive.

Corporate income taxes are paid at rates that range up to 36 percent of profit. They are the third most important source of tax revenue for the federal government.

Other sources of income for the federal government include excise taxes, tariffs, estate taxes, and borrowing.

A paycheck stub shows two kinds of federal taxes—income tax and Social Security tax. Income tax is also deducted in many states.

EMPL. NO.	DATE	SALARY	TOTAL EARNINGS (GROSS PAY)	FEDERAL INCOME TAX	SOCIAL SECURITY TAX	STATE INCOME TAX
09706	9/10/92	$400.00	$400.00	$31.70	$30.60	$4.10

CHECK NO. 5139   NET PAY $333.60

EMPLOYEE _____

Figure 9–2 *Sources of Federal, State, and Local Revenue, 1988*

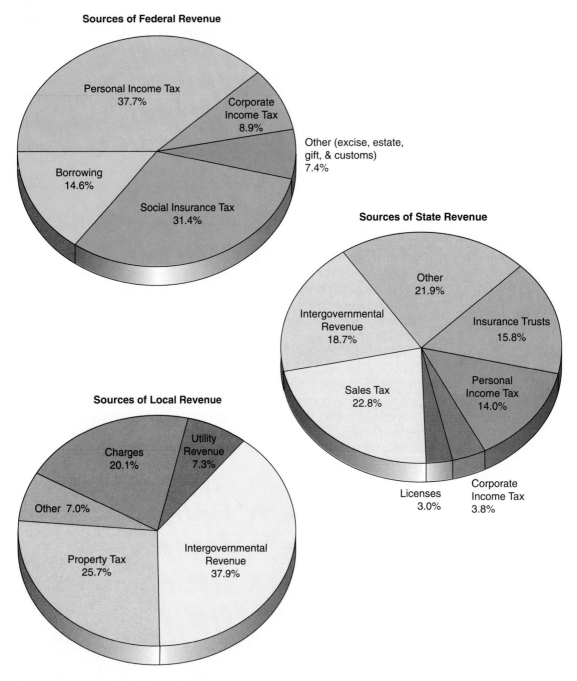

Sources of Federal Revenue

Personal Income Tax
37.7%

Corporate Income Tax
8.9%

Other (excise, estate, gift, & customs)
7.4%

Borrowing
14.6%

Social Insurance Tax
31.4%

Sources of State Revenue

Other
21.9%

Intergovernmental Revenue
18.7%

Insurance Trusts
15.8%

Sales Tax
22.8%

Personal Income Tax
14.0%

Licenses
3.0%

Corporate Income Tax
3.8%

Sources of Local Revenue

Charges
20.1%

Utility Revenue
7.3%

Other 7.0%

Property Tax
25.7%

Intergovernmental Revenue
37.9%

Source: *Statistical Abstract of the United States,* 1991.

State and Local Revenues

The greatest source of tax revenue for most state governments are **sales taxes.** The largest part of local tax revenue is made up of **property taxes.** Many state and a few local governments also have income taxes. These income taxes are progressive in most cases. However, most other state and local taxes are regressive.

For example, assume Joe earns $10,000 a year and pays $200 in sales tax, while his boss Steve earns $50,000 a year and pays sales taxes that total $750. Steve's sales tax is a lower percentage of his income because he spends a lower percentage on taxable items. The tax is regressive because Joe's tax is 2 percent of his income, while Steve's is only 1.5% of his.

An additional source of funds for state and local governments is **intergovernmental revenue.** Intergovernmental revenue is money paid by one level of government to another. Examples include state aid for local school districts, federal aid for roads, and payments received by local governments to help provide social services. The size and complexity of programs that make these payments can make it difficult to determine the original source of revenue for state and local governments.

The graphs in Figure 9–2 show the importance of different sources of revenue for the federal, state, and local governments.

■ *Self-Check*

1. What are the two basic principles of taxation?
2. What is the difference between progressive and regressive taxes?
3. What is the most important source of tax revenue for the federal government, state governments, and local governments?

■ *Applying What You Have Learned*

Look back at the story at the beginning of this section, and find an example of a tax for each of the following principles or characteristics of taxation.

a. progressive tax
b. regressive tax
c. proportional tax
d. the benefits received principle
e. the ability-to-pay principle

Section C Government Spending

This section will discuss how the government chooses to spend money.

Personal Narrative

They Closed the City Swimming Pools

This has been the hottest summer in recorded history, or at least the radio announcer said so. I believe it. We've had 16 days in a row that were over 100 degrees. It hasn't rained for over three weeks. Sometimes I think I'm going to die. Some older people have. What has made it worse is the fact that the City Council couldn't afford to keep the municipal swimming pools open this summer.

There was a big debate over taxes and spending last winter when they were making up the budget. The city's expenses for various social programs had gone way up. They had to either increase taxes 28 percent or cut back on services. They ended up doing some of both. Taxes went up 21 percent and programs, including summer recreation, were cut.

I know something about this because I wrote a report for my economics class last year on how local governments spend their money. I was surprised to find how little spending they really have control over. The city government is required by the state to support both education and social programs. They have to pay interest on money they have borrowed. It could be dangerous to have less police or fire protection. When all is said and done, there is less than a third of the budget that could be cut. People wouldn't stand for all of these programs being eliminated. The city council had no choice but to raise taxes. I'm sorry the program they cut was one I would have used, but I understand why they did it.

I read in a newspaper that the government is giving away millions of dollars to foreign governments. I think it would be nice if they did the same to help local governments pay their bills.

Public Decision Making

It is important to understand that governments do not make decisions in the same way that businesses do. Governments do not exist to make a profit; their purpose is to serve the people. We have a representative form of government. Most government decisions are made by elected officials. Their purpose is often two-fold. People who hold elective office generally want to do what is best for the country and for the people who elected them. Most of them also want to be reelected. One way for politicians to get reelected is to support government spending in the states or districts from which they are elected. Another way is to oppose tax increases even if they might be needed. What is good politically is not always good for the economy. It can sometimes be impossible for politicians to develop policies that are good both politically and economically.

Another problem common to government programs is that once they are begun it is often difficult to end them. When the objective of a government program is to provide money or benefits to people, it is very hard to measure its efficiency. A private business that is inefficient or wasteful will lose money and go out of business, but government programs that are inefficient and wasteful can just go on and on. Programs sometimes do not help the people they are intended to help. In those instances they may be a waste of money. What might the opportunity cost be for money spent on programs that do little to accomplish their basic purpose?

There Go My Consumer Dollars

In recent years, about one out of every five dollars of Gross Domestic Product has been spent by the federal, state, or local governments. Almost one more dollar out of five passed through the government to the people for transfer payments and transfers in kind. Government spending decisions have a great impact on what happens in our economic system.

Redistribution of Income

Federal spending can redistribute income not only from one person to another but from one part of the country to another. Federal taxes are collected primarily on the basis of income. Areas with the greatest income pay the most taxes. However, government spending can be concentrated in specific parts of the country, according to need. For example, the "War on Poverty" of the 1960s concentrated federal spending in Appalachia, a depressed area in the mountains of the central East Coast. Unfortunately, government spending can also be concentrated in the districts of members of Congress who have the most power.

Writing the Budget

The President prepares the federal budget and submits it to the House of Representatives and the Senate for their approval. Federal law requires a new budget to be passed by October 1 of each year. The federal government frequently misses this deadline, and often the budget that is finally approved by Congress bears little resemblance to the one originally submitted by the President.

The process of completing the federal budget has become more complicated since the federal **deficit** has become a major issue. In years when the government spends more than it collects in taxes, it must borrow money. The borrowed funds represent the deficit. Concerned by the rapid growth of the national debt, in 1985 the federal government passed a law to help reduce the deficit. Popularly known as Gramm-Rudman-Hollings after the Senators who designed it, the law required deep cuts in government spending if the President and Congress could not agree on a budget that met the law's spending target.

In 1990, despite amendments that set lower targets for deficit reduction, Congress and the President were unable to agree on a budget before the October 1 deadline. Although congressional leaders did meet the deadline with a tentative agreement, Congress rejected the agreement when it was put to a vote the following day. After this rejection Congress passed a series of stop-gap measures to keep the government running for the next four weeks. Finally, the President and Congress reached an agreement that provided for some tax increases and spending cuts. It was supposed to reduce the budget deficit to about $100 billion in 1990-1991. The actual deficit in that year turned out to be about $270 billion.

Although a new budget was approved, the problem of how to write and approve a fair and realistic budget on time each year was not solved. The 1990 budget, for example, totally ignored the cost of the military buildup in the Persian Gulf that allowed the United Nations and the United States to wage war against Iraq. It cost about $90 billion.

The federal budget frequently contains many parts that have been called **pork barrel legislation.** Such legislation is passed to gain political support in the home district of a member of Congress, not because it is either necessary or even good for the country. It has been suggested that a large portion of money spent for the military and for government construction projects is carried out for this reason.

Figure 9–3 *Federal, State, and Local Expenditures, 1988*

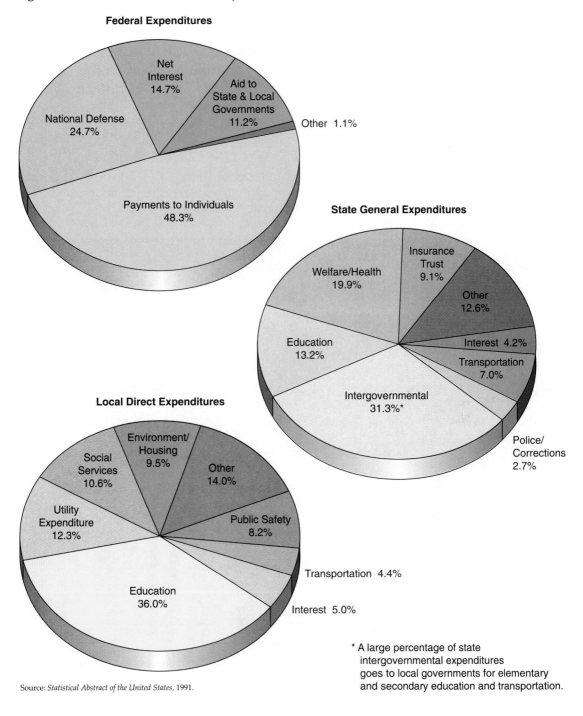

Federal Expenditures

Net Interest 14.7%

Aid to State & Local Governments 11.2%

Other 1.1%

National Defense 24.7%

Payments to Individuals 48.3%

State General Expenditures

Welfare/Health 19.9%

Insurance Trust 9.1%

Other 12.6%

Interest 4.2%

Transportation 7.0%

Education 13.2%

Intergovernmental 31.3%*

Police/Corrections 2.7%

Local Direct Expenditures

Environment/Housing 9.5%

Social Services 10.6%

Other 14.0%

Utility Expenditure 12.3%

Public Safety 8.2%

Education 36.0%

Transportation 4.4%

Interest 5.0%

* A large percentage of state intergovernmental expenditures goes to local governments for elementary and secondary education and transportation.

Source: *Statistical Abstract of the United States,* 1991.

■ *Self-Check*

1. How are public decisions made differently from business decisions?
2. Who is responsible for writing the federal budget?
3. What political body must approve the federal budget?
4. What is the most important type of spending for the federal government, for state governments, and for local governments?

■ *Applying What You Have Learned*

Examine the photograph below. Find at least three different types of government spending that are shown taking place (or that have already taken place) in the photograph.

Section D The Problem of the National Debt

This section will discuss the importance of the *national debt*.

Personal Narrative *My Neighbor Didn't Pay His Bills*

George is my neighbor. Yesterday they came and took his car away. He didn't pay his bills. George says he's going to file for bankruptcy before his creditors get everything he has. I don't understand how he could let this happen. I get nervous if I owe a library fine. We talked about his problems last week. George doesn't really think it's his fault. He blames the banks and finance companies.

George never tried to cheat anyone. About five years ago he got his first credit card, with a $500 line of credit. He used the card and paid his bills. After a while he noticed that the bank had raised his credit limit to $1,500. He thought, "Oh good, they trust me. Maybe I could use the card and buy that boat I've wanted."

George bought the boat. Soon other banks started sending him applications for their credit cards. They offered him "pre-approved" limits of one and two thousand dollars. George filled them out and sent them in. He took out credit cards from oil companies, department stores, and mail-order catalogs. At one point he had 23 different charge cards with a total credit limit of $41,000. George got to the point that he spent money with the cards without really thinking about it.

George owed everyone, at least it seemed that way. His minimum payment for all the loans came to over $800 a month. But after George paid his other bills, he only had $1,000 left a month for his loan payments and for his other living expenses. He went to a finance company and took out a "bill consolidation loan." This reduced his monthly payment a little, but the interest rate was 18 percent. It would have been seven years before he paid it all off.

Last month George's factory announced a six-week shutdown to reduce inventories. George hasn't been paid for three weeks. He missed his last two car payments and he couldn't pay this month either. The bank took his car and soon the mortgage company is going to try to take his house.

George says, "If the government can live on borrowed money, I don't understand why I can't too."

Individual consumers borrow money for personal consumption. The federal government borrows money to support programs that provide public goods and services. The total money the government has borrowed is called the national debt.

The Government's Debt

George is at least partially correct. The federal government does pay for some of its services with borrowed money. In 1992 the **national debt**—the total borrowing of the federal government—passed four trillion dollars. The importance of this debt is a subject of wide debate and disagreement among both economists and politicians.

Until recently the government borrowed almost all of this money from just four sources. It borrowed from:

a. people who bought savings bonds. A savings bond is really just a loan to the federal government. When people buy bonds, they let the government use their money and in exchange they are paid interest;

b. banks and the Federal Reserve System, which buy large-denomination bonds with a specific date of maturity (you will learn more about this in Chapter 10);

c. businesses that buy the same type of bonds purchased by the Federal Reserve System and banks;

d. government trust funds that buy bonds with extra money. For example, if the Social Security System had extra money, it could purchase and hold federal bonds until it needed the funds it had loaned.

In the last few years, a large part of the federal debt has been financed through the sale of government bonds to people and businesses in foreign nations. This is a significant change from the past. Until recent years, interest payments on the debt went to Americans or American organizations. Now a significant portion of the interest payment leaves the country.

Is the National Debt Bad?

There are many different points of view concerning the importance of the national debt. Some people are upset by the size of the debt alone. They point out that the debt was over 15 times as large at the end of 1992 as it was in 1945. Other people argue that the debt should be evaluated in terms of our ability to carry or pay on the debt.

Suppose two people were in debt. Mr. *A* owed $20,000 while Ms. *B* owed $50,000. You might think that Ms. *B* was further in debt, but you might be wrong. If Mr. *A* earns $12,000 a year while Ms. *B* earns $100,000 a year, Ms. *B* is in a better position to pay her debt, even though she owes much more money.

The same argument can be made for the United States. In 1945 our debt of 230 billion dollars was more than our entire GDP. In 1991 the debt was about half of the GDP. From this point of view, the debt was less of a burden in 1991 than it was in 1945.

Some economists believe that the trend of the debt is more important than its size. Between 1945 and 1980 the GDP grew more rapidly than the debt. Therefore the debt seemed less important. But between 1980 and 1992 the debt grew more rapidly than GDP. It was therefore becoming more significant.

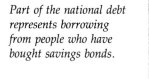

Part of the national debt represents borrowing from people who have bought savings bonds.

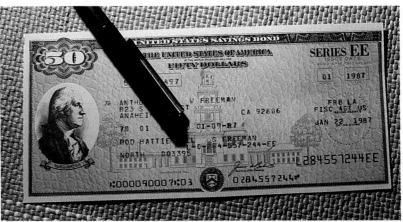

There is debate over the significance of the national debt. One important change in recent years is that now a significant portion of the debt is owed to people and businesses in foreign nations.

Others argue that the size of the payment is more important than the size of the debt. High interest rates in the early 1980s caused the payments on the debt to grow even more rapidly than the debt itself.

Still others suggest that the debt should be evaluated according to its effect on the rest of the economy. Borrowing comes from people's and organizations' savings. Large amounts of government borrowing could reduce the amount left over for people or businesses that also want to borrow. Some economists believe that deficit spending reduces the amount of spending people and businesses are able to do.

Some people don't feel that the debt is as important as the government's responsibility to provide necessary services to the people. They may believe that there will be enough growth in the economy for the government to make its payments even if the debt does grow rapidly.

However, an important part of our debt payments are leaving the country. Many economists believe the debt held by foreign interests can harm us more than debt held by our citizens and businesses. One fact is clear: there is little agreement concerning the significance of the national debt.

Figure 9–4 shows a series of graphs concerning the national debt. Study them and try to decide which one gives you the most accurate picture of the debt between 1945 and 1990.

Figure 9–4 *Aspects of the National Debt*

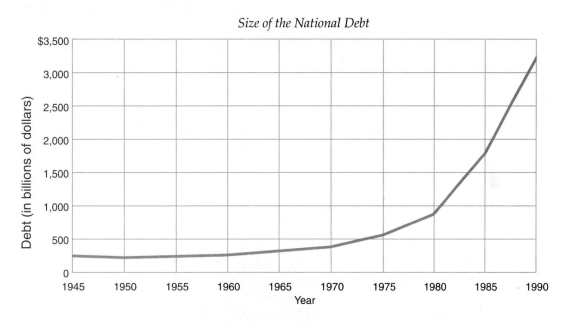

Size of the National Debt

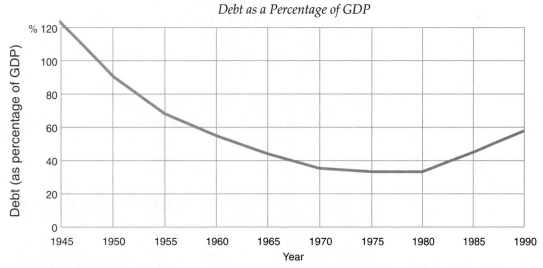

Debt as a Percentage of GDP

Source: *Economic Report of the President*, 1991.

Figure 9–4 (continued) *Aspects of the National Debt*

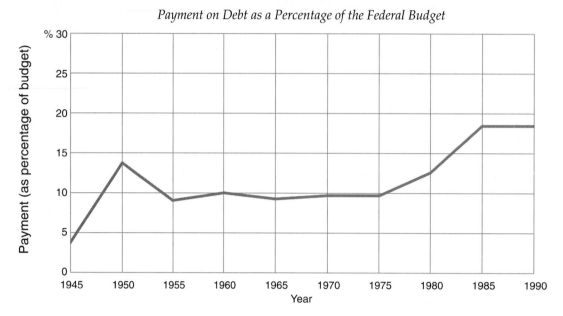

Payment on Debt as a Percentage of the Federal Budget

Source: *Economic Report of the President*, 1991.

Self-Check

1. What four sources of borrowing were used most frequently by the government until recently?
2. What new source of borrowing has been used by the government in recent years?
3. How much agreement is there over the importance of the national debt?

Applying What You Have Learned

1. Economists believe that George's debt and the national debt are different. George borrowed to buy things for himself. The government borrows to support programs that help us all. George must earn the money to pay back his loan himself. The U.S. Government has the entire economy to support its debt. Explain two others ways in which George's debt and the national debt are different.
2. In the preceding section, seven different points of view concerning the debt were described. Restate four of them in your own words. Identify the one which you feel is the best point of view and explain why you feel this way.

CURRENT CONSUMER ISSUES

When Should Consumers Borrow?

At one time or another most American adults have purchased consumer goods on credit. If you are like most Americans, sometime you will borrow money to buy goods or services you want.

A common decision consumers make is whether to borrow money for a new car, or to pay cash for a less expensive used one. In 1991 more than 80 percent of all new cars sold in the United States were financed. There are advantages to owning a new car, but there are also significant costs consumers should keep in mind when they make this decision.

Many people feel a new car is less likely to break down and is worth the extra cost. A new car is covered by a warranty that may last from three to seven years. New cars are more comfortable and easier to drive than older cars. Another reason to buy a new car is to get new safety features like anti-lock brakes.

Some people buy new cars for other reasons that may include impressing their friends or neighbors. Consumers may even be influenced by advertisements suggesting that members of the opposite sex are attracted to owners of certain new cars.

Probably the greatest cost of a new car is rapid depreciation. A general rule of thumb says a car will lose about a fifth of its value each year. This means that a typical $16,000 car would only be worth $12,800 after one year. The same car would lose another 20 percent, or $2,560, in its second year and so on. Used cars depreciate less each year because they are worth less in the first place.

The interest a consumer pays on a new car loan is a significant part of its cost. Insuring a new car costs more than insuring a used car because new cars are more likely to be stolen or vandalized. Finally, there is more sales tax to pay for a more costly new car.

Arguments in Favor of Borrowing to Buy a New Car

1. New cars are more reliable and covered by warranties.
2. New cars may impress other people.
3. New cars are usually more comfortable and easier to drive.

Arguments Against Borrowing to Buy a New Car

1. New cars depreciate more rapidly than used cars.
2. New cars cost more for insurance than used cars.
3. Consumers pay more interest and sales tax when they borrow to buy new cars.

What Do You Think?

If you were in the market for a car, would you buy a new or a used one? Why? What difference do you see between a consumer borrowing to buy a car and government borrowing to provide public goods and services?

Chapter 9 Review

What Have You Learned?

In this chapter you have learned the following important principles of economics:

■ The government plays many roles in the economic system. It provides important *public goods and services* that most people could not afford as individuals. These include roads, military protection, schools, and parks. Public goods are not subject to the *principle of exclusion,* while *private goods* are.

■ In some cases, a firm's activities can harm people who are neither producers nor consumers of the goods or services that the firm is producing. Such harm is called a *negative externality.* Our government tries to correct negative externalities. Anti-pollution laws are one type of corrective measure. Although most people believe this is an important job for the government, there is disagreement over how strict regulations should be.

■ The government has taken on the responsibility of ensuring a minimal income for all Americans by *redistributing income.* The largest part of the federal budget is used to support payments to individuals through programs like Social Security, unemployment compensation, and welfare.

■ Two principles of taxation are the *benefits received principle,* and the *ability-to-pay principle.* In addition, some taxes are based on two other ideas called the *productivity principle* or the *least-likely-to-offend principle.*

■ Taxes may be *progressive, regressive,* or *proportional.* Progressive taxes increase as a percentage of income as income goes up. Regressive taxes decline as a percentage of income as income goes up. Proportional taxes tax all income at the same rate. Most state and local taxes are regressive, while the federal income tax is somewhat progressive for most people.

■ Government decisions are often not made in the same way as decisions in private firms. Private firms make decisions that are intended to increase their profit. Government decisions are intended to help people by providing public goods and services. Many government decisions also serve the political interests of government leaders. Decisions that make political sense do not necessarily make economic sense. Decisions that help individual politicians through spending government funds in their elective districts are sometimes called *pork barrel legislation.*

■ The *national debt* has often been the topic of public debate. Some people suggest that the debt is not a great problem. We have been able to support it in the past. Others believe that its rapid growth will lead to major economic problems in the future.

■ In the past, money that was borrowed by the government came from people and businesses in the United States. However, since 1980 a growing part of this money has come from foreign nations. This means that an important part of our debt payments in the future will be leaving the country. Economists believe the debt held by foreign interests can harm us more than debt held by our citizens and businesses.

Words and Terms

public goods and services
  (p. 238)
principle of exclusion (p. 239)
private goods (p. 239)
negative externality (p. 240)
redistribution of income
  (p. 242)
transfer payments (p. 242)
transfers in kind (p. 242)
benefits received principle
  (p. 243)

ability-to-pay principle (p. 244)
productivity principle (p. 244)
least-likely-to-offend
  principle (p. 244)
progressive taxation (p. 245)
regressive taxation (p. 245)
proportional taxation (p. 245)
personal income tax (p. 245)
social insurance tax (p. 245)
corporate income tax
  (p. 245)

sales tax (p. 247)
property tax (p. 247)
intergovernmental
  revenue (p. 247)
deficit (p. 250)
pork barrel legislation
  (p. 250)
national debt (p. 254)

Building Your Vocabulary

On a separate piece of paper, write the vocabulary word or term that best completes each of the following statements.

1. I can say, "It's mine. You can't have it" if the product is subject to the _____.
2. Taxes that encourage people and firms to make more goods and services are examples of the _____ of taxation.
3. Taxes on people who use the government service supported by that tax are examples of the _____ of taxation.
4. Taxes passed to increase government revenue without causing public protest are examples of the _____ of taxation.
5. Taxes that fall most heavily on the rich are examples of the _____ of taxation.
6. Products that are provided on an equal basis to the people by the government are generally _____.
7. Products that are owned by individuals are generally _____.
8. Laws that support spending that is intended to help politicians keep their jobs is often called _____.
9. _____ increase as a percentage of income as the taxpayer's income goes up.
10. _____ decrease as a percentage of income as the taxpayer's income goes up.
11. _____ tax everyone at the same percentage of their income.
12. When the government takes money from some individuals and uses it to pay for benefits given to others, it is involved in the _____.
13. A _____ occurs when a cost is paid by someone who is neither the producer nor the consumer of a product.
14. _____ occur when the government pays money to people for social programs, while _____ happen when the government provides goods or services.
15. Each federal budget _____ is borrowing that adds to the total _____.
16. Funds paid by one level of the government to another are called _____.
17. The second greatest source of revenue for the federal government is _____.
18. The _____ is progressive, but less so than before the tax changes in 1990.
19. The federal government's third most important tax is the _____.
20. Most state governments get most of their tax revenue from _____.
21. The largest part of local government tax revenue comes from _____.

Chapter 9 Review

Understanding Economics

1. Explain the difference between public and private goods.
2. Describe one example of a negative externality that you know about.
3. Explain one example of each of the four principles of taxation that were identified in Section B of this chapter.
4. If Joe pays $2,000 in taxes and Phil pays $4,000, what else would you need to know before you could say whether the taxes are progressive, regressive, or proportional?
5. Explain why decisions are made differently in government than they are in private businesses.
6. What are the four most important sources of borrowed money that the government used before the 1980s? What additional source is now used?

Thinking Critically About Economics

1. Identify five public goods or services that you often use. For each, explain how you would be affected if these things were not provided by the government.
2. In the 1980s, automobile manufacturers were required to install various pollution-control devices on all new cars. It has been estimated that this has increased the price of a new car by about $800. Explain what this law has to do with the government's responsibility to correct negative externalities.
3. Go back and study the graphs in Figures 9–2 and 9–3. Then answer the following questions.
   a. For each level of government, what type of tax brought in the greatest amount of revenue?
   b. For each level of government, what type of spending accounted for the largest part of total expenditures?
4. Explain why a decision to cut federal income taxes by 5 percent could not be an example of pork barrel legislation, while one to build a new seaport could be.
5. Explain why some economists are worried about the government borrowing from foreign sources.
6. What happened to the size of the national debt in relation to the value of GDP between 1945 and 1980? What happened to this relationship between 1980 and 1991?

Consumer Skills Projects

1. Suppose that to balance its budget your state government must cut spending by 7 percent. Of each dollar, your state spends 39 cents for education, 15 cents for welfare, 9 cents for health services, 5 cents for police and corrections, 12 cents for highways, and 3 cents for the environment. The remaining 17 cents is for state obligations such as interest that cannot be cut. Interview 5 adults and 5 students, asking each to choose how to divide the spending cuts. Record these responses and compare them with other class members' results.
2. Make a bulletin board that shows pictures of goods or services people in your community receive from the government. Discuss whether most consumers could afford these goods or services if they were not provided by the government. What part of our consumption is made possible by government spending?

Developing Your Economic Skills

Using a *Percent-of-Total* Graph

Skill: In this lesson you'll learn how to interpret a percent-of-total graph, showing the changing sources of federal tax revenue. To complete this lesson you'll follow these steps:

1. Examine the vertical and horizontal axes of the graph and understand what they represent.
2. Identify each of the four categories on the graph.
3. Interpret what the graph says about (a) how the percentage in one category compares to the percentage in another, and (b) how the percentages have changed over a period of years.

Application: The federal government has three major taxes which account for the bulk of its tax revenue. They are the *personal income tax* (PIT), the *social insurance tax* (SIT), and the *corporate income tax* (CIT). A fourth category, which we'll call "other," makes up the remainder of federal tax revenue, and includes tariffs, excise taxes, and estate taxes.

Suppose that you want to show what percentage of the federal government's tax revenue comes from each of these four categories. Suppose also that you want to see how these percentages may have changed over the years. Both of these types of information are shown on the graph to the right.

On the graph, the two vertical axes have been divided into percentage values from 0 percent through 100 percent. The years have been placed on the horizontal axis. You can see that personal income taxes (PIT) occupy the bottom area of the graph. The percentage of total tax revenue from the PIT is plotted for each year and connected with a line. The same has been done for each of the

other four categories. Notice that each line represents the percentage for the *total of all the categories below it*. For example, read up from the year 1965 and you'll see that the PIT value for 1965 is about 42 percent. Read further up for the same year, and you'll find that PIT and SIT values together are about 61 percent. As you can see from the graph, most of that 61 percent comes from the PIT.

By looking at this graph, it is possible to quickly see what has happened to the sources of federal tax revenue. In 1985, the percentage from PITs was just slightly larger than it was in 1965. But the percentage from SITs has grown substantially. During the same time, the percentage from CITs has fallen by more than half. The share that comes from other taxes is also smaller as a percentage of the total. This information is clearer on a graph than it would be on a table.

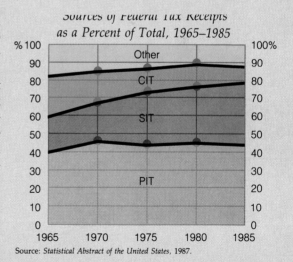

Sources of Federal Tax Receipts as a Percent of Total, 1965–1985

Source: *Statistical Abstract of the United States, 1987.*

Practice: Copy the graph on a separate sheet of paper and add 1990 figures. In 1990 PIT was 46%; PIT and SIT were 82%; and PIT, SIT, and CIT were 92% of the total.

Inflation, Unemployment, and the Distribution of Income

Objectives

In the sections of this chapter, you will learn:

A

how unemployment has been classified by economists and why some types of unemployment create greater problems than others;

B

how inflation is measured through the consumer price index and how cost-push inflation and demand-pull inflation differ;

C

how the government defines poverty and how the distribution of income and wealth can be shown with a Lorenz Curve.

Introduction

Of all the problems faced by the American economy, unemployment, inflation, and poverty must be ranked among the most important. The burden of these problems is not shared equally by all Americans. A person who has a job might not worry about unemployment. Inflation is no problem if your income goes up with prices. Poverty has little impact on those who are wealthy. The people who suffer from these problems are often those who are least able to help themselves. The responsibility of finding fair and workable solutions falls to those who are less affected by the problems but who have power to do something about them.

In this chapter you will learn that there is more than one type of unemployment. Some types create greater problems than others. Policies to deal with unemployment need to vary depending on the situation.

You will discover that inflation can be the result of several different problems. Because there are different causes of inflation, there are also different ways to fight inflation.

Poverty is real, but it is difficult to define. Just how poor does a person have to be to deserve help from the government? How much and what type of help should be given? Most Americans agree that something should be done to help the poor. The problem is in agreeing on what to do.

As you study this chapter you will find that these problems are related to each other. People who are unemployed are often those who are hurt by inflation and end up living in poverty. When the government attempts to solve one problem, it can make others worse. You will learn that there are no easy answers. Finding solutions to these problems will take time, effort, cooperation, and understanding.

Unemployment, infla-tion, and poverty are im-portant problems that confront the economy. The problems are related to each other. While most Americans are employed and enjoy a comfortable standard of living, some people live in poverty. Unemployment is a cause of poverty, and poverty can make it more difficult to acquire the training necessary to get and hold a good job. The problem is complicated by infla-tion, because payments to the poor through gov-ernment social programs have frequently not kept up with increased price levels. This causes the poor to be hurt more by inflation than many other people. There continues to be much discussion on how to best deal with these problems.

Section A The Costs of Unemployment

This section will introduce the four types of unemployment identified by economists—*frictional, seasonal, cyclical,* and *structural.*

Personal Narrative

I Stood in Line All Day

Four people are standing in line at the State Employment Office. They are waiting to sign for their compensation checks. A conversation begins:

Jerry: "So how'd you lose your job?"

Tina: "I told my boss what I thought of my job so he fired me. I kept his books, typed his letters, and made his coffee for over three years. He only paid me $6.20 an hour. I know more about his business than he does. I wish I could be there when he tries to find something in his files. I'll get a better job soon."

Shawn: "You're lucky. I work on construction jobs and I haven't been able to find a job since last fall. Building slows down every winter. I have to wait until the spring. Then I'll be able to work again."

Tina: "If you know you are going to be laid off, why don't you save for it?"

Shawn: "I try to, but it isn't always possible. I only worked 30 weeks last year and my wife had another baby. We just couldn't save enough. Besides, it's hard for me to find other work because everyone knows I'll quit as soon as anything opens up in construction."

James: "At least you can look forward to getting your job back soon. I got laid off from my job at a tire factory because sales were so bad. The whole industry is in a recession. I'm number 381 on the recall list. I'll be lucky to get my job back even if business picks up next year. If I can't find a decent job soon, I'm going to have to go to work in my uncle's grocery store."

Jerry: "Yeah, but things could be worse. I got laid off because a robot took my job. I used to put motors together with 30 other workers on an assembly line. The firm bought machines that do it twice as fast as we can and never make a mistake. I worked that job for nearly 20 years. I never graduated from high school. There is no way I'm going to find a new job that pays anywhere near the $10.23 an hour I used to get. I don't know how I'm going to support my family."

James: "That's tough. How about going back to school?"

Jerry: "How am I going to do that? I've got a wife and three kids. There's the mortgage and the car payments. You think the bank's going to take my IOU? Besides, I'm 44 years old. I'm going to look pretty silly in a classroom."

The clerk says, "Next, please." Jerry steps up to sign for his check and the conversation ends.

Unemployment, What Kind?

Unemployment is measured through a scientific survey carried out by the Bureau of the Census. Roughly 50,000 households are questioned each month to determine employment and unemployment statistics. These homes are chosen from all geographic, ethnic, racial, and occupational groups to represent a cross-section of the American population. The result of this survey is then projected for the entire country.

In September of 1992 there were roughly 7.5 percent of Americans who were officially counted as unemployed. To be considered unemployed a person must be 16 years old or older and actively seeking work. There are different kinds of unemployment. Some types are a greater problem than others. Four specific types have been identified by economists. The types are *frictional, seasonal, cyclical,* and *structural* unemployment.

Frictional unemployment is made up of workers who are between jobs. These workers are short-term unemployed and will suffer little economic hardship from their lack of employment. Many chose to leave their old jobs to look for better work. Others, like Tina in the Personal Narrative above, have lost their jobs but will quickly find others.

Some frictional unemployment is the result of new people moving into the labor force. Unemployment of this nature is not a problem in the economy and cannot be eliminated. It is necessary for workers to be able to move to the jobs where they are most needed. Because of frictional unemployment, there will always be at least a 4 to 5 percent rate of unemployment.

Seasonal unemployment is made up of workers who have been laid off because their jobs exist only during certain parts of each year. Agricultural and construction workers, like Shawn, are often seasonally unemployed. Although this type of unemployment can be painful to the individual, it is at least expected and can be planned for.

Cyclical unemployment is made up of workers who have lost their jobs because of a recession or downturn in the economy.

These workers can be long-term unemployed and can go through great personal hardship. However, there is an expectation that eventually they will be called back to their jobs as the economy improves. In the Personal Narrative for this section, James was cyclically unemployed.

Structural unemployment is made up of workers whose skills or abilities are no longer in demand. This is the most serious type of unemployment, for both the individual workers and for the economy as a whole. Like Jerry in the Personal Narrative, these workers need retraining. They are often middle aged or older. Many of them have family responsibilities. The impact of their unemployment is often much more than economic; it can also be psychological and emotional. It can destroy families and lives.

Structural unemployment can lead to a fifth type of unemployment that the government calls **the discouraged worker.** These are workers who have given up looking for a job. They are not counted as unemployed when labor statistics are gathered. There are many thousands of people in this country who are discouraged workers. They tend to be our least educated and least able workers. Some discouraged workers are homemakers who look for work from time to time but not on a regular basis. The

There are four types of unemployment. Frictional unemployment is made up of workers who are between jobs, and who will quickly find new ones. Seasonal unemployment is made up of workers laid off because their jobs exist only during certain parts of the year. Cyclical unemployment is made up of workers who have lost their jobs because of a recession or a downturn in the economy. Structural unemployment—the most serious—is made up of workers whose skills are no longer in demand.

fact that these people are not actively seeking work in no way means that they suffer less from unemployment than anyone else. However, they are less able to speak out for themselves and are more easily ignored than many other groups. These people truly need government help if they are ever to escape poverty.

The problems of unemployment do not affect all groups of workers equally. The chances of being unemployed vary greatly depending on a worker's sex, race, and age. Table 10–1 shows rates of unemployment for various groups.

Table 10–1
Unemployment Rates for Various Groups, 1975–1991

	1975	1980	1985	1991*
All Workers	8.5%	7.1%	7.2%	6.7%
Male Workers	7.9%	6.9%	7.0%	7.2%
Female Workers	9.3%	7.4%	7.4%	6.1%
White Teenagers	17.9%	15.5%	15.7%	15.7%
Black Teenagers	39.5%	38.5%	40.2%	38.7%

Source: *Statistical Abstract of the United States,* 1991.
*June, 1991

■ *Self-Check*

1. Why will there always be at least 4 to 5 percent unemployment?
2. Why is structural unemployment the most serious type of unemployment?
3. What type of person does government call a discouraged worker?

■ *Applying What You Have Learned*

1. In the story above, each person was unemployed for a different reason. Identify the type of unemployment represented by each person (frictional, seasonal, cyclical, or structural).

   a. Jerry represented _____ unemployment.
   b. Tina represented _____ unemployment.
   c. Shawn represented _____ unemployment.
   d. James represented _____ unemployment.

2. Describe three steps you could take in preparing for a career that would reduce your chance of becoming cyclically or structurally unemployed in the future.

Section B   Life With Inflation

This section discusses how *inflation* affects people. The discussion introduces the *consumer price index* and the terms *demand-pull* and *cost-push inflation*.

Personal Narrative

When I Was Your Age, I Earned a Dollar Forty an Hour

Yesterday evening I went to the show with three of my friends. We each took $8.00. We thought that would give us money for our tickets and popcorn. When we got there we found they had raised the price of a ticket from $6.00 to $7.00. We only had $4.00 left, so we shared two $2.00 boxes of popcorn. That worked out for us, but it would have been embarrassing if we hadn't brought extra money for food.

My friend Shelly works at the candy stand in the theater. I asked her why the price of tickets had gone up. She told me there were really three reasons. The rent on the theater had just been increased. The workers had been given a 5 percent raise. And finally, the manager was worried because attendance was down. He wanted to protect his profit.

On our way home we stopped by Jose's Burger Haven to see who was there. We didn't have any money left, but there's always the chance of seeing someone we know. We found Ted and Phil standing around outside the door. We could hear Phil complaining half a block away. He was saying, "Three fifty for a lousy hamburger? He has to be out of his mind!"

Ted mumbled something we couldn't hear, but it was clear he agreed with Phil. "What's happening?" I asked.

"All the prices at Jose's were raised," Ted answered. "You can't eat there for less than five or six dollars any more. What a rip-off!"

"But look at it!" I said. "There must be a hundred people waiting to get in. Those fools must not care about the price. Jose is making a fortune."

We all walked home wondering how we could be like Jose. The idea of making a fortune sounded pretty good, particularly with prices going up all the time.

When I walked in the door, I told my father I needed an increase in my allowance because prices were up. As soon as I said it I knew I had made a mistake. My father started, "When I was your age I earned my own spending money washing dishes and I only got paid a dollar forty an hour. If you want any more money you should look for a job."

What is Inflation?

Economists define **inflation** as a general increase in the price level. This does not mean that all prices have to be going up. Some prices could be going down, but most are increasing. One of several methods of measuring inflation is the **consumer price index** (CPI). The CPI is found through a survey of several hundred goods sold in about 21,000 outlets. The prices for the goods and services are totaled and compared with their levels at an earlier point in time, called the **base year** (in 1992 the average for prices in 1982–1984). Base years are usually chosen because they are considered typical of most years. Some of the products are counted more than once, or *weighted*, because people buy them more often. Milk, for example, would be counted more times than radios because people buy milk more frequently.

Prices in the base year are given an index value of 100. Changes in price levels cause the index to either rise or fall. Although this may sound difficult, it is easy to work with. If the index for the current year is 140, it means that prices have gone up 40 percent since the base year (140 − 100 for the base year = 40 percent increase).

In Figure 10–1, Graph #1 shows the growth in the consumer price index from 1975 through 1991. Notice the rapid increase in the index in the late 1970s and early 1980s. Graph #2 shows the rate of inflation from 1975 through 1991.

The two graphs are based on the same data, but they do not look the same. Graph #1 does not show the sharp changes in the rate of inflation Graph #2 shows. That is because Graph #2 shows only the rate of inflation each year, while Graph #1 shows the cumulative effect of inflation on prices. Which graph provides the most accurate picture of inflation?

Types of Inflation

Like so many other things in economics, there is more than one type of inflation. One type is called **demand-pull inflation.** Demand-pull inflation is the result of demand for goods and services exceeding their supply. This type of inflation is often found in times of war. Shortages force prices up in demand-pull inflation.

A second type of inflation is called **cost-push inflation.** Cost-push inflation happens when prices go up because there has been an increase in the costs of production. This kind of inflation can be caused by increases in wages, rent, interest rates, or the

Figure 10–1   *Inflation and the Consumer Price Index*

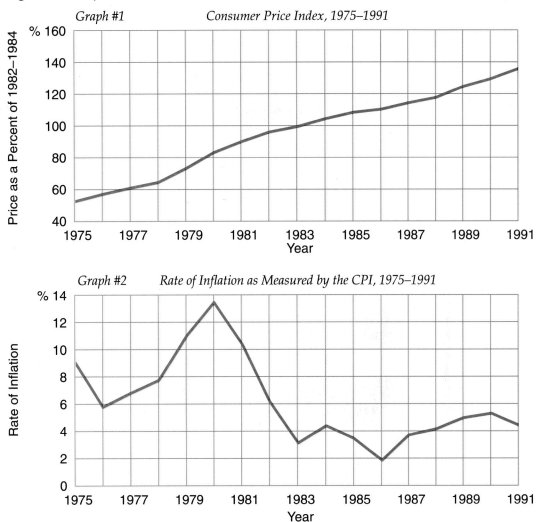

Graph #1   *Consumer Price Index, 1975–1991*

Graph #2   *Rate of Inflation as Measured by the CPI, 1975–1991*

Sources: *Economic Indicators*, 1991 and *Statistical Abstract of the United States*, 1991.

costs of raw materials. Manufacturers attempt to pass their increased costs on to their customers in the form of higher prices.

The difference between these two types of inflation can be shown clearly on a set of graphs. Study the two graphs in Figure 10–2. Graph #1 shows *cost-push* inflation. Graph #2 shows *demand-pull* inflation. You can see that the equilibrium price and quantity for each product is the same at the start, which is represented by P^1 and Q^1.

Air travel is an industry where prices are subject to demand-pull inflation. In holiday seasons, when many people want to travel, fares are usually higher than in off-seasons, during which airlines often lower their fares.

On Graph #1, an increase in the cost of production shifts the supply curve to the left. This causes a new point of equilibrium and a higher market price (inflation), represented by P^2. However, production has fallen to Q^2. A sign of cost-push inflation is a shift of a product's supply curve to the left.

On Graph #2, the demand curve shifts to the right, showing an increase in demand. (This shift could have been caused by a change in any of the determinants of demand that were discussed in Section B of Chapter 3.) As a result, there is a new point of equilibrium with a higher market price (inflation), represented by P^2 on Graph #2. This time production has grown to Q^3. A sign of demand-pull inflation is a shift of a product's demand curve to the right.

Notice that the lower production shown on Graph #1 (showing cost-push inflation) will result in unemployment and a recession in the economy. The higher production on Graph #2 (showing demand-pull inflation) will cause an expansion in the economy and greater employment.

Who Wins? Who Loses?

Inflation hurts different people in different ways. Probably those who are hurt the most are those with fixed incomes. Many retired people are forced to stretch their incomes when prices go up. A second group of people who are hurt by inflation are *creditors*—people who have loaned money. If prices have gone up, the dollars with which they are repaid will buy less than those that they loaned out.

Figure 10–2 *Types of Inflation*

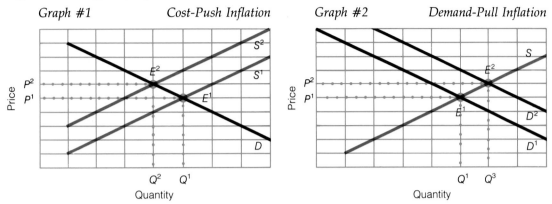

Debtors, who have borrowed money, can be helped by inflation. Higher prices often result in higher incomes, which make it
easier for debtors to pay back their loans. The dollars they repay
buy fewer products than those that they borrowed.

High rates of inflation can discourage business activity. When
there is inflation, interest rates tend to increase. High interest
rates discourage both businesses and individuals from borrowing
and spending. This can lead to a recession. Most economists
agree that rates of inflation that exceed 3 to 4 percent are too
high.

The rate of inflation in the United States grew in the mid-
1960s and again in the mid-1970s. The reasons for these two periods of inflation were very different. In the mid-1960s the United
States was involved in the Vietnam War. Many billions of dollars
were being spent to support the war effort. At the same time, the
government was spending additional billions on expanding social
programs in what President Johnson called "The War on Poverty." Unemployment was only slightly more than 4 percent in
those years, so people had money to spend. The increase in
prices in the 1960s was an example of demand-pull inflation.

In 1974 the Organization of Petroleum Exporting Countries
(OPEC) increased the price of crude oil from about $2.60 a barrel
to around $11.50. This caused the cost of all energy to increase.
Firms found they had to pay more to manufacture goods and
services, so they increased prices. This caused many unions to
demand higher wages, which again increased the cost of production. A recession followed in 1975. The inflation of the mid-1970s
was cost-push inflation.

Gas prices today are considerably higher than they were in the 1960s. The increase is largely due to increases in the cost of crude oil, resulting in cost-push inflation.

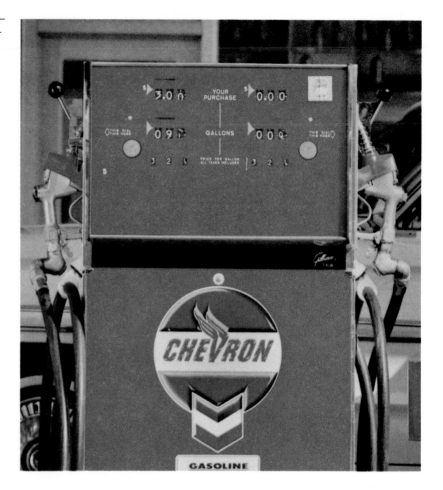

▩ *Self-Check*

1. How is the consumer price index found?
2. If there is cost-push inflation, is the supply or the demand curve likely to shift, and in which direction?
3. If there is demand-pull inflation, is the supply or the demand curve likely to shift, and in which direction?

▩ *Applying What You Have Learned*

Increases in the price of one product or service can sometimes cause increases in the prices of other products and services. In the Personal Narrative for this section, find at least one example where this occurs.

Section C   The Distribution of Wealth and Income

This section will discuss problems that are related to the *distribution of income and wealth* and will introduce the *Lorenz Curve*.

Personal Narrative   *I'd Like to Try Being Rich*

When I'm out of school in the summer, I like to watch daytime quiz programs. It's fun seeing people win prizes. They always get excited and look foolish. I remember one woman who won a trip to a hunting lodge in Wyoming. She was about 25 years old and probably had no interest in hunting at all. I had to laugh when she tried to act really excited in front of the camera.

The host asked another contestant why he wanted to be on the show. The man said he had been laid off and his wife was sick. He wanted to win money to help with his bills. I felt sorry for him. They made him wear a clown suit and get hit with a pie. For his prize he got an electric golf cart. What could he do with it? Maybe they let him take cash instead. I wouldn't have been very excited if I had been him. He was all smiles while they wiped cream off his face.

It would be nice to win a prize, but unless you hit the lottery for a million dollars it wouldn't make any real difference in your life. A trip to Wyoming or a golf cart won't get you a good job, a nice home, or a big bank account. If I had my choice of prizes, I would take a job in a large corporation that paid a hundred thousand dollars a year. That would make a real difference.

Sometimes my family drives out to the beach. On the way we go through an area of estates. Most of them are so far back from the road that we can't see them. They have walls with gates. There are security patrols driving around to be sure that no one tries to get in. I wonder what it would be like to live like that. Those estates must be worth millions of dollars. The taxes and maintenance probably cost a hundred thousand dollars or more each year. I wonder how those people got to be so rich.

My family isn't poor, but I know people who are. Some students I go to school with don't know if there will be food at home for supper. A few of them come from families where their parents don't care about them. Others just seem to always have bad luck. It's hard to figure out why some people have so many things when others have so little. If I ever get rich I'm going to help the poor. If I could, I would just hand them all a lot of money. That would solve the problem.

What is Poverty?

There are many different ideas about what poverty is and what causes it. **Poverty** is a relative term. That means poverty can be defined by comparing what poor people have with what other people have.

Poverty in the United States is not the same as poverty in many other places. In many parts of the world, poverty can mean starving to death. Although some Americans may suffer from a lack of proper nutrition, most people in the United States are not in any danger of starvation. Public and private programs supply at least a minimal diet for most of our poor.

Poverty for some Americans means not having enough money to buy a car or good furniture. Other Americans experience greater hardship when they are unable to pay for heat or electricity. The fact that few Americans go hungry does not mean we have no poverty. It shows us that our poverty is different from that found in many other nations.

The government has an official definition of poverty. In 1991 it was having an income of less than $13,924 for a family of four. This level is a government estimate of what is necessary to provide an adequate diet for a family of four living in the city.

The government's measurement of poverty is based only on money income. It does not reflect noncash benefits such as food stamps, Medicaid, and public housing. In 1991, 14.2 percent of all Americans were officially designated as living in poverty by the federal government. Some were just barely living in poverty. Others were far below the minimum poverty income level. The distribution of income is unequal even among the poor.

Income and Wealth

The government defines poverty in terms of income people receive and not in terms of what they have. This points out the difference between *income* and *wealth.* To an economist, **income** is a flow of value. It is what you receive over a period of time. **Wealth,** on the other hand, is an accumulation of value. It means that there has been saving from past income. The two terms are related, but they are not the same. It is possible for a person to have a house (wealth) but little income. It is also possible to have income but no wealth because all income is spent.

Income Distribution

Poverty is closely related to the distribution of income and wealth. Economists can show the distribution of income through a graph called the **Lorenz Curve,** such as the one shown in Figure 10–3.

Figure 10–3 *A Lorenz Curve*

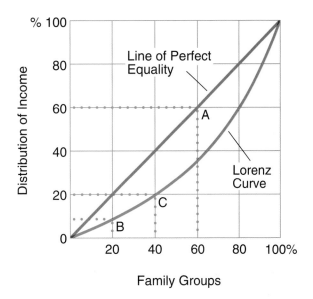

The vertical axis of the graph represents percent of income. The horizontal axis is for percent of family groups. The graph is split by a diagonal, called the *line of perfect equality.* At every point on this line, the horizontal percentage is exactly the same as the vertical percentage. Point *A,* for example, would show that 60 percent of the family groups got 60 percent of the income. *Please note that point 'A' is not on the Lorenz Curve.*

The Lorenz Curve falls below the line of perfect equality. To read a Lorenz Curve, find the percentage of family groups on the horizontal axis. From that point, go up to the Lorenz Curve and across to the vertical axis. The value on the vertical axis is the percentage of income going to these family groups. Point *B* shows that the 20 percent of family groups with the lowest income got 10 percent of the income. Point *C* shows that the 40 percent of family groups with the lowest income received about 20 percent of the income.

The closer a Lorenz Curve is to the line of perfect equality, the more equal the distribution of income. In a competitive economic system we do not want to have totally equal distribution of income. If everyone knew they would have the same income as everyone else no matter what they did, there would be little reason (incentive) to work hard. Businesspeople would not invest their time, money, and effort if they did not expect to earn more than people who did not do these things.

Lorenz Curves do not always stay in the same location. In the 1920s the Lorenz Curve for the United States was further away from the line of perfect equality than it is now. Income distribution has become more equal. In the 1980s, however, 50 percent of added income went to the top 5 percent of family groups.

Figure 10–4 *Lorenz Curve, 1920/1990*

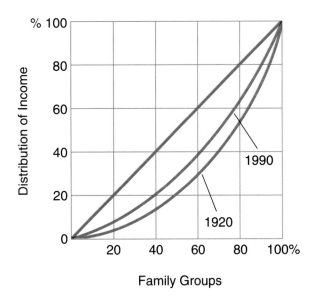

Lorenz Curves can also be used to show income distribution in different types of occupations. For example, the income distribution for teachers is quite equal while the amounts earned by lawyers vary widely. This fact can be seen on Figure 10–5.

We do not want a totally equal distribution of income; on the other hand, we do not want people to be starving in our streets either. We need to create a balance between encouraging people to work and being sure that others do not go hungry.

Figure 10–5 *Lorenz Curve, Teachers/Lawyers*

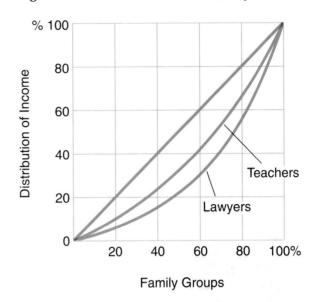

Capitalism could not work efficiently with a totally equal distribution of income. People in businesses would have little reason to produce goods and services if they did not expect that by doing so they would earn a larger income than people who did not produce as much. However, most Americans feel some help should be given to the poor. Study the photograph. Do you believe any Americans should have to live in such conditions? What steps can you think of that can reduce poverty without destroying our incentive to work and produce?

In Figure 10–6 you will find another graph that shows the percentage of various racial or ethnic groups that were officially designated as living in poverty in different years. Study the graph and think about its possible meanings.

Figure 10–4 *Percentage of Groups Below Poverty Level, 1976–1989*

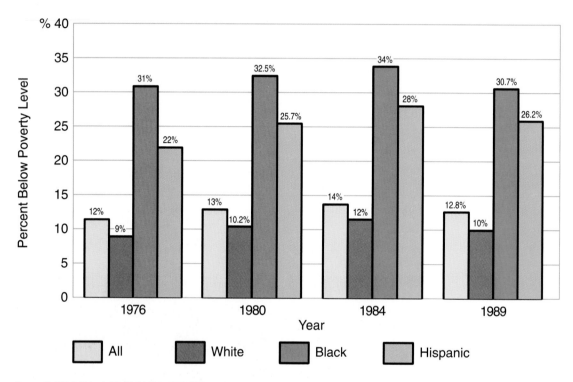

Source: *Statistical Abstract of the United States, 1978–1991.*

■ *Self-Check*

1. What cost does the federal government study when it defines poverty?
2. What is the difference between income and wealth?
3. What is a Lorenz Curve used to show?

■ *Applying What You Have Learned*

The person in the Personal Narrative for this section said that he would give money to the poor if he could. Would this solve all the problems that the poor have? Explain three different reasons why it would or would not.

CURRENT ECONOMIC ISSUES

Should Welfare Recipients Be Required to Train for Work?

In January 1992, Governor James Florio of New Jersey signed a bill into law that cut off benefits to mothers on welfare who refused to train for work or go to school. Under this law the state provides day care for children while mothers attend classes. The New Jersey welfare program pays for tuition, fees, and cost of books. The mothers in the program are required to attend class regularly and to make satisfactory academic effort. They are not required to achieve passing grades.

The purpose of the law is to force welfare recipients to obtain skills that will allow them to become self-supporting. Under the law mothers who complete their education and take jobs may earn up to 50 percent of their benefits without having their welfare payments cut. Governor Florio stated that this law will help people escape a system that "entraps our children in a cradle-to-grave cycle of dependency." However, not everyone believes it is a real solution to the problem.

Some people have stated that the new law will cost too much money. They also argued that welfare mothers may train for jobs that do not exist, and that they do not need to succeed, but only participate to keep receiving benefits. One political leader suggested that the most effective solution would be to reduce welfare benefits for women who have more children.

Is requiring welfare mothers to train for a job a good idea? Consider the following arguments.

Arguments in Favor of the Plan

1. It forces welfare mothers to attend classes and learn a skill.

2. It may eventually reduce the number of people who receive welfare and the cost of the welfare program.

3. It may break the cycle of welfare that some people believe goes from generation to generation.

Arguments Against the Plan

1. It has a high cost at the present.

2. It does not require welfare mothers to succeed in their studies or guarantee that they will find a job.

3. It takes welfare mothers away from their children while they are attending school.

What Do You Think?

What are the costs and benefits of this plan for welfare mothers and their children? Do you believe welfare recipients should be forced to train for a job? What other suggestions would you make for ways to reduce our nation's welfare burden?

Chapter 10 Review

What Have You Learned?

In this chapter you have learned the following important principles of economics:

- There are different types of unemployment, which affect people differently. People who are between jobs are *frictionally* unemployed. People who have jobs that exist only during certain parts of each year are often *seasonally* unemployed. People who are laid off because of a recession are *cyclically* unemployed. The most serious type of unemployment is *structural*, because these people do not possess skills that businesses need. They must be trained before they can get what most people would regard as a good job.

- People who have given up looking for work but who would like a job are called *discouraged workers*.

- *Inflation* is a general increase in the price level. One measure of inflation is the *consumer price index*, which is based on the prices of typical products consumers buy.

- Economists have identified two basic types of inflation. *Demand-pull* inflation happens when prices go up because the quantity demanded exceeds the quantity supplied. *Cost-push* inflation is the result of an increase in the costs of production being passed on to customers in the form of higher prices. Both types of inflation can be shown on a graph of demand and supply.

- Not all people are affected equally by inflation. People who live on a fixed income are hurt the most. Individuals or organizations who have loaned money are also hurt by inflation because the dollars repaid to them buy less than those they loaned out.

- *Poverty* is defined in terms of the economic and social conditions in each country. In the United States poverty is closely related to unemployment, inflation, and the distribution of income.

- The desire to earn money is the basic incentive to produce under capitalism. It is therefore necessary for income and wealth to be distributed unequally for our economic system to work. However, it is also important that we assure a minimum standard of living for all Americans. There is a trade-off between our need for an economic incentive and our desire to treat people fairly.

- Our distribution of income can be demonstrated through a *Lorenz Curve*. When this curve moves closer to its line of perfect equality, it shows that income is being more equally distributed. Between 1920 and 1990 the distribution of income became more equal in the United States. Even so, in 1991 the government classified more than 14.2 percent of our population as living in poverty.

Words and Terms

frictional unemployment (p. 268)
seasonal unemployment (p. 268)
cyclical unemployment (p. 268)
structural unemployment (p. 269)
discouraged worker (p. 269)
inflation (p. 272)
consumer price index (p. 272)

base year (p. 272)
demand-pull inflation (p. 272)
cost-push inflation (p. 272)
poverty (p. 278)
income (p. 278)
wealth (p. 278)
Lorenz Curve (p. 279)

Building Your Vocabulary

On a separate piece of paper, write the vocabulary word or term that best completes each of the following statements in the appropriate place on your answer sheet.

1. A general increase in the price level is referred to as _____.
2. The most common measure of inflation used in the United States is called the _____.
3. _____ occurs when prices go up because of an increase in the costs of production.
4. _____ occurs when prices go up because the demand for goods and services exceeds their supply.
5. Economists say _____ represents a flow of value, while _____ is an accumulation of value.
6. The consumer price index measures percentage increases from a _____, which is given a value of 100.
7. People who are briefly unemployed as they change jobs are part of _____.
8. People who require training to be employed are classified under _____.
9. People who have been laid off due to a recession are victims of _____.
10. Economists call people who have given up looking for a job _____.
11. People who regularly lose their jobs during a part of the year are subject to _____.

12. The _____ is a graph that shows the distribution of income.
13. _____ is a term that can mean different things in different countries depending on social values and economic conditions.

Understanding Economics

1. Describe a specific example of each of the following (do not use any of the examples from this text):
   a. frictional unemployment
   b. seasonal unemployment
   c. cyclical unemployment
   d. structural unemployment
2. Explain what the difference is between a person who is designated as *unemployed* by the government and someone who is a *discouraged worker*.
3. Describe two things that could cause a supply curve to shift to the left. What type of inflation would this cause?
4. Describe two things that could cause a demand curve to shift to the right. What type of inflation would this cause?
5. In your own words, describe how the consumer price index is found.
6. Explain why people who lend money can be hurt by inflation.
7. Explain how poverty in the United States is different from poverty in many other countries.
8. Explain the difference between income and wealth.

Chapter 10 Review

Thinking Critically About Economics

1. Explain why structural unemployment is worse for the economy and for individual workers than other types of unemployment.
2. Make a list of three reasons that could cause a person to become a discouraged worker.
3. Explain three different reasons that might explain why different groups of workers in Figure 10–6 have different unemployment rates.
4. In 1974 the price of crude oil increased from about $2.60 per barrel to $11.50. What type of inflation did this cause? Explain how you know this.
5. Everyone seems to believe that inflation is bad. Describe four specific things that inflation does that hurt people.
6. Explain what might happen to the economy if the government decided to redistribute income so that everyone had about the same standard of living.
7. Describe what you think living in poverty in the United States means.

Consumer Skills Projects

1. Interview someone who has been unemployed for an extended period of time (at least 10 weeks). Ask how the person's life changed when he or she became unemployed. Does the person look at life differently now? If so, what has changed? Classify the person's unemployment as being frictional, seasonal, cyclical, or structural.
2. Go to a library and ask for help to find a copy of a newspaper from ten years ago. Make a list of ten different prices of common household items from advertisements in the newspaper. Find the current prices for the same items now. Measure the rate of inflation for these items over the past ten years. Make a table of your findings and present it to your class.
3. Make a copy of a Lorenz Curve using data from the most recent edition of the *Statistical Abstract of the United States*. Compare your results with Figure 10–4 in this text. Have there been any important changes since 1990? How can you explain these changes or lack of change?

Developing Your Economic Skills

Constructing an Index

Skill: This lesson will show you how an index can be constructed from the prices of specific products purchased in different years. You'll follow these steps:

1. List the prices of products commonly purchased in two different years.
2. Multiply these prices by the number of times you usually purchase each item in a year.
3. Total the spending in each year and divide the value from the first year into the value for the second year.
4. Multiply the result by 100 to obtain the index value.
5. Interpret the index value.

Application: How does an index work?

You have read about the consumer price index in this chapter. This example shows how to create an index.

Suppose you want to compare your cost of living two years ago with your cost of living today. You can't possibly compare the costs of *all* the items you purchased then with those you purchase now. So you'll make a list of only the more common items.

Use the list as the left-hand column of a table. Next to each entry you'll list its price two years ago. Multiply each of these prices by how many times you buy that type of

item each year. This gives you the amount you spent on each type of item. Add these values together to reach the total you spent on *all* of the items two years ago. Follow the same procedure for the items at their current prices. These totals provide you with the information you need to figure a price index.

Use these steps to find the index value:

1. Divide the total spent on the items from the current year by the amount from two years ago. This gives you the value 1.233.

$$\frac{\$252.66}{\$204.86} = 1.233$$

2. Multiply this value by 100. This assigns a value of 100 to the first year and moves the decimal two places to the right.

1.233 becomes an index value of 123.3

To interpret this index value, it's helpful to convert the number to a percentage. To do this, subtract 100 (the value assigned to the first year) from the index value. This gives you the percentage increase (23.3%) in your cost of living between the base year and the current year.

Practice: Find prices for five similar items in the current year and in a prior year. Follow the above example to construct a price index and to find the index value.

Item Often Purchased	Price Two Years Ago		Number Bought		Value Spent	Price Now		Number Bought		Value Spent
Hamburgers	$ .85	X	80	=	$ 68.00	$1.10	×	80	=	$ 88.00
Batteries	$ .79	X	10	=	$ 7.90	$ .99	×	10	=	$ 9.90
Hair spray	$2.49	X	4	=	$ 9.96	$3.19	×	4	=	$ 12.76
Candy bars	$ .35	X	100	=	$ 35.00	$ .40	×	100	=	$ 40.00
Movie tickets	$3.50	X	24	=	$ 84.00	$4.25	×	24	=	$102.00
					Total $204.86					Total $252.66

Money and the Economy

Objectives

In the sections of this chapter, you will learn:

A

how money functions in the economy;

B

how banks *expand* the money supply through checking accounts and loans;

C

how banks earn profit; and

D

how the Federal Reserve System can take actions to affect the money supply.

Introduction

What is it like to be rich? You probably believe that having lots of money would be wonderful. You might be right, but you could be wrong. Fifty million dollars is a lot of money, but it would do you very little good if you were marooned on a desert island. Money has little usefulness of its own. It makes people rich only because of the things it allows them to buy. These goods and services are what people really want from money. Any value money has is the result of what it can buy.

Money can be studied from several points of view. In this chapter you will learn about the functions of money and what its characteristics are, and you will investigate its role in our economic system.

In Section A of this chapter you will learn what makes money what it is and how it contributes to the production of goods and services. You will find that there are several different functions for money within the economic system. Then you'll explore the relationship between money, prices, employment, and economic growth.

In Sections B and C of this chapter you will examine the American banking system and its relationship to the economy. Banks are businesses. Their owners intend to make a profit. At the same time, banks

_In the Personal Narrative
for this section, a young
man inherits a watch
from his grandfather.
What reasons can you
think of for the young
man treating the watch
differently than he would
a gift of money?_

have a vital role to play in helping other businesses succeed. It is
important that banks balance their own needs for profit and security with the need of the economic system for a reliable source
of credit.

Section D of this chapter discusses the Federal Reserve System. This is an agency of the federal government that was established to oversee the operation of the American banking system.
It has been given the job of controlling the supply of money in
the economy. The Federal Reserve System also regulates banks
and has the power to influence interest rates. Although many
people do not understand the Federal Reserve System, it is one
of the most powerful parts of our government. It affects all of us
in many important ways.

There is some mathematics in this chapter. If you follow directions carefully, none of it should be a problem to you.

Section A What Money Is and Where It Came From

This section defines *money*, explains the functions of money within our economy, and describes the characteristics of money. It also explains the relationship between prices and the *money supply*.

Personal Narrative

I Don't Know Much About Money, But I'd Like Some On-The-Job Training

My grandfather Amos died last year. Amos was very special to me. He was a friend. Every time I got in trouble with my parents or things went wrong at school, I could talk to Amos and he'd understand. I know he wasn't always pleased with what I did, but I don't think he ever yelled at me.

Amos didn't have much money. He lived with us for as long as I can remember. He gave my parents the little income he got from his pension. When he died, he left me a gold watch that had belonged to his father. I was happy with it because it had been his and I knew how much he cared about it. Some of my friends said I should be happy because it was old and probably worth a lot of money. They convinced me to take it to an antique shop and have it appraised.

The first man I took it to wanted to buy it for $20. I knew he was trying to rip me off. I finally found someone who I think was honest. He said the watch was probably worth between $500 and $800 but I would have to find a collector who wanted to buy it. He offered me $300 if I needed money in a hurry. I thanked him and left.

Knowing how much the watch was worth kind of frightened me. I was afraid I'd lose it or someone would rob me. I also was tempted by the money I could sell it for. I would have liked to sell just part of it for $80 so I could order a new jacket I had seen in a catalog.

If the man had offered me $800 right away, I might have taken it. I'm glad I didn't now. I would have spent the money on clothes or something. Soon it would have been gone and I wouldn't have anything to remember my grandfather by.

I talked with my neighbor about the watch. He was interested and asked to see it. It really impressed him. He wanted to buy it. I told him "no." Then he offered to trade me his canoe for it. I like to fish and it sounded good. I almost agreed before I realized that the canoe was worth much less than $800 and I had no way to get it to the lake. My parents don't own a car and I couldn't take it on the bus. I thanked him for the offer but told him to forget it.

I've still got the watch and I guess I'll keep it. My father said it will probably grow in value over the years. Maybe when I'm old I'll give it to my grandson.

What is Money?

The young man in the story would probably have acted differently if he had been left money instead of a watch. How is money different from the watch? They both have value but they aren't the same type of thing. Economists view **money** as a *claim* on something that has value. Money usually has little value of its own, but it *represents* value. People must agree that something is money. In some places, beads or special rocks are money because the people there accept them as representing value.

Money in the United States is **fiat money.** This means that it is money because the government says it is. Look at any dollar bill. To the left of George Washington's picture you will find a statement that the bill is "legal tender." This means that it must be accepted to satisfy a debt.

The Functions of Money

Economists have identified the following functions of money in our economic system:

■ **Money is a medium of exchange.** This means that most sales or exchanges are carried out with money. For example, if you buy your lunch at school, you pay with money.

■ **Money is a measure of value.** This means that we can compare the value of different products by studying their prices. If you have $20 you might be able to buy one shirt or ten pairs of socks. This would show you that the shirt is worth ten times as much as a pair of socks.

■ **Money is a store of value.** This means that money can be accumulated and saved, hopefully without losing value. If there were no inflation, the value of a dollar today would be the same as its value was five years ago.

The Characteristics of Money

For money to perform its functions in the economy, it must have the following characteristics.

■ **Money must be accepted.** This means that everyone within the economic system must agree that the money has value and be willing to take it as payment for debts.

This piece of Yapese stone money has all the functions in that society that money has in ours: it is a medium of exchange, a measure of value, and a store of value.

Although Yapese stone money fulfills the functions of money, it lacks some of the usual characteristics. You can see, for example, that it is not divisible. Small transactions on Yap take place with other units of money, which include beads of various colors and sizes. As you would imagine, these stones are not portable. But this is not a problem on Yap, because the island is small. Each piece of money is named and its ownership can be transferred without actually moving the stone.

- **Money must be divisible.** This means that units of money can be divided into smaller units without losing their relative value. For example, the value of ten dimes is the same as one dollar.

- **Money must be portable.** This means that it must be possible to move the money from one place to another with ease. One reason we use more paper money than coins is the fact that it would be difficult to carry large quantities of coins from place to place. Think of trying to buy a new car with the coins we now use.

- **Money must have a reasonably stable value.** This means that a person will be able to buy about the same number or value of products with an amount of money today, next week, or next year.

Money in the United States is made up of currency (coins and paper money), and of checking deposits. A check is a call on money that is deposited in a checking account. Although checks are not legal tender (that is, a person is not necessarily obligated to accept a check as payment for a debt), most large transactions in the United States are carried out through checks. Checks are safer than cash and provide a record of the transactions in which they are used.

Money and Prices

The amount of money that consumers, businesses, and the government have available to spend is closely related to prices. This amount of money to be spent is called the **money supply.** It is important to keep the money supply under control. Rapid changes in the money supply can cause inflation or deflation and other problems for the economy.

Inflation and Deflation

Study Figure 11–1. Suppose that the total money supply at the start of each example is represented by the solid box on the left. The solid box on the right represents production—the amount of goods and services available to buy. In example A there is no change in either the money supply on the left, or the amount of production on the right. Therefore, prices stay the same.

In example B, the money supply on the left and the amount of production on the right both grow the same amount, and again prices stay the same.

In example C, the money supply on the left increases while the amount of production on the right stays the same. There is more money trying to buy the same amount of production, so prices go up. This is **inflation.** More dollars are chasing too few goods and services.

In example D, the money supply remains the same but production grows. The same amount of money must be used to buy more products, so prices will go down. This is **deflation.** Less dollars are chasing more goods and services.

Later you will learn how the Federal Reserve System tries to keep the amount of money in circulation from changing very rapidly. This helps to reduce the chances of having either inflation or deflation and helps to stabilize the economy.

The relationship between the amount of money in circulation and prices was demonstrated by events in the American Civil War. At that time our country was on a gold standard. That meant holders of dollars could exchange them for gold. However, from 1862 through 1864 the U.S. government issued 450 million dollars worth of paper money, called greenbacks, to help

Figure 11-1 *The Money Supply, Production, and Prices*

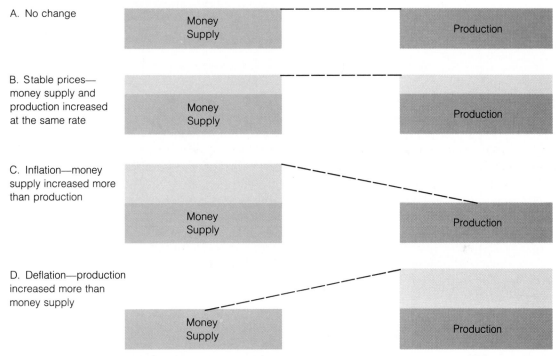

A. No change

B. Stable prices—
money supply and
production increased
at the same rate

C. Inflation—money
supply increased more
than production

D. Deflation—production
increased more than
money supply

pay for the war. This money could not be converted into gold. The resulting increase in the supply of money contributed to inflation. Also contributing to this inflation was the fact that much of our production was devoted to making military goods. This meant that the box representing money was increased, while the box for production that civilians could purchase was reduced.

When more money is spent on the same number of products, prices go up. Between 1860 and 1865 the price of meat, fuel, and rents increased over 50 percent, the price of flour doubled, and the price of textiles quadrupled. As more and more greenbacks were put into circulation, their value fell. At one point in 1864, the value of a greenback was only 39 percent of a gold or silver dollar.

A more recent example of inflation is illustrated in Figure 11–2. Many economists believe inflation between 1970 and 1990 was partially caused by growth of the money supply. Between 1970 and 1990, production grew by 55 percent, but the money supply increased by 249 percent. Because the money supply grew more rapidly, there were more dollars to buy each product.

Figure 11–2 _Percentage of Growth in the Money Supply, Production, and Inflation, 1970–1990_

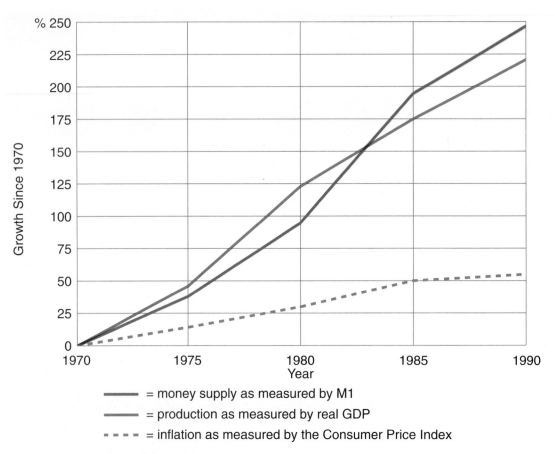

= money supply as measured by M1

= production as measured by real GDP

= inflation as measured by the Consumer Price Index

Source: _Statistical Abstract of the United States_, 1991.

■ Self-Check

1. How do economists define money?
2. What were two of the three functions of money identified in this section?
3. If the supply of money grows more rapidly than the number of goods and services that are offered for sale, what will probably happen to prices?

■ Applying What You Have Learned

Identify and describe four specific problems the young man in the story would have had trying to use his watch as money.

Section B Checks, Money, and the Economy

This section will explain the process through which banks *expand* the money supply and will introduce the *reserve requirement*.

Personal Narrative

My Father Paid the Bills Today

I learned long ago that it is best not to be home when my father pays the bills. Once a month he goes into his study and starts writing checks. He never stays there very long. Soon he is out asking my mother what this bill is and what we needed that for. If any kids are around, he's sure to tell us how much easier we've got things than he did as a child. His other speech is about how we're going to go to the poor house. Then, after he's had his say, my dad always calms down—at least until next month's bills.

When I was young I didn't understand about checks. I thought all you had to do was write them. I couldn't figure out why my father got so upset. If he was short on cash, why not just write a bigger check? I thought it was easy.

Later I found out you had to deposit money in the bank before you could write checks. I wondered what would happen if the bank gave our money to someone else instead. When my father told me that is exactly what they do, I got really worried. I imagined the bank running out of money just when we had to pay our mortgage or something. My father laughed when I told him what I thought.

Eventually I discovered that banks are required to keep money in reserve for people who want to make withdrawals or write checks. They can also borrow cash from the Federal Reserve System if they run short. That made me feel better, but I still didn't understand how checks worked.

I understood more after I got a job. I work as a general helper at a shoe store. Two of my jobs are to take the mail to the post office and to make deposits at the bank. I put checks in the mail to our suppliers and deposit checks from our customers. For all the money that goes through the store, we handle very little cash. Any cash that we do receive we deposit at the end of the day. It seems to me that cash spends most of its time in one bank or another. Even my pay is in the form of a check, which I usually put in my savings account.

If the government wants to control the economy, it will have to control checking first.

Checking Accounts and the Supply of Money

Most spending in the American economy is done through checking accounts. (Cash transactions are more frequent, but they tend to be small.) More than half of the value of all spending is done through checks. You can follow the path of a check through the economy by studying Figure 11–3.

Figure 11–3   *A Check's Path Through the Economy*

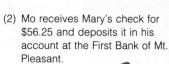

(1) Mary writes a check on her account in the State Bank of Mt. Pleasant to Mo's Garage for $56.25 for fixing her car.

(2) Mo receives Mary's check for $56.25 and deposits it in his account at the First Bank of Mt. Pleasant.

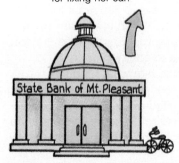

(5) The State Bank of Mt. Pleasant receives Mary's check from the Federal Reserve Bank of Chicago. It debits Mary's checking account for $56.25 and returns the canceled check to Mary.

(4) The Federal Reserve Bank of Chicago credits the account of the First Bank of Mt. Pleasant with $56.25. It also debits (charges) the State Bank of Mt. Pleasant's account for $56.25 and sends it Mary's check.

(3) The First Bank of Mt. Pleasant credits Mo's account for $56.25 and deposits the check in its account in the Federal Reserve Bank of Chicago.

People and businesses deposit money in banks for many different reasons. Deposits in checking accounts are frequently spent quickly. Savings deposits are usually left in banks for longer periods of time. Some deposits, called certificates of deposit, are placed in banks for a specific period of time, such as six months or a year. Banks pay higher rates of interest on these deposits, because they know how long they will have the use of the money and because they are not required to maintain as large a reserve for such deposits. All deposits serve the purpose of enabling banks to make loans to their customers, which increases our ability to buy goods and services.

To measure the amount of money in circulation, it is necessary to measure the flow of money through checking accounts. For the same reason, regulating the amount of money in circulation requires control over these accounts.

The Expansion of Money

Banks have the ability in effect to allow more than one person to spend the same money. They do this by approving loans from money deposited in checking accounts. Economists call this process the **expansion** of money. The expansion process is described below. Study Figure 11–4 while you read the explanation.

a. Suppose a new deposit of $1,000 is made in a checking account at a bank. This deposit is shown in yellow on row 1 of the figure.

b. The bank has a **reserve requirement** that it must meet. This is the percentage of the deposit which the law says the bank must keep on reserve. The reserve requirement for the checking deposits of most banks was 10 percent in 1992. 10 percent of $1,000 is $100. The bank must keep $100 on reserve and can lend the remaining $900 to someone else. The amount kept on reserve in row 1 is shown in blue, while the amount loaned out is shown in green.

c. Money the bank lends out is almost always spent. Therefore, someone else receives it and probably deposits it somewhere in the checking system. This is another new deposit, which becomes the basis for additional loans and spending. This process can be seen in rows 2 and 3 of Figure 11–4. Each time a loan is made on the right side of the figure, it is spent and becomes a new deposit on the left side of the figure. This new deposit allows more money to be held on reserve and still more money to be loaned out. By studying the figure you can see how this expansion process allows total

Figure 11–4 *The Expansion of Money*

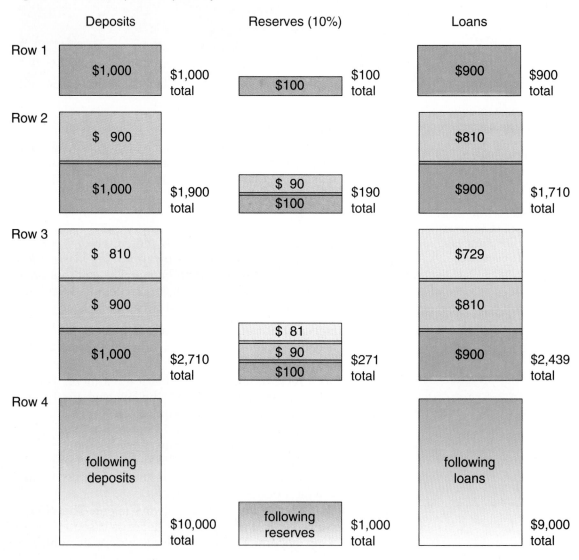

deposits, loans, and spending to grow far beyond the original deposit of $1,000.

d. Although only three steps of the expansion process are shown on the figure, you should realize that it goes on and on. The total expansion of money can be found by using what is called an *expansion multiplier*. This is found by dividing the reserve requirement of 10 percent into 1. The result is a value of 10. When this value is multiplied times the original new deposits of $1,000, the total "following deposits" figure of $10,000 is found. Likewise, multiplying the value of 10 times the amount held on reserve ($100) and the original loan ($900) completes these totals in row 4. If every possible step in the expansion process took place, the totals in row 4 would be reached. (The scale on the graph in row 4 is smaller than the scale on the other rows.)

What Limits and Controls the Expansion Process?

A number of factors limit the expansion process. One factor is that banks normally keep more money in reserve than is required. This provides the banks with a sort of "safety margin," which prevents them from falling below their reserve requirement if deposits are withdrawn. Banks may also choose to invest in other securities rather than make loans.

Another limit on expansion is the fact that people hold cash. People keep some money to pay for things they intend to buy. In addition, some people save cash at home rather than depositing it in a bank. Money that is not put into circulation either by banks or by people cannot become part of the expansion process.

Actions of the Federal Reserve System may also limit the expansion of money. These will be discussed in Section D of this chapter.

◼ *Self-Check*

1. About what part of spending is done with checks?
2. What is the meaning of the reserve requirement?
3. What two factors limit the expansion of money?

◼ *Applying What You Have Learned*

Since most money is spent in the form of checks, there must be important advantages to this form of spending. List and describe three such advantages. It may help to consider the characteristics of money that were explained to you in Section A.

Section C Banks Are in Business to Make a Profit

This section will introduce the FDIC and will discuss how banks operate as businesses, with *assets* and *liabilities*.

If You Really Need a Loan, the Bank Won't Give You One

My father works as a gardener for several local businesses. His job is to make sure that the trees and flowers outside their buildings look good. Up until this year he did pretty well. We weren't getting rich, but we could pay our bills. Last spring the city's dam broke and we've had a water shortage ever since. The new dam won't be done until fall. The city council passed an ordinance against watering anything. Have you ever tried to grow flowers without water? It can't be done. Most of my father's customers decided not to have flowers at all. Some of them stuck plastic plants in the ground. My father hasn't had much work this year.

Last year my father bought a new truck with spraying equipment for his business. It cost over $25,000. Every month his payments are almost $700. With our mortgage and other expenses, he owes at least $2,500 a month. He hasn't been able to earn much more than seven or eight hundred dollars from his work and doing odd jobs. My mother took a job as a waitress, but they are still short several hundred dollars. We really need some help to get through this year.

My parents applied for a loan at the bank, but didn't get one. The loan officer said we weren't a good risk. Used trucks aren't worth much. We have little value built up in our house. We don't own anything else to use for collateral. The loan officer said there is no guarantee my father's customers will hire him back even after the dam is fixed. She said she couldn't risk the depositors' money.

I can understand the bank's point of view, but it doesn't seem fair. When my father was doing well, they were happy to lend him money and take his interest payments.

My father finally borrowed $5,000 from a doctor he works for. The doctor loaned him the money mostly as a favor. Still, my father has to pay him 10 percent interest on the loan. The doctor's going to make money.

Banks as Businesses

Banks are businesses. They are in business to make a profit by providing services to their customers. Two of their primary services are to provide safety and interest income for their depositors' money. Another major service is to provide a source of loans for individuals and businesses that need to borrow money.

The money on deposit in a bank is the merchandise the bank has to sell. Banks earn their profit by charging borrowers a higher rate of interest than they pay their depositors. There is usually a difference, or "spread," of four to five percent between what a bank pays its depositors and what it earns from its loans. Banks are hesitant to make risky loans. One bad loan can wipe out the profits from many good loans.

Economists believe that banks would act in a **pro-cyclical** way if the government allowed them to. *Pro-cyclical* means that their policies would increase any existing economic trends. For example, if the economy were doing well, businesses would make good profits and the banks would be willing to make more loans. More loans would cause the economy to grow even faster, possibly causing inflation.

Banks are able to compete with each other by offering different rates of interest to depositors. Therefore, it is important to determine what interest rates are paid at different banks before making a deposit. The difference in what the savings will earn over several years can be substantial.

If the economy were in a recession, businesses would make little profit. Banks would have a difficult time making profits from loans. Fewer loans would result in less spending and a deeper recession.

In other words, without government intervention bank policies would make expansions larger and recessions deeper. These would be pro-cyclical policies. **Countercyclical** policies, however, are policies that *reverse* trends in the economy. Depending on the circumstances, countercyclical policies are usually better for the economy than pro-cyclical ones.

In Section D of this chapter you will learn about Federal Reserve policies that attempt to stabilize the economy or to prevent pro-cyclical actions by banks.

Insuring Depositors

In the past there were times when people lost confidence in banks. Mass withdrawals, or runs on banks, accompanied the Great Depression in 1932. The government established the **Federal Deposit Insurance Corporation** (FDIC) in 1935 to raise confidence in banks by insuring deposits. In 1992 the FDIC

The Federal Deposit Insurance Corporation was established in 1935, to prevent the kinds of mass withdrawals that occurred in 1932 during the Great Depression. The FDIC insures savings, thereby maintaining depositors' confidence in their banks.

insured deposits up to a maximum of $100,000 per depositor.

New government regulations in the 1970s and 1980s increased competition among banks and reduced their profits. The new rules also encouraged banks to make higher-risk investments. As a result, bank failures increased dramatically in the late 1980s. In 1991 the federal government arranged a new source of funds for the FDIC, so that it could pay depositors of failed banks.

Savings and loan associations (S&Ls) work much like banks today, but they were quite different in the past. These institutions expanded in the 1930s to give small savers a place to deposit their money and to provide home loans at low interest rates. The government created the Federal Savings and Loan Insurance Corporation (FSLIC) to protect depositors.

S&Ls made billions of dollars of long-term loans at low fixed interest rates in the 1950s and 1960s. High inflation in the 1970s forced S&Ls to pay higher interest on deposits. Most S&L income, however, came from previous low-interest rate mortgages. S&Ls were not competitive.

In 1982 Congress decided to allow the S&Ls to make higher-risk loans and investments. When these investments went bad, hundreds of S&Ls failed in the late 1980s and early 1990s. The Federal Savings and Loan Insurance Corporation ran out of funds. Congress created the Resolution Trust Corporation (RTC) in 1989 to take over the failed S&Ls and sell off their property. The FSLIC was replaced with the Savings Association Insurance Fund (SAIF). Some economists estimated that the S&L disaster would cost taxpayers a half trillion dollars.

■ *Self-Check*

1. How do banks earn a profit?
2. What does "pro-cyclical" mean?
3. What was the reason for the creation of the Federal Deposit Insurance Corporation?

■ *Applying What You Have Learned*

List and explain three different reasons why the man in the Personal Narrative was not a good risk for a loan.

Section D   What the Federal Reserve System Does

This section will explain the role of the *Federal Reserve System* (the Fed) in our economic system.

Personal Narrative

Give Me the Sports Section, You Can Have the Rest

Whenever I bring in the paper, my family splits it. My mother takes the front page, my sister reads the clothing ads, my little brother finds the comics, and I get the sports section. My father takes what's left. No one wants the financial pages.

Earlier this year I was assigned to read and cut out articles from the business section. One article I read was about the Federal Reserve System and interest rates. It said that the amount of money in circulation was growing faster than the Federal Reserve System wanted it to. Market analysts thought that the Federal Reserve System would slow the growth of the money supply, which would force interest rates up. There was some fear that this could contribute to a downturn in the economy. A discussion of how this would affect attempts to reduce the federal debt followed. I copied over some of the things that I read and handed it in. My teacher gave me a *B* on my paper. To be honest, I didn't understand more than two words I wrote.

We have been thinking of moving to a new house this year. We put our home on the market three months ago. At least one hundred people have come to see it. Some of them came back two or three times. We have had offers, but none my parents were willing to accept. The real estate agent said that interest rates have gone up lately and people are putting off buying a home until interest rates go down.

My father sees the same problem at work. He is an industrial architect. His business has been slow recently because there has been less construction. He believes his customers have been cutting back on new building because of the high interest rates. If the Federal Reserve System slows the growth of the money supply, Dad says interest rates may go up even more.

When I studied the Federal Reserve System, my teacher said that money acts just like anything else people want. If the supply is reduced when people want the same amount, prices will go up. The price of borrowed money is the interest rate. If interest rates go up even more, I wonder what will happen to my father's job.

I realize that the Federal Reserve System is important. Its actions have a major effect on businesses and people, but I don't really understand how it works.

The History of the Federal Reserve System

Following a run on banks in 1907, the **Federal Reserve System** (also known as "the Fed") was created to oversee banking in this country in 1913. Since then its powers have grown to the point that it now has the ability to influence the entire economic system.

In 1935 Congress established a Board of Governors for the Federal Reserve System. The seven members of this board set Federal Reserve policies. Each member is appointed by the President and approved by the Senate to serve a 14-year term of office. These appointments are staggered, so that there are always experienced people on the board.

Individual banks may or may not belong to the Federal Reserve System. Banks that have been chartered (given the right to operate) by the national government *must* belong. Those chartered by state governments have the choice to belong or not. Generally, larger banks have chosen to belong and smaller ones have not.

In the past, member banks were required to follow rules set by the Federal Reserve System while nonmember banks were not. Since the passage and implementation of the Banking Act of 1980 (Depository Institutions Deregulation and Monetary Control Act), there has been little difference between banks that choose to belong and those that do not. All depository institutions, including banks, saving banks, and savings and loan associations, must now meet reserve requirements set by the Fed.

Tools of the Fed

The most important job of the Federal Reserve System is to maintain a stable supply of money for the economy. There are three basic tools the Fed has to carry out this responsibility: the *reserve requirement*, the *discount rate*, and *open market operations*.

The Reserve Requirement

The *most powerful tool* the Fed has is the power to change the reserve requirement on demand deposits to any value between 3 and 14 percent. A change in the reserve requirement would have a large effect on the expansion of money that was described in Section B of this chapter, and on the economy in general. If the reserve requirement is lowered, more money becomes available for loans. If the requirement is raised, less money becomes available. For example, if the Fed sets the reserve requirement at 12½ percent, the expansion multiplier would be 8. However, if the Fed sets the reserve requirement at 10 percent, the expansion multiplier would be 10. With a lower reserve requirement, the expansion multiplier becomes greater—and the amount of money in circulation increases.

The Fed has not used this power very often. Between 1980 and 1992, the reserve requirement on checking deposits remained at 12 percent. The Fed lowered it to 10 percent in May 1992 to encourage lending.

The Discount Rate

The Fed has the power to change the **discount rate.** This is the rate of interest the Fed charges banks to which it lends money. Private individuals and businesses cannot borrow from the Fed. Banks can, and frequently do. If the discount rate goes up, fewer banks will want to borrow from the Fed. This will reduce the amount of money these banks have available to loan to their customers and will force interest rates up. Changes in the discount rate usually result in similar changes in other interest rates.

Open Market Operations

The *most important tool* the Fed has is **open market operations.** To understand how this works you need to know that there is a market for previously owned government securities in New York City. Every business day millions of dollars worth of "used" securities are bought and sold. By buying and selling government securities in this open market, the Fed exercises control over the money supply.

The Fed is the largest single owner of government securities in the country. It also buys and sells more securities than anyone else. When the Fed buys securities from banks, businesses, or individuals, it puts money into the banking system in exchange for the securities that it buys. When it sells securities, it takes money out of circulation.

Table 11-2 will help you understand how this works. In example 1, the Fed *buys* a government security from Joe. The Fed pays money to Joe, and Joe will deposit the money in the banking system. This will be a new deposit, which can be expanded. There will be additional money in circulation. This should make it easier for people or businesses to borrow money.

In example 2, the Fed *sells* a government security to Frank. Frank will pay with money he withdraws from the banking system. This will reduce the amount of money banks have to expand. There will be less money in circulation. This should make it more difficult for people or businesses to borrow money.

In this way the Fed regulates the amount of money available for new deposits in the expansion process. The Federal Reserve System carries out most of its responsibility to control the money supply through open market operations.

Monetary Policy

Federal Reserve actions that are intended to stabilize the economic system make up what is called **monetary policy.** The Fed uses open market operations most frequently to carry out monetary policy. For example, if the Fed wanted banks to have more money to lend, it would buy government securities. This would add more money to the expansion process and increase the ability of banks to make loans.

The Fed does change the discount rate from time to time. In the early 1990s the discount rate was lowered from 7 percent to just 3½ percent in 1992. This drop may have encouraged banks to borrow from the Fed to make loans. It allowed them to reduce the interest they charged their customers, which would encourage businesses and consumers to borrow.

On a few occasions the Fed has changed the reserve requirement. The results of these changes on the economy have been so great that it is doubtful such changes will be made frequently in the future.

Over the past 50 years the Fed has had different objectives for its monetary policy. In World War II it tried to keep interest rates low to help the government pay for the war. In the mid-1960s it tried to reduce the amount of money banks had available to loan in order to fight inflation. In the early 1980s Federal Reserve actions helped force interest rates to very high levels. These high interest rates contributed to the recession of 1981–82, but

Table 11-2

Example 1. The Federal Reserve Buys a Security

Federal Reserve System	Joe	Joe's Bank

Federal Reserve System	Joe	Joe's Bank
The Federal Reserve buys a government security from Joe. The Fed receives the security and pays Joe.	Joe sells his government security and is paid by the Fed. Joe puts the money in his bank.	With Joe's deposit, the bank now has additional money to make more loans.

Example 2. The Federal Reserve Sells a Security

Federal Reserve System	Frank	Frank's Bank
The Federal Reserve sells a government security to Frank. The Fed receives a check from Frank. The Fed sends the check to Frank's bank for payment.	Frank buys a government security from the Fed. He writes a check to pay for it, so money comes out of his bank and flows to the Fed.	Frank's bank pays the Fed on Frank's check and reduces Frank's balance in his account. Since the bank now has less money on deposit, it is able to make fewer loans.

eventually helped to reduce the high rate of inflation. Figure 11-5 shows the levels of prime interest rate (the rate that banks charge their best customers) for the years 1977–1990.

Some politicians and economists feel that the Fed has made many mistakes. Others feel that it has done a good job most of the time. It is clear at least that the Federal Reserve is an important power in our economic system.

Figure 11–5 *Average Prime Interest Rates, 1977–1990*

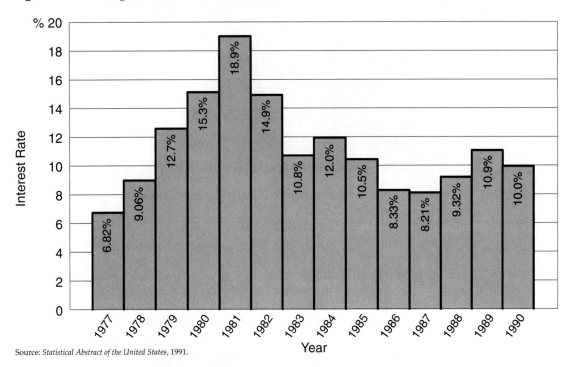

Source: *Statistical Abstract of the United States*, 1991.

Self-Check

1. What is the most important job of the Federal Reserve System?
2. Why hasn't the Federal Reserve's Board of Governors changed the reserve requirement very often?
3. What is the purpose of monetary policy?

Applying What You Have Learned

There is a list of possible Federal Reserve actions below. In each case the action is intended to either increase or decrease the amount of money in circulation. Identify the purpose of each action.

a. The Fed increases the discount rate.
b. The Fed lowers the reserve requirement.
c. The Fed buys government securities.
d. The Fed sells government securities.
e. The Fed raises the reserve requirement.
f. The Fed lowers the discount rate.

PROFILE

Paul Volcker
(1927–   )

In a survey of national leaders made in the early 1980s, Paul Volcker was rated the second most powerful man in the United States next to the President. What could give a man such power? Paul Volcker served as the Chairman of the Board of Governors of the Federal Reserve System at a time when monetary policy squeezed inflation from 13.5 percent in 1980 to 3.3 percent in 1985. During this time our country went through the worst recession since the Great Depression, and experienced unemployment of nearly 10 percent. In 1981–1982 real GDP actually declined 2.5 percent.

Paul Volcker was appointed Chairman of the Board of Governors in 1979 by President Carter and was later reappointed by President Reagan. He left the Board in 1987.

He brought a wide and impressive background with him to the job. He was a brilliant student at Princeton, Harvard, and at the London School of Economics. He held several important banking positions before accepting the post of Undersecretary for Monetary Affairs for the Department of the Treasury. While holding this position he was influential in establishing a new system for setting exchange rates. Before being appointed Chairman of the Board of Governors, he served as President of the District Federal Reserve Bank in New York.

How did Volcker accomplish the "miracle" of whipping inflation? He had the Fed sell government securities to reduce the money supply. At the same time the discount rate was increased to an unprecedented 14 percent. These actions forced interest rates above 20 percent for car loans, mortgages, and businesses. Sales of these items fell, leading to a recession. Many people called for Volcker to resign. He seemed to be winning the battle to reduce inflation, but at what cost? Was it worth having nearly 11 million people unemployed? In the latter part of 1982 the Fed allowed the money supply to grow more rapidly. This gradually brought down interest rates and helped the economy recover without a return to inflation.

CURRENT ECONOMIC ISSUES

Should Controls Be Placed on the Powers of the Federal Reserve System?

Although there are effective checks-and-balances on powers held by the Congress and the President, there are few checks on the monetary power of the Federal Reserve System's Board of Governors. Under current law, the Board of Governors is free to act within broad limits established by Congress and the President. Actions taken by the Fed are important to the success of government economic policy, yet there is no guarantee that members of the Board of Governors will cooperate with Congress and the President in implementing economic plans. Some political leaders have suggested that the powers of the Fed's Board of Governors should be limited, or that they should be made responsible to the President.

Supporters of controlling the Fed believe such a policy would assure the country of a unified economic policy. Some argue that it is wrong for people with so much power not to be elected by the people.

Other people are against the plan because it would allow the Fed's powers to be used for political reasons instead of the good of our economic system. They argue that politicians would be too slow to act, that decisions would be made to help people get elected, and that politicians would probably put too much

money into circulation to keep interest rates low and make voters happy. There is a fear that this would lead to inflation.

How would putting the Fed under the control of the President affect you or your friends? What would be good or bad about this idea?

Arguments in Favor of the Idea

1. It would lead to a more unified government economic policy.
2. It would give voters a choice in who carried out monetary policy.
3. It would prevent the Board of Governors from making important decisions with no checks.

Arguments Against the Idea

1. It would make monetary policy subject to political pressure.
2. It would make monetary policy very slow to react to change.
3. It could lead to more money being put into circulation and result in inflation.

What Do You Think?

Consider the arguments for and against this idea. Do you believe it is a good idea? Do you feel politicians would be able to regulate our banking system properly? What might happen if they made mistakes?

Chapter 11 Review

What Have You Learned?

In this chapter you've learned the following important principles of economics:

- Money plays many important roles in our economic system. Money serves as a *medium of exchange*, a *measure of value*, and a *store of value*. To carry out its economic functions, money must be acceptable, divisible, portable, and stable in value.

- The amount of money in circulation is closely related to prices. When more money becomes necessary to buy the same number of goods and services, there will be *inflation*. On the other hand, if the same amount of money is used to buy more products, there will be *deflation*.

- The largest part of spending in this country is done with checks. It is necessary to control checking to control the money supply. When banks loan money, the banking system is *expanding* the money supply. This is accomplished by a series of deposits and loans that pass through checking accounts.

- Money that is withdrawn from accounts and not redeposited, or that is deposited but not loaned out by the bank, reduces the expansion process.

- The *Federal Reserve System* was established in 1913 to oversee the American banking system. It is now administered by a seven-member Board of Governors. These governors set what is known as *monetary policy*. Monetary policy is intended to help keep our economic system from going into a recession or from hav-

ing inflation. It does this by ensuring a reliable banking system and supply of money.

- The *Federal Reserve System* can control the expansion process and the supply of money by adjusting banks' *reserve requirement*, by buying and selling government securities in the open market, or by changing the *discount rate* to affect bank borrowing from the Federal Reserve System. These tools make up the Fed's monetary policy. In recent years the Fed has been hesitant to change the reserve requirement on checking deposits and has relied on *open market operations* most of the time.

- In trying to earn a profit, banks would run in a *pro-cyclical* way if they were able to. In bad times they would find it hard to make as many safe loans. In good times they would make many loans. This would tend to make expansions greater and recessions deeper. The Federal Reserve System takes actions to influence banks to run counter to the business cycle.

- In 1935 the *Federal Deposit Insurance Corporation* was established to insure deposits in our banks. This organization has faced challenges because of increased bank failures in recent years.

- There is often disagreement over the proper role of the Federal Reserve System. Some people feel the Board of Governors has made too many mistakes. Still, it is clear that the Fed has an important function to carry out in our economic system.

Words and Terms

money (p. 292)
fiat money (p. 292)
functions of money (p. 292)
characteristics of money (p. 292)
money supply (p. 294)
inflation (p. 294)
deflation (p. 294)
expansion of money (p. 299)
reserve requirement (p. 299)
pro-cyclical (p. 303)

countercyclical (p. 304)
Federal Deposit Insurance
  Corporation (p. 304)
savings and loan associations
  (p. 305)
Federal Reserve System (p. 307)
discount rate (p. 308)
open market operations (p. 308)
monetary policy (p. 309)

Building Your Vocabulary

On a separate piece of paper, write the vocabulary word or term that best completes each of the following statements.

1. The _____ was established to build trust in the banking system by insuring bank deposits.
2. _____ were institutions that expanded in the 1930s to provide small savers a place to deposit their money and that could offer home loans at low interest rates.
3. An increase in the average price level is called _____.
4. The process that allows banks to increase the amount of money in circulation through checking accounts is called the _____.
5. Economists define _____ as a claim on something of value.
6. The _____ include medium of exchange, measure of value, and store of value.
7. The _____ include acceptability, divisibility, portability, and stability of value.
8. A decrease in the average price level is called _____.
9. Something that is money because a government has said that it is money is called _____.
10. The part of a deposit that a bank is required to keep on hand is called the _____.
11. The interest that a bank must pay when it borrows from the Federal Reserve System is called the _____.
12. The _____ was established in 1913 to oversee banking in the United States.
13. _____ policies make expansions greater and recessions deeper.
14. _____ policies make expansions smaller and recessions less severe.
15. The Federal Reserve carries out _____ to try to maintain a steady supply of money in this country.
16. When the Federal Reserve System buys and sells government securities, it is carrying out _____.
17. The amount of money in circulation is called the _____.

Chapter 11 Review

Understanding Economics

1. Explain why a valuable watch or gold ring would not make good money. Explain what this has to do with the functions of money.
2. Describe what would probably happen to prices if the amount of money in circulation increased by half. Explain why this would happen.
3. If you deposited $100 in a checking account when the reserve requirement was 10 percent, how many dollars would the bank have to keep and how much could it loan out?
4. If the bank loaned this money out (from question 3), describe how it would be expanded through the banking system.
5. What are the two ways that the expansion process can be controlled?
6. Explain why banks would tend to act in a pro-cyclical way if they could.
7. Describe what the Federal Deposit Insurance Corporation does and why it is important to the banking system.
8. Identify the group that makes decisions for the Federal Reserve System.
9. Describe each of the three tools that the Fed has for carrying out monetary policy.

Thinking Critically About Economics

1. Suppose you inherited a piece of land in the country. You want to use it to pay your tuition at school next year. Describe the problems you would have if you couldn't sell the land for money.
2. Draw your own table to show the relationship between the money supply, products for sale, and prices. Use Figure 11–1 to give you ideas, but don't just copy it.
3. Explain how a deposit of $500 in a checking account could be expanded into a total increase in deposits of thousands of dollars.
4. Describe what would happen to the expansion of money if the Federal Reserve System increased the reserve requirement for checking deposits from 10 percent to 12 percent.
5. Explain why the Federal Deposit Insurance Corporation is important to our banking system.
6. Describe what would probably happen if the Federal Reserve System increased the discount rate to 6 percent from 3½ percent.

Consumer Skills Projects

1. Go to various local banks and find out what interest rates they are offering for deposits. Make a large chart that shows these different rates. Show it to your class. Try to think of several reasons that could explain any differences in interest rates. You could do the same project for interest rates on loans.
2. Interview a person who makes loans for a bank. Ask this person about the things a young person could do to establish a good credit rating. Report your findings to your class.

Developing Your Economic Skills

Using Tables to Compare Interest Costs

Skill: This lesson will show you how to use two types of tables to evaluate the cost of borrowing money. To complete this lesson you'll follow these steps:

1. Study the two tables and identify specific values on each.
2. Consider why the two tables could lead people to different decisions.
3. Evaluate the meaning of each table.

Application: How important are interest rates?

Many people who borrow money are only interested in knowing their monthly payments. They ignore the interest rate and the total interest cost of their loan. This may be a costly mistake. Low monthly payments can hide high interest costs when loans are spread out over many years. The tables below demonstrate this fact.

The first table lists the term of the loan (the number of years over which it must be paid off) on the left side and various interest rates across its top, and shows the monthly payment for each possible combination. The second table is set up the same way, but in-

Interest Cost of a $1,000 Loan at Different Rates, Over Different Terms

Term of Loan (in years)	Interest Rate/Monthly Payment		
	12%	14%	16%
1	$88.85	$89.79	$90.73
2	$47.07	$48.01	$48.96
3	$33.21	$34.18	$35.16
4	$26.33	$27.33	$28.34
5	$22.24	$23.27	$24.32

stead of showing the monthly payment, it shows the total interest paid. Loan officers at banks have tables similar to these.

If you looked at the first table without really thinking about what it means, you might conclude that a 3-year loan at 12 percent was more expensive than a 4-year loan at 16 percent. The monthly payment for the 3-year loan is $33.21, while the 4-year loan at a higher interest rate has a payment of only $28.34 (find these values, underlined on the table). Your conclusion would be wrong. The interest expense would be much greater with the higher interest rate loan. The next table demonstrates this fact.

Total Interest Paid at Different Rates

Term of Loan (in years)	Interest Rate		
	12%	14%	16%
1	$ 66.19	$ 77.45	$ 88.77
2	$129.76	$152.31	$175.12
3	$195.71	$230.40	$265.65
4	$264.02	$311.67	$360.33
5	$334.67	$396.10	$459.08

This table shows you that the total interest you would pay on the 4-year loan at 16 percent would be $360.33, while the 3-year loan at 12 percent would cost only $195.71.

Which of the two tables do you believe provides more important and useful information?

Practice: A customer wants to borrow $1,000 for 2 years with monthly payments of $47.07. Determine how much more interest the lender could earn by offering a lower monthly payment of only $27.33 on a $1,000 loan at 14% interest for 4 years. If you were the customer, would you accept the offer?

Government Decisions and Economic Success

Objectives

In the sections of this chapter, you will learn:

A

how the government uses *fiscal policy* to attempt to promote employment, production, and purchasing power, and how Classical economists and Keynesian economists disagree about using fiscal policy;

B

how government price controls and supply-side policies have been used in an attempt to control inflation and unemployment, and why they have met with only limited success;

C

how the ability to regulate our economy is limited by the global nature of our economy; and

D

about programs that are intended to guarantee a minimum level of economic security for all Americans.

Introduction

The Declaration of Independence states that governments are created to secure the rights of "life, liberty and the pursuit of happiness." We believe that our government exists to serve the people. Among other things, our government assures us an opportunity to earn a decent living. To carry out this responsibility the government must be involved in our economic system.

The Laissez-Faire System

In the early days of the United States, the government played a relatively small part in the economic system. The role of the government was limited to protecting property rights, making sure that contracts were carried out, establishing a fair civil code (laws dealing with business transactions), and enforcing general rules for how businesses could operate. In general, the government stayed out of the everyday affairs of individual firms. There was a **laissez-faire** economic policy. This means that the government tried to let the economic system run on its own with as little government involvement as possible.

In a laissez-faire economy (also known as a *free-market* economy) the forces of demand and supply are allowed to make the basic economic decisions of *what, how,* and *for whom.* People who favored this type of

In the early days of the United States, the government played a very limited role and attempted to let the economy operate on its own. This was known as a laissez-faire, or free-market economy. But over the years, as businesses and society have become more complex, it has been necessary for the government to play a greater role in the economic system.

economy were called **Classical economists.** The Classical theory said the economic system would take care of itself and that unnecessary government intervention could only cause problems. Classical economists believed that if the government made too many decisions in the economic system, the result would be inefficient use of the factors of production (land, labor, capital, and entrepreneurship).

The Role of Government

However, over the years it has become necessary for our government to play a greater role in our economic system. Most businesses and products were relatively simple 200 or more years ago.

There were few big monopolies and practically no labor unions. Today we have giant firms that negotiate contracts with powerful unions and sell complex products in monopolistic markets. Individual consumers are no longer able to protect themselves from economic abuse. As our economic system has grown and become more complicated, our government has taken on more responsibilities.

This chapter will discuss problems regarding the role of the government in today's economy. Unlike businesses, the federal government is not run to make a profit. Its purpose is to provide services to the people (you read about some of these services in Chapter 9).

A relatively new service of the government is its attempt to provide economic stability. Because of its immense size and power, the government is able to influence economic conditions in many areas. It can create more jobs by cutting taxes or increasing its spending. It can carry out policies that encourage investment or reduce inflation. And government decisions can increase or decrease our trade with other countries.

Although the government plays a vital role in our economic system, there is often disagreement over how the government can best use its powers. There are several general areas of disagreement concerning government economic policy. One is a lack of agreement over what our economic objectives should be. However, even if we could agree on our objectives, we would still have a second problem. We would have to set priorities—that is, we would have to decide which goals to try to achieve first. It is impossible to deal with all problems at the same time.

Important questions need to be answered. Is it more important to reduce poverty or to increase investment? If unemployment and inflation are both too high, which should we work on first? What is the best trade-off between individual freedom and government protection? It is difficult to set government economic policy until we agree on what we want to achieve.

Another problem is that even if we do agree on our objectives, we still need to choose the policies that can best achieve our goals. Is it better to reduce unemployment by giving a tax cut to businesses or to individuals? Should inflation be fought through increased production or through reduced demand? What effect will attempts to control the size of the federal deficit have on the rest of the economy? There is widespread disagreement over the specific policies that would be most effective in achieving our objectives.

In this chapter you will study the debate over our economic objectives. The basic ideas of several economic theories will be outlined for you. You will learn about what the government tries to do, and why there is so much disagreement over government policies.

Section A   Government Spending and Jobs

This section will discuss the role our government plays in creating jobs for American workers.

My Mother Got a Job with the County

About two years ago my mother lost her job when the shirt factory shut down. There used to be lots of mills and clothing factories in this area, but they were hurt by imported goods. Now most of them are closed.

Mom had supported four kids on her salary. (My father died about the same time my little sister Jessica was born.) We have been through some hard times. For years we lived on welfare in a government low-income housing project. Food stamps helped, but there never seemed to be enough to eat. My mother couldn't take a part-time job. She said it would cost us more in lost benefits than she could earn. We all did what we could. I delivered newspapers and my older sister did babysitting in the evening. Mom wouldn't let us quit school to find work.

Finally last month things began to look up. The government has set up a program to retrain workers. My mother knows how to type and keep records. She got a job working for the county in the retraining program. She helps people fill out applications and keeps files up to date. They are teaching her how to prepare reports for the federal government. She earns almost as much now as she did when she worked in the factory, and she likes her work. Mom isn't worried about being unemployed any more. She is learning skills that will help her get a better job in the future.

We've been lucky, but I wonder about all the other local people who are out of work. They are supposed to be training for new jobs, but there aren't any jobs around here for them to take. I think most of them will have to move if their training is going to do them any good. Many people won't want to do that. They have families, friends, and homes here. I think most of them will stay and remain unemployed.

Our representative visited town last week to talk about getting "high-tech" firms to move into the old mill buildings. He said something about giving tax breaks to encourage them to move here. That sounds good, but I doubt it would help people who live here now. We don't have "high-tech" skills. The businesses would probably bring people in from outside for most of the jobs. Any work we could get would probably pay minimum wage.

My social studies teacher said there was a tax cut a few years ago. It was supposed to get the economy moving again. Last year my family's income was almost nothing. We paid no income tax at all. Reducing taxes did not help us very much.

There is a debate in Congress over ways to balance the federal budget. They talk about increasing taxes or cutting aid for the poor. One suggestion was to get rid of the program that pays for my mother's job. If they cut her job, we might have to go back on welfare. The government would end up supporting us, but they would get no work from my mother in return. It desn't sound like a very efficient way to save money to me.

Theories of Government Involvement in the Economy

The **Employment Act of 1946** stated that it is the responsibility of the government to promote employment, production, and purchasing power. This law said the government should take actions that would help people find work. The law stopped short of guaranteeing everyone a job, but it did say the government should help achieve full employment.

Although full employment is a goal that most people could agree with, there are many different ideas about what the best way is to achieve it. In the preceding story you saw several examples of things the government can do to try to affect the economy and increase employment. There is disagreement over which actions the government should take. There has also been disagreement over how much government involvement there should be. Two important schools of thought have been the *Classical theory* and the *Keynesian theory*.

The Classical Theory

Before the Great Depression of the 1930s, most economists thought that the economy did not require government involvement. **John Baptiste Say,** a Classical economist who wrote in the early 1800s, believed that a market economic system would naturally have full employment. He suggested that if there was a recession, the market would quickly bring it to an end by lowering prices, interest rates, and wages. He said that unemployed workers would accept lower wages, which would encourage employers to hire them. Banks would reduce interest rates to encourage borrowing, and firms would lower their prices so they could sell their products. The result would be that the market, through the forces of demand and supply, would adjust the economy and bring the recession to an end. Classical economists believed there was no need for government intervention in the economy. But when the Great Depression did not automatically

John Baptiste Say (top left), a Classical economist, believed that the economy worked best without government involvement.

When the Great Depression failed to come to an end of its own accord, attention focused on the theories of John Maynard Keynes (top right). Keynes said that capitalist market economies are not self-regulating. He believed the government should take the responsibility for seeing that there is full employment and economic stability. Keynes said that governments could encourage spending and increase employment in a recession by having a deficit budget; that is, by spending more than it took in from tax revenues.

come to an end, it became clear that other theories would have to be found to explain how the economy worked.

The Keynesian Theory

An alternative theory was suggested by an English economist, **John Maynard Keynes.** Keynes believed that economic activity and jobs depend on the rate of *spending* in the economy. Keynes said that there were three types of spending—spending by *people* (for personal consumption), spending by *businesses* (for investment), and spending by the *government* (to provide goods and services for the people). In a recession, people and businesses become worried and cut back on consumer spending and investment. This results in lower sales, unemployment, and lower production.

Increased government spending for services is one example of Keynesian policies to end a recession. If government spending increases and taxes stay the same, more money is introduced into the economy. An alternative Keynesian approach is lowering taxes without decreasing the current level of spending. Either policy could cause a budget deficit.

Keynes believed that in a recession, the third spending group (the government) should try to make up for the decreased spending from consumers and businesses. The government should help the market along by spending more than it took in from tax revenues. This could be accomplished in two ways. The government could cut taxes without changing its spending. This would give households more disposable income (income after taxes) to increase their spending. An alternative would be for the government to increase its own spending without changing taxes. For example, building roads or providing more services would create more jobs. It would also be possible for the government to do some of each of these policies.

If the economy was expanding too rapidly, Keynes believed the government should take the opposite actions and increase taxes and/or reduce its own spending. This would decrease total spending and reduce the possibility of having inflation.

According to Keynes, ensuring full employment would require continual adjustment of government spending and taxing to achieve the correct level of total spending. This amount of spending would create enough jobs for everyone who wants to work.

During the past several decades, Keynesian economic policy has been used in varying degrees by the federal government. Presidents Kennedy and Johnson, in particular, relied on Keynesian ideas to "fine tune" the economy.

The types of products needed and produced in our society have changed dramatically in recent years. In a number of cases, the government has stepped in to help businesses and workers whose livelihoods were threatened by changes in technology. Special tax breaks for businesses, and training programs for workers, have allowed some factories that were closed to reopen and pro-duce in high-tech fields.

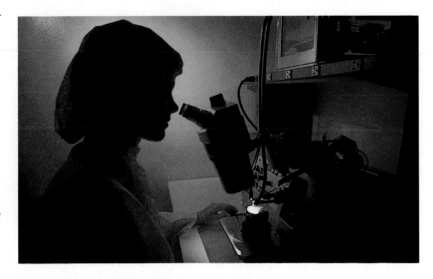

Fiscal Policy

Economists call the federal government's attempt to stabilize the economy through taxing and government spending **fiscal policy**. Fiscal policy involves planning a budget that has either surpluses or deficits that are intended to maintain a steady level of total spending in the economy. Fiscal policy can be either *discretionary* or *automatic*.

Discretionary fiscal policy is policy that someone must *choose* to implement. It requires an action by either the Congress and the President, or by an agency of the government, to take effect. For example, in 1964 there was a tax cut to encourage economic expansion. Four years later, in 1968, there was a tax increase to reduce inflation. In 1992 the economy was in a period of slow growth. Candidates in the 1992 presidential campaign debated whether or not to lower taxes to encourage investment.

Individual government departments have the ability to either speed up or slow down their spending. An advantage of discretionary fiscal policy is the fact that it can be targeted to specific areas of the country that have special problems. For example, in the 1960s large amounts of money were spent in depressed areas in the eastern part of our nation. In the early 1980s, President Reagan frequently suggested that "urban development zones" be identified in depressed areas of our cities. His plan called for re-duced taxes and special aid for firms that moved into or ex-panded in such areas.

Fiscal policy that reacts automatically (referred to as **automatic stabilization**) is different from discretionary fiscal policy in that it does not require new or special action to go into effect. It reacts automatically when the economy changes. Several examples of automatic stabilization are welfare, unemployment compensation, and income taxes. To see how automatic stabilization works, consider what happens to these examples in a recession.

When the economy goes into a recession, additional people automatically become eligible for government transfer programs. As a result, government expenditures to support welfare and unemployment compensation automatically increase. Neither Congress, the President, nor any government agency has to make a new decision in order for this to happen. This automatic increase in expenditures injects more money into the economy.

At the same time, people who become unemployed in a recession would pay less income tax. This results from people falling into lower tax brackets as well as from people paying taxes on lower incomes. This also puts more money into the economy. When the economy recovers, the opposite events would take place, automatically reducing the amount of money going into the economy. Generally, automatic stabilization goes into effect much more rapidly than discretionary fiscal policy. On the other hand, it is more difficult to target specific problems with automatic stabilization.

Classical economists would say that the free market, through changing wages, prices, and interest rates, is all the automatic policy that is needed. Keynesian economists answer that the market needs help from the government because it works too slowly.

Weaknesses in Keynesian Theory

There are several limitations on the effectiveness of Keynesian economic policy. One problem is the difficulty the government has in predicting what the economy is going to do in the future. It is hard to formulate policies to deal with problems if you don't know what the problems will be.

Another limitation on Keynesian policy is that discretionary policy—an important tool in the Keynesian approach—takes a long time to put into effect. Some economists believe that the "lags" between the beginning of a problem and the government's taking action are so long that we would be better off if the government did not try to use discretionary fiscal policy.

Discretionary policy may not only be slow, it may also be misguided. In the Personal Narrative for this section, the government was training workers for jobs that did not exist in their local area. The young man believed most of the workers being trained would have to move to find jobs. It is also possible for jobs to be brought to an area which has few qualified workers. The tax breaks for "high-tech" firms supported by the member of Congress in the narrative would be an example of this problem. Spending money to create jobs does not guarantee that the money will be well spent.

A third problem is the fact that Keynesian policy cannot fight both inflation and unemployment at the same time. Keynes believed that the government should deal with inflation by cutting spending and/or increasing taxes.* He said it should fight unemployment by increasing government spending and/or cutting taxes. The government can't follow both of these policies at the same time.

Finally, there is the problem called the "**crowding-out effect**." This idea states that government borrowing to support Keynesian policy in a recession could force interest rates up. Higher interest rates would discourage consumers and businesses from borrowing and spending. Therefore, extra government spending could cause lower private spending, so that total spending might not change much. Government borrowing could crowd consumers and businesses out of the credit market.

The crowding-out effect can be seen in Figure 12-1. Suppose that the demand curve, D^1, is for money that people, businesses, and the government want to borrow. The supply curve, S, is for money that is available to be loaned. If the government decided to borrow $100 billion more, D^1 would shift to the right to D^2. This would result in the interest rate (vertical axis) at the equilibrium point going from 8 to 10 percent. The higher interest rate would discourage people and businesses from borrowing and spending. Although the government increased its borrowing by $100 billion, the amount of money loaned (the horizontal axis) would go up by only $50 billion, from $150 to $200 billion. This would happen because higher interest rates would cause people and businesses not to borrow and spend $50 billion that they otherwise would have.

---

*It is also possible to use monetary policy to encourage investment and spending, by increasing the money supply and causing interest rates to decrease. See Section C of Chapter 10.

Figure 12-1 *Private and Public Demand and Supply for Loanable Funds*

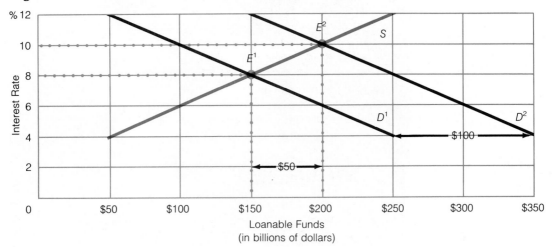

In spite of such problems, there are many economists (called *neo-Keynesians*) and politicians who believe in a modified Keynesian approach as a basis for the best government economic policy.

Keynes supported the idea of helping unemployed people through government job programs. One example of such a program was the Comprehensive Employment and Training Act of 1973 (CETA). This law was enacted to provide training and job opportunities for America's "hard-core" unemployed. The program grew from a budget of just over $2 billion in 1974 to almost $12 billion in 1979. The program was specifically directed to help "offenders (of the law), persons of limited English language proficiency, handicapped, women, single parents, displaced homemakers, youths, older workers and people who lack education." At its peak, CETA provided 725,000 public service jobs.

On the other hand, many people believe that CETA wasted a great deal of the people's money. The dropout rate from many CETA training programs ranged up to 50 percent. Frequently people were trained for jobs that did not exist. One example of this problem involved 2,000 classroom aides who completed CETA training in 1976. Of this group, only about half found jobs in the fields they had been trained for.

Many local governments found that they could pay for their ordinary employees out of CETA funds. In 1979, New York City paid for 20,000 of its 200,000 municipal employees through the

Keynes supported the idea of government spending to provide training and job opportunities for the unemployed. The CETA programs of the 1970s were an example of this, as were public works programs of the 1930s.

program. Cleveland, Washington, D.C., Detroit, Miami, and many other cities did the same. Relatively few of the nation's poorest people were helped through the program.

CETA was gradually eliminated under the Reagan administration.

■ *Self-Check*

1. What did Classical economists, like John Baptiste Say, believe would happen when there was a recession?
2. What did John Maynard Keynes believe the government should do if people and businesses reduced spending in a recession?
3. What is the difference between automatic and discretionary fiscal policy?
4. Why do some economists believe that "lags" make discretionary fiscal policy ineffective?

■ *Applying What You Have Learned*

The young man's mother in the Personal Narrative worked for a government-sponsored job training program. Such a program would be created through discretionary fiscal policy. Identify and describe two things the program did that were good for the people of her community. Then, identify and describe two specific weaknesses in the program.

PROFILE

*John Maynard
Keynes*
(1883–1946)

Most economists would rate John Maynard Keynes as the most influential contributor to economic theory in the twentieth century. Born in England and educated at Cambridge, Keynes had a wide variety of famous friends in music, literature, the dance, and government. He worked for his government in several ways including the settling of England's debts with France. He became very wealthy by trading currencies on the foreign exchange market and spent many years editing the *Economic Journal*.

Keynes used his knowledge of economics to help his government, his college, and himself. He developed many important ideas concerning macroeconomic theory, which he explained in his book, *The General Theory of Employment, Interest, and Money*. This book was published in 1936 during the Great Depression. It provided an explanation of what had caused the Depression and proposals for bringing it to an end.

Keynes believed that the forces of demand and supply in the market would not always bring about full employment and stable prices. He said that total spending of consumers, business investment, and government spending might not produce enough total demand to provide jobs for everyone who wanted to work. Government could regulate total spending through its taxes and spending. By creating a budget deficit, it could stimulate the economy to provide more jobs in a recession. In times of inflation, the government could reduce total spending by having a budget surplus. Keynesian policy was most successfully used in the first half of the 1960s, when taxes were cut for the purpose of increasing jobs.

Although John Maynard Keynes called for limited government action to help market forces create full employment, he did not believe in central planning.

Keynes led a full life. He accomplished most of his personal objectives, helped his government, and gave the world a better understanding of economics.

Section B Government Policies and Inflation

This section will discuss government policies intended to limit inflation.

Why Don't They Do Something About Prices?

My grandmother talks about the "good old days." She remembers when bread cost 10 cents a loaf and eggs were 20 cents a dozen. She believes that life was better then. Maybe she's right. Prices certainly were lower.

Prices are a real concern for Grandma. She lives on Social Security and a small pension. Social Security payments have increased over the years, but her pension is the same as it was ten years ago. Rent for her apartment cost $95 a month when she first moved in. Now it's $380 and she thinks they are going to raise it again next year.

Grandma can't drive anymore, so she takes the bus. She likes to go downtown to shop or see a show. She can get into senior citizen bargain matinees for $2.00, where she meets her "boyfriend." Often they go out for something to eat after the show. The city gave Grandma a special card so she can ride the bus for half price. Even with the discount, she thinks about the 1950s when she took the bus to work for a dime. Grandma doesn't think older people should have to pay the higher prices.

Grandma isn't the only person who is affected by higher prices. I'm going to attend a junior college about 20 miles from here next year. The school sent me a letter saying the tuition had been raised by $200 a semester. I've been told to expect to spend about $200 to $250 on books. My father was not happy to hear this news.

I needed to buy a car to get back and forth to school. My father and I went to look at new cars. I thought he was going to have a heart attack right there in the showroom. It's practically impossible to buy a new car for less than $9,000. I had to listen to him talk about his first car that cost less than $2,000 in 1966. We finally agreed on a small used car for $4,500. I hope nothing goes wrong with it.

When we got home from buying my car, Dad opened the mail. There was a letter from the school district, explaining why our school taxes had to go up 12 percent this year. It was not a good day for my father. I wish the government would do something about inflation.

Controlling Inflation Through Fiscal Policy

The federal government does take steps to try to control inflation. These steps can be part of the fiscal policy that you learned about in Section A of this chapter. Keynes believed that the government could limit inflation by reducing demand. He said that higher taxes, or reduced government spending, or any combination of the two that would result in a government budget surplus, could reduce the total demand for goods and services. He believed this would lead to a lower rate of inflation or even to stable prices. Most economists agree that in cases of demand-pull inflation, such a policy should succeed in reducing price increases (see Chapter 10). However, it would not be effective against cost-push inflation.

In cost-push inflation, prices go up because of higher costs of production. This type of inflation is caused by increases in the cost of labor or raw materials, not by increased demands. Steps to reduce demand probably will not eliminate this type of inflation, but they are likely to cause more unemployment. What can the government do to reduce cost-push inflation?

Price Controls

On a number of occasions the government has tried to reduce inflation by regulating prices. In World Wars I and II there were price controls and rationing of many products. A more recent example came between 1971 and 1974, when the federal government attempted to control inflation through price and wage regulation.

On August 15, 1971, President Nixon announced a 90-day price and wage freeze. During this time it was against the law to increase either prices or wages for any product other than agricultural production. At the end of the 90 days, a program called **Phase II** was established. Its purpose was to keep price and wage increases within reasonable levels. An organization known as the "Cost-of-Living Council" was given the job of making sure that increases were not excessive. Although this program lasted for more than a year, its success was questioned by many economists. Some people felt it gave the government too much power. It was gradually eliminated between 1972 and 1974.

Any time the government sets an artificially low price for a product, it increases the possibility of a shortage of that product. The graph in Figure 12–2 demonstrates this problem. When the

Figure 12-2 *Effects of Price Regulation on Production*

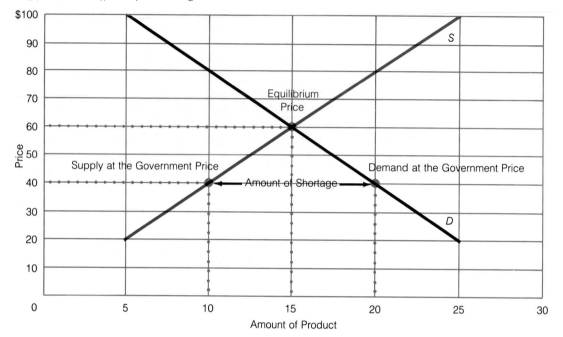

This graph shows the demand and supply curves for a product. These curves intersect at a point of equilibrium that indicates a price of $60 and a quantity of 15. If the government decided that $40 was the highest price a firm could charge, producers would be discouraged from making any more than 10 units of the item. However, the lower price would cause customers to want to buy 20 units. The result would be a shortage of the product, equal to the difference between the demand (20 units) and the supply (10 units).

government set the maximum price below the equilibrium price, customers demanded more items than producers were willing to supply. The result of government price control was a shortage of the product.

In general, since the 1970s there has been less pressure on the government to regulate prices. Most economists seem to doubt that such plans work very well.

A Policy for Unemployment and Inflation?

It is difficult for either monetary policy or fiscal policy to deal with the twin problems of inflation and unemployment at the same time. (You learned about monetary policy in Section D of Chapter 11.) The government cannot raise taxes to fight inflation

In 1971, President Nixon announced a 90-day price and wage freeze. The freeze was followed by Phase II, during which wage and price increases were restricted. Phase II lasted more than a year, and it may have contributed to a reduced rate of inflation in 1972. However, many people felt the system was unfair, that it did not allow the market system to operate efficiently, and that it would eventually result in shortages and the misallocation of resources. Phase II was eliminated in January of 1973.

and at the same time lower taxes to fight unemployment. Nor can the Federal Reserve System take steps to increase interest rates to fight inflation at the same time it is lowering interest rates to fight unemployment. Is there a way to deal with these two problems at the same time? In the 1980s a group of people who were known as "supply-side economists" thought they had found the answer.

Supply-side economics says that the best way to fight unemployment combined with inflation is to reduce the costs of production. The reasoning is that if it costs businesses less to produce their products, they will not need to raise prices (less inflation) and they will sell more products. Selling more products, they will need more workers to make more goods and services (less unemployment). Supply-side economists argue that the objective of government policy should be to help businesses reduce their costs and therefore increase **productivity.** Productivity is a measure of the value of products that can be created from a quantity of factors of production. When a firm becomes more efficient, its productivity improves and its costs of production are lowered. An improvement in productivity should increase the supply of products manufactured and offered for sale. This is why people are called supply-side economists.

In recent years, many American businesses have invested in new, more efficient machinery. As a result, many workers who lack the training to run new machines have lost their jobs. These investments have caused a dilemma for the American economy. We need to use new technology to keep our businesses competitive in a world economy. However, in doing this, we may be creating a class of people who cannot keep their old jobs and are not qualified for the new ones being created.

Although there were a number of ways that supply-side economists thought the government could help businesses reduce costs of production, the most important method was to encourage investment in new, more efficient technology. Supply-side economists reasoned that if businesses bought more efficient machines they could reduce their labor costs and their consumption of energy, therefore becoming more productive. Many of the policies of the Reagan administration from 1981 to 1989 were basically supply-side economics.

From 1981 through 1983 federal income tax rates were reduced by 25 percent. One reason for this reduction was to encourage people to work harder and produce more because they would be able to keep a larger part of the money they earned. At the same time businesses were allowed to reduce their taxes if they bought new machinery. People were encouraged to invest when taxes were reduced for capital gains. Provisions were made that allowed people to put off paying taxes for money they saved in special individual retirement accounts (IRAs). All of these changes were intended to increase investment and therefore productivity.

There is little evidence that these policies actually resulted in much greater investment or productivity. They were criticized because they provided more benefits to people who were wealthy than those who were not. For these and other reasons, most of the supply-side policies passed in the early 1980s were eliminated when federal tax laws were reformed in 1986.

Table 12–1
Measurements of Economic Growth, 1981–1986

Year	GDP in billions of constant (1982) dollars	Gross Private Saving (billions of dollars)	Percent of GDP saved
1981	$3,249	$550.5	16.0%
1982	$3,166	$557.1	17.6%
1983	$3,279	$592.2	18.1%
1984	$3,501	$673.5	19.2%
1985	$3,619	$665.3	18.4%
1986	$3,722	$681.6	18.3%

Source: *Statistical Abstract of the United States*, 1989.

Some people believed that the government had not passed laws that would make supply-side theories work. One of President Clinton's priorities was tax credits for industries that invested in new technologies—a plan that served the goal of supply-side economics.

■ *Self-Check*

1. Do most economists feel fiscal policy would be more effective in controlling demand-pull or cost-push inflation?
2. What problem may result from government price controls?
3. What do supply-side economists believe must be done to fight inflation and unemployment at the same time?

■ *Applying What You Have Learned*

In the Personal Narrative, "Grandma" thinks older people shouldn't have to pay higher prices. Suppose the government passed a law that made it illegal to charge people over 65 higher prices. Describe three different problems that would result.

Section C   Government Policy in a Global Economy

This section will introduce the effect of the global economy on the financial policies of individual nations.

Personal Narrative

When Iraq Invaded Kuwait I Lost My Job

In 1990 I was 19 years old and had a job making plastic counter tops that were used in new homes. My wage rate was more than $11 an hour. My employer gave me health insurance and other benefits. I borrowed $14,000 to buy a new car and was planning a skiing trip to Colorado in the coming winter. Everything looked fine to me. I could never have dreamed the leader of Iraq, Saddam Hussein, could do anything that would matter much to me. I was wrong.

After Saddam's forces invaded Kuwait on August 4th, the price of oil shot up from about $17 a barrel to nearly $30 in only a few weeks. Oil was the basic raw material that was used to make the plastic for our counter tops. Only a few weeks after the invasion, my employer had to pay almost twice as much for the plastic we used. He raised the price of our products 20 percent and sales began to fall. But the problem was larger than that. Lots of people who had been thinking of buying homes got worried about the war in the Middle East and put off making any purchases. Many new housing developments were stopped and others slowed down. With fewer homes being built there was less demand for our products. Our sales fell almost 50 percent.

After the invasion, President Bush sent American soldiers to Saudi Arabia and other countries as part of the U.N. forces. There was talk of a war that would go on for months or even years. Estimates of its costs were as high as several hundred billion dollars. At the time I paid little attention to these events. I put in my time on the job and took long drives in the country. The only thing I noticed was that the price of gasoline was about 25 cents a gallon higher. Then I got my pink slip.

My employer laid off more than 40 percent of the factory's workers. I received a letter with my pink slip that explained why the layoffs were necessary, but it didn't make me feel any better. Without a job, I couldn't make the payments on my car. I had to sell it to pay off the loan. Then I started taking the bus to look for a new job. Eventually, I found one as a shoe salesperson, but I only earned $7 an hour. I bought a used car for $4,000 and forgot about my plans for a trip to Colorado.

I never did get called back to the factory. The managers bought new equipment from a company in France that required fewer workers, and they laid off even more employees. I still sell shoes for a living. I enjoy the work, but I feel poor. The government spent a lot of time and money protecting Kuwait. I wonder why the government doesn't do more to help people like me.

What the Government Can't Do

The individual in the story above wonders why the government did not prevent or solve the economic problems that resulted from the invasion of Kuwait in 1990. The answer is, once the invasion began there was very little that the government could have done to help. The United States is part of a global economy. Events that take place in other parts of the world often impact the American economy. There are limits to what the government can do with its economic policies to prevent these events from affecting Americans. For example, in 1990 Saddam Hussein did not care what interest rates were in the United States, or whether the U.S. government's taxes or spending changed. His invasion of neighboring Kuwait and the resulting economic events would have taken place no matter what internal economic policies the U.S. government had. With the invasion, there was nothing our government could have done to stop the price of crude oil in world markets from increasing. The effects of the price increase were dramatic in the United States because of our dependence on foreign oil. As long as the United States imports more than half of the oil we use, we must pay the world's prices.

Similar events had happened in the 1970s when tension and wars in the Middle East affected oil supplies. Trouble in the Middle East caused shortages of imported oil in the United States. This drove up prices for gasoline and most consumer goods, affecting the whole American economy. There is no reason to believe that these types of events will not take place in the future, with the same results. One cost of living in a global economy is the risk of experiencing economic problems that are beyond our control.

The Reduced Power of the Federal Reserve

Thirty years ago interest rates in the United States were largely determined by actions of the Federal Reserve System. This is much less true today. Our interest rates are more likely to be affected by the rates of other nations. This is because the United States government finances part of the federal deficit by borrowing funds from other nations. It does this by selling bonds. In the 1980s and 1990s the United States government and

U.S. businesses sold more that $1 trillion worth of bonds to people in other countries. To attract foreign investors the United States must pay interest rates that are at least as high as those offered in other countries. We cannot expect German or Japanese investors to buy United States bonds if our bonds pay less than those sold in Germany or Japan. Therefore, when interest rates go up in Germany or Japan, they are likely to increase in the United States as well.

Many economists believe that the Fed has less power over the United States economy than it had in the past. This is in part the result of global influences on the United States economy. An example of the effect of foreign interest rates on the United States rates happened in 1990. That year the Fed took steps to try to force interest rates down in the United States. However, interest rates were going up in other nations at that time. As a result, interest rates went up in the United States too, despite the actions of the Fed.

Another reason that the Fed may exercise less control over interest rates is the attitudes of its own board members. In the early 1990s, the Fed concluded that it was not very effective in controlling short-term economic conditions, especially interest rates and unemployment. Instead, the Fed aimed at the long-term objectives of price stability and steady, low interest rates. When the economy is sluggish, rather than trying to stimulate growth quickly through inflationary policies, the Fed may decide to move cautiously. Rather than seeing itself as the cure-all for economic ills, sometimes the Fed tries to avoid being the source of economic disturbances.

Economic Conditions Flow from Nation to Nation

Different economic systems (including that of the United States) are no longer immune from problems that happen in other countries. A good example occurred in October 1987 when the United States stock market crashed, losing about one-third of its value in just several weeks. The fall in the U.S. stock market was mirrored in other stock markets throughout the world. It is difficult to tell which fall started the worldwide slide, but it is clear that when American investors read that the London stock market fell 18 percent, they were influenced to sell their stocks too.

Economic changes in one nation do not always influence every other nation as directly as the above examples. Changes in a small economy such as that of Bolivia may have little impact on the global economy. Changes in the economy of a major power such as the United States are more likely to be felt throughout the world. Sometimes even economists, however, cannot predict the effect that changes in one major economy may have on that of another nation. For example, in the spring of 1992 the American stock market hit a series of all-time highs. At the same time the Tokyo stock market hit a five-year low. Still, Americans worried that the problems in Japan would affect the United States market. At the time, however, foreign investors controlled only 4 percent of the Japanese stock market and only 6 percent of U.S. stocks. Investors realize that as international investing increases the effects of changes in one market will be more likely to cross national boundaries.

Economists continue to study the effect of the global economy on individual nations. In some instances international financial changes clearly have influenced the individual nations' financial markets. In other cases, the connection is not so clear. For example, U.S. interest rates did not rise or fall with foreign rates in 1989. Beginning in 1990, however, U.S. rates did seem to do so. Economists who wanted to find out how closely interest rates in different economies were linked could create a graph showing two nations' interest rate changes over a period of time. The following graph shows U.S. and Japanese interest rates over an 18-month period.

Figure 12–3 *Interest Rates of United States and Japan, 1989–1990*

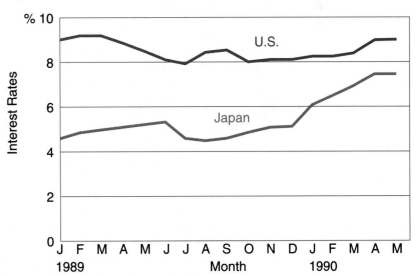

The graph on the previous page shows that Japanese and United States interest rates did not move in the same direction during most of 1989. Beginning in the first half of 1990, they did move in the same direction. To provide a clearer answer as to how interest rates in one nation's economy affect interest rates in another nation's economy, an economist might track rates in both economies over a longer period.

The International Economy

Many of the reasons that the United States economy is becoming more international in nature will be discussed in Chapter 13. Two important aspects of the global economy are international trade and the growth of multinational corporations. There are important benefits that the United States receives from international trade as well as from having multinational corporations. There are also costs that we must pay. As we have learned in this chapter, one of the costs of playing a major role in the international economy may be the loss of some of our ability to control our own economic climate.

■ *Self-Check*

1. Why can't the U.S. government control the price of oil sold in the United States?
2. Why should Americans care if interest rates go up in Germany or Japan?
3. How may an American investor be affected by a fall in the value of stock on the London market?
4. What are two reasons why the Fed may have less power over the United States economy than it has had in the past?

■ *Applying What You Have Learned*

Many people tend to think of the negative things that happen as a result of the global nature of our economy. Perhaps this is because negative news, being more dramatic, captures more headlines. When a large factory closes down, it is big news. If several small new firms each hire 50 people, it is not such big news. Can you find positive news related to the global nature of our economy? Search through newspapers and magazines to find examples of international events that have helped American consumers or workers. Summarize each news article by writing a positive statement about its effect on the United States economy.

Section D Government Social Programs

This section will discuss the role of the government in providing a minimum standard of living for all Americans.

Personal Narrative

Dignity at the City Mission

I belong to a youth group at my church. One of the projects we work on is taking food to the poor. Each Saturday morning we all get together in the church kitchen and cook. We don't make anything fancy, but we make well-balanced meals. We take some of the food to shut-ins, and the rest goes to the city mission. I usually ride in the van to the mission.

I live in the suburbs. My family seems to have enough money to take care of our needs. The first time I went to the mission I got a real education. I knew that there were poor people, but I didn't know any myself. I thought only drunks or drug addicts were poor. So far as I was concerned, their poverty was their own fault because of the way they lived. I found that although I was right in some cases, for most poor people I was wrong.

Many of the poor people at the mission are mentally or emotionally disabled. They are people who would have been in an institution 30 years ago. The government decided that they should be returned to the community, but there were few programs set up to help them after they were released. Many of them are unable to care for themselves. They go to the mission because they have nowhere else to go.

Another large group at the mission is made up of the elderly. They come for a free meal because they can't afford to feed themselves. Many receive welfare and use food stamps, but they still can't afford enough food. They have a particularly hard time in the winter when heating bills are high. They need to be warm, but often must live in old places that are not well insulated. Some of them use up almost all their income on their heating bills.

I was told that in the last few years entire families have started coming to the mission. In most cases the parents of these families have been out of work for months. They have run out of unemployment compensation benefits. Often they have no place else to go. I met one family that slept in their car. It's true that many of these people are not well educated, but they want a chance in life just as much as anyone else.

Each Saturday I help serve over 500 people. They are always polite and say, "Thank you." It makes me feel kind of strange. I have

never done anything to earn my standard of living. I live well
because my father has a good job. I wonder what my life would have
been like if I had been born in a poor family. When I'm at the mission
I know that in a few hours I will be home with plenty to eat. But these
people will still be at the mission with nowhere to go. I wonder why
the government doesn't do more to help them.

Searching for Security

The **Social Security Act** of 1935 started the federal government
on the road toward helping the nation's poor. This law included
the foundations for today's Social Security program, unemployment insurance, and welfare. Although these programs have
been expanded over the years, many of their basic concepts still
come from the original Act.

Social Security covers about 90 percent of the workers in the
United States. The only major group that is excluded are federal
government workers who were hired before 1984 and some state
government employees. These workers are covered by other retirement programs.

Among the important programs that stem from the Social Security Act are *retirement benefits* (including Medicare), *unemployment insurance*, and *welfare*.

Retirement Benefits

To be eligible for retirement benefits under the federal program, an employee must have paid into the system through a
withholding tax over a number of years. Employee withholding
is matched by employers. Self-employed people must make their
own payments into the system at a higher rate than employees
because their payments are not matched. People with low incomes pay a greater percentage of their income than the wealthy.
However, social security benefits are more important to people
with low incomes. As the system exists today, people who live
for a reasonable length of time after they retire will receive more
from the system than they paid in. Since 1972, benefits have been
indexed—that is, adjusted upward to keep pace with rising inflation. A 1965 amendment to the Social Security Act created the
Medicare program. Medicare provides basic medical insurance to
retired people in the Social Security program.

It is often pointed out that it is difficult to live on Social Security benefits. There is little doubt that this is true. However,

Although the Social Security system was established only to supplement private savings, many Americans rely on this program for all or most of their support. Some elderly people may not have saved for their retirement through lack of planning. Others may not have earned enough income to save. For whatever reason, society is now faced with the responsibility of caring for a growing number of people who are not financially able to support themselves.

the original intent of the law was to supplement private savings, not to provide total retirement needs. People are still expected to save for their own retirement.

The trend toward smaller families and longer life has put financial pressure on the Social Security system. In the future we will have more beneficiaries and fewer employed people who will work to pay the bills. It is probable that either increased taxes or decreased benefits will become necessary in the future.

Unemployment Insurance

The Social Security Act provided a federal mechanism to help states set up unemployment compensation programs, but each state has its own program. Therefore, programs and benefits vary widely from one state to another. All benefits are paid for by taxing employers. There is a federal minimum tax of 3.9 percent on wages paid, but states can tax firms at higher rates. States that tax more are able to pay greater benefits. Recipients are paid up to half of their former weekly earnings for as long as 26 weeks. In 1989 the average weekly benefit for the nation was $152. The lowest payments were in Louisiana, with an average of $105. The highest were in Massachusetts, which paid a weekly average of $212.

The inequality in payments and taxes in different states may cause both firms and workers to move from one state to another. Businesses might move to low-tax states, while workers might migrate to states with higher benefits. It is clear that there is inequality in the burden and benefits of the unemployment insurance program.

Welfare

Millions of Americans receive unemployment compensation, but even more are given some form of welfare. In 1989, roughly 11 million Americans received cash assistance through the welfare system. More than two-thirds of these individuals benefited from Aid to Families With Dependent Children **(AFDC)**. Other groups to receive benefits were the aged, disabled, and the blind.

Welfare programs, like unemployment insurance, are set up by each individual state. Welfare benefits vary from state to state. In 1989 the benefit for an average family in Mississippi was just over $1,400 a year, while a California family received over $7,400. Again, there are many questions of fairness and equity in the nation's welfare system. Table 12–3 shows the differences in payments among states.

Although there is aid available to the nation's poor, there is serious doubt about whether the welfare system is run efficiently or if its benefits are distributed equitably. There are many states where the poor have to eat in city missions or other private establishments because their aid from the government will not support them at even a minimum standard of living.

Table 12-3
Average Aid to Families with Dependent Children, 1989

State	Average Payment per Month	Total Recipients
California	$620	1,833,000
Connecticut	$534	117,000
New York	$530	964,000
Rhode Island	$483	44,000
Ohio	$314	623,000
West Virginia	$253	109,000
South Carolina	$208	105,000
Texas	$168	581,000
Mississippi	$118	178,000
Alabama	$114	130,000

Source: *Statistical Abstract of the United States,* 1991.

This table shows the average aid paid to families with dependent children in various states. What factors might explain the differences in aid among states?

Millions of children are supported on welfare. Some people worry that children who have grown up in families that depend on welfare will come to accept it as a way of life. They argue that such children may lack self-respect and a belief in their ability to succeed. Others feel that children who have lived on welfare will desire better things for themselves and be willing to work for them. Do you believe that being raised in a family that depends on welfare would change a child's outlook on life?

In recent years there has been a significant increase in people who have been called the "new poor." These are people who have recently become poor because of changes in the economy, social conditions, or government programs. A large part of this group is made up of households headed by women and their children. Some of these households have fallen into poverty because they receive less support from the government. Others are poor because of separation or divorce. Regardless of the reason, there are many new poor in the United States who need help.

In 1985, private help for the nation's poor was organized through the "Hands Across America" program. Almost five and a half million Americans joined hands in one long chain from New York City to Long Beach, California. Each participant collected an average of $35 in pledges, bringing the total raised to almost $200 million. Although this seems like a large sum of money, it is only about $13 for every person living in the United States who is designated as living in poverty by the government.

Private aid of this nature helps, but the problem of hunger is so great that many people doubt there can be a solution without more government support.

■ *Self-Check*

1. What are three social programs that were started under the Social Security Act of 1935?
2. What has the trend toward smaller families and longer lives done to the Social Security system?
3. Name two programs described in this section that are administered by state governments and two that are run by the federal government.

■ *Applying What You Have Learned*

Over 70 percent of the people who receive welfare are either children, aged, or disabled. Another 20 percent have either part-time or full-time jobs. With this fact in mind, answer the questions below. Explain your answers.

a. Would it be useful to make recipients work for their benefits?
b. How much would cuts in welfare benefits affect the number of recipients who are looking for work?
c. What type of people would be most affected by cuts in welfare benefits?

PROFILE

Paul Samuelson
(1915–   )

Do we need to tinker with the market to make the economy run well? Two economists of powerful reputation answer the question differently. Paul Samuelson, the best known and most influential Keynesian economist in the United States, would say, "Yes." Milton Friedman, America's most famous conservative economist, would say, "No."

Paul Samuelson

Paul Samuelson, the first American to win the Nobel Prize in Economics and author of the most successful college economics textbook in this country, believes that it would be a waste of resources to wait for the market to adjust production when unemployment is high. He suggests that by using countercyclical fiscal policy to create temporary budget defi-cits, total spending can be increased to create needed jobs. When inflation is a problem, he would create a budget surplus through increased taxes, reduced government spending, or a combination of these actions. Total spending should be reduced, resulting in lower prices.

Samuelson recognizes the importance of controlling the money supply, but he feels it works more slowly than fiscal policy.

Many economists have improved their understanding of and ability to analyze the economy by studying Samuelson's book, *Foundations of Economic Analysis*. The public has come to know his ideas through his journalistic writings on current economic problems. Presidents and the Congress have often asked his advice, although he has never taken a government post. No economist questions Samuelson's knowledge and skill, but conservative economists find fault in his approach to economic problems.

Milton Friedman

Like Paul Samuelson, Milton Friedman has been awarded the Nobel Prize in Economics. But unlike Samuelson, Friedman believes the market should be left alone.

Continued on page 350.

PROFILE (Continued)

Milton Friedman
(1912–   )

Friedman is best known among economists for the book he coauthored with Anna Schwartz, *A Monetary History of the United States, 1867–1960*. His stand against government involvement in the economy and against Federal Reserve countercyclical adjustments in the money supply assures him a large audience whenever he speaks.

Friedman believes nothing regulates the economy better than the free market. Like Adam Smith, he respects the ability of individual consumers, workers, and businesspersons to decide what is in their own best interest. This self-interest is shown in consumer demand and businesses' willingness to supply products to satisfy this demand. These forces interact in the market to determine prices, wages, and profits. Resources will be allocated most efficiently when the government does not interfere in the market.

Friedman has shocked liberals with his opposition to almost all existing social welfare programs. He would provide help for the poor through a negative income tax, a direct payment to the poor to supplement their income. He would allow the poor to decide how to spend the money they receive, rather than give food stamps or subsidized low-income housing.

As a monetarist, Friedman would have the Federal Reserve System increase the money supply between three and five percent per year, or at about the same rate as the increase in production. His studies have shown the Federal Reserve to have such a poor record of implementing monetary policy that he feels we would be better off not letting them adjust the money supply other than at a constant annual rate.

Friedman taught for many years at the University of Chicago. He and his colleagues made that university famous for its conservative economic position. Samuelson of the Massachusetts Institute of Technology, and Alvin Hansen and John Kenneth Galbraith at Harvard, made their respective institutions famous for a liberal economic point of view.

CURRENT ECONOMIC ISSUES

Has Tax Reform Been Fair for All Americans?

In 1986 and again in 1990 the structure of federal income taxes was changed. The intent of the changes was to create a tax system that was more fair. To accomplish this, the amount of the exemption that could be subtracted from taxpayer income for each person supported was increased to $2,000. The standard deduction that could be subtracted was raised to $5,000. These amounts were increased each year after 1988 according to the rate of inflation. As a result, a married couple with two children could earn $14,300 in 1991 before they had to pay any federal income tax. The new rates reduced the number of tax-paying Americans by more than 10,000,000 people.

The number of different tax rates was also reduced from 14 to only 3. The maximum rate that had been 50 percent in 1985 became 31 percent in 1991. After 1988, the federal income tax rate for most taxpayers was 15 percent.

How could the government give so many tax breaks? This was done by getting rid of "loopholes" or deductions that had allowed people to reduce their taxable income in the past. Deductions for sales taxes, medical expenses, losses, business expenses, and many types of investments were reduced or eliminated. As a result, the government collected about the same amount of money that would have been taken in under the old laws.

The reforms did reduce tax rates for many. However, the law increased taxes on investments and may have discouraged businesses from investing in new factories that would have created jobs. Also the law did not seem to benefit middle income taxpayers as much as those with lower and higher incomes. How have these tax changes affected your family?

Arguments in Favor of the Reforms

1. They eliminated taxes for many low-income Americans.
2. They made it difficult to avoid paying taxes.
3. They were intended to make the tax laws easier to understand.

Arguments Against the Reforms

1. They did not eliminate all tax loopholes.
2. They did not eliminate the growth of the national debt.
3. They may have discouraged people from investing in the economy to create more jobs.

What Do You Think?

Consider the arguments for and against the reforms. What information can you find that shows how they have worked? Is the tax system more fair because of the changes introduced in these reforms? Do they appear to have helped the country or harmed it?

Chapter 12 Review

What Have You Learned?

In this chapter you've learned the following important principles of economics:

- The government's role in the economy has grown over the past 200 years.
- *Classical* economists believed the natural state of the economy was full employment.
- The Great Depression of the 1930s showed the ideas of Classical economists were wrong, and an alternative theory was offered by *John Maynard Keynes*.
- Keynes believed the government should implement policies to stabilize the amount of total spending so that there would be jobs for all people who want to work.
- Although Keynes's ideas have been widely accepted, there are problems with his theory. These include our limited ability to predict the future, the time it takes the government to make policy changes, its inability to fight inflation and unemployment at the same time, and the effect government borrowing may have on interest rates.

- Government attempts to limit inflation through price controls have often led to shortages and have met with only limited success.
- In recent years a theory called *supply-side economics* has been accepted by some economists. This theory suggests that policies to encourage business investment should be carried out by the government. Supply-side economists believe these policies will result in economic growth, greater production, and more jobs.
- The global nature of our economic system has limited the ability of the United States government to regulate our economy through fiscal and monetary policy.
- Although we have attempted to provide jobs and limit inflation, there are still many people in the United States who live in poverty. Our government has established a number of programs which are intended to help these people.
- The foundations for our Social Security, unemployment compensation, and welfare programs were established by the Social Security Act of 1935. Although unemployment compensation and welfare programs exist in all states, differences cause inequity in taxes and benefits from state to state.

Words and Terms

laissez-faire (p. 319)
Classical economics (p. 320)
Employment Act of 1946 (p. 323)
John Baptiste Say (p. 323)
John Maynard Keynes (p. 324)
fiscal policy (p. 326)
discretionary fiscal policy (p. 326)
automatic stabilization (p. 327)

crowding-out effect (p. 328)
Phase II (p. 333)
supply-side economics (p. 335)
productivity (p. 335)
IRA (p. 337)
Social Security Act (p. 344)
indexed (p. 344)
AFDC (p. 346)

Building Your Vocabulary

Answer each of the following by placing the word or term which best completes each of the following sentences in the appropriate space on a separate answer sheet.

1. The idea that additional government borrowing will lead to reduced consumer spending and business investment is called the _____.
2. The largest number of people who receive welfare are mothers and children who are paid _____ benefits.
3. Welfare, Social Security, and unemployment compensation were all started by the _____ of 1935.
4. Social Security benefits have been adjusted for inflation, or _____ , since 1972.
5. If the government does not become involved in the economic system, it is following a _____ economic policy.
6. _____ was an economist who believed that prices, interest rates, and wages would fall to end any recession.
7. _____ was an economist who believed that it was necessary to regulate total spending for economic success. He also felt that governments should either adjust taxes or their own spending, or a combination of both, to achieve the correct amount of total spending.
8. _____ was a system for government regulation of prices established by President Nixon in 1971.
9. When a firm's costs of production fall, its _____ will increase.
10. The attempt of the Congress and the President to stabilize the economy through taxing and government spending is called _____.
11. Before the Great Depression of the 1930s, many people believed in _____, which stated that the economic system would regulate itself and that the government should stay out of the system to the greatest extent possible.
12. An _____ is a special type of savings account that allows depositors to put off paying tax on the part of their income they save.
13. _____ suggests that it is possible to fight both inflation and unemployment by lowering the cost of production.
14. _____ will go into effect without any new action by either the President or the Congress or a government agency.
15. _____ requires the action of either the President or the Congress or a government agency to go into effect.
16. After World War II, Congress passed the _____, which placed a responsibility on the government to carry out policies that would promote full employment.

Understanding Economics

1. According to Classical economists, what three things would happen in a recession that would lead to economic recovery?
2. What were the three sources of spending that Keynes identified?
3. According to Keynes, what are two ways the government could achieve higher levels of spending in a recession?
4. Explain the difference between automatic and discretionary fiscal policy. Give an example of each.
5. If the government tries to fight unemployment by increasing spending, what is this policy likely to do to the rate of inflation?

Chapter 12 Review

6. If the government tries to fight inflation by cutting spending, what is this policy likely to do to the rate of unemployment?

7. Explain why many people were opposed to President Nixon's Phase II policy of the early 1970s.

8. Supply-side economists want the government to have policies that would encourage businesses to produce more goods and services. What are two results they believe would come from such policies?

9. Explain why the price of oil cannot be controlled through fiscal and monetary policy.

10. Describe why welfare and unemployment compensation programs may have caused people to move from state to state.

11. Explain why many people feel private programs are not able to do an adequate job of helping the poor in the United States.

Keynesian economist and a *supply-side* economist.

3. In 1981–82 there was a recession in the U.S. economy. In November of 1982, Congress passed a five cent per gallon increase in the tax on gasoline. The increase took effect on April 1, 1983. The money was to be used to provide needed jobs by rebuilding the nation's roads. It was late summer of 1983 before any contracts were awarded with this money. Construction actually began at the end of 1983. Describe what this shows you about fiscal policy that involves government spending and the time it can take to implement it. Would a tax cut work more quickly? Explain why or why not.

4. Suppose the government borrows and spends large amounts of money to carry out Keynesian economic programs. Some people believe a result of such a policy would be to reduce consumer and investment spending. Explain why they believe this.

Thinking Critically About Economics

1. When this country was originally formed in the 1700s, our government had a relatively small role in our economic system. Describe three things that have changed to cause our government to take a larger role in our economic system.

2. Suppose there was a recession in the United States. Describe the policies a *Classical* economist would want the government to follow. Do the same for a

Consumer Skills Projects

Go to a local social services office. Obtain copies of the forms that have to be filled out to qualify for welfare in your state. Show them in class. Discuss whether the questions the forms ask are reasonable. Be sure to address the question of whether people who receive aid from the government should have the same rights to privacy and individual choice as people who are able to support themselves.

Developing Your Economic Skills

Interpreting Pie Graphs

Skill: A pie graph is especially useful for showing how the parts of a whole amount (the pie) are divided. In addition, two or more pie graphs can be compared to show how a whole amount—for example, total expenditures—has changed over time.

In this lesson you'll look at pie graphs to see how total payments for social service programs have grown and how proportions of the payments are divided between federal, and state and local governments. To complete this lesson, you'll follow these steps:

- Compare the total sizes of the three graphs to see how total spending for social services has grown.
- Examine the sections within each individual graph to see how the expenditures for that year were divided between federal, and state and local governments.
- Compare the sections between the three graphs to see how the distribution of the spending has changed.

Application: How are social service benefits paid for?

Social programs supported by the federal, state, and local governments have grown dramatically in recent years. In 1970 a total of $146 billion was spent by all levels of government for social programs. By 1988 this spending had grown to $887 billion. The graphs below illustrate this.

The increasing size of the graphs from left to right shows growth in total spending of all governments.

Each graph is divided into two sections. The orange section represents spending that was supported by the federal government. The blue section is for spending supported by state and local governments. By studying these graphs, you can see that the share supported by the federal government grew between 1970 and 1980, but fell between 1980 and 1990.

Practice: These graphs allow you to see both the total spending and the distribution of support for that spending. How would you determine whether total federal spending increased or decreased between 1980 and 1990? Why do you think the share of spending supported by the federal government fell in the 1980s?

Spending on Social Service Programs by Federal, and State and Local Governments, 1970/1980/1990

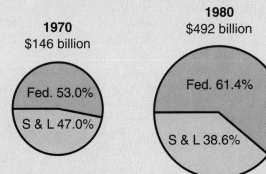

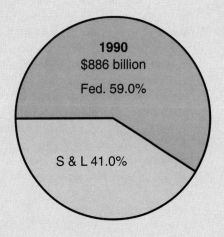

Part 3 Review

Summary of Major Economic Principles

In Part 3 you have learned the following basic economic principles concerning the function of our economic system and concerning government involvement in the economy. These principles are part of what is called *Macroeconomics*.

- The basic measure of production in the United States is the *gross domestic product*, which is measured through the expenditure and income approaches by our government.
- The GDP is used as a measure of the *business cycle*, which changes over time from *expansion* to *recession*. The business cycle can be predicted through the use of *leading indicators*.
- Our government provides *public goods* and *services* that most people could not afford as individuals. It also tries to correct *negative externalities* and to assure all Americans a minimal income by *redistribution of income*.
- Taxes may be based on the *benefits-received principle*, the *ability-to-pay principle*, the *productivity principle*, or on the *least-likely-to-offend principle*, and may be *progressive*, *regressive*, or *proportional*.
- The *national debt* has grown rapidly in recent years. Some economists are concerned over its size and the fact that much of the borrowing to support the debt has been from foreign sources.
- The several types of unemployment are *frictional*, *seasonal*, *cyclical*, and *structural unemployment*. People who give up hunting work are called *discouraged workers*.

- *Inflation* is a sustained general increase in prices. *Demand-pull* inflation is the result of demand that exceeds supply. *Cost-push* inflation happens when producers pass increased costs of production on to customers in higher prices.
- People are not hurt equally by inflation. Those who live on fixed incomes or who have made loans are likely to be hurt the most by inflation.
- *Poverty* is defined in terms of economic and social conditions in each country. In the United States, poverty is associated with unemployment, inflation, and the distribution of income. In 1989 more than 12 percent of our population were identified as living in poverty.
- Money serves as a *medium of exchange*, a *measure of value*, and a *store of value*.
- If the money in circulation grows more rapidly than the supply of products offered for sale, there will be inflation. If the supply of products offered for sale grows more rapidly than the supply of money, there will be deflation.
- Most spending in the United States is done through checks. Banks have the ability to *expand* the money supply through a process that involves checking deposits and loans made in repeated cycles.
- The *Federal Reserve System* oversees the American banking system. It also sets *monetary policy*, regulating the money supply by changing the *reserve requirement*, by adjusting the *discount rate*, or by buying and selling government securities in *open market operations*. There is often disagreement over the proper role of the Federal Reserve System and the actions of its Board of Governors.

- The role of the government in the economy has increased during the past 200 years. *Classical economists* believed the economy would regulate itself and the government should not attempt to interfere with it. This policy did not work in the Great Depression.
- *John Maynard Keynes* developed a new theory that said the government should implement policies to stabilize the amount of total spending, so that there would be jobs for all people who want to work. Although his ideas have been widely accepted, there also have been problems in using his theory to form government policy.
- In some cases, the government has tried to limit inflation with price controls. This policy has often led to shortages. There has been less pressure on the government to use price controls in recent years.
- A theory called *supply-side* economics was used as the basis for many government decisions in the 1980s. Supply-side economists believe policies that encourage investment will result in economic growth, greater production, and more jobs.
- Although we have attempted to provide jobs and limit inflation, there are many people in the United States who live in poverty. Our government has established programs that are intended to help these people. They include Social Security, unemployment compensation, and welfare.

Understanding Economic Concepts

Each of the following questions emphasizes one or more of the important economic concepts you have learned in Part 3. The important concept is listed in parentheses after each question. Answer the questions in complete sentences that *show you understand the*

meaning of the concepts. The first question has been answered for you as an example.

1. What are the two methods used by the federal government to measure the gross domestic product? (Discuss the *expenditure* approach and the *income* approach.)
   (*Answer*: In the expenditure approach, the government measures GDP by counting all spending on new products. In the income approach, the government counts all earnings.)
2. What is the most important problem in accurately measuring GDP? (Discuss the *underground economy*.)
3. The producers of what type of goods will be affected most by a recession? (Discuss *durable goods*.)
4. How can businesses predict economic conditions in the near future? (Discuss *leading indicators*.)
5. Why is it necessary for governments to supply many things to its citizens? (Discuss *public goods and services*.)
6. When the government requires a firm to stop polluting a river, what economic problem is it trying to resolve? (Discuss *negative externality*.)
7. What are the two basic principles of taxation? (Discuss the *benefits-received* principle and the *ability-to-pay* principle.)
8. What name has been given to parts of many government spending bills? (Discuss *pork barrel legislation*.)
9. What is an important difference between most state and local taxes and the federal income tax? (Discuss *regressive* and *progressive* taxation.)
10. What are the basic types of unemployment? (Discuss *frictional, seasonal, cyclical,* and *structural* unemployment.)
11. What is the difference between the two basic types of inflation? (Discuss *de-*

Part 3 Review

mand-pull inflation and *cost-push* inflation.)

12. What is often associated with unemployment, inflation, and the distribution of income in this country? (Discuss *poverty*.)

13. What are the three functions of money in our economic system? (Discuss *medium of exchange, measure of value,* and *store of value*.)

14. What process do banks participate in when they make loans based on money deposited in checking accounts? (Discuss the *expansion process*.)

15. What is the name of the policy the Federal Reserve System carries out? (Discuss *monetary policy*.)

16. What are the three things the Fed can do to affect the amount of money in circulation? (Discuss the *reserve requirement*, the *discount rate*, and *open market operations*.)

17. How would banks act if they were allowed to? (Discuss *pro-cyclical*.)

18. How was confidence in the banking system restored in the Great Depression? (Discuss the *Federal Deposit Insurance Corporation*.)

19. What is a description of the economic theory that supported government involvement in the economy? (Discuss *Keynesian* economic theory.)

20. Why does the global nature of our economy limit the government's ability to regulate the United States economy? (Discuss *fiscal* and *monetary policy*.)

Writing About Economics

Each of the questions below requires you to write a brief essay. Follow these steps:

■ Demonstrate your understanding of the identified economic concept(s) in your essay.

■ Explain how the economic concept(s) is involved in the situation.

■ Describe how you would resolve the situation and on what basis you would make your decision.

1. Pretend you have a pen pal named Helga who lives in Norway. She writes you that she has been assigned to do a report for her social studies class on the economy of the United States. She would like you to explain how production is measured in the United States economy. Write Helga a letter that answers her question. (Discuss *gross domestic product*, the *income* approach, and the *expenditure* approach.)

2. You have been employed as an advisor to your city's mayor. She wants to attract more businesses to the area. Members of the city council have presented her with three ideas (listed below) on how this could be done. Your job is to write a report that identifies the best plan and explains why it is better than the others. You may also reject all of the plans, but you must explain why. (Discuss the *ability-to-pay* principle, the *productivity* principle, and *negative externalities*.)

    The plans are:

■ Reduce property taxes on new businesses or on new investments made by existing businesses. Increase the sales tax to make up for lost property taxes.

■ Reduce all property taxes and cut back on public services such as schools, roads, and police protection, so that the city government can still balance its budget.

■ Let new factories bury their waste on city land if they agree to provide jobs to local people.

3. Suppose you are a newspaper reporter. A local politician is running for Congress. You are assigned to listen to a speech he gives to a group of local businessmen. In his speech he makes these points:

■ He wants to reduce taxes for businesses that invest or hire more workers.

■ He wants to reduce taxes on money that is saved.

■ He wants to reduce public service programs to encourage more people to find work.

Your job is to write an article for your newspaper that explains what he wants to accomplish and what problems might result if his ideas are put into use. (Discuss *supply-side economics*.)

Discussing Economics

The following paragraphs describe economic proposals that have been the topic of recent public debate. For each issue, decide whether you support or do not support the proposal, and think about how you would present your opinion to the rest of the class. When you present your opinion to the class, follow these steps:

■ Identify and describe the controversial issues of the proposal.

■ Clearly state the decision you have reached.

■ Explain why you think your choice is the best one.

1. Some people believe a law should be passed that would prevent the government from increasing tax rates unless the people vote to approve the tax increase. Supporters of this idea argue that the government is too large and that we could prevent it from getting larger if politicians could not increase tax rates by themselves.

Other people say such a law would make it impossible for the government to provide necessary public goods and services. They argue that few people would vote to increase their own taxes even if an increase was needed. Such a law would probably hurt the poor and elderly the most.

Would you support such a law? On what basis would you make your decision?

2. According to our government, there are slightly over 30 million people in the United States who live in poverty. It would cost the government between $80 and $100 billion dollars more than it now spends to give these people enough money to escape poverty. Some people say the United States is rich enough to do this. They feel no American should have to live in poverty.

Other people disagree. They suggest that giving people so much money would destroy their desire to work. They argue that if it cost $80 billion to get rid of poverty this year, it would cost much more in the future because many poor people would give up working. They also point out that the extra benefits would probably be paid for through taxes on people who are working to escape poverty through their own effort.

Part 3 Review

Would you support such a law? On what basis would you make your decision?

3. Some people believe that all banks should be required to make loans to small firms or minority-owned businesses that would not otherwise be able to get loans. They argue that banks earn money from the entire community and should therefore have to make loans to all parts of the community. If banks only make loans to people and businesses that are already successful, then few new people will have a chance to succeed.

Other people disagree. They say that banks must protect their depositors. Making risky loans to new or small businesses could hurt these people and force the cost of banking up. They argue that such a law would treat people unequally. Banks could end up looking for small or minority-owned businesses to make loans just to abide by the law. This could make less money available for slightly larger businesses to borrow.

Would you support such a law? On what basis would you make your decision?

Problem-Solving in Economics

Chapter 8

1. It has been said that the "American Dream" is to see your children have a better life than you have. To most people, the idea of a better life means having more things. List four things you would like to have in your life that your parents didn't have. Explain why each is important to you.

2. Make a list of four things that add to your quality of life but that do not involve money or goods and services. Explain why each is important to you.

3. When additional products are made and sold, how much do they add to the add to the quality of life? Not everyone agrees on the value of different products. Below you will find a list of percentage increases in sales of certain items between 1989 and 1990 in the United States. Explain how much each added to the quality of life, *in your opinion.*
   a. Sales of bottled water increased by 13 percent.
   b. Sales of cosmetics increased by 6.5 percent.
   c. Sales of snack foods increased 2.8 percent.
   d. Sales of soap beauty-bars increased 7 percent.
   e. Sales of antacids increased 3 percent.

4. Explain whether each of the following would indicate that the economy would expand or contract soon.
   a. New building permits are down.
   b. Interest rates are down.
   c. Employees are working more hours.
   d. It takes longer to get deliveries.
   e. People are saving less of their income.
   f. Few new businesses are being started.

Chapter 9

1. Suppose you are on the town board. There is a suggestion to build a new harbor on a river that flows through the town. If the project is completed it should increase tourism, but it will re-

quire a 10 percent increase in property taxes to pay for it. Explain how—and why—each of the following people would react to the plan.

a. a person who owns land on the river
b. a person who has a farm on the other side of town
c. a person who owns a bait shop
d. a person who owns a house on the river and likes peace and quiet
e. a person who owns a factory along the river

2. Below you will find a bar graph showing how the federal government spent its money in 1970, 1980, and 1990. You will notice that the percentage of spending in some categories increased over these years, while the percentage of spending in other categories decreased. Study the graph and answer the following questions. (Your answers from the graph do not have to be exact, but try to make them as close as possible.)

a. What percentage of federal spending went to payments to individuals in 1970?
b. What percentage of federal spending went to payments to individuals in 1990?
c. What percentage of federal spending went to national defense in 1970?
d. What percentage of federal spending went to national defense in 1990?
e. Describe the change in emphasis for federal spending between 1970 and 1990 that is shown by the answers to questions *a* through *d*.
f. What has happened to the importance of the federal government's interest payment between 1970 and 1990?

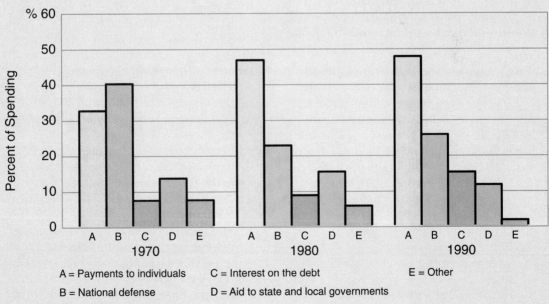

A = Payments to individuals   C = Interest on the debt   E = Other
B = National defense   D = Aid to state and local governments

Source: *Statistical Abstract of the United States*, 1991.

Part 3 Review

Chapter 10

1. Identify the type of unemployment described in each of the following examples (frictional, seasonal, cyclical, or structural). In each instance, think of at least one action that the person could have taken in advance to help avoid a lengthy period of unemployment.
   a. Joe loses his job when inventories grow too large.
   b. Max quits his job to look for a better one.
   c. Jan loses her job after the Christmas sales rush.
   d. Sue loses her job when a new computer is installed.
   e. Ted is replaced on his job by a college graduate.

2. Unemployment can cause many problems other than economic hardships. Describe three different problems that could result from long-term unemployment. Be specific.

3. People can react to higher prices in different ways. Suppose you really wanted a particular type of car and you found that its price had just increased from $12,000 to $15,000. There is a list of possible things you could do below. Rank each action from 1 to 5 (1 is most likely, 5 is least likely), according to which you would be most likely to do. Then explain each ranking.
   a. Give up on buying the car.
   b. Buy a used one instead.
   c. Save longer and buy it at the higher price.
   d. Buy one, but with fewer options than you had wanted.

   e. Try to find someone to share the car and cost with.
4. Identify what you consider to be one of the major causes of poverty. Suggest at least one action that you think could be taken to help eliminate that cause.

Chapter 11

1. Identify each of the situations below as an example of one of the functions of money—as a medium of exchange, as a measure of value, or as a store of value. Then explain your answer.
   a. Your little brother puts money in his piggy bank to save for a pair of roller skates.
   b. You pay for your milk with a dollar bill.
   c. Your mother shops where the prices are lowest.
   d. A firm borrows $50,000 from a bank to pay for a new machine.

2. Decide whether each of the following actions would *increase* or *decrease* the amount of money in circulation.
   a. The Federal Reserve System lowers the reserve requirement to 10 percent.
   b. The Federal Reserve System reduces the money supply.
   c. People hold less cash, deposit more.
   d. Banks decide to hold more cash and make fewer loans.
   e. The Federal Reserve System increases the money supply.
   f. The Federal Reserve System raises the reserve requirement to 14 percent.

3. Suppose that your aunt has several thousand dollars that she wants to lend out as an investment, and she asks you how she should go about finding someone to

lend it to. What qualifications for a borrower would you suggest, and why?

4. In the end, the Fed has only the power to make it easier or more difficult to borrow money. It does this by increasing or decreasing the money supply. With this in mind, answer each of the following questions.

a. If there is inflation, would the Fed probably try to increase or to decrease the amount of money in circulation to reduce demand?

b. If there is unemployment, would the Fed probably try to increase or to decrease the amount of money in circulation to increase sales and jobs?

c. Study your answers to questions *a* and *b* above. If there is both unemployment and inflation, can the Fed attack both of them at the same time?

d. If prices go up because of an increase in the price of imported raw materials (such as oil), will monetary policy solve the problem? (Hint: think of what type of inflation this might cause.)

e. In a recession, people and businesses are often worried about being able to pay their bills. What effect would lower interest rates probably have on people's willingness to borrow and spend?

f. Describe the three limitations on monetary policy that you have learned about in answering the preceding questions.

Chapter 12

1. It has been suggested that jobs created by the government only last as long as the government is willing to pay for them. Almost everyone knows of a relative or an individual who has been unemployed. Briefly describe one such person you know of. What type of work did he or she have? How did he or she become unemployed? What hardships has the person experienced, and what prospects does he or she have for the future? Describe at least two actions you believe the government should take to help people like this. Be realistic by considering the political and economic consequences of your suggestions.

2. Suppose that you own your own business. Inflation in general has been 6 percent. The cost of your raw materials has gone up 10 percent in the past year. You are negotiating with your workers for a new contract. They want a 9 percent pay increase and you are convinced that they will go on strike if they don't get it. You have seen your profit margin fall from over 12 percent to just 3 percent in the last year. Most of your competitors have increased their prices more than you have.

The government has sent you a letter asking you to limit your price increases to no more than 4 percent this year. Write a letter back to the government telling them what you plan to do and why you intend to do it. Include at least three specific reasons for your plan.

3. Programs to help the poor, retired, and unemployed also help those who have jobs. If there were a recession and these programs did not exist, what would the answers to the following questions be?

a. What would happen to the number of products that could be purchased by the poor?

b. What would happen to the number of foreclosures and repossessions?

c. What would happen to the number of jobs in the economy?

d. How do programs to help the poor help those who keep their jobs?

4

Understanding International Economics

Part 4 will help you understand how the American economy fits into and has become part of the world economy. In Chapter 13 you will learn why nations trade and why they limit trade. Problems related to international payments and exchange rates will be discussed. You will then examine multinational corporations and see what part they may play in bringing national economies closer together. In Chapter 14 you will study developing nations and the difficulties they have producing enough to satisfy their people's needs. You will evaluate the arguments for and against industrialized countries providing aid to developing nations. Finally, in Chapter 15 you will look at different ways of answering the basic economic questions in other countries. Part 4 will help you understand how the world's economy has become interrelated and global.

Why Countries Trade

Objectives

In the sections of this chapter, you will learn:

A

why countries trade according to the theories of *absolute advantage* and *comparative advantage,* and why countries try to restrict trade through tariffs, quotas, and other methods; and how there are costs and benefits to both *positive* and *negative* balances of trade;

B

how the *exchange rates* for the dollar affect the U.S. economy and are related to the balance of trade; and

C

why corporations become multinational, and how they affect jobs and trade.

Introduction

The economic system of the United States is just one part of the world economy. Like all other countries, we depend on international trade. Each year we export and import hundreds of billions of dollars worth of goods and services. As we have already learned, specialization allows us to produce products of better quality and lower prices. Florida and California produce oranges in exchange for Idaho potatoes and corn from the Midwest. Specialization in international trade is merely an extension of the same principle. We import fuel, bananas, and textiles and export grains, airplanes, and computers. We must import some products, such as coffee, aluminum ore, and sugar. Without our wheat, selected medicines, and coal, however, other countries would have a lower standard of living.

We not only need to buy products from other countries, but other nations provide markets for many of the goods we produce. It has been estimated that more than 10 million jobs are created by our exports.

Although we need and benefit from trade, there are problems associated with it. Money spent on imported goods is money that cannot be spent on American products. Importing too many foreign products can reduce the demand for prod-

Trade—both importing and exporting of goods— is essential to our economy. But there are trade-offs in importing goods from foreign nations. Different people have different viewpoints on the costs and benefits of importing foreign-made cars and other products.

ucts that are made in this country. This can cause unemployment in some industries in the United States.

In this chapter you will study the trade-off between using foreign goods and domestic goods. Buying foreign goods, which are often less expensive, can help keep inflation under control. On the other hand, purchases of domestic goods create jobs for Americans. There is something to be gained and something to be lost with either course of action.

Another problem you will investigate is the fluctuation in U.S. exports. In the early 1980s, American producers found it increasingly difficult to sell their products to other countries. At least part of this problem was the result of the high value of our dollar. To buy American products, foreign nations must trade their currency for dollars. When the dollar's value is high, foreign nations receive fewer dollars in exchange for their money. Beginning in 1986 the value of the dollar declined in relation to foreign currencies. That was like putting American products on sale to foreign buyers. U.S. exports increased sharply.

This chapter will show you how Americans are affected by trade, and how it helps most of us.

Section A The Benefits of Trade

In this section you will learn about the theories of *absolute advantage* and *comparative advantage* and why nations trade. You will then explore why nations sometimes use *tariffs* and *quotas* as barriers against trade.

Personal Narrative

My Father Sells Nissans For a Living

My father has always earned his living selling cars. He started in 1973, selling Chryslers. In 1979, when Chrysler almost went bankrupt, he took a job selling Nissans. Now he says he likes his job more than before, because he believes in the product he sells.

According to my father, you can't be a good salesperson unless you're excited about what you're selling. Customers sense how you feel, and are more likely to buy because of it. My father thinks Nissans are great. He says they are well designed, carefully assembled, efficient, and reliable. He feels good when someone buys one of his cars. He must believe in his product; he's won sales awards in each of the last four years.

Some of my friends at school think what my father does for a living is wrong. They say Americans should buy only products that were made in the United States. My father has heard this argument many times and has several answers for it. They are:

a. Americans believe in freedom. They should be free to buy the best products at the lowest prices, no matter where the products were made.

b. American firms used to be too lazy. They had years to improve their efficiency and quality, but they didn't really try until there was foreign competition. Foreign imports have forced American firms to produce better products.

c. Many parts in American cars are made in other countries. U.S. manufacturers have found that foreign parts are inexpensive and have high quality. Today many products that are called "American Made" have parts that were produced in other countries.

d. Many Americans are employed selling and servicing foreign products that are sold in the United States. There are salespeople, mechanics, distributors, and people in advertising who earn their livings because of imports. If we didn't buy imports, these people would have to find other jobs.

e. If we didn't buy foreign products, foreigners would not have money to buy from us. Many Americans earn their living by producing goods and services that are sold abroad.

When I try to explain these arguments at school, most of my friends don't listen. I can understand why. There is a big General Motors plant near town that has laid off many workers in recent years. If my father had lost his job because of imported cars, I probably wouldn't want to hear these arguments either.

Why Trade?

No country in the free world is forced to trade, yet all countries import and export goods. If no country is forced to trade, only one conclusion makes sense: countries trade because they want to.

Economists have developed two theories to explain why countries trade. They are called the theories of *absolute advantage* and *comparative advantage*. Both of these theories state that countries should specialize in making products that they are most efficient at and trade for products that they do not make as well. If this were done, all countries would make the things they do best, causing total production to increase. These theories say that after trade, all countries would have more products.

An example that demonstrates the theory of **absolute advantage** would be U.S. trade with Central American countries for bananas. The United States could never produce bananas efficiently. It would be a waste of our time to try. On the other hand, we do manufacture machinery more efficiently than most Central American nations. Therefore, it makes sense for the U.S. to buy bananas from these countries and to sell them our machinery. We both benefit from the exchange because we each have a type of production that we do best.

Should a country trade even if it is better at all types of production than other countries? The theory of **comparative advantage** says yes. Suppose that an executive who earns $50 an hour can type better than her secretary, who is paid $7 an hour. It would be inefficient for the executive to do her own typing, because she has more important things to do. Even if the secretary took twice as long as the executive to do the work, it would still be less expensive for the secretary to do it. The same is true of countries. Suppose that the United States produces both airplanes and watches cheaper than does Switzerland. However, its relative efficiency in airplanes is 3 to 1 (one-third the cost of Swiss airplanes), while its relative efficiency in watches is 2 to 1 (one-half the cost of Swiss watches). Both the U.S. and Switzerland would be richer if they specialized, the U.S. in airplanes and Switzerland in watches, and traded with each other.

Barriers to Trade

Although countries benefit from trade, they also want to control their imports and exports. This can be done through *tariffs, quotas,* or other types of restrictions.

Tariffs

A **tariff** is a tax on an import. Tariffs make imports more expensive and therefore less attractive to consumers. Tariffs can be used to reduce a nation's imports, as well as to provide revenue for government expenditures.

There are three major types of tariffs, classified according to their main purposes. The three types are *revenue, protective,* and *restrictive.*

Revenue tariffs are intended to raise money to run the government. Many U.S. tariffs in the 1800s were of this type.

Protective tariffs are intended to increase the price of imported products to a competitive level with products made in the country that sets the tariff. Tariffs on imported cars and steel are examples of this sort of tax.

Restrictive tariffs are intended to reduce or eliminate the flow of a particular type of product into a country. Tariffs on luxury goods imported into many poorer nations are examples of this type of tax.

Quotas

A **quota** is a limit on the amount of a product a nation will allow to be imported. The United States uses both tariffs and quotas to control imports.

U.S. Trade Policy

From its beginnings until the mid-1860s the United States encouraged trade with other nations, protecting only a few industries from foreign competition. We encouraged the world to buy American agricultural products and traded for manufactured goods. Beginning in the 1860s, Northern industrial interests in control of the government passed high protective tariffs to prevent foreign competition from threatening our young industries. With some fluctuations, these tariffs remained high until the 1930s. President Franklin Roosevelt tried to increase trade by lowering tariffs and encouraging our trading partners to do the same. That policy of encouraging free trade has remained, only recently encountering any serious opposition.

When World War II ended, the U.S. knew it would be necessary to help Europe rebuild its economy. The government did this through the Marshall Plan, which provided the resources needed to reconstruct European economies. Along with other nations, the U.S. set up a World Bank for Reconstruction and Development from which all nations could borrow. We also led in the development of the International Monetary Fund, so that nations could borrow foreign currencies in short-term loans in order to trade. Finally, the U.S. helped organize the General Agreement on Tariffs and Trade (GATT). Under this agreement nations meet regularly to discuss mutual tariff policies. Each of these meetings, called "rounds," has resulted in the removal of many trade barriers. In short, the U.S. has been responsible for much of the increase in world trade, as you can see in Figure 13-1.

Figure 13–1   *U.S. Merchandise Exports and Imports, 1950–1991 (billions of dollars) and Total Merchandise Trade as a Percentage of Gross Domestic Product*

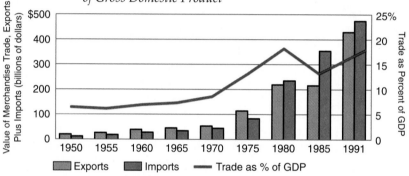

Source: *Office of Trade and Investment Analysis, U.S. Department of Commerce.*

The best measure of how important trade has become to the U.S. economy is the line showing trade as a percentage of the nation's GDP. From 1950 to 1965 it averaged about 6.5 percent. From 1980 to the present it has averaged about 15 percent.

Voluntary Export Restraints (VER)

Because import quotas are no longer permitted under GATT, exporting countries may be induced by special agreements to limit shipments of specific goods to an importing country. The most well-known of these was Japan's agreement to limit exporting automobiles to the United States. The announced reason was to save American jobs. The trade-off was that the American consumer had to pay a higher price for an automobile. Hundreds of other items have been placed on VER lists.

Regulations and Certification

Most nations have import restrictions that are supposed to protect the safety and health of their citizens. In some instances, imported products must be certified for standards of quality. In reality, these often turn out to be devices for keeping out foreign goods and protecting home industries. The European Community barred imported American beef because it was treated with hormones. The United States bars tomatoes unless they are a certain size, which hurts Mexican exports. Japan requires foreign firms to team up with Japanese firms in order to do business there. Brazil requires all imported cars to have a certain percentage of their value produced in Brazil. These are some of the many restrictions that countries use to protect their own producers but which cost their own consumers millions to billions of dollars.

The Costs and Benefits of Trade Barriers

Why Restrict Trade?

Although the theories of absolute advantage and comparative advantage tell us that as countries trade more they will become better off, all countries have some barriers to trade. Some people believe barriers to trade are able to *protect infant industries*, to *improve national security*, to *protect domestic jobs*, and to *maintain economic stability.*

a. The **infant industry** argument states that countries should protect new industries with tariffs. An infant industry is one that is just starting out. Such an industry won't be as efficient as established industries in other countries. If it is not protected, it may fail. For example, when India started to manufacture steel in the 1950s, it put high tariffs on imported steel. This allowed its new firms to compete successfully against cheaper foreign steel.

b. The **national security** argument states that a country should produce vital military products for itself, even when they can be purchased for less in other countries. A country would not want to depend on others to supply weapons that it needs to defend itself. For example, France, at great expense, has chosen to build its own nuclear weapons rather than rely on the United States for its defense.

c. The **protection of domestic jobs** argument points out that many foreign workers are paid much lower wages than

American workers. Because of the lower wages, foreign producers are able to charge lower prices and increase their sales in the U.S. Tariffs would increase the price of foreign goods to levels that U.S. products can compete with.

d. The **maintaining economic stability** argument states that nations that depend on trade are more likely to be hurt by disruptions in trade. An example of this problem came in 1973 when Arab countries cut off exports of oil to the United States. If we relied less on imported energy we would be less vulnerable to actions of this nature.

Keeping Trade Balanced

Turn back to Figure 13-1. You can see that before 1980 U.S. exports were greater than imports. The difference between the value of exports and of imports is called the balance of trade. From 1950 to the 1970s our merchandise exports were greater than our imports, and we had a favorable or **positive balance of trade.** In 1980 that balance was negative—called an unfavorable or **negative balance of trade.**

The advantages of a positive balance of trade include (1) greater employment, (2) higher profitability, (3) increased economic growth, (4) larger income for the government to tax, and (5) the ability to buy things from other nations.

Unfortunately, if some countries have positive balances of trade, then other countries have negative balances of trade. They import more than they export. The disadvantages of a negative balance of trade are the opposite of those above. Negative balances of trade tend to (1) reduce employment, (2) decrease profitability, (3) slow economic growth, (4) reduce taxable incomes, and (5) make it more difficult to buy things from other nations.

Not all effects of a negative balance of trade are bad. For example, less expensive imports help keep inflation under control. Many economists believe that having more goods and services enter instead of leave the country is better for the economy. However, most people believe the benefits of a positive balance of trade are much better than those of a negative balance.

In the 1980s Presidents Ronald Reagan and George Bush vetoed legislation that would restrict trade, because they both believed in free trade. The United States opened talks with Canada and Mexico to eliminate trade restrictions. In 1991 Congress authorized President Bush to begin negotiating a North American Free Trade Agreement (NAFTA) that would link the three nations in a trading bloc. The federal government earlier had taken steps to help individuals who had been hurt by trade. For ex-

In the early 1980s, foreign production of some parts for electronic goods became so inexpensive that American firms gave up making them in this country. Some Americans asked whether Japan was competing fairly.

ample, the Trade Adjustment Assistance program was established in 1974 to help workers who lost their jobs because of imported goods. The program paid extended unemployment benefits and helped with the cost of retraining.

Protectionism and Politics

In the 1980s many advocates of free trade changed their position to support "fair trade." They pointed out that U.S. trade policy had far fewer restrictions than many of its trading partners. Political pressure led to the passage of the Omnibus Trade and Competitiveness Act of 1988. Much of the act supported free trade, giving the President authority to negotiate reductions and even elimination of trade barriers on dozens of products. Nearly $1 billion was made available to retrain workers who were displaced because of imports. In addition, the so-called "super 301" provision required the administration to list the names of all countries that practiced "unfair trade," and to negotiate the removal of these practices. In May 1989 the first listing designated Japan, Brazil, and India as having unfair trade practices. Negotiations have resulted in Japan and Brazil being removed from the list, but the threat of retaliation by the United States remains.

One practice the government tries to prevent is **dumping** of products. Economists define dumping as selling goods in foreign markets for less than they are sold in the producing nation. Most countries agree that this practice is unfair competition. The United States imposes special taxes on a country found guilty of dumping. This policy is not often needed, because actual cases of dumping are relatively few.

Pressure to keep out foreign competition grew even stronger as the recession of 1990 to 1992 caused the closing of many automobile plants. Presidential candidates ran on platforms of America first. It became popular to blame the Japanese for our foreign trade troubles. While the United States was still the most efficient overall producer in the world, other nations were improving efficiency. American producers sought protection on products that others produced more efficiently.

Protection is an expensive and inefficient way to save jobs, however. Economists have estimated that Americans have spent more than $20 billion in higher prices on automobiles because of restrictive policies. To save one job in some industries, it is estimated that consumers have had to pay $250,000 in higher prices. When consumers pay higher prices they cannot afford to save and invest as much. This, in turn, reduces funds for business expansion and new jobs.

■ *Self-Check*

1. What do the theories of absolute advantage and comparative advantage state countries should do?
2. What is the difference between a tariff, a quota, and voluntary export restraints?
3. According to the infant industry argument, why should developing countries establish tariffs?
4. What are the benefits and the costs to countries from a favorable (positive) balance of trade? From an unfavorable (negative) balance of trade?
5. Explain how American trade policy has fluctuated. Explain why.

■ *Applying What You Have Learned*

In the Personal Narrative for this section, five arguments were given that favored free trade. State an answer to three of these arguments that could be given by someone who was against free trade.

Section B The Value of The Dollar and Trade

This section will discuss the relationship between the value of the U.S. dollar and our balance of trade.

Personal Narrative

Sometimes Business Conditions Are Beyond Our Control

My father used to work for a firm that manufactured high-quality machine parts, almost half of which were exported. For the first 15 years he worked for Mert's Machine Parts his employer's business grew steadily. Mert's profits increased and Dad's income gave us a good living. During the recession of 1980-1982, Mert's sales fell. Everyone thought business would improve when the recession ended, but it didn't. The problem was that after 1983 Mert's sold almost nothing to foreign nations.

I remember one evening in 1986 when Dad called a family meeting. His expression told me he was worried. He said his manager had announced that all hourly employees would only be allowed to work 30 hours a week until Mert's business improved. Dad explained that the value of the American dollar had almost doubled in relation to some other types of currency. Although Mert's prices had not changed very much in dollars, it could cost foreigners twice as much of their money to trade for the dollars they needed to buy Mert's products. Most of them could buy similar products from other countries for less. Mert's tried to keep its customers by cutting costs and lowering profits, but there was a limit to what they could do. The only real solution was a lower value for the dollar. In the meantime Dad said we all had to cut back on our spending.

About a month after our family meeting, I read a newspaper article that described an agreement between leaders of industrialized nations to lower the value of the dollar. It said the American balance of trade was getting worse each year. The article explained that the high value of the dollar allowed Americans to buy more yen, francs, and marks, encouraging imports and discouraging exports. I realized this was bad for American businesses that depended on exports.

About two years later the value of the dollar was lower and Dad was back working full-time. The value of the dollar had fallen to about the same level it was in 1980, making Mert's products less expensive to foreigners. I guess the value of the dollar in the foreign exchange market makes a big difference.

Exchange Rates

Foreign trade requires converting one type of money for another. The price of an imported good depends on the **exchange rate** between the American dollar and the money of the country that manufactured the product. Exchange rates are set in an international market according to the demand and supply for different types of money.

For example, if German prices were very low, many Americans would want to buy German products but few Germans would want to buy American products. Once again we can apply our simple model of demand and supply. As Americans went to banks to trade their dollars for German marks, the banks would find that they had an increasingly large supply of dollars and a deepening shortage of marks. The banks would react by making Americans pay more dollars for German marks. Economists would call this increase in the value of the mark **appreciation.** The decrease in the value of the dollar would be a **depreciation.** German prices would seem more expensive to Americans because it would take more dollars to get the marks to buy the German products. On the other hand, American prices would appear lower to Germans because they could get more dollars for their marks. Fewer Americans would buy German products and more Germans would buy American products. If prices were the only things that affected exchange rates, the system would work more easily. Unfortunately, many other things can affect exchange rates.

Causes of Changing Rates

Anything that causes people to trade one type of money for another will affect exchange rates. In the early 1980s, many foreigners traded their money for dollars for reasons that had little to do with trade or prices.

American interest rates were higher than interest rates in other countries in the early 1980s. Many foreigners traded their money for dollars so they could invest in U.S. banks or buy U.S. securities to earn these higher interest rates. Demand for dollars increased and the value of the dollar went up.

At the same time, there were many political and economic problems in other parts of the world. Wealthy individuals and firms wanted to put their money where it would be safe. Many of them bought dollars and invested in United States firms because they were secure. Again, the demand for U.S. dollars increased.

A final reason for the appreciation of the dollar was the early recovery of the U.S. economy from the recession of 1981–1982. Our economic problems started to improve before most other countries. As a result, many foreigners invested in U.S. businesses. This required them to convert their money into dollars.

For these reasons the value of the dollar went up more than 50 percent on an average between 1980 and 1985. After 1985, the trend has reversed itself. By 1992 the dollar had declined to about the same value it had in 1981 against other currencies.

This reversal was at least in part the result of actions taken by the governments of the United States and other countries. In January of 1986 a meeting was held in London to discuss steps that could be taken to reduce the value of the dollar. Although no public announcement was made concerning any agreements, it seems that the foundations for international cooperation were laid there. In 1986 interest rates fell in the United States. The U.S. economy slowed its expansion and economic conditions improved in other nations. These factors combined to reduce the value of the dollar. Figure 13-2 shows the sharp upturn in U.S. exports when the dollar began to decrease in value. As foreign buyers received more dollars in exchange for their own currencies, they bought more American products. American consumers bought less foreign goods, because they received less yen, less francs, and less marks for their dollars.

From 1987 to 1991 the U.S. unfavorable balance of trade dropped sharply. The change in the value of the dollar accounts for only part of the change in the balance of trade, however. A recession also slowed American purchases of foreign products, while American businesses increased their exports.

Figure 13–2 *Value of U.S. Merchandise Exports and Fluctuations of the Dollar in Relationship to Currencies of U.S. Trading Nations*

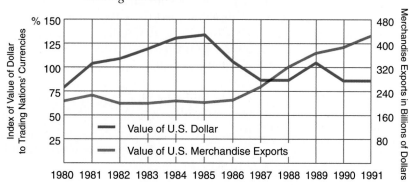

Basic Solution

The Omnibus Trade and Competitiveness Act of 1988 allowed the U.S. government to restrict imports from nations we believed were not practicing "fair trade." It also gave aid to firms hurt by imports through worker retraining and other programs. Motorcycle producer Harley Davidson and many U.S. steel companies took advantage of this act to improve competitiveness in the world market.

A study of U.S. imports and exports shows that most of our negative balance of trade is caused by imports of oil and automobiles. Foreign nations have had both absolute and comparative advantages in supplying these products. Some people suggest the solution to our trade problem is simply to stop buying as many foreign products. A better answer is to improve our productivity and increase our exports. Lower costs allow businesses to reduce prices and increase sales. American producers can become more productive by improving education and technology.

■ *Self-Check*

1. How and where are exchange rates set?
2. What is the relationship between the value of the dollar and foreign trade?
3. What factors besides trade influence the value of currencies?
4. How can the U.S. increase its productivity and be more competitive in the world market?

■ *Applying What You Have Learned*

In each of the cases below, you are asked to use the changing value of foreign currency (or of the dollar) to find an answer to buying or selling decisions.

a. If you wished to buy a specific Japanese camera whose price in Japan stayed the same, which would have been the better year to buy it, 1985 when the dollar was worth 238.5 yen or 1992 when the dollar was worth 133 yen?
b. In 1989 the Italian lira was worth $.00073 and a dollar would buy 1372 lira. In 1992 the lira was worth $.0008 and a dollar would buy 1250 lira. Which would have been the better year to buy Italian shoes?
c. Would you have been better off buying or selling Swiss francs in 1992? A franc was worth $.70 in 1990, $.69 in 1991, and $.67 in 1992.

Section C Multinational Corporations

This section will define and show the growth of multinational corporations. It will explain why they have spread throughout the world and point out their contributions and the harm they may cause both the parent and host countries.

Personal Narrative

What's American?

There is a business in town that makes auto parts. A few weeks ago the owner had a big sign installed in front of his building that read, "Only American Cars Allowed in This Parking Lot!" I wonder what the owner thinks an American car is.

My Uncle Bob works in Ohio making Honda Accords. At a Chrysler dealership my father sells Plymouth Colts and Dodge Stealths that are made in Japan. In the same area there are dealers who sell Jaguars produced by a factory owned by Ford in Great Britain, Geo Prizms manufactured by General Motors and Toyota in California, and Mercury Grand Marquis that are assembled in Canada. Even cars produced by American-owned firms in the United States have many parts that were made in other countries.

I have a friend whose father is a stockbroker. He told me that most of the big corporations in the world are multinationals, doing business in many different nations. Businesses become multinationals to improve their ability to compete in the world market. He said that Tropicana Orange Juice, for example, used to be restricted in the types and amounts of juice it could sell in Japan. By agreeing to allow a Japanese company to buy a portion of Tropicana, their quota was increased and they were allowed to export all types of orange juice to Japan. He said we have similar rules in the United States.

This information left me a little confused. Is it good for the United States to have a Honda factory in Ohio or an IBM factory in Japan? Is my father taking away American jobs when he sells cars that were made in Japan? Would it make any difference whether I took a job working for SONY or for RCA in this country?

Multinational Corporations

Any business that is headquartered in one country but carries on business activities in one or more foreign countries is a **multinational corporation.** With the great expansion of trade after World

War II and the increase in sales by U.S. businesses abroad, firms like Ford, ITT, General Electric, and IBM set up plants in other countries. They did so for many reasons. Sometimes it was to avoid the high cost of labor here, sometimes to avoid quotas and tariffs. Coca-Cola did it to expand the market size. Encouraging foreigners to invest in their company was a reason for some.

While the largest U.S. firms started the trend, it soon spread. Today there are more than 10,000 large multinationals with more than 90,000 subsidiaries in different nations.

Types of Organizations

Multinationals may be organized in several different ways. Most started out with control by the parent corporation over the branches (subsidiaries) in other countries. Later, many subsidiaries were given more decision-making power. In some corporations, such as IBM, more than half of the company's income is now generated by its foreign operations.

Some companies have *joint ventures* involving mergers of corporations from different countries. Car manufacturers and electronics firms have many such arrangements. Firms which take minerals from the earth, usually from developing countries, often have a partnership with the host country's government.

Hiring employees from the labor force of the host country depends on the types of skills needed and those that are available. Usually managers and technicians are sent abroad to start production and train local workers.

What Are the Benefits of Multinationals?

Corporations choose to operate outside the borders of their own countries to take advantage of opportunities in other nations or to maintain their competitive position in the market. Originally most multinationals were involved in extracting oil, minerals, or other natural resources. Their investments helped develop the resources of developing countries and provided jobs, education, capital, and taxes to the host countries. Their motivation may have been to earn a profit for their owners, but the results provided benefits to citizens of the host nations as well.

Recently, multinationals have more often been involved in exporting more efficient methods of production. U.S. cars have better quality today in part because of new technology that was developed in other countries and brought to the United States.

Multinational corporations may provide another benefit that is not directly economic. With the nations of the world becoming so intertwined in their economic interests, there may be a greater opportunity for understanding and world peace.

What Harm May Multinationals Cause?

While more U.S. jobs may be created when multinationals move into the American economy, U.S. corporations often take away jobs when they move production to other countries. Frequently this results in exploiting cheap foreign labor. This can cause bad feelings toward the United States in other countries, and resentment of foreign workers by Americans who have lost their jobs. Critics can also cite examples of U.S firms that have interfered in the internal affairs of host countries.

There is also a real question as to whether or not these firms pay their fair share of taxes. While some profits made by a foreign multinational may stay in the host country, much of it will return to the parent country. This often contributes to trade and financial problems of the host country. Most economists, however, welcome the low-cost production and quality that competition in our global economy brings. They also believe a greater use of research and new technology will raise the standard of living for all people.

Multinationals may cause short-term upheavals that force some people to lose their jobs and businesses to fail as our economy changes. It is difficult to think of the benefits of multinationals when you are out of work and are in danger of losing your possessions. Another problem is finding a way to control the power of multinational corporations when their interests are in conflict with those of the host nations.

■ *Self-Check*

1. What reasons are there for a company to go multinational?
2. What advantages may a multinational bring to a host nation?
3. Many developing countries fear multinationals. Why?

■ *Applying What You Have Learned*

In the Personal Narrative these questions are raised: 1) What is an American company? and 2) Who benefits from multinationals?

CURRENT CONSUMER ISSUES

Should the United States Use Trade Barriers to Help Its Industries?

The traditional argument for protecting businesses with tariffs has been to give *new* industries a chance to become more efficient so they can compete with foreign industries at home and in the global market. Should tariffs be used to protect *established* U.S. firms that have not kept up with foreign competition? Should the American consumer be asked to pay the costs for trade protection? The problems of the American steel industry illustrate this controversy.

In the 1950s and early 1960s the United States dominated the world steel market. However, construction of new facilities in other countries left our steel industry in a noncompetitive position by the 1980s. The United States imported millions of tons of steel, while American plants closed. Leaders of U.S. steel firms pleaded for tariffs or quotas that would give them a chance to improve their productivity.

During the next ten years U.S. steel firms closed inefficient plants, improved production methods, and reduced hourly wages. The number of worker-hours required to produce a ton of steel fell from 10.5 in 1980 to just 5.3 in 1990. This improvement was made possible at least in part by trade protection. This trade protection cost roughly $175,000 for each job that was saved.

Was this policy inconsistent with an earlier agreement? The United States helped establish the General Agreement on Tariffs and Trade (GATT) in 1947. Objectives of GATT included the reduction of tariffs and elimination of quotas among participating nations. Had the United States disregarded the rules for trade that it had helped create?

Arguments in Favor of Protection
1. It helped the U.S. steel industry recover.
2. It protected many American jobs.
3. It reduced the United States's dependence on other nations for a basic product.

Arguments Against Protection
1. It cost American consumers billions of dollars.
2. It may have diverted American investments into a business that had little comparative advantage.
3. It may have cost the United States some respect in the GATT organization.

What Do You Think?
Do you believe the government should protect other industries from foreign competition in the future?

Chapter 13 Review

What Have You Learned?

In this chapter you have learned the following important principles of economics:

- The United States trades because our benefits from trade exceed our costs. The theory of *absolute advantage* states that countries should specialize in products they produce most efficiently and trade for products they produce less efficiently. *Comparative advantage* differs by saying countries should specialize in producing things in which they have the greatest relative efficiency and trade for things in which they are relatively least efficient.
- U.S. trade policy began with *revenue tariffs*, shifted to moderately *protective tariffs*, and then became very protective from the Civil War to the 1930s. Since then the U.S. has led the world in trying to end trade restrictions. This has led to a boom in world trade. Trade is a significant share of U.S. GDP.
- Although theories suggest countries should have free trade, there are reasons that cause nations to impose tariffs, quotas, and other measures to restrict trade. Four such reasons are the *infant industry*

argument, the *national security* argument, the *protection of domestic jobs* argument, and the *maintaining economic stability* argument.

- In general, countries prefer to have a *positive balance* rather than a *negative balance of trade*. A positive balance of trade contributes to a nation's employment, economic growth, and taxable income.
- Some steps have been taken to help those who have been hurt by foreign competition. The Omnibus Trade and Competitiveness Act provided help for those who lost their jobs. Rules have been made against *dumping*.
- The price of imported products is partially the result of *exchange rates*. Part of the reason for the U.S. negative balance of trade in the early 1980s was the increased value of the dollar. Our high interest rates, political and economic problems in other parts of the world, and our early recovery from the recession of 1981–1982 all contributed to the dollar's rise in value. When the dollar declined beginning in 1985, U.S. exports increased sharply.
- U.S. businesses were the first to start the trend toward *multinational corporations*.

Words and Terms

absolute advantage (p. 370)
comparative advantage (p. 370)
tariff (p. 371)
revenue tariff (p. 371)
protective tariff (p. 371)
restrictive tariff (p. 371)
quota (p. 371)
infant industry (p. 373)
national security (p. 373)

protection of domestic jobs (p. 373)
maintaining economic stability (p. 374)
positive balance of trade (p. 374)
negative balance of trade (p. 374)
dumping (p. 376)
exchange rate (p. 378)
appreciation (p. 378)
depreciation (p. 378)
multinational corporation (p. 381)

Chapter 13 Review

These giants operate outside the borders of their parent countries providing jobs, education, capital, and taxes to host countries. Their power can also cause problems in the host countries.

Building Your Vocabulary

On a separate piece of paper, write the vocabulary word or term that best completes each of the following statements.

1. When the value of a country's money increases in comparison to other types of currency, it is called _____.
2. When the value of a country's money decreases in comparison to other types of currency, it is called _____.
3. A _____ is a tax on an imported good.
4. The theory of _____ states that a country should specialize and trade even if it is better at doing everything than other nations.
5. The theory of _____ states that each country should specialize in making the products that they are most efficient in producing and should trade for other products they do not make as well.
6. A _____ is an upper limit on the quantity of a good that can be imported into a country.
7. A tariff intended to increase the price of imported products to a competitive level with domestic products is a _____.
8. The _____ argument states that countries should limit trade to help control unemployment.
9. The _____ argument states that coun-

tries should limit trade to avoid being too dependent on other nations for important goods.
10. The _____ argument states that countries should limit trade to allow their new industries to grow and become efficient.
11. The _____ argument states that countries should limit trade so that they do not become too dependent on only a few types of production.
12. A tariff intended to reduce or eliminate the flow of a particular type of product into a country is a _____.
13. A _____ is a firm that is headquartered in a parent country with branches in host countries.
14. The value of different types of currency in terms of each other is called _____.
15. A _____ will tend to increase employment, economic growth, and business profitability.
16. A _____ will tend to decrease employment, economic growth, and business profitability.
17. _____ happens when a nation sells its products to other countries for a lower price than it charges its own people.
18. A tariff intended to raise money to run the government is a _____.

Understanding Economics

1. What do countries need to do in order to follow the theories of comparative advantage and absolute advantage? Explain how they should benefit from this.
2. Explain why many countries that are not advanced technically choose to place tariffs on imported goods.

3. Many countries choose to manufacture their own military equipment when they could buy these products from the other countries for less money. Explain why they do this.
4. Describe three advantages a country would enjoy if it had a positive balance of trade.
5. Many Americans benefit from lower prices and better quality that can result from imported goods. However, the costs of trade are not paid equally by all Americans. Explain why this is true.
6. Explain why some Americans were hurt by the decline of oil prices in the mid-1980s.
7. Describe the results of the voluntary limit Japan put on its exports of cars in the early 1980s.
8. Explain what it means when we say, "Between 1980 and early 1985 the U.S. dollar appreciated about 40 percent."
9. Describe three reasons for the increase in the value of the U.S. dollar in the early 1980s *that were not directly related to trade.*
10. Why did the U.S. dollar decrease in value after 1985? Explain the consequences.
11. Why do corporations go multinational? What undesirable results might occur?
12. What are the benefits to the host country of having a multinational corporation? What might be the costs?

Thinking Critically About Economics

1. Suppose you have been placed in charge of setting tariffs for a country that has high rates of unemployment and inflation. Explain why it will be very difficult for you to please everyone.
2. Some economists believe that foreign competition will be good for U.S. indus-

tries because it will force them to invest in new equipment and become more efficient. They point to the new factories that have been built by U.S. automakers to support this idea. Explain why you either agree or disagree with this argument.
3. Is the Omnibus Trade and Competitiveness Act of 1988 the work of protectionists, free traders, or a compromise to help the United States deal with an economic problem? Explain your answer.
4. "Dumping" is selling products to foreign countries for less than the price charged in your own country. Describe what a country could gain from doing this.
5. If interest rates go down in the United States, the value of the U.S. dollar should go down or depreciate (assuming nothing else changes). Explain why this might happen.
6. Explain why it is becoming increasingly difficult to identify an American product or company. Do foreign multinationals in the United States help or hurt our economy? Explain.

Consumer Skills Projects

1. Take a survey of the kinds of cars that are owned by students (and parents) in your class. What are the reasons for purchasing these particular cars? Do students' reasons differ from parents' reasons?
2. Bring a month-old issue and a current issue of *The Wall Street Journal* to class. Look up exchange rates under the title "Foreign Exchange." Find out whether the value of the dollar is going up or down in terms of other currencies. What generalizations can you make from the changing value of the dollar?

Developing Your Economic Skills

Positive and Negative Values on a Line Graph

Skill: In this lesson you will learn how to draw a line graph that includes both positive and negative numbers. This graph will plot information that shows a change in the financial position of the United States in relation to other countries. To complete this lesson, follow these steps:

■ Study a table that shows the U.S. international investment position, over a period of years.
■ Plot a graph of this information, in which positive amounts are shown above the horizontal axis and negative amounts are shown below it.
■ Evaluate the importance of the information provided on the graph.

Application: Is the United States a debtor nation?

Americans conduct many financial transactions with other nations. International trade, travel, and investments represent huge dollar transactions each year. Governments loan to each other; banks loan to businesses in other countries; people buy securities (stocks and bonds) issued by foreign businesses or governments. For many years the results of these exchanges made the United States a creditor nation. This means that each year our investments abroad were greater than foreign investments in the United States.

In the 1980s this changed. The United States developed large trade deficits as

Americans bought more goods and services from other countries than we sold to them. Many dollars returned to the United States in the form of foreign investments in American business and foreign purchases of U.S. government securities. Our international investment position changed from being a creditor nation to being a debtor nation. By 1987 the balance of U.S. foreign investment debt was greater than that of any other country, and still growing.

The following table shows the change in the U.S. financial position. **Balance** indicates the difference between U.S. investments abroad and foreign investments here.

United States Net International Investment Position 1980-1990 (in billions of dollars)

Year	Balance	Year	Balance
1980	$392.5	1986	$ 18.7
1981	$374.3	1987	$- 26.6
1982	$378.9	1988	$-183.8
1983	$337.4	1989	$-312.3
1984	$232.9	1990	$-294.8
1985	$139.0	1991	$-361.5

Source: *Survey of Current Business*, June 1992.

Practice: Plot these values on a line graph to show the trend more clearly. Make a copy of the following graph, with numbers on the vertical axis running from a positive value of 400 to a negative value of 400. A positive number represents a *surplus* U.S. investment position; a negative number represents a *debt* position.

The great size of this debt is causing economic problems for the U.S. economy, and could cause greater problems in the future. For example, payments made on this debt in the form of interest and other earnings send money out of the United States and reduce our purchasing power. Foreign companies are able to expand in the United States, while domestic firms lay off workers. How does the visual help you understand the trend in the U.S. international investment position? What might reverse this trend?

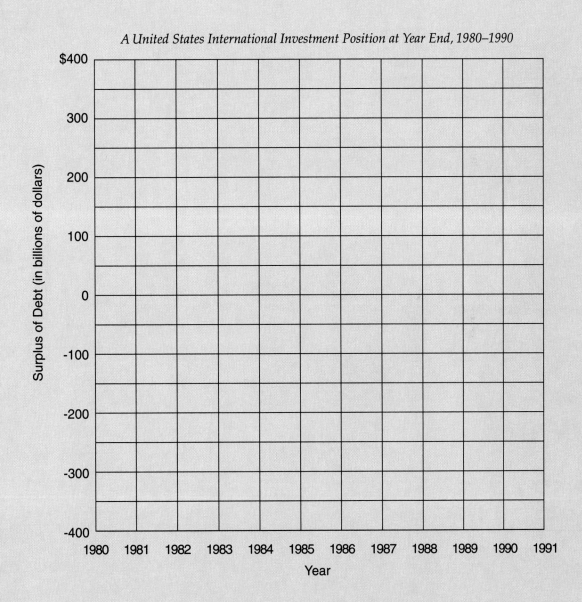

A United States International Investment Position at Year End, 1980–1990

Developing Nations, Growth, and Population

Objectives

In the sections of this chapter, you will learn:

A

what is meant by *developing nations*, what hampers their growth, and what is needed by these nations to speed development;

B

what type of aid is available, the controversy over whether aid should be given, and, if so, what type of aid; and

C

why many developing nations also have a problem with *population*, and how economic growth is linked to control of population growth.

Introduction

Most Americans have at least an adequate standard of living. They eat regularly, have clothing to wear, and a place they can call home. Many of us have a great deal more than just enough. This cannot be said of many other people in the world. There are nations in which the majority of people do not have even a minimal standard of living. Over the years these nations have been called "less developed," "underdeveloped," "emerging," or "disadvantaged countries." In this text they will be referred to as **developing nations.** All of these countries have at least one thing in common—low average incomes. The term **developed nations** will refer to industrialized countries like the United States, Germany, and Japan. The term **newly developed nations** will mean those middle-income countries with some developed industry, such as Poland, Mexico, and South Korea.

Average per capita income shows vast differences among the peoples of the world. The average personal income in the United States was about $20,000 in 1992. The World Bank lists 56 countries whose per capita income is below $1,000 per year. More than half of these countries had incomes of less than $500, and 350 million people living in 14 countries had incomes no higher than $250 per year.

The people of Ethiopia, Zaire, Kenya, and some other developing nations have experienced repeated famines in recent years. In many cases, there were steps that could have been taken to reduce or solve this problem. Unfortunately, internal conflicts prevented people from helping themselves and stopped outside aid from achieving its intended effect on development.

In this chapter you will learn some of the reasons for poverty in other nations as well as suggested solutions for increasing growth. The United States, other developed nations, and multinational corporations have attempted to help developing nations, with varying degrees of success. Nations and businesses that offer aid usually want some control over that aid. The developing nations, however, want freedom to do what they choose with the money. The cultural values of developing nations, their internal political instability, insufficient capital for investment, and lack of adequate educational systems often prevent developing nations from making economic progress. In some developing nations less than half the people can read, and rapid population growth strains already scarce resources.

The last section of the chapter will deal with population growth. Countries with the highest rates of population increase are often those that are least able to support and feed more people. Projections of future population trends offer little hope for the future in some parts of the world. Demands for help are likely to be made on wealthy nations by the people of less fortunate nations. The time may come when you will be asked to help make decisions that are related to this problem.

Section A The Problems of Developing Nations

This section will discuss problems that are faced by developing countries in their attempts to improve their standards of living.

Personal Narrative

Why Don't They Help Themselves?

My ancestors came to North America from Africa some time around 1750. There is no way to know exactly when they came, or where they came from, because they were black and brought here as slaves. I have never been to Africa and I probably never will go. I would know nothing about the language or customs there. But I feel a kinship for people who live in Africa. I know that I might be living there if history had been different.

I learned about problems in Africa from watching TV. I saw Africans starving on the news. It bothered me more than other problems that were reported. I was upset because I knew it could have been me. I wanted to know why they had these problems and what could be done to help them.

On one television program, I saw a reporter interview an expert on the economic problems of Africa. She explained several reasons for the problems she studies. One of the most important she mentioned is that many people in Africa do not know how to take care of their land and its resources. They often waste things that should be saved and cared for. Many Africans do not have the basic tools for farming or the skills to use tools they have been given. It is difficult to teach new skills because most African countries have limited funds to spend on education. Another important problem is fighting that has gone on in many parts of Africa. There are many cases where land and crops have been destroyed for political reasons. These, and other problems, have combined to make life almost impossible in many parts of Africa.

My church collected money to buy food for people in Ethiopia. I gave what I could. It made me feel a little better to be doing something, but I knew that it wasn't going to solve the real problems in Africa.

What Are the Problems?

Growing food requires more than seeds and rain. It requires tools and fertilizer—and most of all, knowledge. Farmers in many parts of the world learn what they know about farming from their relatives, and not in schools or from books. As a result, their farming methods almost never change.

A Traditional Economy

Traditions play a role in all economic systems, but they play a larger role in some countries than in others. In Medieval Europe, 900 years ago, there was an economic system called *feudalism*, which was based on tradition. In that system, everyone was expected to do the same job as their parents. All the land belonged to a king, a feudal lord, or to the church. The peasants farmed it and got to keep part of what they grew. This system went on for several hundred years with almost no social or economic change. We can find similar situations in regions of many developing nations today.

Even in the United States, what we consider right and wrong depends on what we were taught by our parents and families. However, we also learn from schools, books, and through other institutions in our society. In many countries most people learn almost everything they believe in from their families. These countries have what are called **traditional economies.** It is very difficult to bring about change in such economic systems.

If your father fed cattle in a drought by cutting down trees to get the leaves, you would do the same. You would not realize that you were destroying the environmental balance of the land. If your mother told you that a sign of power and status was a large family and lots of cows, you would believe this was true. The problem is that when everyone believes this, the number of cattle and people can grow beyond the ability of the land to support the population.

This is what has happened in large parts of Africa. The people could solve some of their own problems if they knew how, but they don't. Trying to teach new methods to people who have done things the same way for generations is not an easy task.

What is Needed for Change?

There is general agreement among economists that in order for developing nations to improve their economies they need to better educate their people, to increase their capital, to improve their management, and to have stable governments that other people and governments can trust.

Investment capital usually comes from savings, but how can poor people save? When capital becomes available, it may be invested in industries such as steel that offer prestige but little economic value to the nation. Management is frequently placed in

Although enrollment in schools and the literacy rate are improving in developing nations, many classrooms lack the basic educational tools that most schools in developed nations take for granted.

the hands of the politically powerful or inherited by the upper class instead of entrusted to the best trained and hardest-working people. Governments may hold power by favoring the few and controlling the army. Much of the money taken in may be used to put down rebellions and uphold the ruling powers.

If people know how to read, they can learn how to improve their health, develop skills, and better their living conditions. Unfortunately, only a little more than half of the children in developing nations attend primary school, and in most poorer nations less than ten percent attend high school. The ratio of teachers to pupils is more than double that of high-income countries. Books, chalkboards, desks, and even pencils and paper are scarce. Learning skills by example is useful, but few volunteers are willing to leave their own comfortable environments to provide such needed service.

Another problem of many developing nations is a lack of **infrastructure.** Infrastructure refers to the physical developments necessary for efficient production and distribution of goods and services. Such things as roads, ports, electric generators, telephones, and sewers are considered infrastructure. Without these things, it is difficult for an economic system to function efficiently. The lack of infrastructure makes it impossible for such countries to compete successfully with more developed nations. Building an infrastructure is very expensive. Many developing nations cannot afford to invest in these improvements.

The following table compares six nations in some key areas of infrastructure and of secondary school enrollment.

Roads are an example of infrastructure—the physical developments necessary for efficient production and distribution of goods and services. A major problem for many developing nations is that they cannot afford the investment necessary to create enough infrastructure to become competitive with the more developed nations.

Table 14–1

Infrastructure and Secondary School Enrollment for Various Nations

Nation	Km Roads per sq. Km*	Km RR Tracks in Thousands of Miles**	Percent of Adults Enrolled in Secondary School	Energy Production Per Person in Kg of Coal Equivalents
United States	.68	225.4	98	9,542
Japan	2.93	19.9	95	3,741
Brazil	.20	22.1	38	767
Thailand	.15	3.7	28	493
Nigeria	.01	3.5	29	166

*Generally, more densely populated nations have more roads, but all countries need roads to develop resources.
**Geographically larger countries are more likely to have more Km of railroad tracks. The United States is about 18 times as large as Thailand, but has 80 times as many miles of track.

What Has Happened to Growth in Developing Nations?

Table 14.2 shows the average annual percentage changes in GDP per capita in industrial and developing nations for three groups of years. It also gives World Bank projected growth for the 1990s. Both for the industrialized countries and all of the developing nations, with the exceptions of East and South Asia, growth rates have declined or remained at a plateau from 1965 to 1989. With a few exceptions, the poorest countries are part of the

Sub-Saharan or Latin American and Caribbean regions. Both of these show negative growth for the decade of the 1980s. They also have negative projections for the 1990s. Compare these figures with those of East Asia and South Asia. What are the reasons for growth in Asia?

Table 14–2

Growth of real GDP per capita, 1965–2000 (average annual percentage change, unless noted)

Group	Population, 1989 (millions)	1965–73	1973–80	1980–89	Projection for 1990s[a]
Developed countries	773	3.7	2.3	2.3	1.8–2.5
Developing countries	4,053	3.9	2.5	1.6	2.2–2.9
Sub-Saharan Africa	480	2.1	0.4	−1.2	0.3–0.5
East Asia	1,552	5.3	4.9	6.2	4.2–5.3
South Asia	1,131	1.2	1.7	3.0	2.1–2.6
Europe, Middle East, and North Africa	433	5.8	1.9	0.4	1.4–1.8
Latin America and the Caribbean	421	3.8	2.5	−0.4	1.3–2.0

Sources: World Bank data and World Bank 1991[a].

Taiwan, South Korea, Hong Kong, and Singapore, sometimes called newly developed nations, have had the fastest growth rates in the world. They have also had fairly stable governments, have provided good education for their people, and have high savings and investment rates. In the poorest Sub-Saharan and Latin American and Caribbean nations, political unrest has kept the economies from growing. There the rich have spent a high portion of their income on luxuries and have invested in other countries. Meanwhile, these governments have spent little for education and the work force is discouraged, with little hope of improving its income or position.

■ *Self-Check*

1. How is a traditional economy hampered in its growth?
2. What are the major factors necessary for growth in developing nations?
3. Which regions of the world recently have the best record of growth? Which have the poorest?

■ *Applying What You Have Learned*

If you were in charge of economic growth in a developing nation and the United States gave your country $30 million as a development gift, how would you spend it? Explain why.

Sir William Arthur Lewis
(1915-   )

Sir William Arthur Lewis is one of the rare individuals to have succeeded in combining a life of scholarship, teaching, and doing. He was honored with the Nobel Prize in Economics in 1979 for his work on theories of economic development. He has been a Professor of Economics at Princeton and at the University of Manchester in London. He was also made an Honorary Fellow of the Weitzman Institute and the President of the American Economic Association.

At the same time that Lewis was accumulating these impressive academic achievements, he was also working with a United Nations group on developing countries, was a consultant to the governments of the Gold Coast and Western Nigeria, and was an economic advisor to the Prime Minister of Ghana.

Lewis's keen interest in human problems brought him into the service of developing nations. His studies of the policies that worked and that failed in such nations led him to write his most important publication, *Theory of Economic Growth.* In it, Lewis explained his belief that developing nations must recognize the importance of agriculture and develop their industrial sectors slowly. Too often, poor countries pour resources into industrialization, only to find them wasted for a lack of a trained work force. The key to success, Lewis thought, was to be found in dual economies that have a large farm sector and a small industrialized urban sector. The small industrialized sector should make use of the surplus labor from the agricultural sector. Lewis believed that the wages of factory workers could not go up until surplus labor from rural areas was entirely employed. Although not all economists agree with his model, the foundations for much of our economic development theory were laid by Lewis.

Lewis served as an administrator in several Caribbean universities and was knighted by the British Government in 1963. He also founded the Caribbean Development Bank of Barbados. Few scholars have devoted as much time or effort to the problems of the poor as Sir William Arthur Lewis.

Section B The Relationship Between "Have" and "Have Not" Nations

This section will discuss the role of the United States and other developed countries in assisting developing nations.

Personal Narrative

Is There Anything We Could Do?

Students at my school earned money to pay for sending food to people in Africa last year. We sold candy door-to-door. Some other schools in town held paper drives or collected soda bottles to turn in for money. My homeroom won a free pizza party for earning the most money. The total for all the schools in town was almost $7,000. The president of our student council, and a bunch of other students, got their picture in the paper giving the money to leaders of the Red Cross. They said our money would save hundreds of lives. It made us feel good to know we had helped, but I know our money only made a small dent in the problem of world hunger.

I read that it would take billions of dollars to solve the problems of poverty and hunger in the world. I doubt that anyone except the government could afford to do it. We had a debate in English class about how much aid the government should give to other countries. I was surprised to find that many students were against the government giving anything at all.

I remember one student who said she was more worried about poverty in the United States than in other countries. She thought the government should spend its money here until all Americans had a "decent" standard of living. Many other students seemed to agree with her.

My teacher thought that sending aid might be a waste of our money because many developing nations aren't able or willing to deliver the aid to the people who need it. He said he had read about thousands of tons of food rotting in ships that were waiting to be unloaded. He also thought that dishonest government officials in some countries might steal the aid for their own use. He said we should only send aid if we were sure it would be used to help people who were really in need.

One of my friends believes that we should only send tools, seed, fertilizer, and educational aid. She said that sending food to developing nations will discourage them from learning to help themselves. Free food from developed nations would compete with food grown by local farmers. This would make it more difficult for farmers to succeed and therefore for the nation to ever be able to feed itself.

Another student said he thought we should only send aid to countries that supported our foreign policy and political ideas. He said that many countries take our aid and then accuse the United States of trying to tell them what to do. For example, he thought we should "cut off" any country that voted against our point of view at the United Nations.

A final idea was that we should only help countries that had a chance to escape poverty. One student said that some countries have so many people and are so poor that there is nothing we could do to solve their problems. He said our aid would only make it take longer for people to starve to death. He wanted to help the countries that were already making progress. He said aid sent to really poor countries was a waste of money and resources.

When the debate was over, I don't think anyone had changed their mind. I hadn't. I think we should all send something, even if it isn't enough to solve the world's problems. The government has more money than we do. I think it should do its part, too.

The Changing Nature of Aid

During the 1950s foreign aid from industrialized countries was considered absolutely necessary for the economic growth of developing nations. European countries and Japan, just beginning to recover from the massive destruction of World War II, were unable to provide aid during that period. The United States, which had helped with Japan's and Europe's recovery, provided the largest share of aid to developing nations during that decade. When Europe and Japan became richer, the distribution burden shifted. From 1960 to 1990 the United States's percentage of total aid supplied by the Western nations to developing countries dropped from 60 percent to 17 percent. Japan became the largest donor, and many European and Arab states provided a larger percentage of their GDP in aid than did the United States.

Total aid to developing nations more than doubled during the 1980s, but the needs of these nations increased even faster. This was a period when recessions hurt developing nations even more than industrialized countries because of the severe drop in the price of basic **commodities,** or products of agriculture or mining. These products made up most of developing countries' exports. Because of the apparent lack of progress in many devel-

When developed nations sent food to Ethiopia and other African nations in recent years, they prevented the deaths of many thousands of people. But many of these nations still have traditional economies, with few tools and a shortage of trained people. Unless these and other problems can be solved, they are likely to experience periods of famine again in the future.

oping nations, people in developed nations questioned whether aid could ever solve the world's economic problems.

The early 1990s brought the collapse of the Soviet Union and the end of its dominant influence in many nations. The former communist nations asked for immediate aid from the wealthy industrialized West. Without such aid, many feared that these nations might return to some form of communism. The industrialized nations estimated that $24 billion worth of aid would be needed. At that time the United States government's budget deficit was reaching record levels, however. Americans questioned raising the level of foreign aid.

Other Sources of Aid

Many private organizations and individuals send aid to both governments and foreign citizens to ease their burdens. In some cases, such as aid to India and China, the sum of such aid is fairly large. Emergency relief and United Nations related organizations ease suffering, but this aid has little to do with development.

Commercial banks grant loans that are important sources of investment capital to developing nations. Many of the nations that ask for such loans have had good growth records or possess mineral deposits that are in demand. Commercial banks charge high interest rates for such loans, making them financially profitable. There is a risk that a developing nation may not pay back its loans. However, the risk is offset by the hope that the United States government would come to the rescue if American banks faced large losses.

Multinational corporations are another source of investment capital for developing nations. As we studied in Chapter 13, multinationals can be very helpful to developing nations' economies, or they can attempt to get what profits they can without really contributing much to growth and development. Negotiations between multinationals and developing nations largely determine how much each will benefit.

The Debt Crisis

A number of factors brought on a debt crisis for many developing nations in the 1980s. The value of many of their exports, including oil, dropped sharply. Many loans had to be paid back in dollars at a time when the value of the dollar was increasing. Economic growth slowed, and poor management and inflation contributed to doubling the size of developing nations' debt compared to their GDP. By 1990 the accumulated international debt of developing nations was $1.3 trillion.

In the early 1990s interest fell to the lowest rates in many years. Lenders seemed more willing to renegotiate developing nations' loans. The alternative, in some instances, was to lose most of the money they had loaned. The International Monetary Fund and the World Bank played key roles in setting up new terms for payments and requiring the developing nations to discipline themselves in spending, saving, and moving toward free trade. These actions seemed to help developing nations with their debt problems.

Whose Attitude Is Right?

Developing nations are sometimes called the "have nots." They fear and resent being told what they can and cannot do by foreign nations, multinational corporations, or international organizations. They often feel that rich countries are trying to exploit them. Wealthy nations do see advantages in helping poorer nations develop. Developing nations can be sources of good quality products, inexpensive suppliers of raw materials, and good cus-

Investments in training, tools, and new seeds and fertilizer helped India develop from an importer of food in the 1970s to an exporter of food in the 1980s. Aid that promotes self-help is essential if developing countries are to overcome their problems.

tomers for industrialized nations' merchandise. However, multinationals will not risk their stockholders' money unless there are safeguards against losses. Regional and international agencies acting as neutral overseers may be able to establish ground rules acceptable to both developing nations and multinational corporations.

▢ *Self-Check*

1. What has happened to United States aid to developing nations in the last 40 years?
2. How has the source of international aid changed in recent years?
3. What world events caused the developing nations' debt crisis?

▢ *Applying What You Have Learned*

Reread the Personal Narrative and explain why you believe aid should continue or stop to developing nations during a recession in the United States.

Section C The Population Explosion

This section will discuss problems related to population growth in developing nations.

Personal Narrative

Will There Be Enough Resources for Tomorrow?

I like people. I enjoy talking with my friends. Crowded dances are fun. Being at a concert when everyone is excited makes me feel alive. I think New Year's Eve with crowds of people is the best night of the year. But, as much as I like people, sometimes I want to be alone. I believe that most people need a place of their own. It doesn't have to be big or luxurious, it just has to be a place where you can think in peace with no one else to bother you. When I look at newscasts about poor people in Africa or Asia, I wonder how they can stand to be so poor and so crowded together with nothing of their own. I also wonder if they did this to themselves.

I ask questions that aren't very popular. I can't help myself, I need to ask them. For example, if there are hundreds of millions of people in the world who are starving, doesn't it mean that millions of people had babies they couldn't support? When people can't educate their children, why do they have more of them? Does it make sense to have more children if your house is already too crowded? When I ask these questions at school, lots of people get mad at me, but others agree with my point of view. Few people are able to answer my questions.

I remember watching a news special on the famine in Africa. There were pictures of hundreds of thousands of people living in tents or out in the open. Most of them were starving. There were flies and garbage everywhere. The people were too weak to do anything for themselves. A reporter said that for every person in the camp there were probably five or six more back in their villages who were also starving.

I felt sorry for the kids, but not for the adults. Didn't they know what they were doing to themselves? How could a person bring children into a life like that? I don't understand it.

Poverty and Population Control

Many countries that have high rates of population growth are the same countries that are least able to support more people. To understand why poor people have large families, you need to know about their values and social systems.

Developing countries with high rates of population growth face great difficulty in trying to improve their standards of living. In such countries, most increases in production are used to support new children as they are born. Many economists believe these nations will not be able to achieve economic growth until they control their birthrates.

Truly poor people have few or no possessions. Their countries can't afford to pay them social security or pension benefits. Any economic security they have must be provided for by their families. If you expect your children to support you in your old age, it makes sense to have many children. One of them may do well and be able to take care of you.

Conflicts in Values

Most poor people are also poorly educated. They often do not know how to limit their family size. Attempts to educate people in methods of family planning have met with limited success in many developing nations. Some leaders in developed countries feel that family planning is not an appropriate answer to the problems of the developing countries, or that it is something that developed countries should not be involved in.

In the past, population growth was often limited by sickness. For example, the **mortality rate** (average number of deaths per thousand people per year) in Egypt was over 16 as recently as 1960. Advancements in medicine reduced this number to 10 by 1991. Health programs supported by the United States and other developed nations have helped people live longer, but in doing so they have made the population problem worse.

Effects of Growing Population

Population growth in many developing nations has made economic growth almost impossible. Countries that have population growth rates of 2 to 3 percent per year will double their population every 30 years. If these nations can't increase their production at an equal or faster rate, their standard of living will go down.

High population growth rates mean that there will be more children to take care of. Children do not contribute to production for at least the first few years of their lives. They also create a greater need for schools. When young workers do join the labor force, they may be less productive than more experienced older workers. Countries with high birthrates are likely to be less productive than those with lower birthrates (see Table 14–3).

Some countries have reduced their poverty in recent years. Most of these countries have first reduced their population growth rate. This has often been accomplished through harsh regulations on family size. An example of this happened in the People's Republic of China during the 1970s and 1980s.

The government of China took strong steps to encourage smaller families in recent years. They tried to convince their people that having fewer children is good for both social and economic reasons. Their government used schools, printed materials, and public advertising to make this point. To a large extent, they have succeeded.

Table 14–3
Population Growth Rates and Per Capita GDP for Various Nations

Country	Population Growth Rate (Average for 1980–1989)	GDP Per Capita (1989)
United States	1.0%	$20,910
West Germany	.0%	$20,440
France	.4%	$17,820
Argentina	1.4%	$ 2,160
Pakistan	3.2%	$ 370
Kenya	3.9%	$ 360

Source: *Statistical Abstract of the United States, 1991.*

In the 1950s, China's population was growing more than 3 percent per year. By 1990 this rate had fallen to 1.4 percent. At the same time, GDP per person in China increased from less than $100 to about $350 per person. To accomplish this, the Chinese government attempted to set a limit of one child per family. There has been resistance to this program, particularly in the countryside, where large families were important to farmers. Nevertheless, the Chinese population problem has become much less severe in recent years.

■ Self-Check

1. What is one reason that people in developing nations often want a large family?
2. How has a reduced mortality rate added to the population problems of many developing nations?
3. What special demands does a high birthrate put on a nation's economy?

■ Applying What You Have Learned

Make a list of three advantages and three disadvantages to having a large family in the United States. For each one, explain why the problem would be either more or less important in a poor country.

CURRENT ECONOMIC ISSUES

Should the United States Increase Its Aid to Developing Nations?

In 1964 the United Nations Conference on Trade and Development was created largely through the efforts of developing nations. This agreement established guidelines to govern the relations between rich and poor nations. Later the developing nations signed the New International Economic Order, calling on rich nations to favor poorer countries in purchasing their products, to increase aid and loans with no strings attached, to help raise commodity prices, and to allow host nations to buy foreign property holdings in their countries at fair prices. While the developed countries agreed to a few requests, they rejected ideas that would have changed the world economic order at their expense.

Businesses in industrial nations do see the potential of large markets for exports in developing nations. However, in the United States support for granting aid to developing nations has weakened in recent years. Many Americans believe that the United States should solve some of its own economic problems before extending more aid to other nations. In addition to this argument, Economic growth has been slow in developed countries, and recessions have hurt their economies. Few nations have been willing to increase their foreign aid, because many are not satisfied with the results.

Do you believe rich nations should increase aid to developing nations?

Arguments in Favor of More Aid
1. Developing nations can become markets for developed nations' exports.
2. Economic growth helps developing nations pay back their loans.
3. Unlike private investments, aid may be used for improvements in education, health, infrastructure, and agriculture.

Arguments Against Aid
1. The United States should reduce its federal deficit and its negative balance of trade, and help its own poor before aiding developing nations.
2. Much aid winds up in the pockets of politicians or is wasted on projects never completed.
3. Many developing nations that the United States aids do not support our positions when important issues come before the United Nations.

What Do You Think?
Consider the arguments for and against giving aid to developing nations What personal factors might influence your position? If you were older, owned a business, or worked in an exporting company, how might your position change?

Chapter 14 Review

What Have You Learned?

In this chapter you have learned the following important principles of economics:

- *Developing countries* have many special problems that make it hard for them to increase their production and the standard of living of their people.
- Developing nations often have *traditional* economic systems that are difficult to change. They often are unable to provide an adequate education to their people.
- Developing nations generally do not have an adequate *infrastructure* of roads, electrical generating facilities, water, sewage systems, or other capital improvements to allow efficient production.
- Developing nations often have political problems with origins that can be traced to times when they were colonies of other nations.
- When developed nations try to help developing nations, they must deal with many different problems at the same time.

- In the past 40 years the share of aid given by the United States has declined. Recently, developing nations have benefited from bank loans and investments by multinationals.
- In the 1980s many developing nations experienced a debt crisis as the prices of their exports fell and interest rates on their loans increased.
- Many developing nations have a population problem. Social values in many of these nations encourage people to have many children. High population growth rates require even higher rates of growth in production if people are to live better.
- In general, the developing nations that have been most successful in improving their standard of living have been those that were willing and able to place limits on family size.
- The problems of developing nations are so great and complicated that it is unlikely that any amount of aid would solve all their problems. Developing nations will have to do much of the work for themselves.

Words and Terms

developing nations (p. 391)
developed nations (p. 391)
newly developed nations (p. 391)

traditional economy (p. 394)
infrastructure (p. 395)
mortality rate (p. 405)

Building Your Vocabulary

On a separate piece of paper, write the word or term that best completes each of the following statements.

1. The United States, Japan, Germany, and many other industrialized countries are often referred to as _____.
2. While economic growth has slowed in much of the world, some of the _____, especially in South Asia and East Asia, have experienced impressive rates of growth in recent years.
3. In a _____ people learn most of what they know from their relatives rather than in school or from books.
4. A lower _____, made possible through advancements in medicine, has contributed to the rate of population growth in many developing nations.
5. Many developing countries lack an adequate _____, or roads, electric power systems, schools, and other physical improvements necessary for economic growth.
6. Nations in which the majority of people do not have even a minimal standard of living are called _____.

Understanding Economics

1. Explain why it would probably be more difficult to bring about change in a traditional economic system than in a developed country like the United States.
2. Describe why a lack of infrastructure makes it difficult for developing nations to produce goods efficiently or to increase their economic growth rates.
3. Identify two reasons why international economic conditions caused many developing nations to experience a debt crisis in the 1980s.
4. It is possible that some U.S. aid has been wasted by developing nations because their people did not know how to use the aid that was given. Explain why sending tools to these nations is not enough to ensure economic growth.
5. Summarize the arguments for and against investments by multinational corporations in developing nations.
6. Explain why countries with high rates of population growth tend to have difficulty in achieving economic growth.
7. Explain why many people believe that a strong government is needed to reduce the rate of population growth.

Thinking Critically About Economics

1. Make a list of five important things you know about that you would not understand if you only knew what you had learned in your home.
2. Suppose that someone suggested the countries in Africa be joined together into one big nation to make it easier to assist their development. Explain why this would not be a good idea.
3. If you wanted to open a large paper mill in a South American rain forest, what problems would you have to overcome to achieve your goal?
4. Suppose that you are in charge of educating people in a developing nation. What sort of education would you emphasize? Explain why you would do this.

5. Why do you believe many foreign banks have been willing to allow developing nations to renegotiate their loans and reduce their payments?

6. Do you believe that most Americans would be willing to give more aid to developing nations? Would *you* be willing to give more aid? Explain why you feel the way you do.

7. Suppose that you are in charge of improving the standard of living in a developing nation. Although the production of goods and services has been increasing by 2 percent a year, your nation's population has been growing at 3 percent a year. Your people are worse off today than they were five years ago. Describe two realistic steps that could be taken to solve the problem.

Consumer Skills Projects

1. Interview ten adults. Ask each of the first five whether they would support giving more aid to developing nations. Tabulate their answers. Ask the next five if they would support sending more tools to poor countries to help them feed themselves. Tabulate their answers. Identify any differences between the answers from the two groups of adults. Try to explain these differences.

2. Look at a map of your neighborhood. Identify as many examples of infrastructure as you can on the map. Explain how these things help local firms compete to sell their products.

3. Take a poll of the students in your class, asking how many children there are in each of their families. Also find out how many brothers and sisters each student's parents and grandparents had. Using this information, find the average size of the family for today's students, for their parents, and for their grandparents. Has this average increased or decreased? What reasons could explain this change? Try to explain what this has to do with social and economic changes.

Developing Your Economic Skills

Interpreting Economic Data on Maps

Skill: In this lesson you will learn how to use a map to compare data about different nations.

Maps can enable a reader to easily relate economic data to geographic and political areas. Economists often make use of political maps (showing boundaries of nations) and adapt them to show economic data. In this lesson you will study a map of South America that shows levels of per capital Gross Domestic Product (GDP) in different nations. The map will allow you to make general comparisons of the probable standards of living in these nations. To complete this lesson, you will follow these steps:

- Look at the map to see what types of areas are represented.
- Study the key to determine what kind of information is being shown and how it is being presented on the map.
- Examine the map and relate it to the key.

Application: Every map contains a *key* (or *legend*) that shows you how to interpret the map. When you study the key for this map, you will see that each color shown on the key represents a different level of per capita GNP. By matching each nation with a color shown on the key, you can determine the level of per capita GNP for that nation. Notice that the levels are broadly drawn. A country that falls in the second level, for example, can have a per capita GNP of any amount between $500 and $1499.

When you study this map, you will see that there is some variation among the per capita GNPs of different South American countries. There is much greater variation, however, between these countries and the United States and Canada, both of which have per capita GNPs greater than $20,000.

Practice: List the names of all South American countries in four sets, from the highest GDP per capita to the lowest.

South America, Per Capita GDP

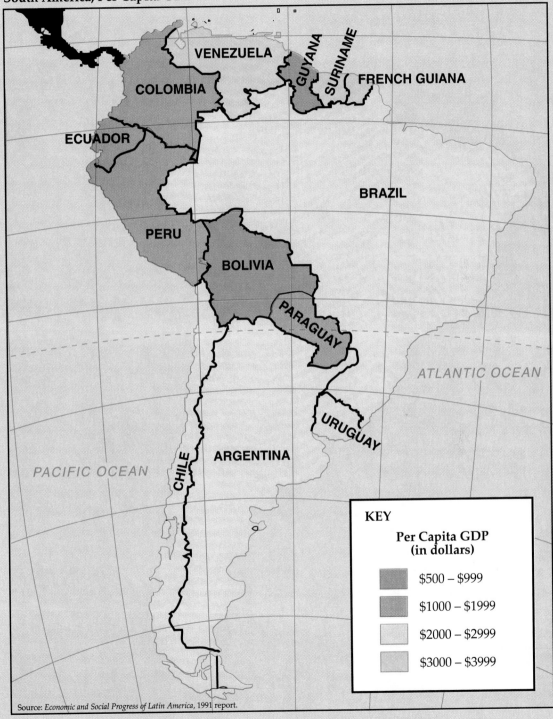

VENEZUELA

GUYANA

SURINAME

FRENCH GUIANA

COLOMBIA

ECUADOR

BRAZIL

PERU

BOLIVIA

PARAGUAY

ATLANTIC OCEAN

URUGUAY

PACIFIC OCEAN

CHILE

ARGENTINA

KEY

**Per Capita GDP
(in dollars)**

$500 – $999

$1000 – $1999

$2000 – $2999

$3000 – $3999

Source: *Economic and Social Progress of Latin America*, 1991 report.

Alternative Economic Systems

Objectives

In the sections of this chapter, you will learn:

A

how different economic systems may be identified and evaluated;

B

about differences between theories and the realities of how different types of economic systems work; and

C

how the values and cultures of different nations are reflected in the economic systems they use.

Introduction

In Chapter 2 you learned about differences between market and command economies. In this chapter you will look more closely at a variety of ways nations choose to answer the basic economic questions *what*, *how*, and *for whom*. You will discover that the way different nations answer these questions is closely related to their political systems, their values, and cultures.

Economic systems are often said to be based on economic theories or models. As you read about the systems that exist in various nations, you will realize that the way they work in reality is not exactly like the theories economists have developed. These theories have value, however, because they may be used as guides to help you understand real economic systems more easily. As you learned in Chapter 2, economic models provide a foundation on which students of economics may build a better understanding of the way economics works in the real world.

Studying a nation's economic system tells you a great deal about that nation's goals, values, and human relations. This will be clearly demonstrated when we compare the differences between the capitalistic economies of Japan and the United States in Section C.

Section A A Variety of Economic Systems

This section will identify different economic theories and explain differences between these theories and real economic systems that exist or have existed in the world.

An Island of Socialism

My name is David Goldberg. I am 17 years old. Last summer my parents sent me to Israel to live and to work on a **kibbutz.** They said they wanted me to "get in touch with our people," and to learn about "life." When I left I didn't really know what they meant. After spending two months living in what often seemed to be a dream world, I think I understand why they sent me.

A kibbutz seemed like a combination of a community and a family to me. The 270 or so kibbutzim (plural) in Israel are villages in which all residents work together for their common good. No one owns private property except for a few personal possessions. All the buildings, tools, cars, trucks, land, and other resources are owned collectively by the community. Like most others, the kibbutz where I stayed was largely involved in farming. It had orange groves, a fish farm, and a recently built small factory where it assembled parts for computers. In many ways the kibbutz was self-sufficient. The people who lived there grew almost all of their own food, built their own buildings, and produced many of their own clothes.

At the kibbutz I was assigned a place to live with many other young men. We all received work clothes and shared a telephone, TV, radio, and bathroom. We all ate in a community dining hall. None of us had any real privacy. We were assigned jobs by the Work Coordinator, who tried her best to give us jobs we liked. However, disagreeable jobs, like cleaning toilets, were shared by all. What really surprised me was how hard everyone worked in spite of the fact that no one got any more for their work than anyone else. In fact, the only money we received was just enough to buy candy or a few souvenirs to take home.

At first I wondered why everyone worked so hard. What was the point, if no one could earn much money or own cars or houses of their own? I discovered that many members of the kibbutz wanted the praise and admiration they received from others when they worked hard. The few people who did not seem to do their share were not respected in the community. I learned that a few had even left. I found that the kibbutz would pay for its members' college educations and support them in their old age. So, people worked because they wanted to be respected by other members of their community, and because it gave them a sense of security.

The kibbutz was run by an elected General Assembly, which chose officers and an Economic Committee. The Committee made the basic economic decisions of what, how, and for whom. I soon realized that the kibbutz was really an example of a small command economy like the ones I had learned about in school. Most economic decisions were made by a small group that told the others how to use the community's resources.

Almost everyone seemed happy at the kibbutz. Anyone who became dissatisfied had the right to leave. There were a few specialists who worked in the computer parts factory who were not members but were hired for their special skills. They received a salary like workers in capitalism. They preferred the individualism, personal income, and private property that are found in most of the Israeli economy.

At the end of the summer I was invited to come back again next year. This made me feel good because it showed I had been accepted. I have decided not to return but to take a job in my uncle's store, where I will earn almost $2,000. I guess having my own TV in my own bedroom and only having to share a bathroom with one sister may have something to do with my decision. I don't regret having visited Israel; I just like our system better.

Some societies do not value individualism as highly as the United States. Instead, they emphasize a spirit of community. Many workers in Japan begin the day with 10 minutes of group exercise.

Answering the Basic Questions

You learned in Chapter 1 that all nations face the same basic economic problem of having limited resources and unlimited wants. They try to choose the economic system that will provide them with the greatest satisfaction possible, given the limited resources they have. All nations must answer the basic economic questions of what to produce, how to produce, and for whom the production is created.

The model shown in Figure 15-1 illustrates a range of ways that these key questions may be answered. On the far left is a command economy where the *what, how,* and *for whom* are decided by a central planning agency. This was the approach used by the former Soviet Union and that is being used by the Economic Committee of the kibbutz in the Personal Narrative. In a command economy productive resources are owned collectively by all, and a planning agency determines how the resources will be used. Individuals have little voice in making the basic economic decisions.

On the far right side of the model is a market economy where the basic economic questions are answered by individuals through the forces of demand and supply. In a market economy resources are owned by individuals, who determine how they will be used.

Figure 15–1   *The Range of Economic Systems*

Command Communism	—	Socialism	—	Welfare Capitalism	—	Industrial Capitalism	—	Market Capitalism
North Korea China		Cuba		Sweden United Kingdom		Germany Japan		Singapore United States

In the range between the two extremes of the model are communism, socialism, welfare capitalism, industrial capitalism, and capitalism. Each of these systems has different degrees of government ownership and control over the system's productive resources. No country fits either extreme of the model perfectly. All nations have mixed economies that range from near capitalism to near communism. The position of the countries listed below the range of systems shows about where the economic systems of these nations were located in 1993. One way to place a country on this range is to find what share of total spending is carried out by the nation's government. The larger the share, the farther to the left the country is likely to be.

The Importance of Political Systems

Trying to classify countries strictly by their economic systems does not provide an accurate picture of how they work. We should also consider their political systems. In all countries there is a division of political power between the people and the government. In some countries people hold most of the power, in others the power belongs largely to political leaders. How this power is distributed provides a clue to how the system works.

Any country that has a command economy must tolerate a strong government role in its system. In these countries political leaders are likely to hold more power. In market economies most economic decisions are made by individuals who own and control the productive resources. Less government intervention in the economy is needed or tolerated. In such nations more of the political power is likely to be held by the people.

The balance of power between people and their political leaders is likely to change over time. As societies become more complex, the need for government power tends to increase. As the economic system of the United States developed, the country found a need for social security, public schools, government transfers for welfare and medical care—the list goes on and on. These additional government programs required giving both more political and economic power to the government. In the twentieth century the United States economic system took on more characteristics of a command economy and increased the power of the central (federal) government and its influence over the individual's life.

Economists, politicians, and citizens have debated the issue of how power should be divided between the people and the government. Under President Franklin Roosevelt, government economic powers grew rapidly. Many government agencies were established that limited the economic rights of businesses and people. Minimum wage laws replaced negotiations over wages in some industries. Fifty years later, under President Ronald Reagan, attempts were made to reduce the power of the government in the economy. Tax rates were lowered and some government regulations were eliminated.

Look at Figure 15-2. It shows a relationship between the political and economic systems that are likely to be associated with each other in a nation. In the left column more of the economic and political power is given to the government and less to the people. In the right column the opposite is true—more power is in the hands of the people and less power belongs to the government. There are costs and benefits associated with each distribution of power. The left column represents a system that provides greater security and less individual opportunity for a nation's citizens. The right column shows a nation that provides its people with greater individual opportunity but less security.

Figure 15–2

The Distribution of Political and Economic Powers

More reliance on central political control and a command economy

More reliance on individual political choice and a market economy

▨ *Self-Check*

1. Where should a kibbutz be placed on the range in Figure 15-1?
2. Why do countries have mixed economic systems?
3. Why do countries with centrally controlled economic systems usually have governments with strong political powers?

▨ *Applying What You Have Learned*

Identify a current debate over government spending in your community. Describe how this debate is related to the role of government in the economy of your community and its ability to use its political power.

Section B Economic Theory vs. Economic Reality

This section will explain the ideas of Karl Marx and discuss differences between economic theories and the mixed economic systems that exist in nations today.

Personal Narrative

The Theory and the Reality

Yesterday I saw an old movie of a news program from 1960 in my economics class. At first I thought I was going to be bored, but it turned out to be interesting even if the sound wasn't too clear. The subject of the movie was an interview with a man named Gus Hall, who was introduced as a leader of the American Communist party.

I learned from the film that in 1960 there was a recession in the United States economy. That was the year John Kennedy and Richard Nixon were running against each other to be President. The film showed Mr. Hall saying neither of these men had an answer to the people's problems. He told the interviewer the real problem was America's capitalist businesses that were only run to earn profits for their owners. According to him, the owners didn't care about consumers or workers. They charged the highest possible prices and paid the lowest possible wages. Mr. Hall said capitalists were exploiting American workers as well as people in other countries. He said business owners were getting richer, while workers were becoming poorer. The answer to our economic problems, according to Mr. Hall, was to get rid of the capitalists and their economic system. Then, he said, we could produce the products ordinary people needed and everyone would have a fair share of our nation's wealth and income. The whole idea seemed strange to me, but I think Gus Hall really believed what he was saying.

Yesterday evening when I talked about the movie at supper, my father became really angry. He said, "Don't you know that communism stuff is dead? It was nothing but a bunch of ideas that didn't work. Even the Russians got rid of it when the Soviet Union broke up. People didn't work in communism, because they had nothing to work for. The few products they produced fell apart. Most of the time people couldn't find anything to buy at all. The only people who gained in communism were the leaders who told everyone else what to do. That Hall guy was just plain crazy and I don't want to hear any more about him!" I think my father reacted too strongly, but I understand. I told him it was just a history lesson and excused myself from the table as quickly as I could.

Communism: The Theory

Only a handful of people through history have had as much influence on people's lives as Karl Marx (see his Profile on page 427). Through most of the twentieth century hundreds of millions of people lived in countries that had economic and political systems based on his ideas.

Marx believed history is mostly the story of the struggle between capitalists, who owned the means of production (land, factories, machines, etc.) and other people, who owned little and usually worked for the capitalists. During the industrial revolution, according to Marx, the means of production became too large and expensive for most people to own. Fewer and fewer capitalists earned increasingly larger profits by exploiting workers who received less and less wages. When workers became unable to buy the products they made, there was overproduction that caused recessions and widespread misery. Marx predicted that when conditions became intolerable, the workers would revolt and take over the means of production from the capitalists. Then, he said, the workers would join together in a spirit of brotherhood to produce the products that were needed by all and share the fruits of their labor equally—a system called **communism**. Although the revolution Marx predicted never happened in the way he thought it would, his ideas had a strong influence on many people in the twentieth century.

Communism: The Reality

Karl Marx never laid out careful plans for how a communist economic system should be set up or controlled. Therefore, when a revolution in Russia made that nation the world's first communist country (the Soviet Union) in 1917, no one knew how to run its economic system. Between late 1917 and 1924 Nikolai Lenin was the leader of the Soviet Union. He tried to start a system of complete government ownership and control of the means of production, but his attempt was a dismal failure. There was economic chaos and little production. Lenin revised his system to mix government ownership with a degree of private ownership of farms and smaller businesses. Although this mixed system worked reasonably well, after 1928 it was replaced with almost total government ownership and control by Joseph Stalin.

Under Stalin's leadership private ownership of the means of production was eliminated and the basic economic choices of *what*, *how*, and *for whom* were made by a government planning agency. The government set wages and prices and determined how resources would be allocated. The result was shortages of

The basic theory of communism was developed by Karl Marx in the late 1840s. Although Marx laid the foundations for modern communism, many of his ideas have been changed to fit the needs of communist countries in the world today.

many consumer products at the same time there were surpluses of other goods that often had low quality or that no one wanted.

Many of Stalin's goals for the Soviet Union were achieved. In the 1930s the Soviet Union (Union of Soviet Socialist Republics, or USSR) became a major military power. Basic industries were established and thousands of miles of railroad tracks were built. These accomplishments came at the price of great human suffering. Under Stalin, the government forced workers to work through fear. When the government eased its oppressive policies under later leaders, workers were left with little **incentive,** or motivation, to work hard. The standard of living for most people in the Soviet Union was very low. The central planning agency set production goals, but plant managers chose to produce the quantity of goods demanded by sacrificing the quality of the goods. Millions of people, without incentives, seemed only to be "putting in time" on their jobs. This inefficient economic system remained essentially the same until the late 1980s. Then it collapsed because it could not provide basic necessities. This was perhaps the greatest cause for the breakup of the Soviet Union.

Many Eastern European nations were close allies of the Soviet Union. For many years they also attempted to make communist economic systems work. More recently, these nations have tried varying mixtures of socialism and capitalism as their economic systems. The People's Republic of China remains as the largest nation that continues to use the communist model. Even China, however, has opened up part of its economy to private ownership, using the **profit motive** as an incentive to en-

Which is more productive, a command economy or a market economy? Hoping to improve productivity, some socialist governments in Europe have returned some government-owned industries to private business.

courage greater production. Communism in theory supported a democratic state, but in reality communism has never existed in a democracy. When the people have political power they are not likely to allow any government to have so much control over their economic choices.

Socialism: The Reality

Both communism and **socialism** trace their main ideas to the thinking of Karl Marx. However, socialists did not predict a revolution by workers against owners. Various forms of socialism developed in democratic nations, especially in Europe. Although communism seems to have failed as a political and economic system, various mixtures of socialism still exist in many countries. Several nations of Western Europe have relied on socialist ideas including government ownership of large industries and utilities. Some prices have been set and many resources were allocated by government agencies. Incomes in these nations were more equal and tax rates higher. People in these nations have enjoyed personal security through extensive social programs provided by their governments. Some economic systems have been called **welfare capitalism** because of these benefits. In exchange for security, the people have given up a degree of individual economic freedom.

In the past several years most countries have reduced the amount of socialism they mix into their economic systems. They have turned more toward capitalism, mainly to encourage greater productivity. In France, for example, a socialist president sold some government-owned industries to private businesses and reduced government regulation of the economy. Similar steps have been taken in Scandinavian countries that have reduced benefits of government social programs and lowered tax rates. Even in the United States many local governments have stopped providing services like garbage collection and public transportation. They let private businesses sell these services in their communities.

Capitalism: The Reality

According to the theory of capitalism, private individuals have the right to use resources they own to produce the goods and services they believe will earn them the greatest profit. The basic economic questions of *what, how,* and *for whom* are answered by people making individual economic choices. The problem of allocating resources is not centralized in government but **decentralized** in the market. The government's role in this system is limited to setting and enforcing basic rules for how businesses are organized. In such a system the government collects and spends a very small portion of the total national income.

If a country chooses to become less capitalistic, the government's role in the economy grows along with the share of income it collects and spends. One simple way to measure the degree of capitalism or socialism that exists in a nation's economy is to look at the share of national income that is spent by its government. Using this method, we can see that the United States is far from pure capitalism. In the United States government support for education, welfare, health services, retirement programs, and many other services takes up nearly one-third of the income earned in this country. In most European economies the share of income spent by the government is even larger. In these nations people have given up some individual economic freedom to gain a degree of economic security and equality for all.

Table 15–1
Tax Revenues of Selected Countries, 1988

Country	Tax Revenue as Percent of GDP
United States	29.8
Japan	31.3
United Kingdom	37.3
France	44.4
Sweden	55.3

Present and Future Systems

We live in a world that has steadily become more complex and interdependent. Many nations have moved away from pure market or pure command economies in an attempt to provide the best features of both capitalist and socialist systems. There is little reason to believe current economic systems will remain the same over time. As long as people have the right and power to control their governments there will be changes in the mixtures of economic systems.

In this chapter we have compared economic theory with reality. Theories are important because they provide direction. If one change does not work, a theory may suggest another approach. For most of the twentieth century the United States experienced a gradual growth of government involvement in its economic system. Much of this government involvement came in reaction to abuses that many people believed had developed because government had been reluctant to change the economic system. This trend reversed in the 1980s and 1990s. Many people in the United States and in other nations believed government had become too powerful. They felt it was time to return to greater individual economic freedom. How long will this most recent trend last? No one knows. However, we can say with a reasonable amount of certainty that the exact mix of market and command economies in the United States will continue to change throughout our lives.

▪ *Self-Check*

1. How did the economic system in the former Soviet Union answer the basic economic questions of *what, how,* and *for whom?*
2. What are several characteristics of the United States economic system that are more socialist in nature than capitalist?
3. Why have many countries chosen to change the mix of economics in their systems to less socialism and more capitalism in recent years?

▪ *Applying What You Have Learned*

Investigate the economic statements of politicians running for a government office in a recent or a coming election. Which of these candidates seems to favor more government control? Which would have less? What reasons does each candidate provide to justify his or her point of view?

PROFILE

Karl Marx
(1818–1883)
and
*Joseph Alois
Schumpeter*
(1883–1950)

Karl Marx

Few people in history are as closely identified with revolution and economic struggle as Karl Marx. In *Das Kapital*, he interpreted the history of capitalism through his economic and social theories. He also wrote *The Communist Manifesto*, with Frederick Engels, in which he said that capitalism would fall and that communism would triumph.

Marx believed that history showed a never-ending class struggle between those who owned capital (machines, buildings, etc.) and those who had to work for the capitalists. He thought capitalism was a necessary evil that enabled society to create the tools of production. However, he believed that firms in capitalism were run only to earn a profit for the owners, and not to produce what people needed. Marx said that capitalists earned a profit by paying workers less than the value of their labor. As a result, capitalists grew richer while workers got poorer.

Marx believed that as time went by, there would be more poor people and fewer rich people. At some point the workers would revolt, seize control of the means of production, and establish a dictatorship of the proletariat (the workers). While Marx never explained

exactly how a communist country should be run, countries that called themselves communist lagged far behind more capitalistic countries in terms of their ability to produce goods and services. Marx's predictions seem far from the way the real world turned out.

Joseph Alois Schumpeter

Born in 1883, the same year that Karl Marx died, Joseph Schumpeter believed that capitalism would lay the seeds for its own destruction through its success rather than through its failure. Schumpeter was born and educated in Austria and later taught at Harvard.

In his book *Capitalism, Socialism and Democracy*, Schumpeter started with his economic hero, the entrepreneur. Business owners were anxious to produce goods and services so that they might earn large profits. These risk-taking capitalists would bring prosperity to themselves as well as to society.

However, at a certain point in their success, firms would become overly cautious. The spirit of the risk-taking entrepreneurs would give way to bureaucracy and socialism. In Schumpeter's view, capitalism and the economic advantages it offered would decline, and the world would be poorer, not richer, when capitalism disappeared.

Section C Different Kinds of Capitalism

This section will compare the different types of capitalism that are practiced in the United States and Japan.

Personal Narrative

Two Views of Japan's Economy

Last week a new student named Eric registered in my economics class. He had just returned from spending a year living with his father, who works for the Motorola Corporation in Japan. My teacher asked him to tell us about his experience there. Some of the things he said surprised me, some made me angry, and others made me worried.

Eric told us that the economic system in Japan is a different form of capitalism than we have in the United States. Although their businesses are owned by people, there are different rules for what these firms may do and how they treat their workers. Probably the thing that surprised me most was that many Japanese workers are hired for life by their employers. Employees agree not to work for any other firm, and the employer guarantees them a job until they retire. It sounded like a really good deal to me. My father had worked making electronic parts for automobiles for almost 20 years. Then he was laid off because his employer started buying electronic parts from Japan. They gave my father a couple of months of salary and advised him to train to be a computer operator, and that was just about it. Now both my parents work in retail stores, so we can make ends meet.

When Eric lived in Japan he spent a day at a factory that produced VCRs. He said everyone started the day with 10 minutes of exercise. Workers were divided into groups that were allowed to decide how to do assigned tasks. Managers walked around the factory asking questions and talking to workers as if they were equals. The tour guide told Eric that the difference between workers' and managers' salaries is not too large. Eric learned that unemployment and inflation in Japan are very low. The rate of economic growth has been roughly 50 percent faster than that of the United States in the past 20 years. They have earned hundreds of billions of dollars from exports and have invested in other nations' businesses. He made it sound like everything in Japan was great. I felt really depressed.

I guess our teacher was concerned about the reaction of the class. The next day she invited an American of Japanese heritage to speak to us about another side of the Japanese economy. Mr. Shento told us that the United States is still the most productive country in the world. Production per worker in the United States is

$55,300 compared to only $38,800 in Japan. Mr. Shento praised Japan for the economic progress they have made, but he also pointed out that most Americans have better material lives than the Japanese. He said housing costs in Japan are almost twice as high as they are in the United States. An imported melon can cost $60 in Japan. I felt a little better, but I am still worried about my father finding a good job.

Testing for Capitalism

There are several tests that may be used to determine the degree of capitalism that exists in an economic system. One is whether people own the means of production. Another is if resources are allocated according to profits or controlled by the government. A third method that was discussed earlier in this chapter is the share of national income that is spent by the government. In the United States and Japan government spending is a much smaller share of the national income than in many more socialistic nations.

Market forces determine most resource allocation in the United States. Different businesses buy resources based on their profitability. The Japanese government, on the other hand, takes a leading role in allocating resources. In the Japanese economy businesses and government cooperate to direct resources to firms that are expected to be most successful in producing and exporting goods. Some 700 large corporations have organized into the Federation of Economic Organization, whose chief executive officer is sometimes called the "prime minister of Japanese industry." In the United States such an organization of producers working together would be challenged and broken up under the government's antitrust laws.

Different Trade Responsibilities for the Government

The United States Commerce Department tries to help American firms compete in world markets by providing them with information and advice. However, it tries to show no favoritism to any particular industry or firm.

This is not the case in Japan. The Japanese Ministry of International Trade and Industry (MITI) picks industries that it believes will be successful in international competition. It helps these industries by providing low-cost loans, research grants, tax breaks, and advice. Also, restrictions on how goods may be imported put foreign producers at a disadvantage competing in Japanese markets. This type of economic system is sometimes called **industrial capitalism.**

Different Labor-Management Relations

In the United States labor and management are usually on opposing sides. The U.S. government has passed laws to protect the rights of workers. These laws include minimum wages, rights of unions to negotiate collectively, protection against discrimination, and safety regulations. The U.S. government avoids becoming involved in labor-management relations most of the time. Although the United States has a National Labor Relations Board, more than 95 percent of labor disputes are settled without government intervention.

Japanese workers treat some firms almost as if they were part of the family. They see the firm's success as their personal responsibility and sacrifice their needs for those of the group. This is only a part of the picture, however. Only about 30 percent of the labor force in Japan has this type of lifetime worker-employer relationship. The other 70 percent are either self-employed or work for firms that do not provide guaranteed jobs with good benefits. Many Japanese workers have no job security. Social benefits provided by the Japanese government are less extensive than those of the United States. Workers who retire without a pension in Japan often must rely on the support of their children in their old age.

Other Differences

Many economists believe the most important factor in Japan's economic success is that country's high saving and investing

Japanese culture places more value on conformity than does American culture. Children learn some cultural values in school.

rates. Japanese people save a share of their income that is about twice as large as Americans save. This may be caused by their different values or by the fact that their government provides smaller retirement benefits. Japanese firms pay lower dividends than American corporations, investing a larger share of their profits back into their businesses. The Japanese devote more of their income to education for both children and adults. Japanese culture places a value on conformity and not showing emotion. These and other social values may contribute to Japan's productivity. On the other hand, many people suggest that the desire for conformity reduces creativity. The Japanese government and some businesses have experienced cases of corruption that some say surpass the U.S. Savings and Loan disaster. As in all nations, there are both good and bad aspects of the Japanese economy.

Defending Japan

Another factor that may have aided Japan's economic growth is the national defense provided by the United States for many years. United States defense efforts directed toward keeping peace around the world have cost an average of about 8 percent of its U.S. GDP since World War II. The Japanese have spent less than an average of 2 percent of their GDP for defense. This has left Japan with more resources to devote to investment and production. Japan also benefited from U.S. investment and technical help immediately after World War II. Today and in the future the United States and other nations expect Japan to contribute more to world security and growth.

Self-Check

1. Explain whether you would want to work for a Japanese corporation based on Eric's report in the Personal Narrative.
2. Why can we say that both Japanese and American economies are capitalistic, while those of Scandinavian countries are more socialistic?
3. What types of help do Japanese businesses receive from their government that cause many Americans to feel that they have unfair advantages over competing American firms?

Applying What You Have Learned

"The world would be a better place if the Japanese worked less and consumed more." What do you think this statement means? Is it consistent with the principles of economics? Explain.

CURRENT CONSUMER ISSUES

Should Our Government Provide Medical Insurance for All Americans?

At the time of the 1992 presidential campaign more than 35 million Americans had no medical insurance. Millions more had inadequate coverage. Members of both major political parties supported government intervention to assure all Americans a minimum amount of medical insurance. However, each party had a different plan. Americans heard the candidates explain their differing approaches to providing medical insurance in the campaign.

President George Bush suggested that the government should issue vouchers to low-income Americans. These papers could be used by consumers to buy insurance coverage of their own choice, at the government's expense. Under this plan middle-income people would benefit by being able to deduct their insurance payments from their taxes. The main point was that consumers could buy their own insurance from private companies.

Democrats argued that some people would not buy insurance under President Bush's plan. President Bill Clinton came into office with a different plan. The government would be the provider for those workers whose employers did not provide a health plan. Employers would have to pay into a government insurance fund for these employees. People with-

out jobs would receive a tax subsidy to help pay the premium for a basic package of health benefits.

Which plan do you believe was best?

Arguments in Favor of President Bush's Plan
1. It would allow individual consumers to choose their own insurance coverage.
2. Middle-income people would be allowed to deduct their insurance payments from their taxes.
3. It would limit the involvement of the government in determining the type of insurance people have.

Arguments in Favor of President Clinton's Plan
1. It would cover all people, regardless of their income.
2. People without jobs would receive government tax subsidies to help pay their premiums.
3. It would eliminate the need for inefficient private insurance programs.

What Do You Think?
Are all Americans qualified to choose their own insurance? Could the government run a large insurance program efficiently?

Chapter 15 Review

What Have You Learned?

In this chapter you have learned the following important principles of economics:

- Many types of mixed economic systems exist between the extremes of command and market economies. Although there are differences between these systems they must all answer the basic economic questions of *what*, *how*, and *for whom*. They must also have a way to allocate scarce resources. All economic systems are mixed, having a combination of central control and individual freedom that suits their values and political system.
- People who live in economic systems that rely more on a central authority trade a degree of economic freedom for more security. Other people who live in nations that rely more on the market system enjoy more personal freedom and less economic security. As always, there is a trade-off when economic choices are made.
- One way to judge the degree of central control in an economic system is by studying the share of national income that is spent by the government. Countries with a higher percentage of government spending tend to also have more central control. These nations are also likely to have government leaders with greater political power.

Words and Terms

kibbutz (p. 416)
communism (p. 422)
incentive (p. 423)
profit motive (p. 423)

socialism (p. 424)
decentralized (p. 424)
welfare capitalism (p. 425)
industrial capitalism (p. 429)

- Communism is an economic system that has both centralized control of the means of production and of the political system. The theory for this system was developed by Karl Marx in the mid-1800s. Communist theory suggests that once workers are given the opportunity to work together for their common good they will enjoy peace and prosperity. In reality communism proved inefficient and restrictive of people's rights. Most nations that have had communist systems have replaced them with various forms of market economies.
- Many countries, including the United States, have some characteristics of socialism mixed into their economic systems. The nations of Western Europe and Scandinavia have used extensive government ownership and control of resources for many years. Their governments commonly spend 40 percent or more of their national income. In recent years most nations have reduced the amount of central control over their economies in an attempt to improve their productivity.
- Both Japan and the United States have economic systems that are forms of capitalism. However, the ways each of these nations uses capitalism are quite different. The government of the United States allows most economic decisions and the allocation of resources to be accomplished through decisions made by indi-

See Chapter 15 Review Answers, page T156.

viduals. The Japanese government takes a more active role in deciding which businesses will receive resources and how investments will be made. Japanese firms are often encouraged to work together to develop new products and export goods to other countries.

■ There are advantages and disadvantages to the Japanese brand of capitalism. Although some Japanese workers have guaranteed jobs and many benefits, others lack these advantages. The Japanese economy has grown rapidly for many reasons that may include their greater rates of saving and investing, a closer relationship between their workers and employers, and the fact that Japan has been spared the cost of maintaining a large military to defend itself. Some people believe that a Japanese desire for conformity stifles creativity in that nation. Japan's growth and production will force it to take a larger role in world affairs in the future.

Building Your Vocabulary

On a separate piece of paper, write the vocabulary word or term that best completes each of the following statements.

1. _____ is an economic system that relies on centralized control over a nation's productive resources and political system.
2. The basic _____ to run a business in capitalism is the desire entrepreneurs have to earn a profit.
3. The _____ is an incentive that encourages greater production in capitalism.
4. In _____ the government assures all citizens a basic standard of living by pro-

viding extensive social programs that are paid for through relatively high taxes.
5. In capitalism most of the power to make economic decisions is _____.
6. A _____ is a community in Israel that has a command economy which makes most of the basic economic decisions.
7. In _____ the government helps businesses work together and often takes part in the allocation of resources to encourage greater productivity.
8. Generally the greater the share of national income that is spent by a country's government, the more _____ is mixed into its economic system.

Understanding Economics

1. What types of rewards are supposed to give people an incentive to work in command economies?
2. What does it mean to say that all countries have mixed economic systems?
3. If a nation's government is taking and spending a growing share of national income, what is probably happening to the mixture of capitalism and socialism in its economic system?
4. What types of governments are most often found in nations that have strong central control over their economic systems?
5. Why did Karl Marx think workers would revolt and replace capitalism with communism?
6. What are three economic problems that were experienced by nations that had communist systems before the 1990s?
7. Why have most nations reduced the amount of socialism mixed into their economic systems in recent years?

8. What are three measures that are often used to tell if a nation's economy is a form of capitalism?
9. What type of help is provided to Japanese businesses by their government that the American government does not give to its businesses?
10. What are three possible reasons for the rapid growth of the Japanese economy in the past 20 years?

Thinking Critically About Economics

1. Suppose that you visited a kibbutz and were asked the following questions by children in one of their schools. How would you answer each question?
   a. Why are there many poor people in a nation that is as wealthy as the United States?
   b. What is the purpose of the billions of dollars your businesses spend on advertising each year?
   c. Why are so many schools in the United States in need of repair?
   d. When so many people compete against each other in the United States, how can you expect people to live together in peace and harmony?
2. Make a list of four questions you would ask a student who lives on a kibbutz about his or her life.
3. Suppose you run a business that employs several hundred workers who build public housing projects in large cities. List and describe four different

ways that the government would limit your freedom to run your firm as you see fit. How does this demonstrate our mixed economic system?
4. Explain why firms in the former Soviet Union could make low-quality products and continue to exist year after year. What would happen to such a firm in the United States economy?
5. Explain why many people believe the extensive social programs in nations with socialist economic systems reduced the incentive people felt to work hard.
6. What reasons may Japanese managers have to work hard when the salaries they receive are not much more than ordinary workers are paid?

Consumer Skills Projects

1. Interview five adults. Ask each to explain reasons for the changes that took place in the economic systems of nations in Eastern Europe and the former Soviet Union in the early 1990s. Record their answers and report them to your class. What conclusions can you draw about the knowledge many adults have about the events in these nations?
2. American consumers purchase auto insurance under the market system. Imagine how auto insurance might be provided in a command economy. Describe the advantages and disadvantages of such a system.

Developing Your Economic Skills

Interpreting a Bar Graph To Compare Related Information

Skill: In this lesson you will learn how to interpret a bar graph that is used to compare information that is different but may be related. In this example the rates of inflation and changes in production in Japan and the United States will be compared. Some economists believe inflation may sometimes cause increased production. They feel businesses may respond to increased demand and higher prices by producing more goods and services. This graph may be used to evaluate this belief. To complete this lesson, you'll follow these steps:

1. Examine the vertical and horizontal axes of the graph to see what kind of information they show.
2. Examine the types of bars on the graph to see what they compare.
3. Evaluate the significance of the information provided on the graph.

Application: What were the rates of inflation and growth in real (adjusted for inflation) GDP in the United States and Japan in 1990 and 1991?

On this graph the percent of change in prices (inflation) and in real production (measured by GDP) appear on the vertical axis. The graph's horizontal axis shows various categories that include the years 1990 and 1991, which country is being considered, and the type of change that is being measured.

When you compare the bars you will notice that the United States had almost no change in its real GDP in both 1990 and 1991. However, the American economy did experience inflation that was greater than 5 percent in 1990 and more than 4 percent in

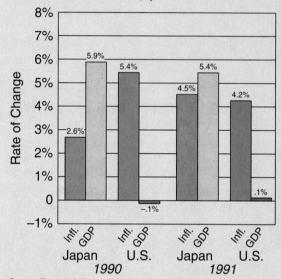

Inflation and Rates of Change in Real GDP in the United States and Japan, 1990 & 1991

Sources: *Economic Indicators*, April 1992; *Economic Trends*, Federal Reserve Bank of Cleveland, November 1991.

1991. Inflation did not seem to encourage more production in the United States in these years. In both 1990 and 1991 Japan had a real rate of growth in its GDP of over 5 percent. Although Japan also experienced inflation its rates were lower than those in the United States. Japan experienced a growth in production although it had a relatively low rate of inflation. The information provided on this graph does not seem to support the idea that inflation causes growth in production.

Practice: Is this explanation correct, or may other factors explain the growth in production in Japan and the lack of growth in the United States? To further test this explanation, prepare a graph that shows the relationship between inflation and changes in production in the United States over a longer period of time or in more countries.

Part 4 Review

Summary of Major Economic Concepts

In Part 4 you have learned the following basic economic principles concerning relationships between the economy of the United States and those of other nations.

■ The United States and other countries trade because the benefits of trade exceed the costs. The theories of absolute and comparative advantage state that countries should specialize in making the goods they produce most efficiently and trade for others they produce less efficiently.

■ Countries may limit trade with tariffs, quotas, or standards imported products are not likely to meet. This is done to protect industries and domestic jobs, and to maintain national security and economic stability.

■ Countries prefer to have a positive balance of trade, which contributes to employment, growth, and taxable income.

■ Multinational corporations have been taking an increasingly important role in the world economy. Although countries benefit from the increased trade, employment, and investment these organizations bring, they may also cause problems. Multinationals may not pay their fair share of taxes, and they may interfere in a nation's internal affairs.

■ The United States had a negative balance of trade through most of the 1980s and into the 1990s. This was caused by many factors that included an increased value of the U.S. dollar, inflation, and a desire of some Americans to buy foreign products they believed had high quality. When the value of the dollar fell in the late 1980s the U.S. balance of trade improved but remained negative.

■ Developing nations have special problems that make it difficult for them to improve the standard of living of their people. These problems include economic systems that resist change, inadequate educational systems, a lack of infrastructure, rapid population growth, and political instability.

■ In recent years, the share of foreign aid given to developing countries by the United States has fallen. However, developing countries have benefited from bank loans and investments made by American businesses.

■ Many types of mixed economic systems exist between the extremes of command market economies. Although there are differences between these systems they must all answer the basic economic questions of *what*, *how*, and *for whom*.

■ Many countries, including the United States, have characteristics of socialism mixed into their economic systems. Many nations of Europe in recent years have reduced the amount of central control over their economies in an attempt to improve their productivity.

■ Both Japan and the United States have economic systems that are forms of capitalism. However, the ways each of these nations uses capitalism are quite different. The government of the United States allows most economic decisions to be made by individuals. The Japanese government takes a more active role in deciding which businesses will receive resources and how investments will be made.

■ The Japanese brand of capitalism has advantages and disadvantages. Although

Part 4 Review

some Japanese workers have guaranteed jobs and many benefits, others lack these advantages. The Japanese economy has grown rapidly for many reasons that may include greater rates of saving and investing, a closer relationship between workers and employers, and the fact that Japan has spent little for military defense. Japan's growth will force it to take a larger role in world affairs in the future.

Understanding Economic Concepts

Each of the following questions emphasizes one or more economic concepts or terms from Part 4. The concept is listed in parentheses after each question. Answer in complete sentences that show you understand the concept. The first question has been answered for you as an example.

1. What theories tell us which products countries should produce and which products they should trade for? (Discuss *absolute* and *comparative advantage*.) (Answer: The theory of absolute advantage says countries should produce goods they can make most efficiently and trade for other goods. Comparative advantage emphasizes *relative* efficiency.)

2. What three types of barriers to trade may countries establish? (Discuss *tariffs*, *quotas*, and *standards that discourage trade*.)

3. Why do many developing nations have high tariffs? (Discuss the *infant industry argument*.)

4. Why would countries prefer to export a greater value of goods and services than they import? (Discuss *positive balance of trade*.)

5. What was one important reason for the U.S. negative balance of trade in the 1980s? (Discuss the *exchange rate* for the U.S. dollar.)

6. How have large firms that do business in many nations helped and hurt different nations? (Discuss *multinational corporations*.)

7. Why is it often difficult to bring about change in developing nations? (Discuss *traditional economic systems*.)

8. What is one important form of capital that many developing nations lack? (Discuss *infrastructure*.)

9. Why doesn't sending tools to developing nations guarantee that they will be used effectively to increase production? (Discuss *inadequate education systems*.)

10. What is one important change that has contributed to population growth in developing nations in the past 40 years? (Discuss reduced *mortality rates*.)

11. What basic characteristics are found in different types of command economies? (Discuss *communism* and *socialism*.)

12. What reason probably contributed to the low worker productivity that existed in many communist countries in the past? (Discuss the *incentive* people feel to work.)

13. What advantages are provided to Japanese businesses by their government? (Discuss *industrial capitalism*.)

Writing About Economics

Each of the questions below requires you to write a brief essay. Follow these steps:

■ Demonstrate your understanding of the identified economic concept(s) in your essay.

- Explain how the economic concept(s) is involved in the situation.
- Describe the choice you would make in the situation and on what basis you would make this decision.

1. A politician is going to visit your school to talk about foreign trade. You know from what you have read that she is in favor of reducing tariffs. Write three different questions to ask her, and explain why each is an important question. (Discuss the *protecting domestic jobs argument, dumping,* and *negative balance of trade.*)

2. Pretend you have helped organize a drive to raise money to pay for tools, seed, and training for poor South American farmers. You are going to a meeting at a local church to ask for contributions. You are sure you will be asked to explain why people in developing nations need help from people in the United States. Prepare a written answer. (Discuss *traditional economic systems, infrastructure,* and *inadequate education systems.*)

3. Suppose there is an exchange student from Japan visiting your school. One day he asks you to explain what you believe are the most important differences between the U.S. economic system and the economic system of Japan. Write an answer to his question. (Discuss differences between the *industrial capitalism* found in Japan and the *mixed capitalism* of the United States.)

Discussing Economics

The following paragraphs describe economic issues that have been topics of recent public debate. For each issue, decide whether you support or oppose the proposal, and how you would present your opinion to the class. When you present your opinion, follow these steps:

- Identify and describe the controversial issues of the proposal.
- Clearly state your decision.
- Explain why you think your choice is the best one.

1. There is evidence that American automobile firms have been harmed by imports from other nations. Suppose a bill was introduced in Congress that would require that at least 80 percent of the parts in all cars sold in the United States be made in this country. This law would force foreign producers to make or buy many parts for their cars in the United States, or else stop selling them here. Those who support the bill believe it would increase the number of jobs in this country. Opponents of the bill say it would make our cars much more expensive. What action do you recommend to your congressional representative?

2. Some Americans have become concerned about the large loans that many American banks have made to developing countries. They are afraid that these loans may not be repaid and that U.S. taxpayers will be forced to "bail out" U.S. banks when these loans go bad. They want a law passed that would prevent banks from making loans to developing nations. Other people say such a law would go against the economic principles of our capitalistic system and would harm developing nations that need our loans. Which side of this debate would you support?

Problem-Solving with Economics

Chapter 13

1. Suppose you could afford and wanted to buy each of the products listed below. For each, indicate whether you would

Part 4 Review

expect to buy an American or foreign-made product, and explain the reasons for your belief.

a. VCR   c. automobile

b. home computer   d. suit

2. A number of suggestions have been made for things that could be done to help people who are hurt by imported goods. Describe the costs and benefits that would result from each of the following suggestions. (In considering costs, remember that government programs are paid for by the taxpayers.)

     a. Limit the amount of goods that may be imported.

     b. Increase tariffs on imported goods.

     c. Extend unemployment benefits by two years for people who lose their jobs due to imported goods.

     d. Provide government retraining programs for anyone who loses a job because of imported goods.

     e. Give government jobs to anyone who is unemployed because of imported goods.

Chapter 14

1. Suppose you are in charge of a developing nation. You know that in order to grow, a country must invest in tools and factories, in education and training, and in infrastructure. You have the resources to work on these areas, but not all equally. Explain which type of investments you would concentrate your resources in and why you would do this.

2. Suppose that the following ideas were suggested to help the world's poor people. Explain how well you believe each would work and why.

     a. Have U.S. government pay tuition of foreign students to study in the United States to learn how to help their people.

     b. Encourage U.S. businesses to invest in developing nations by giving them tax breaks if they do.

     c. Send U.S citizens to developing nations to show people how to be more productive.

3. Suppose you are the director of the ministry of health in a developing nation. You learn that a developed nation has recently marketed a vaccine that will prevent a disease that has been a major cause of death in your nation. You also realize that lowering the death rate will cause rapid population growth that will slow economic growth and could later result in famine. Should you recommend that the government purchase the vaccine?

Chapter 15

1. Suppose you live in a command economy and want to achieve economic growth. Describe three steps you might take that would be different than steps you would take in a market economy. Would the steps in the command economy be as likely to increase productivity as those in a market economy? Explain why or why not.

2. The kind of person who is a good business manager is not always the same kind of person who can win an election. Describe the personal traits that would make a good manager. Do the same for a person who could win elections. Use these lists to explain why nations with socialist systems and democratic governments may have economic problems (in these nations elected officials often make basic economic decisions).

CAREERS AND
EMPLOYMENT OPPORTUNITIES

Some of you are working now, some of you will start work when you are graduated from high school, and still others of you will delay work until you leave college. Almost everyone who looks for work can find something somewhere, at least part-time. But most people have in common a desire to find a full-time job that will pay an adequate income now and hold good promise for the future. We look for jobs that have the potential for advancement, with additional responsibilities, greater authority, better job security and more money. We would all like to enjoy our work and be successful at it. Finding such a job is not easy. But you can improve your chances by carefully exploring different job opportunities and by learning about your own abilities.

Every year, the U.S. Bureau of Labor Statistics publishes the *Occupational Outlook Handbook* (OOH). Information about almost all occupations is listed. For each occupation, the Handbook describes working conditions, employment training, qualifications, advancement opportunities, job outlook, and current and expected earnings. It also covers related occupations and provides sources for additional information, career counseling, and financial aid for education and training.

Anyone looking for a job or considering training for a career should consult the latest edition of the *Occupational Outlook Handbook*. This source and other valuable career planning guides can be found in most libraries.

What Is the Job Market?

Like all markets, the job market is made up of buyers and sellers. The buyers are businesses, governments, and consumers who need people to work for them. The sellers are the labor force: all persons sixteen years or older who are working or looking for work. Of the 250 million people in the United States in 1992, about 128 million were in the labor force. They represent supply. Those who hire workers represent demand. The total job market is the sum of many smaller job markets, and it involves individual decisions by millions of people.

In the early 1990s, an average of 93 percent of those in the labor force had jobs. But the job market is much tougher on new job entrants than on experienced workers. New entrants into the work force can improve their chances with more education, additional skills, training, and any work-related experience they can acquire.

What Are the Employment Trends?

Although the total number of people in the labor force continues to grow, the number of new people entering the labor force has slowed in recent years. For the high school or college graduate looking for an entry-level position, it's encouraging to know that not as many new workers are now competing for those positions. However, the growing total number of people in the work force means job advancements might be slow.

In 1948, manufacturing accounted for 27 percent of civilian employment, while workers in services and trades combined made up 25 percent. By 1992, manufacturing had dropped to 20 percent, while services and trades jumped to 57 percent. Manufacturing clearly offers less job security to new entries than do services and trades.

What Are the Occupational Trends?

Almost all occupations will need new workers in the 1990s, even if it is just to replace retiring workers. But some areas will be growing rapidly, some slowly, and still others will be declining.

The health-care field, for example, will expand, because of the increase in the number of elderly. Advancing technology will increase opportunities in some fields, but decrease opportunities in others. Occupations related to computers, word-processing equipment, and industrial robots will expand. But employment of statistical clerks, stenographers, and welders will decrease. Despite these changes, office clerical workers will likely remain the largest major occupational group.

Below are listed (in alphabetical order) some occupations expected to grow rapidly and those headed for decline.

Fastest-Growing Occupations
Accountants and auditors
Computer programmers
Corrections officers
Data processing equipment repairers
Electrical and electronics technicians
Employment interviewers
Lawyers
Mechanical engineers
Medical assistants
Paramedical personnel
Physical therapists
Registered nurses
Securities and finance sales workers
Travel agents

Fastest-Declining Occupations
Central office operators
College and university faculty
Farm management advisers
Farm workers
Furnace operators
Machinery maintenance mechanics
Postal service workers
Railroad brake signal operators
Sewing machine operators
Shoe and leather workers
Statistical clerks
Stenographers
Textile workers
Tractor operators

Making a Personal Choice

While it is important to know as much as you can about the careers you are thinking about, the choice must be a personal one. The market will determine the present and future demand for workers in a particular occupation and the degree of competition. You have no control over the market other than to accept or reject what it offers. What you do have control over is determining your own career goals. In determining a career path, you need to assess your own abilities and evaluate the sacrifices necessary to achieve different possible goals. You need to consider which career paths will likely bring the rewards that will be worth your total investment in money and time.

It is difficult to make such choices without adequate information. Take the time to consult sources such as the *Occupational Outlook Handbook* and seek the advice of a career counselor. Finally, there is a good chance you will be in the work force for about 40 years. If you are like most people, you will change careers, perhaps more than once in your lifetime.

Selected Job Categories

This section contains samplings of the kinds of information that you should consider when you think about your career choices. In the space of this book it is only possible to present a few job categories. There are many other career fields that you can explore. Detailed information about most types of jobs can be found in the *Occupational Outlook Handbook* and in other sources.

The OOH provides earnings information for many job categories in terms of the "middle range." To find this range all people employed in a job category are ranked according to their annual earnings. The highest paid 25 percent and the lowest paid 25 percent of the category are not considered. The range of income of the middle half is reported in the OOH.

Accountant

Nature of the Work

Most people think of accountants as preparers of income taxes. While that is certainly an important task, it is but one of their many responsibilities. Their major purpose is to prepare, analyze, and verify financial reports that furnish information to management in both the public and private sectors.

The four major fields in accounting are public, management, government, and internal auditing. *Public accountants* serve the general public (not government) in privately owned firms. They check clients' financial records, seeing to it that they conform to standard procedures for reporting. They give advice on tax advantages and disadvantages, on setting up an accounting system and on managing cash resources, and they prepare income tax statements.

The largest group are *management accountants*. They usually work for larger businesses in such areas as budgeting, investment, and taxation. The financial information they provide helps management make decisions.

Government accountants are employed at all levels of government. Some deal with the financial management of government agencies and operations, including the preparation of budgets, while others (such as those working for the IRS) examine tax returns.

Internal auditors are hired by a company as full-time employees to audit that company's records. This field is growing faster than the other areas of accounting, as the demands for management to account for their actions increase. Internal auditors approach their examination of records with an attitude of "what can I find that is wrong or wasteful."

Working conditions for accountants are generally pleasant, and hours are frequently regular, with the exception of tax season.

Education and Training

Most firms and government agencies require applicants to have a bachelor's degree in accounting or some closely related field. More selective employers prefer those with a master's degree and who are familiar with computers. Those planning to become accountants must be good at mathematics, be able to compare, analyze and interpret numbers and facts, to make sound judgments, and to communicate well. Patience and accuracy are essential.

Job Outlook

There are approximately 1 million accountants. About 300,000 are Certified Public Accountants (CPAs), which gives professional recognition. About 10 percent are self-employed. Very few accountants work part-time.

The job outlook for accountants is very good, because of increasing demands made on management and by government. Turnover and firings due to decline in business conditions are low. Starting salaries for those with bachelor's degrees average $25,300. For those with experience, salaries average $33,500, while chief accountants or those with supervisory duties average $53,300. Some CPAs earn over $100,000.

Automotive Mechanic

Nature of the Work

Automotive mechanics repair and service automobiles and trucks. When repairs are required, the mechanic must first diagnose the problem, and then make the necessary repair or replacement. Preventive maintenance during routine servicing is considered equally important to treating breakdowns.

Larger shops, particularly automotive dealers, have specialists. These include mechanics for automatic transmissions, tune-up, front end, air conditioning, brakes, radiator, and electrical systems. Mechanics use a variety of tools, both power and hand, some of which they own personally. Machine tools, such as lathes, jacks and hoists, infrared engine analyzers, diagnostic devices, and welding and flame-cutting equipment are usually furnished by the employer.

Working conditions for automotive mechanics depend on the conditions in the garages where they work. These may be fairly pleasant, or they may be noisy, poorly lit, too cold (or hot), or poorly ventilated. Many jobs are greasy and dirty and may require working in awkward positions. Lifting heavy parts and receiving cuts and bruises is commonplace.

Education and Training

Automotive mechanics get their training through apprenticeships, formal schooling, or a combination of both. However, fewer employers are willing to hire people with no formal classroom work in automotive technology. Programs are offered in high school, public and private vocational and technical schools, and in community colleges. Instruction may be concentrated in six months or be extended over two years at a community college where academic courses are combined with automotive training. Employees, particularly at new dealerships, may be sent to factory training centers to learn about new models and to receive specialized training in one of eight different specialized areas. Achievement is recognized by certification from the National Institute for Automotive Service Excellence for having two years experience and passing a written test in each of the eight different service areas.

Job Outlook

In 1988 there were 771,000 automotive mechanics. Most worked for dealers, repair shops, gasoline service stations, and supply stores. Many others worked for organizations that had fleets of cars, such as governments, large companies, taxicabs and automobile leasing firms. Some worked for motor vehicle manufacturers. About 20 percent were self-employed.

The job outlook for those with some formal training is better than average because of an expected increase in the number of motor vehicles and the need to replace experienced workers who move on to other occupations or retire. Earnings for skilled mechanics who are employed by a dealer average $17.40 an hour; less skilled workers average $8.70 an hour. Most mechanics work about 40 to 48 hours per week.

Computer Systems Analyst

Nature of the Work

If a retail chain wants to computerize its inventory or if a research organization wants to improve its efficiency, each will need a computer systems analyst. Some computer systems analysts plan and develop computer "networks" for businesses. These networks connect all the computers in an individual office, department, or building. This allows all the users of microcomputers on the system to retrieve data from a mainframe computer and use it at their workstation machines.

Analysts usually begin an assignment by discussing the needs of the organization with managers or specialists. They define the goals of the system and then use models to develop a plan that meets these needs. They may also prepare a cost-benefit analysis to help management decide whether the proposed system is satisfactory. If a system is accepted, the analyst may determine what specific computer hardware and software will be needed to set it up. They may also prepare specifications for computer programmers to follow or work with programmers to eliminate errors from the system.

The possible uses of computers are varied and complex. Analysts usually specialize in either business, scientific, or engineering applications. They may need training in the field for which they develop the computer systems. Some analysts improve systems already in place or adapt them to handle more tasks.

Systems analysts work in offices. Their work week is usually the same as other professionals and office workers. At times, however, evening or weekend work is necessary. For example, they may have to make changes in a system when system users are not at work.

Education and Training

The qualifications of a systems analyst vary because they depend on the preferences of employers. Many employers, however, expect the analysts to have a college degree in computer science. The college degree indicates that the analyst is familiar with programming languages, computer concepts, systems analysis, and data base management.

A background in accounting or business management is important for a computer systems analyst who wants to work in a business environment. Scientific organizations prefer analysts with a background in science, applied mathematics, or engineering.

Prior work experience is important. Most people entering this field transfer from occupations such as engineer, manager, or computer programmer. The titles Certified Data Processor and Certified Systems Professional are conferred by the Institute for Certification of Computer Professionals. Candidates for certification passed a general test and a specific two-part examination.

Job Outlook

Demand for computer systems analysts will increase with the advancing technology that leads to new applications for computers. There were more than 463,000 people employed as computer systems analysts in 1990 and median annual income was about $38,700. The range of income was fairly broad. The lowest 10 percent of systems analysts earned less than $23,000. The highest 10 percent earned more than $62,000.

Cosmetologist

Nature of the Work

Beauticians or hairstylists are common names to describe cosmetologists. They also may give manicures, clean and style wigs, give scalp and facial treatments, and provide make-up analysis for women.

Working conditions are generally pleasant. However, most cosmetologists must be on their feet for hours at a time. Full-time workers usually have a 40-hour week, but some work in the evenings and on weekends and holidays, when beauty salons are busiest.

While there were 649,000 cosmetologists working in the late 1980s, about 40 percent worked part-time. Most are employed in beauty salons, some in "unisex" salons, barber shops, department stores, hospitals, and hotels. A few leading cosmetologists in large cities set fashion trends.

Those wishing to become cosmetologists should have finger dexterity, a sense of beauty, and should enjoy working with people. They should be able to carry out the instructions of their customers, and should keep up with current hairstyles, so as to offer suggestions when asked. They should expect to begin their first jobs doing simple tasks such as shampooing and gradually increase their responsibilities.

Education and Training

All states require cosmetologists to be licensed, although the qualifications vary. Most states require graduation from a state-approved school, a physical examination, and that the person be at least 16 years old. A few require high school diplomas.

Training is offered in public and private vocational schools and in the evening as well as the day. Attending school full time requires from six months to one year to complete the program. Many high schools offer a course of study along with the usual academic subjects. Much of the program centers around demonstrations and practical experience.

Job Outlook

Job opportunities are expected to be plentiful, at least through the mid-1990s. Most openings will be replacements, because there is a fast turnover as workers seek better-paying jobs. Opportunities for part-time work are excellent.

Average weekly earnings for the middle range are between $175 and $320 per week. The size, location, and reputation of the salon will be most important in determining wages.

Dental Hygienist

Nature of the Work

A dentist is able to expand his or her services with the help of a dental hygienist. Working under the direction of a dentist, a hygienist cleans teeth, takes and develops X-ray films of the teeth, applies topical fluoride to prevent tooth decay, makes impressions of teeth for study models, and performs other services as an assistant to a dentist. State laws control how far a dental hygienist may go in patient care and how closely the dentist must supervise the hygienist's activities.

In school systems, hygienists may examine children's teeth and educate youngsters on good oral hygiene. For those with advanced training, positions in dental hygiene are plentiful.

Working conditions are pleasant, usually in a comfortable office surrounded by professionals. Most hygienists work less than a 35-hour week. Many will hold more than one job. There could be danger of overexposure to diseases or radiation if proper procedures are not followed.

Education and Training

All states require dental hygienists to be licensed. Requirements include graduation from an accredited dental hygienist school and passing both a written and

clinical examination. Most programs are for two years and offer an associate degree. There are four-year programs leading to a bachelor's degree. Many taking the four-year program obtain jobs with school systems. Six schools offer master's degrees. Admission to any of the 200 schools requires a high school diploma. The curriculum includes subjects in the liberal arts as well as basic, clinical, and dental sciences. Those working to become dental hygienists should have manual dexterity, be neat, in good health, and should enjoy working with others.

Job Outlook

There are about 75,000 jobs in dental hygiene, but the number of jobs is greater than the number of people who want to fill them. This is because most hygienists are hired to work only two or three times a week. While most work in private dental offices, many work in clinics, public health agencies, hospitals, and large businesses.

The job outlook is somewhat better than average as the demand for dental care rises. Also, the change to group practices should add more jobs. The factors that may change this increasing demand are the greater supply of dentists and the improvement of dental care as a result of fluoridation.

Earnings vary with training. The average yearly earnings in the late 1980s were $15,000 to $20,000 for the middle range.

Drafter

Nature of the Work

Drafters provide a necessary step between those who create ideas for making objects (such as equipment and buildings) and the actual construction of those things. They prepare detailed drawings from rough sketches made by engineers, scientists, and architects. These include specifications, views from different positions, and any other information needed to carry out the project. Their tools include compasses, dividers, protractors, rulers, triangles, technical handbooks, tables, and calculators. Drafters are also increasingly using computer assisted design (CAD) systems. These systems, which are slowly changing the field, allow the preparation of a design and the change of that design with a minimum of routine work. While CAD can produce designs more quickly, accurately, and thoroughly, it has made only a small dent in the traditional approach used by drafters.

Working conditions are usually pleasant, but sitting for long periods of time can produce eyestrain and be boring. Those thinking of becoming drafters should have good eyesight, patience, and manual dexterity. They should be able to draw freehand three-dimensional objects and do detailed work with accuracy and neatness.

Education and Training

While college training is not a prerequisite, more than 40 percent of recent employees have had some post high-school training, usually at a community college or technical institute. The curriculum usually includes courses in structural design, architectural drawing, engineering, and industrial technology.

Learning how to use computer aided design (CAD) equipment is helpful. However, employers frequently prefer to teach their drafters how to use the company's own CAD system, because not all CAD systems are compatible.

Job Outlook

There were 319,000 working drafters in 1988. About one third worked in manufacturing firms that produced machinery, electrical equipment, and fabricated metals. Another third worked for engineering and architectural businesses. About 16,000 worked for governments, primarily state and local.

The expected impact of CAD on future jobs has not been great. There will be some increase in jobs, but most openings will result from replacement of existing drafters. Job security is less than average because the industries in which drafters are employed are sensitive to economic recessions.

Average earnings for drafters in the late 1980s was $24,000. The middle range was $17,700 to $30,000. A few drafters will continue their studies and go on to study architecture, engineering, landscape architecture, and surveying.

Elementary School Teacher

Nature of the Work

To many, there is no greater calling than to help shape the lives of young children. Elementary school teachers introduce youngsters to the basics of primary skills: mathematics, languages, social studies, and science. Equally important, they try to instill an appreciation for learning. They observe and evaluate both the performance and potential of their students and take steps to overcome weaknesses. They observe the development of their children's health and social behavior and work with parents and school officials to improve each.

Elementary school teachers usually instruct their students in a number of subjects, although specialization is common in art, music, and physical education. Some teachers are trained to offer remedial work, or to deal with emotionally or physically disabled children.

Only a part of a teacher's work takes place in the classroom. Lessons have to be prepared, papers graded, and faculty and committee meetings attended. Teachers are expected to keep up to date on educational materials and subject matter through reading and attendance at workshops. The demands of clerical work and supervision of lunchrooms and playgrounds are sometimes lessened with the help of teacher aides.

The working conditions of teachers vary considerably with the grade level and nature of the class. Attending to children's physical needs are greatest at the lower grades, while coping with those who are disrespectful and emotionally volatile may be more difficult at upper grades. Most elementary school teachers have a nine or ten-month schedule, with week-long or greater breaks in the fall and spring. School days range from 175 to 205, with 184 as an average. After a trial period of about three years, a teacher can be granted tenure, which provides greater job security than in most employment. Not all teachers are given tenure.

Education and Training

All states require public school teachers to be certified, and most states require the same for private schools. Typically, certification will be for early childhood (nursery school through third grade), elementary grades (one through eight), or special education or reading. While requirements vary by states, all now require a bachelor's degree from a college with an approved teacher training program. Course work includes specific subject matter as well as professional education. Information about special state requirements may be obtained by writing the state education department. Teachers should like being with children, and they should be creative, dependable, and patient.

Job Outlook

There presently are about 1.4 million teachers of elementary school. About 85 percent work in public schools, the rest in private schools. Enrollments in elementary school are expected to grow rapidly until the mid-1990s. This will increase demand. Supply, however, is not as predictable. It will depend largely on salaries and the priorities and prestige afforded teachers. Earnings (for both new and experienced teachers as a group) average $28,900 with slightly higher salaries in the Mid-Atlantic and western states and lower salaries in the South.

Hotel Manager

Nature of the Work

Hotel managers are responsible for the successful operation of their establishments. The manager is in charge of all aspects of the hotel (or motel), including marketing and sales, accounting, food service, housekeeping, recreation, personnel, security and maintenance, guest satisfaction, and just about any problem that might arise. In small establishments, the manager may have to supervise all these operations. In large chains, many of these functions are centralized.

Working conditions will vary depending on the circumstances. Because hotels/motels operate around the clock, managers may be on call at all times if emergencies arise. Some managers live on the premises, which in itself can be tiring. Stress may build in dealing with angry guests. Problems with low-paid help may be frequent. Managers should have dispositions that are not easily ruffled.

In larger hotels and motels, the general manager may coordinate the operations of the front desk manager, food and beverage manager, accounts manager, and so on. Frequently these functional managers will rise to become general managers.

Education and Training

Most hotel managers rise to their positions through experience in this and related businesses. More recently, however, employers are seeking people with college training in hotel management. More than one hundred colleges and universities offer four-year programs in this field, and an even greater number are offered in two-year colleges. Typical courses include accounting, economics, marketing, computer science, food service management, and others related to operating a business. Large hotel and motel chains may offer their own courses, with many opportunities for advancement.

Job Outlook

There are currently about 96,000 hotel/motel managers, plus an additional number of owner/managers. The job outlook is better than average, as more hotels and motels are built, tourism expands, and people now in the field retire.

Salaries vary, depending on experience and responsibilities. Front-office managers average $30,000, while general managers average above $53,000. Liberal fringe benefits are given and bonuses are not uncommon. Managers generally receive paid vacations, life insurance, medical benefits, and pension plans. Some earn bonuses up to 15 percent of their basic salaries. Experience and training in hotel and motel management are easily carried over to managing apartment buildings, stores, and offices.

Insurance Sales Worker

Nature of the Work

The purpose of insurance is to protect individuals, families, and businesses from financial loss. Three basic categories of policies are life, property-liability (which includes automobile insurance), and health. There are many specific types of policies within these categories. Insurance sales workers offer professional advice in helping to find the right policy for the circumstances. Some sales workers sell insurance in all three major categories; others specialize in certain fields, such as life insurance. Some workers specialize in group policies that employees or members of organizations may buy at lower prices.

Hours for insurance sales workers are frequently irregular, with evening and weekend appointments commonplace. Long work-weeks and a great deal of local travel may be drawbacks, but insurance sales workers have some control in arranging their hours. About a third of all sales people work for themselves. Most beginners usually need income from some other job until they can get enough clients.

Education and Training

A college degree is not necessary for most insurance sales jobs, although most firms prefer their people to have some college work. Many people enter the field from other occupations, which results in older entrants. Many colleges have courses in insurance and a few have insurance programs leading to a bachelor's degree. In addition, several different insurance associations offer conferences, seminars, and courses. After passing an examination, each offers appropriate designations of achievement that are prized in the industry. These achievement designations go well beyond the required licensing examination that each state requires.

Job Outlook

There were 423,000 insurance sales workers in 1988, many of whom were part-time. The job outlook is for comparatively slow expansion. This is because insurance sales workers are now using more productive methods, even though the amount of insurance sold continues to increase. Most openings will come from high turnovers, since many people find they cannot make a good living in insurance sales.

When new sales workers join a firm, the company will frequently pay them about $1,200 a month. This is a subsidy while they are learning. Most sales workers are paid on a commission. They earn a higher commission on a new policy than on a renewal. The median income after five years is $30,400, after ten years $50,300, and many very experienced sales workers, particularly in casualty insurance, earn more than $100,000.

Lawyer

Nature of the Work

In a nation ruled by law, all of us are affected by laws in most aspects of our lives. Lawyers (or *attorneys*) help connect our system of laws with our actions as individuals, in groups, and as a part of government. Lawyers may act as counselors, advising their clients of the potential legal consequences of their actions, and examining and writing legal contracts and other documents. They may act as advocates, representing their clients in a court of law. Some lawyers perform all of these functions. Some lawyers thrive on trial practice, and some rarely see the inside of a courtroom.

Lawyers frequently specialize in certain areas of law, such as taxes, real estate, administrative law, or personal injury law. Some lawyers specialize in civil cases, where one party sues another. Others deal in criminal cases, where the government brings actions for crimes against society. A few defend the poor in legal aid societies, some teach, and still others have found their training useful in businesses not directly related to the law.

Most frequently, lawyers work in offices, law libraries, and courtrooms. Those who work for government or corporations are likely to have regular hours, while those in law firms or in business for themselves go through periods of great pressure.

Education and Training

Most states require lawyers to pass their bar examination. Educational preparation is usually four years of undergraduate college and three years of law school. Some states accept the results of passing the bar in another state. While there is no national licensing, all but four states require a Multi-state Bar Examination along with the state examination. A few states still permit candidates to take their examinations without formal college and law school training.

Job Outlook

There are about 582,000 lawyers employed in this country. Almost 460,000 are in private practice with most of the remaining working in government, particularly local government.

The job outlook for lawyers reflects an increase in both demand and supply. Increases in laws and litigation in many fields, including consumer protection, environment, and safety, have created a need for more legal services, and this has been matched by a doubling of law school graduates in the last ten years. Job turnover is not frequent, perhaps because income tends to be high. First-time jobs usually begin at $34,000 or more; average salaries for experienced lawyers are above $80,000 and much higher than that in private industry.

Medical Record Technician

Nature of the Work

Doctors and hospitals set up permanent record files for each patient they treat. These files include the patient's medical history, results of physical examinations, laboratory tests, diagnosis and treatment plans, and doctors' and nurses' notes. Medical record technicians work together with other medical record professionals to manage the records system. This management is important because it must meet strict medical, administrative,

ethical, and legal requirements. Recent changes in the way hospitals are paid for their services have made medical records even more significant. Medical record administrators are key members of the hospital management team.

Medical record technicians organize and evaluate records for completeness and accuracy. They ensure that all forms are present and properly identified and signed. Increasingly, this task is done on computers. Each technician has a computer terminal that can retrieve information from the patient's files in the hospital's mainframe computer.

Technicians also assist hospital administrative staff in tabulating and analyzing data from medical records. This statistical information can be studied to determine such things as occurrences of disease by type and length of hospital stay. Technicians may also assemble information in response to inquiries from law firms, insurance companies, government agencies, or researchers.

Medical record personnel usually work a 40-hour week. In hospitals where medical record departments are open 18 to 24 hours a day, technicians may work day, evening, or night shifts.

Education and Training

To gain a credential as an Accredited Record Technician, a person must pass a written examination given by the American Medical Record Association (AMRA). The examination is given to persons who have graduated from an AMRA accredited 2-year associate degree program or who have graduated from the Independent Study Program in Medical Record Technology and have also obtained 30 semester hours of prescribed academic credit. Courses include biological sciences, medical terminology, medical record science, business management, legal aspects, and computer data processing.

Job Outlook

Three out of five medical record technician jobs are in hospitals. In addition, public health departments, insurance firms, nursing homes, clinics, accounting firms, and law firms hire medical record technicians. A change in Medicare reimbursement in 1990 increased the need for detailed records in doctors' offices. Demand for experienced or credentialed technicians as well as for recent graduates is strong. More than 52,000 technician jobs were held in 1990. The average fulltime technician employed by a private hospital earned $9.70 per hour in 1991. Because of overtime pay, average yearly wages approached $25,000.

Photographer and Camera Operator

Nature of the Work

The objective of photographers and camera operators is to capture the visual image and emotion of people, places, and events. Still photography, such as taking portraits, is quite different from camera operation for either video or film. Most photographers specialize in a particular field, because specific skills are required for achieving different effects. Specialization in scientific photography may reveal images not seen by the naked eye. Advertising and industrial photography require taking pictures of a wide range of subjects. The results must be attractive to be effective in newspaper and magazine advertising or in catalogs. Camera

operators are employed by television and movie studios.

Both still photographers and camera operators use a wide variety of cameras, with numerous accessories to meet different circumstances. Some operators develop their own films, others use a laboratory.

Photographers employed by government and commercial enterprises usually have regular hours. Those who work freelance and for the news media may be subject to immediate call and the necessity of traveling. Those who freelance are under pressure to solicit clients.

Education and Training

Formal education is not always required to go into photography, although a good understanding of the technical aspects of equipment is needed. Imagination, creativity, and timing are all important. For specialized photography, some knowledge of the subject matter may be required.

Many colleges and universities offer programs in photography and cinematography, leading to a bachelor's degree. Two-year colleges have programs with associate degrees. Art and design schools usually have classes in photography.

A type of apprenticeship in a studio is a frequent way of moving into the field. Typically the trainee will start in a darkroom, mixing chemicals and developing film. Responsibilities will gradually be increased.

Job Outlook

Slightly more than 105,000 jobs are held by photographers and camera operators. Half of this number are salaried, working in photographic or commercial studios or for the news media. The remainder are self-employed. Photographers are employed almost everywhere, while camera operators, found mainly in television broadcasting and motion pictures, are usually in metropolitan areas.

Job opportunities in photography are expected to grow faster than the average for all occupations until the mid-1990s. Demand continues to grow as businesses rely more on visual aids for both learning and advertising. Demand for camera operators is also expected to grow, but the excitement and glamour of the field will probably attract more applicants than the jobs available.

New and relatively inexperienced photographers average $21,000 a year; those with greater experience usually earn in the range of $24,600 to $33,800, and those most experienced or doing more difficult work average close to $40,000. Camera operators may earn even more than this.

Police Officer

Nature of the Work

Police work can range from keeping order in public places and investigating crimes to controlling traffic and lecturing the public on safety. In small communities, officers may be called on to do all these things. In large cities, work may be highly specialized, including chemical and firearms analysis, fingerprint identification, harbor and border patrol, and work with the canine corps and even helicopters.

All levels of government need law enforcement officers. There are related jobs, such as security guards with private companies. Most police recruits begin with patrol, on foot or riding in a police vehicle. They are expected to be alert to anything that could be dangerous to people and to react appropriately.

Working conditions will vary with particular assignments. Most officers work a 40-hour week, but many must work nights, weekends, and holidays because of the demands of protecting the public. Even when police are off duty, they are subject to immediate call. Such challenges as working long hours outside in severe weather, risking a high injury rate, taking the chances involved in pursuing speeding motorists and apprehending criminals, all demand dedication to the job.

Education and Training

Most police jobs are covered by civil service regulations. Usually candidates must be at least 21 years old and U.S. citizens. Competitive tests are given to determine physical fitness and personal qualifications. Both written tests and interviews are given to determine the candidates' honesty, good judgment, and sense of responsibility. Most jobs require a high school education or more. The more specialized jobs require college training.

Some large cities hire civilian police cadets or trainees right out of high school. They perform clerical jobs and take classroom instruction in job-related areas. This procedure helps select the best candidates for officers.

Job Outlook

Approximately 575,000 men and women are employed as police or detectives. Most work in local government with about ten percent in state agencies and five percent at the federal level.

The job employment outlook through the 1990s is above average. Most openings will come from retirees. Transfer to other jobs is small.

The average starting salary was $20,600 and the average maximum $26,700 a year in 1988. Sergeants, detectives, and lieutenants can expect an average of $4,500 more. Maximums with experience are frequently above $35,000. These low salaries are usually offset by very liberal benefits, including education, vacations, and a retirement pension at half pay after 20 or 25 years.

Registered Nurse

Nature of the Work

Registered nurses (R.N.s) deal with health and illness. Their concern is with the entire person, for whom they observe, assess, record symptoms, and administer care.

More than two-thirds of all nurses work in hospitals or similar health institutions. There they provide skilled bedside care and carry out the physicians' orders. Some nurses specialize in such fields as surgery or psychiatric care.

For patients who need constant care, there are private duty nurses. Office nurses assist physicians in the maintenance of their practice. Occupational health and industrial nurses work for governments or businesses. They treat minor injuries, offer health counseling, give health examinations, and arrange for further medical care. Community health nurses care for patients in clinics, retirement homes, and other community settings.

While most nurses work in good facilities, the physical demands of patient care can be very strenuous. Coping with human suffering and frequent emergencies requires emotional stability. Working at night, during holidays, and on weekends is not unusual, because patients demand constant care.

Education and Training

Programs for nursing vary in length from two to five years after graduation from high school. There were almost 1,500 training programs in the United States in 1988. Programs taken at two-year colleges offer an associate degree. At hospitals, where three years are required, a diploma is given. At colleges and universities the four-to-five-year program leads to a bachelor's degree. Some schools offer masters and doctoral programs. All graduates become eligible to take the national licensing examination, leading to the R.N. Supervisory or administrative positions require a minimum of a bachelor's degree.

All nursing education programs include classroom instruction as well as clinical (practical "hands on") experience.

Job Outlook

There were about 1.6 million nurses in the late 1980s, but about 30 percent were part-time.

Those interested in a career in nursing must be able to show sympathy, accept responsibility, and follow orders. There are numerous opportunities for advancement. These include specializing in some branch of medicine, or becoming a nurse practitioner or a physician's associate. Secretarial, computer, and management skills increase the opportunities and the earnings of nurses.

The job outlook for nurses is excellent, with opportunities in many settings. The shortage in the late 1980s has raised the middle range of annual salaries to about $23,100. The top ten percent make over $32,100.

Retail Sales Worker

Nature of the Work

The primary purpose of a retail sales worker is to interest customers in the merchandise. How successful an establishment is depends in large part on how efficient and courteous its sales force is. The worker should know the product and its construction and design, and the competitors' products. Being able to demonstrate the use of the product, when appropriate, is also important. For those selling complex items such as computers, knowing special features and what they can do is essential.

Retail sales workers are also called on to make out sales slips, receive and record payments, handle exchanges, and help make or keep the sales area attractive.

The working conditions are generally pleasant. However, during sales and holiday seasons the demands on a sales worker can cause stress. Some must stand for long periods of time, while others may have to travel to customers' homes. Many stores are open evenings and weekends. Some workers may have to put in long hours.

In the late 1980s, there were about four million jobs in retail sales. The largest employers are department stores; general merchandise, apparel and accessories stores; drug, food, and furniture stores; and car dealers. Sales workers who sell expensive items are likely to be employed full-time. Almost 60 percent of the others are likely to be part-time.

Education and Training

Employees are expected to be neat and pleasant and to communicate easily. Most people who enter the field have no experience. Usually their main objective is to earn immediate income rather than start a career in selling. Employers generally prefer to hire high school graduates for full-time positions, but high school students are sometimes employed on a part-time basis. Stores may have a training program, or may assign the new employee to work with an experienced sales worker. When employees perform well, they generally are switched to selling more expensive items.

Management positions have sometimes come from the ranks without a college education. However, more stores are turning to college graduates who enter a management training program.

Job Outlook

While sales are expected to grow, so are the number of self-service areas. Therefore, the number of jobs should grow at about an average rate. Opportunities in retail sales will continue to be numerous because of the size of the work force and the rate of turnover.

Average weekly earnings in 1988 for retail workers were about $320. Sales people in motor vehicles and appliances averaged $439, while those in apparel and shoes averaged below $207. Workers may be paid a salary, a commission, or some combination of the two. Fringe benefits for full-time workers are usually generous.

GLOSSARY

This Glossary defines terms that are important in the study of economics. The number in parentheses after each definition indicates the page in the textbook where the term is introduced.

A

ability-to-pay principle: A belief that those with the greatest income should pay the highest tax rates. (p. 244)

absolute advantage: A theory that countries should specialize in producing those products or services that they are most efficient in and trade their surplus for goods and services they produce with less efficiency. (p. 370)

advertising: Attempts by businesses to *inform* and *persuade* consumers to buy their product. (p. 106)

agency shop: An arrangement in which all employees are required to pay union dues whether they join the union or not. (p. 189)

Aid to Families with Dependent Children (AFDC): Government cash assistance (welfare) to families with children 18 or under. (p.346)

allocation of resources: The problem of how to distribute scarce resources given unlimited wants. (p. 45)

antitrust policy: Government policy to enforce competition and stop monopolistic practices. (p. 164)

appreciation: An increase in the value of a nation's money in relation to other types of money. (p. 378)

arbitration: A manner of settling a labor-management dispute by submitting disagreements to a third party for a decision. If a labor contract or law requires all disagreements to be settled this way and both parties must accept the decision, it is compulsory arbitration; otherwise, it is voluntary arbitration. (p. 192)

automatic stabilization: Items in the budget, such as income taxes and transfer payments, that change when the economy changes. Designed to keep the economy stable through countercyclical policy that requires no action by government in order to operate.(p. 327)

average fixed cost: The total costs divided by the number of units produced. (p. 125)

B

balance of trade: The difference between the total value of goods and services exported to other countries and the total value of goods and services imported. (p. 375)

barriers to trade: Obstacles, such as tariffs and quotas, designed to discourage trade, particularly imports. (See *tariff* and *quota*.)

base year: A past year used to compare other years in a variety of economic measurements, such as the consumer price index. (pp. 272, 287)

benefits received principle: The belief that taxes should be paid by those who use the services supported by the tax. The gasoline tax is a good example. (p. 243)

bond: A security representing a debt owed by a borrower to a lender, which pays a fixed rate of interest. Businesses usually issue bonds in $1,000 denominations. Government bonds are issued in many different amounts. (p. 132)

boycott: A group decision designed to put pressure on another group. Usually a union urging its members and others not to buy from an employer in order to make the employer come to terms. (p. 190)

business cycle: The expansion and contraction of business activity in four fairly regular periods—expansion, peak, contraction, and trough. (p. 225)

C

capital: A factor of production used by labor in making products; a man-made instrument of production such as a tool, machine, or sheet metal. (p. 15)

capital gain: Occurs when stock can be sold for more than it originally cost to buy. (p. 132)

capitalism: An economic system in which production and the means to produce are owned and controlled by private individuals or groups. Government plays a very small role. The market determines how resources are distributed. (p. 34)

central problem: In economics, how to distribute production when resources are scarce and wants are unlimited. (See *scarcity*.)

characteristics of money: For money to perform its functions in the economy, it must be accepted as payments, be divisible, portable, and have a reasonably stable value. (p. 292)

checking deposits: Money in a bank or thrift institution that may be withdrawn at any time by writing a check or similar instrument. (p. 298)

circular flow model: A simplified diagram of the economy, showing the product market (production flows from businesses to consumers and dollars flow in the opposite direction) and the factor market (households sell their factors to businesses in return for dollars). (p. 65)

classical economist: One who believes that the interaction of demand and supply in the market with no government interference will produce the best economic system. (p. 320)

Clayton Act: Antitrust legislation passed in 1914 that closed some of the loopholes left by the Sherman Antitrust Act, and said that antitrust legislation did not apply to labor unions. (p. 185)

closed shop: A union contract in which the business can only hire union members. Currently, this is illegal. (p. 186)

collective bargaining: A method for reaching agreement on wages, hours, and conditions of work where representatives of workers and representatives of business discuss changes for all. (p. 190)

command economy: An economic system in which decisions on the questions of *what, how,* and *for whom* are made by the government. (p. 34)

communism: An economic system in which goods, particularly capital goods, are owned collectively and payment is made according to need. In practice, decisions are made centrally and the individual has little freedom. (p. 422)

comparative advantage: A theory that states all nations will have more goods if they specialize in producing those items in which they have the greatest relative efficiency and import those things in which they have the least relative efficiency. (p. 370)

complementary good: A good that is used with another good, such as a bow is to an arrow. (p. 72)

compulsory arbitration: The law *requires* that a solution be determined by an unbiased person. (p. 192)

Consumer Price Index: The most commonly used measurement of inflation. (pp. 272, 287)

consumer protection: When government intervenes in the market to protect consumers from harmful products. (p. 103)

consumer sovereignty: The idea that customers determine what products will be produced by showing demand in the market. Also, the belief that competition in the market protects the consumer. (p. 98)

corporate income tax: The third most important source of tax revenue for the federal government (p. 245)

corporation: A form of business organization requiring a government charter granting the company specific powers separate from those of the individuals who own the firm. These include the right to sue and be sued and to issue stock. (p. 117)

cost-push inflation: An increase in prices caused by an increase in the cost of production, such as higher oil prices. (p. 272)

countercyclical: An economic policy that is aimed at changing the direction of the business cycle, such as stimulating the economy when it is contracting and slowing it down when it is expanding. (p. 304)

craft union: An organization of workers who have similar skills (also called *horizontal* union). (p. 183)

crowding-out effect: When government borrows heavily, the additional demand increases interest rates, thus discouraging businesses and consumers from borrowing and spending. (p. 328)

cyclical unemployment: Job layoffs caused by a decline in business conditions. (p. 268)

D

decentralized: Economic questions, *what, how,* and *for whom* are answered by individuals in the market, rather than by centralized government. (p. 425)

deficit spending: It happens when government spends more than it takes in. This may be useful if done when the economy needs to expand in order to increase employment. (p. 256)

deflation: A general decline in the price level. (p. 294)

demand: The willingness on the part of people to buy certain quantities of a product at different price levels. (p. 69)

demand curve: A graphic representation of a demand schedule. It generally slopes downward from left to right. This shows the lower the price, the more people are likely to buy. (p. 70)

demand-pull inflation: When prices rise because there is a greater demand than there is a supply; too many dollars are chasing too few goods. (p. 272)

demand schedule: A table that shows how many products people will buy at various prices. (p. 70)

demand-side economics: The Keynesian idea that total spending, the sum of consumers, businesses and government, will determine the GDP. (See *John Maynard Keynes.*)

depreciation: A decrease in the value of a nation's money in relation to other types of money. (p. 378)

deregulation: The act of reducing the amount of government controls over the economy. (p. 165)

derived demand: The demand for factors of production that results from the demand for a product or service. (p. 176)

determinants of demand: The things that cause demand to change: for example, consumer taste, income, price of substitutes and complementary goods, and a change in the number of potential customers. (p. 71)

developed nation: A country such as the United States which is highly industrialized (p. 391)

developing nation: A nation in which the majority of people do not have a minimal standard of living. (p. 391)

diminishing marginal productivity: At a certain point, adding another worker (or other factor of production) does not increase production as much as the preceding additions of workers. (See also *diminishing returns*.) (p. 177)

diminishing marginal utility: Each additional unit of a product is less valuable than the one that came before it. (p. 94)

diminishing returns: At a certain level of production, the cost per unit of producing additional units increases. This occurs because when one factor of production increases but other factors are held constant, a point is reached where the additional inputs will add less production than the preceding inputs. (pp. 73, 177)

discount rate: The rate of interest the Federal Reserve Bank charges banks that borrow money from it. (p. 308)

discouraged workers: Workers who have given up looking for a job. (p. 269)

discretionary policy: An economic policy that requires a person or agency to take some action. It can be fiscal (budget changes) or monetary (changing the money supply). (p. 326)

diseconomies of scale: A diseconomy of scale exists whenever the per unit costs increase as production increases. The larger the production, the less efficient the operation of that business. (p. 159)

disposable personal income: That income that is left to consumers after they have paid their personal taxes. Some of it will be spent and some saved. (p. 325)

diversification: When a business increases the types of products it sells in order to lower its fixed costs and take advantage of less competitive market conditions. (p. 144)

dividends: That share of the corporation's profit that is distributed to stockholders. (p. 132)

division of labor: Dividing production up into specific tasks in order to increase efficiency and to lower costs. (p. 36)

double counting: Occurs when the value of a contributor is counted more than once when determining GDP using the income approach. (p. 218)

dumping: Selling goods to other countries at below cost to get rid of surpluses or to hurt foreign competition. (p. 376)

durable goods: Goods that do not need to be replaced every year, such as cars and appliances. (p. 226)

E

economics: The study of how people produce, distribute, and consume resources in order to satisfy their wants, and of how people make choices in trying to satisfy their wants with limited resources. (p. 5)

economic system: A set of rules by which a nation answers the basic questions of *what, how,* and *for whom*; how it decides to distribute its resources to satisfy its peoples' wants. (p. 33)

economies of scale: The things that make a large firm more efficient than a small firm. As production increases, unit costs decrease; the larger the production, the more efficient the operation of the business. (p. 159)

elasticity: The effect that a change in price has on demand. (p. 81)

Employment Act of 1946: Law that required the President of the United States to make annual reports to the nation on the condition of the economy and to recommend economic policy, if needed. It established the Council of Economic Advisers and abandoned *laissez faire.* (p. 323)

entrepreneurship: The factor of production that takes the risks and responsibilities of starting a business; an organization that combines the other factors of production. (p. 15)

equilibrium: When economic forces are balanced. If the economic forces of demand and supply are equal, the price will be at equilibrium. (p. 78)

equilibrium wage rate: The wage level that will provide the same number of workers as jobs available. (p. 179)

exchange rate: The value of one nation's currency in relation to other nation's currency. (p. 378)

expansion multiplier: The amount that a dollar of reserves will support in checkable deposits in the bank. (p. 301)

expansion of money: Process by which the granting of credit (loans) by banks results in an increase in the money supply. (p. 299)

expenditure approach: One of three methods for determining GDP. Add consumer spending, plus government spending, plus business spending, plus net spending by foreign purchasers to determine GDP. (p. 217)

externality: When someone who is neither the producer nor consumer of a product pays a cost or receives a benefit from its production. (p. 237)

F

factor market: Where businesses buy natural resources, labor, and capital needed to produce their goods and services. (pp. 65, 176)

factors of production: The inputs used in the production process, including natural resources, entrepreneurship, labor, and capital. (p. 15)

Fair Labor Standards Act: A law passed in 1938 that determined the minimum wage that a worker could be paid. (p. 193)

Federal Deposit Insurance Corporation (FDIC): A government agency that insures deposits up to a certain amount in a bank that is covered if that bank should fail. (p. 304)

Federal Reserve System: An agency created in 1913 to oversee banking and which can influence the economy. (pp. 290, 307)

fiat money: Money that has value because the government orders that it be accepted for payment of debts. (p. 292)

fiscal policy: Planning a federal budget that has either surpluses or deficits intended to maintain a steady level of total spending in the economy. (p. 326)

fixed costs: Production costs that remain the same regardless of the number of units produced. (p. 123)

for whom: One of three major economic questions every economic system must answer. Asks *for whom* is the production meant or what is the method for distribution. (p. 41)

free market economy: An economic system in which individuals and businesses own the factors of production and basic economic decisions are determined by the interaction of demand and supply. (p. 319)

frictional unemployment: Short-term unemployment caused by workers changing jobs. (p. 268)

full employment: A condition in which anyone who wishes to work can. Usually set at 94 to 96 percent of the labor force, or 4 to 6 percent unemployment rate. (See *frictional unemployment*.)

functions of money: Money can be used as a medium of exchange, as a measure of value, and as a store of value. (p. 292)

G

goods: Tangible (physical, touchable) things that satisfy human wants and needs. (p. 5)

Gross Domestic Product (GDP): The retail value of all final products produced in a nation in a given year. (p. 216)

H

horizontal combination: A merger of companies in the same business; occurs when firms that do the same thing join together. (p. 156)

how: One of three basic questions any economic system must answer; namely, *how* goods and services will be produced. (p. 41)

I

imperfect competition: A market condition in which an individual or a group of sellers and buyers is large enough to influence price. It includes natural monopoly, oligopoly, and monopolistic competition. (p. 148)

incentive: An inducement to do something or not do something. In capitalism, profits influence people to produce; higher wages influence workers to work overtime. (p. 423)

income: A flow of value; what you receive over a period of time. (p. 278)

income approach: A method of calculating GDP; total of income, including wages, profits, rent, interest, some taxes, and the cost of wearing out capital (machinery). (p. 218)

indexed: Adjusted income that overcomes the decline in the value of money through inflation. (p. 344)

individual retirement account (IRA): A retirement plan that allows individuals to put off paying taxes on money they save. (p. 337)

industrial capitalism: An economic system that relies on the market to make most decisions but allows the government to allocate some resources to some firms. (p. 429)

industrial union: A union in which all workers in an industry belong to the same union regardless of their job (also called *vertical union*). (p. 183)

infant industry: An argument used to justify a temporary tariff to allow new industries to learn how to produce more efficiently. (p. 373)

inflation: A general increase in the price level resulting from a decline in the value of money. (pp. 272, 294)

informative advertising: Advertising that is intended to inform. (p. 108)

infrastructure: Facilities such as roads, water systems, communications, etc., that help a nation to produce and distribute production. (p. 395)

injunction: A court order to stop some kind of action. (pp. 185, 191)

interest: Payment for the use of money. (p. 130)

intergovernmental revenue: Revenue paid by one agency or level of government to another. (p. 247)

invisible hand: Business owners serving the interests of society when they attempt to serve their own self-interests. (p. 100)

K

Keynes, John Maynard: An English economist who believed that economic activity and jobs depended on the rate of spending in the economy. (p. 324)

kibbutz: A community in Israel that has a command economy. (p. 416)

L

labor: A factor of production contributing human effort in the production process. (p. 15)

labor force participation rate: The percentage of people, 16 years of age or older who could work, who are either working or looking for work. (p. 179)

labor union: An organization of workers formed to give them greater bargaining power, that attempt to improve their wages and working conditions through collective action. (p. 182)

laissez faire: A policy that believes government should not intervene in the economy. (p. 319)

law of demand: States that people will buy more of a product at a lower price than at a higher price, if nothing else changes. (p. 69)

law of supply: At higher prices producers are willing to offer more products for sale than at lower prices. (p. 74)

leading indicator: A measurement that anticipates changes in the direction of the economy. (p. 226)

least-likely-to-offend principle: In evaluating taxes, politicians frequently choose those which will offend their voters least. Taxes on liquor and cigarettes are the best examples. (p. 244)

limited liability: The legal doctrine that protects stockholders in corporations from losing more than the money they invested. (p. 119)

limited life: The condition that proprietorship and partnerships cease upon the death of an owner. Corporations have unlimited life. (p. 117)

lockout: When management closes the work place to prevent unionized employees from working. (p. 191)

Lorenz Curve: A graphic method of showing the inequality in the distribution of income. (p. 279)

M

macroeconomics: The study of the economy as a whole. (p. 213)

maintaining economic stability: An argument which states that nations that depend on trade are more likely to be hurt by disruptions in trade. (p. 374)

marginal physical product: The amount of additional product that is added to the total when an additional factor (such as another worker) is added. (p. 178)

marginal revenue product: Same as marginal physical product, but converted to the money value of the additional product. (p. 177)

marginal worker: Generally, workers who are hired last because they are least qualified. Usually such workers earn the minimum wage and have other means of support. (p. 195)

mediation: A method for settling a labor dispute in which a third party helps union and management arrive at an acceptable compromise. (p. 191)

microeconomics: The study of how decisions are made by individual parts of the economy, such as businesses and consumers. (p. 61)

minimum wage: A law setting the lowest wage that may be paid to a worker. (p. 193)

model: A tool used by economists to show how different factors act and react on each other, such as a demand and supply graph; a simplified picture of the real world. (p. 18)

monetary policy: Actions to control the money supply by the Federal Reserve system to achieve full-employment, stable prices, and economic growth. (p. 309)

money: Medium of exchange that is accepted for payment of debts; a claim on something that has value. (p. 292)

money supply: The amount of money that is available to be spent in the economy. (p. 294)

money wages: The number of dollars workers receive for their labor (as opposed to *real wages*). (p. 180)

monopolistic competition: Imperfect competition in which there are many firms selling similar products; the seller tries to make his/her product appear different from others. (p. 149)

mortality rate: The average number of deaths per thousand people per year. (p. 405)

multinational corporation: Any business that is headquartered in one country but carries on business activities in one or more foreign countries. (p. 381)

N

national debt: The amount of money the federal government owes. (p. 254)

National Labor Relations Act: Legislation passed in 1935, which recognizes labor's right to bargain collectively as a union. (p. 185)

national security: Used to justify trade barriers against military products, on the grounds that the country should not depend on another nation for such items. (p. 373)

natural monopoly: When an industry requires such large capital investments that it would be inefficient to have more than one firm in that area. (p. 150)

natural resources: A factor of production that has not been changed by people. Also called *land*. (p. 15)

negative balance of trade: When the value of a nation's imports is greater than the value of its exports. (p. 374)

negative externality: Occurs when someone who is neither the producer nor the consumer of a product pays a cost associated with the product. (p. 240)

newly developed nation: A country that has experienced rapid economic growth in recent years. (p. 391)

nominal values: The numbered value of measurements in the economy such as GDP, prices, and wages. Not adjusted for inflation, in contrast to *real values.* (p. 222)

nondurable goods: Those goods that need to be replaced frequently, such as food and clothing. (p. 226)

normative statement: A statement involving value judgments as opposed to a purely objective, factual statement. (p. 22)

O

oligopoly: An imperfect market in which a few firms dominate. (p. 149)

open market operations: Buying and selling of U.S. Government securities by the Federal Reserve Bank in order to control the money supply. (p. 308)

opportunity cost: The value of the second choice that is given up when the first choice is taken. (p. 11)

P

partnership: A form of business organization with two or more owners, having limited life and unlimited liability. (p. 117)

perfect competition: A market in which there are numerous buyers and sellers seeking to trade a similar product. There is easy movement in and out of the market and no seller can control the price. (p. 143)

perfect monopoly: A market in which there is only one producer, thus offering some control over price. (p. 147)

personal income tax: The federal governments most important source of revenue. (p. 245)

persuasive advertising: Advertising that is intended to persuade. (p. 108)

Phase II: The attempt by government in 1971–1973 to keep price and wage increases within reasonable levels after a 90-day price and wage freeze. (p. 333)

picket line: A union weapon in which striking workers walk in line carrying placards which express their grievances. (p. 191)

point of equilibrium: The intersection of the demand and supply curves, indicating the price and quantity at which a product will be sold in the market. (p. 78)

political action committees: Groups that intend to put pressure on politicians to support their points of view. (p. 191)

pork barrel legislation: Laws passed by Congress to gain political support in the home district of a member of Congress, not because it is either necessary or even good for the country. (p. 250)

positive balance of trade: When the value of a nation's exports is greater than the value of its imports. (p. 374)

positive statement: A statement of fact, as opposed to a statement of personal values. (p. 21)

poverty: A relative term; defined by the U.S. government in 1991 as an income of less than $13,924 for a family of four living in the city. (p. 278)

price control: A policy that prevents prices of designated items from going above or below a specified level. (p. 333)

price elastic demand: A change in price causes a change in the quantity sold. Demand for luxuries is elastic. (p. 82)

price inelastic demand: People want the same amount no matter what the price. Demand for necessities is inelastic. (p. 81)

prime rate: The lowest interest rate that banks charge their best customers. (p. 131)

principle of exclusion: A claim of sole use of a product. (p. 239)

private goods: Goods owned by individuals and subject to the principle of exclusion. (p. 239)

pro-cyclical: Economic policies that increase the direction in which the economy is moving. (p. 303)

production: The creation of various kinds of goods and services. (p. 14)

production possibilities frontier: A graph showing different attainable combinations of two possible outputs that a given amount of resources (inputs) can produce. (p. 25)

product market: Sales of consumer products; the final goods and services that are bought by households. (p. 65)

productivity: The measure of the value of products that can be created from a quantity of factors of production. (p. 335)

productivity principle: A tax incentive given to business to encourage greater productivity and efficiency. (p. 224)

profit: The basic incentive for operating a business in capitalism, consisting of the amount of money left over after all costs are paid. (p. 44)

profit motive: The incentive that causes people to work hard to make money because they know they can retain the profit. (p. 423)

progressive taxation: A tax in which the tax rate increases with the tax base (higher incomes pay a higher percentage of income). (p. 245)

proletariat: A term used by Karl Marx and his communist followers, meaning *workers*. (p. 423)

property tax: A local tax on buildings and land. (p. 247)

proportional taxation: A tax in which the tax rate stays the same regardless of the tax base. (p. 245)

protection of domestic jobs: An argument to increase tariffs on lower priced foreign goods to make U.S. products more competitive with foreign products. (p. 373)

protective tariff: A tax placed on foreign goods, meant to discourage their being imported and to protect home producers. (p. 371)

public goods and services: Goods and services provided to the public by the government. (p. 238)

Q

quota: A limit placed on the amount of imports or exports. (p. 371)

R

rational choice: Decisions made on the basis of selecting things with greater value in return for giving up things with lesser value. (p. 20)

real GDP: The retail value of a nation's annual output stated in constant dollars. Converts nominal or current dollar GDP into constant dollars using the purchasing power of a given base year. (p. 222)

real hourly wage rate: Hourly earnings as adjusted for inflation. (p. 223)

real values: Stating wages, interest rates, income, or other measurements in constant dollars in order to correct for the changing value of money. (p. 222)

real wages: How much can actually be bought with the wages paid (as opposed to *money wages*). (p. 181)

recession: The contracting portion of a business cycle, when output declines and unemployment increases. The opposite of recovery. (p. 226)

recovery: The expanding portion of a business cycle, when output is increasing and unemployment is decreasing. (p. 226)

redistribution of income: Changing the income of households by the way government taxes and spends. Generally, it reduces the income of those having high income and increases the income of those with low income. (p. 242)

regressive taxation: A tax in which the tax rate declines as the tax base increases (lower incomes pay a greater percentage of income). It hurts the poor in favor of the rich. (p. 245)

regulatory agency: A board appointed by the executives of a state which sets rates that natural monopolies can charge. (p. 150)

relocation: A firm moves the plant to another place where wages, taxes, or other costs may be lower, making profits greater. (p. 191)

rent: Payment for the use of a natural resource. (p. 130)

reserve requirements: The percentage of a deposit that a bank must put aside and not use for loans. It is determined by the Federal Reserve Bank. When stated as a fraction, it is the reserve ratio. (p. 299)

resources: All the things that are necessary for production. (p. 14)

restrictive tariff: A tariff designed to reduce the flow of a particular kind of product into a country. (p. 371)

revenue: The income of a business or government. (p. 247)

revenue tariffs: Tariffs intended to produce revenue for the government. (p. 371)

right-to-work laws: State laws that make contracts requiring employees to join a union as a condition of work illegal. (p. 186)

S

sales tax: A tax on retail products made at the time of purchase. (p. 247)

savings: The part of disposable income that is not spent. (p. 233)

Say, John Baptiste: A French classical economist who believed that the production of goods and services (supply) would create enough demand so they would be bought. (p. 323)

scarcity: The condition in the economy where wants are greater than the resources to satisfy them. The central problem in economics. (p. 9)

seasonal unemployment: Decline in employment due to seasonal conditions, such as lay-offs in outdoor construction in the North in the winter. (p. 268)

secondary boycott: Where unions encourage the public not to buy from a firm's suppliers. Now illegal. (p. 190)

services: Intangible things that satisfy human wants or needs. (p. 5)

Sherman Antitrust Act of 1890: Said that plans to restrain trade, or to monopolize or attempt to monopolize production, were against the law. (p. 164)

shortage: When the equilibrium price is below the offered price, a shortage develops. At that price, the quantity demanded is greater than the quantity supplied. (p. 79)

single proprietorship: Form of business organization that places full responsibility on a single owner. (p. 117)

sit-down strike: When workers refuse to leave the plant which is being struck. (p. 191)

slowdown: An organized attempt by workers to slow down their production in order to put pressure on the company to meet workers' demands. (p. 190)

social insurance tax: Taxes used to support Social Security programs. (p. 245)

socialism: An economic system in which most of the means of production are owned by government and in which there is much central planning. (p. 424)

Social Security Act: A 1935 act which established the Social Security program, unemployment insurance, and welfare. (p. 344)

specialization: Concentrating a person's labor (or other function of production) on a single task in order to increase efficiency. (p. 36)

specialized capital: Tools designed to increase the efficiency of a particular task in production. (p. 36)

stock: Ownership in a corporation, expressed as shares. (p. 132)

strike: When workers withhold their services in order to pressure management to yield to the workers' demands. (p. 191)

strike breakers: Workers called in by a firm to replace workers who are out on strike. (p. 191)

structural unemployment: Loss of jobs for workers whose skills are no longer in demand; caused by changes in consumer tastes or in technology. The skills of workers looking for jobs do not match the skills employers are looking for. (p. 269)

substitute good: A good that is interchangeable with another, such as butter and margarine. (p. 71)

supply: The quantity of goods and services that sellers will offer at various prices during a given time and place. (p. 73)

supply curve: A graph of a supply schedule, showing the relationship between price and quantity. (p. 75)

supply schedule: A table showing the relationship of price and the quantity sellers will offer in the market. (p. 74)

supply-side economics: The theory, associated with President Reagan, that emphasizes increasing supply, in contrast to Keynesian economics where aggregate demand is stressed. (p. 335)

surplus: When the equilibrium price is above the intersection of supply and demand, a surplus remains. At that price the quantity demanded is less than the quantity supplied. (p. 79)

T

Taft-Hartley Act: Legislation passed in 1947 that outlawed the closed shop, prohibited federal employees from striking, permitted the President to seek an injunction delaying strikes that harm the national interest, and permitted state "right-to-work" laws. (p. 186)

tariff: A tax on an item that is imported. (p. 371)

tax: A charge made by government on individuals and businesses, usually for the purpose of shifting resources from the private to the public sector. (p. 243)

tax base: The value of what is being taxed; for example, the value of a person's taxable income. (p. 245)

tax rate: The percentage of the tax base (for example, a person's taxable income) that is taxed. (pp. 244, 245)

trade-offs: Choices between alternatives

with the understanding that using resources for one purpose must be at the expense of another purpose. (p. 11)

traditional economy: An economic system in which the basic questions of *what, how,* and *for whom* are decided by custom (doing things the way they were done in the past). (pp. 34, 394)

transfer in kind: Redistribution of income through non-cash payments such as food stamps, medical care, or low-income housing. (p. 242)

transfer payment: Redistribution of income through the payment of cash, such as welfare payments or unemployment compensation. (p. 242)

U

underground economy: The unreported economic activity, sometimes illegal, that is never reported. Results in large losses in government revenue, and causes reported GDP to be smaller than actual production. (p. 219)

unemployment rate: The percentage of those in the labor force who are not working but who are actively looking for work. (p. 270)

union label: By sewing a union label into garments, unions try to encourage the public to buy only products that were manufactured by union workers. (p. 191)

union shop: An agreement between labor and management that all workers must join the union after they have been hired. (p. 189)

unlimited liability: If an unincorporated business (proprietorship or partnership) goes bankrupt, much of the owners' personal property may be taken over by creditors. (p. 117)

unlimited life: A condition that allows a corporation to continue doing business even after the death of its owner. (p. 119)

V

value judgment: Decision-making based on personal values rather than on facts. (p. 6)

variable costs: Costs that increase as production increases. (p. 123)

vertical combination: A merger of businesses that perform different stages of production. (p. 156)

voluntary arbitration: An agreement between labor and management that a labor dispute be settled by an unbiased person. (p. 192)

W

wages: Payment for labor. (p. 181)

wealth: The total value of accumulated goods and services. (pp. 37, 278)

welfare capitalism: An economic system that relies on the market to make most economic decisions but which provides many benefits paid for by relatively high taxes. (p. 424)

what: One of the three major questions every economic system has to answer, namely, *what* to produce. (p. 41)

wildcat strike: When workers strike without approval of the union. (p. 191)

workable competition: Sufficient competitiveness so that consumer interests are protected, but where the economic advantages of large scale production are recognized. (p. 163)

INDEX

Photography

Cover, Will Shively.

iii, Dan DeWilde; iv, Mike Yamashita/Woodfin Camp & Associates; v, Robert Brenner; vi, © Nobiru Kimine 1987/Photo Researchers; vii, © Jeffrey A. Rycus, courtesy City Center Mall, Columbus OH; viii, Boroff\TexaStock; ix, courtesy NY Convention & Visitors Bureau; x, Glennon P. Donahue; xi, Frank Wing; xiii, Eastcott-Momatiuk/Woodfin Camp & Associates; xiv, Frank Wing; xv, David Zalaznik of the Peoria Journal-Star; xvi, George Hall/Woodfin Camp & Associates; xvii, Michael D. Sullivan/TexaStock; xviii, Frank Wing; xix, Susan Friedman; xxi, Adam Woolfitt/Woodfin Camp & Associates; xxii, Sepp Seit/Woodfin Camp & Associates; xxiii, Karen Rantzman; xxiv, Adam Woolfitt/Woodfin Camp & Associates; xxv, Tom Craig/FPG; xxvi, Jeff Bates; 2-3, Dan DeWilde; 4, Mike Yamashita/Woodfin Camp & Associates; 6, © Don & Pat Valenti/Tony Stone Worldwide; 7, clockwise from top: Christopher B. Kuhn/TexaStock, Sepp Seitz/Woodfin Camp & Associates, AP/Wide World Photos, Dan DeWilde; 10, U.S. Air Force Photo; 12, Tony Freeman; 16, NASA; 18, Jeff Bates; 21, Barrera/TexaStock; 22, Patricia Fox-Smith/TexaStock; 23, Elliot Varner Smith; 25, Paul Light/Lightwave; 32, Robert Brenner; 38, courtesy The Ford Archives, Henry Ford Museum, Dearborn, MI; 39, (t) Terry Wild Studio, (b) courtesy Caterpillar Inc., Peoria, IL; 42, (t, bl) David E. Kennedy/TexaStock, (br) William Rogers; 45, O. Abolafia/Gamma-Liaison; 46, Gene Fitzer; 48, © Nobiru Kimine 1987/Photo Researchers; 60-61, © Jeffrey A. Rycus, courtesy City Center Mall, Columbus OH; 62, Boroff/TexaStock; 67, Alec Duncan; 68, Bettmann Archive; 71, Grant Heilman Photography; 74, Frank Cezus; 85, Gene Fitzer 86, 92, courtesy NY Convention & Visitors Bureau; 95, Robert Brenner/PhotoEdit; 96, George Hall/Woodfin Camp & Associates; 99, Susan Friedman; 100, David R. Frazier Photolibrary; 103, Susan Friedman; 105, James M. Mejuto; 107, (t) courtesy Microsoft Corp., (b) Dennis Monarchy Photography, courtesy Nike Inc.; 114, Glennon P. Donahue; 118, (t) Joseph A. DiChello Jr., (c) Elliot Varner Smith, (b) Michael L. Abramson/Woodfin Camp & Associates; 123, Patricia Fox-Smith/TexaStock; 126, © Bob Daemmrich/Tony Stone Worldwide; 127, 131, Susan Friedman; 140, Frank Wing; 142, (t) David E. Kennedy/TexaStock, (b) Michael D. Sullivan/TexaStock; 144, Kolvoord/TexaStock; 146, Susan Friedman; 148, Dennis Barnes; 149, Bill Gallery/Stock Boston; 150, PhotoEdit; 152, Arthur Grace/NYT Pictures; 154, Jim West; 155, Tony Freeman; 157, courtesy Chevron Corporation, San Francisco, CA; 159, Tom Pantages; 160, Al Levy; 163, Jim West; 165, Susan Friedman; 172, Eastcott-Momatiuk/Woodfin Camp & Associates; 174, Bettmann Archive; 180, Library of Congress; 183, Bettmann Archive; 184, (all) UPI/Bettmann Newsphotos; 185, AP/Wide World Photos; 189, 190, UPI/Bettmann Newsphotos; 194, Paul Light/Lightwave; 195, © Ann States/Saba Press Photos; 212-213, Frank Wing; 214, David Zalaznik of the Peoria Star-Journal; 219, David E. Kennedy/TexaStock; 223, (t) AP/Wide World Photos, (b) Susan Friedman; 227, Barbara Filet; 234, George Hall/Woodfin Camp & Associates; 236, (t) Dale Ahearn/TexaStock, (b) James M. Mejuto; 238, (t) Bettmann Archive, (b) Gene Fitzer; 240, Dennis Barnes; 241, AP/Wide World Photos; 244, Aaron Haupt; 252, 254, 255, Tony Freeman; 256, © Gordon/R.E.A./Saba Press Photos; 264, Michael D. Sullivan/TexaStock; 266, (t) Michael D. Sullivan/TexaStock, (b) Susan Friedman; 269, Alon Reininger/Contact Press/Woodfin Camp & Associates; 274, Lorraine Parrow/First Light; 276, courtesy Chevron Corporation, San Francisco, CA; 281, David E. Kennedy/TexaStock; 288, Frank Wing; 290, Gene Fitzer; 293, Wolfgang Kaehler; 299, Blair Seitz/Photo Researchers; 303, Aaron Haupt; 304, Dennis Barnes; 312, AP/Wide World Photos; 318, Susan Friedman; 320, (t) courtesy the Historical Society of PA, (b) James Wilson/Woodfin Camp & Associates; 324, (l) Historical Pictures/Stock Montage, (r) Bettmann Archive; 325, Steve Allen/Peter Arnold, Inc.; 326, Chuck O'Rear/Woodfin Camp & Associates; 330, Michal Heron/Woodfin Camp & Associates; 331, AP/Wide World Photos; 335, Dennis Barnes; 336, (t) Michael L. Abramson/Woodfin Camp & Associates, (b) Dwight Cendrowski; 345, (all) Barrera/TexaStock; 347, Barbara Laing/TexaStock; 349, 350, AP/Wide World Photos; 364-365, Adam Woolfit/Woodfin Camp & Associates; 366, Sepp Seitz/Woodfin Camp & Associates; 368, © John A. Giordano/Saba Press Photos; 375, Gene Fitzer; 390, Karen Rantzman; 392, David Burnett/Contact Press/Woodfin Camp & Associates; 395, © Marion Patterson/Photo Researchers; 396, Alan Oddie/PhotoEdit; 398, AP/Wide World Photos; 401, Korma Puusa/Woodfin Camp & Associates; 403, Marc & Evelyne Bernheim/Woodfin Camp & Associates; 405, Gianfranco Gorgoni/Contact Press/Woodfin Camp & Associates; 406, Alon Reininger/Contact Press/Woodfin Camp & Associates; 414, Adam Woolfit/Woodfin Camp & Associates; 417, © Fujifotos/The Image Works; 423, AP/Wide World Photos; 424, Tom Craig/FPG; 430, © 1989 Jean Kugler/FPG.

Illustrations

Tom Kennedy; Randy Miyake (technical); Mary Moye-Rowley